Côte d'Az

a photo essay

1 Biot

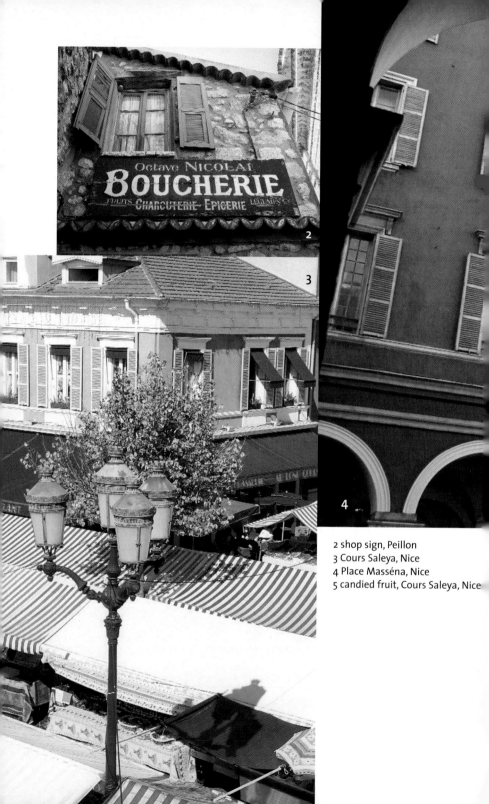

2 shop sign, Peillon
3 Cours Saleya, Nice
4 Place Masséna, Nice
5 candied fruit, Cours Saleya, Nice

5

6 Russian Orthodox church, Nice
7 shutters, Vieux Nice
8 Jean Cocteau sundial, Coaraze
9 La Roue pottery, Vallauris

10, 11 vegetables, local market, St-Raphaël
12 Vieux Nice

12

13 St-Raphael harbour
14 casino, Monte-Carlo
15 street market, Antibes
16 harbour, Menton

17 the Esterel coastline

20

18 Villefranche-sur-Mer
19 Peille
20 view from cactus gardens, Eze-Village

21 Golfe-Juan

Dana Facaros and
Michael Pauls

CÔTE D'AZUR

'aristocrats, dilettantes, artists,
consumptives, literati and glitterati,
expatriates, post-war hedonists,
hippies and poodle-toting retirees...'

CADOGANguides

Contents

About the authors

Dana Facaros and **Michael Pauls** have written over 30 books for Cadogan Guides. They have lived all over Europe, and are currently ensconced in an old farmhouse in southwestern France.

About the updater

Jacqueline Chnéour is a freelance translator and researcher. Brought up in Paris and Nice, she moved to England in 1979 to follow a dream, and has lived in London ever since. She has updated or consulted on several guides in the Cadogan France series, including the Paris guide.

Thanks also to **Vanessa Letts** for help with the Travel and Practical chapters.

Cadogan Guides
Highlands House, 165 The Broadway,
London SW19 1NE
info.cadogan@virgin.net
www.cadoganguides.com

The Globe Pequot Press
246 Goose Lane, PO Box 480, Guilford,
Connecticut 06437–0480

Copyright © Dana Facaros and Michael Pauls 1996,
   2000, 2002, 2004
Updated by Jacqueline Chnéour 2004

Cover and photo essay design by Sarah Gardner
Book design by Andrew Barker
Cover photographs: front © Jon Arnold Images
           back: © John Miller
Photo essay © John Miller
Maps © Cadogan Guides, drawn by
   Map Creation Ltd
Editor: Linda McQueen
Proofreading: Catherine Bradley and Jacqueline
   Chnéour
Indexing: Isobel McLean
Production: Navigator Guides

Printed in Italy by Legoprint
A catalogue record for this book is available
   from the British Library
ISBN 1-86011-149-1

Introduction

The Côte d'Azur is grey old Europe's favourite fantasy escape, its dream of a generous sun on a blue sea drenched in the hot luxurious colours of Matisse and soft lights flickering in warm perfumed nights. From Victorian times, when the casino at Monte-Carlo was known as the 'cathedral of hell', to the carefree era of Brigitte Bardot wiggling on the sands of St-Tropez, this escape has always conjured up a *frisson* of illicit pleasure – temporary freedom not only from rain and sleet and the daily grind but also from the constraints of good behaviour.

The 'sunny place for shady people', as long-time resident Somerset Maugham put it, packs a lot into a small area, a mere 125 miles of irregular coastline from Menton on the Italian border to Bandol, safely beyond the orbit of Marseille. The land may be poor, but it's fragrant, producing mostly flowers, wine and herbs, and the scenery is filled with drama. The Côte d'Azur encompasses three mountain ranges tumbling down to the sea: the Maritime Alps, the porphyry-red Esterel and the dark, ancient chestnut-wooded Massif des Maures. Stunning capes clothed with sub-tropical gardens project into the sea, coves and beaches tucked in their side pockets; wooded islets float temptingly close to the shore; and on a clear day, from the mountain-tops, you can even make out Corsica piercing the horizon.

The ancient Romans, whose Via Aurelia first penetrated the mountain fastness of the coast, were also the first to see it as a playground. Picture, briefly, Flavia and Gaius sunning by their heated pool, before a millennium and a half of trouble intrudes, bringing intermittent third-division battles, with cut-throats in the mountains and pirate raids on the coast, forcing survivors to take refuge high up in *villages perchés*, safe from coastal danger. The French Riviera began to rediscover its Roman vocation for pleasure some 200 years ago, when the first trickle of chilly English and Russian aristocrats moved down for the winter.

This trickle turned into an international flood after 1860, when railways were built and the impoverished Grimaldis opened their casino at Monte-Carlo. By 1887, the phenomenon was packaged once and for all when poet Stephen Liégeard gave it a name: the Côte d'Azur. Although the First World War put an end to its Belle Epoque follies, the Roaring Twenties brought the coast back into fashion as never before, as writers, artists and rich Americans in Paris came down and set the trend for spending summers on the coast. After the Second World War the Côte d'Azur metamorphosed again. Paid holidays democratized the once exclusive Riviera fantasy and inaugurated an orgy of building and property speculation. Corruption, kickbacks and illegal building were rife; everyone from Aristotle Onassis on down wanted a piece of the action. 'The South of France, as far as I am concerned, has had it,' Noel Coward declared in 1960. Or, as the great Sam Goldwyn put it, 'Nobody goes there any more. It's too crowded.'

In the late 1970s the Côte d'Azur began to shift gear again, recreating itself as an international business paradise; Nice in the last thirty years has grown to become the fifth largest city in France. New convention halls and business hotels were built, new companies were drawn to the likes of Sophia-Antipolis, the Riviera's answer to Silicon Valley. Monaco, where courtesans once tickled diamonds from dukes, has become a huge tax-free haven full of trusts and banks. The Cannes Film Festival, for all its glitz, is

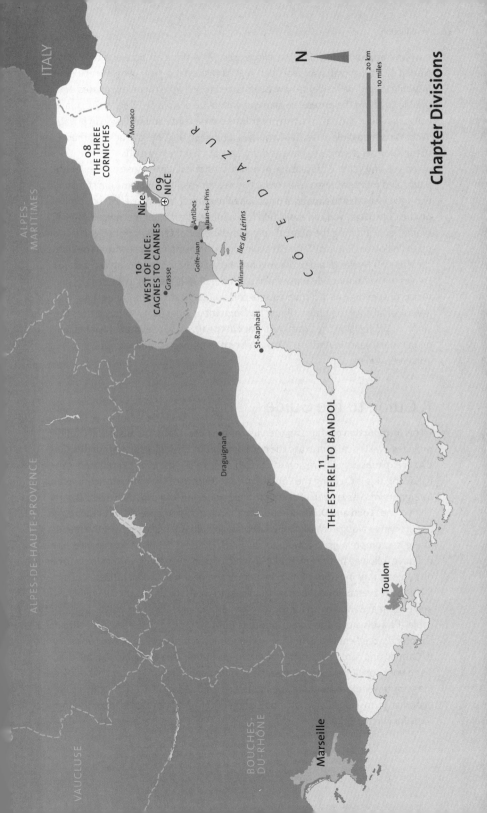

Chapter Divisions

N

20 km
10 miles

ITALY

ALPES-
MARITIMES

08
THE THREE
CORNICHES

Monaco

09
NICE

Nice

10
WEST OF NICE:
CAGNES TO CANNES

Antibes
Jean-les-Pins
Golfe-Juan
Grasse

Miramar

Iles de Lérins

C Ô T E   D ' A Z U R

St-Raphaël

ALPES-DE-HAUTE-PROVENCE

Draguignan

11
THE ESTEREL TO BANDOL

Toulon

VAUCLUSE

BOUCHES-
DU-RHÔNE

Marseille

now an overgrown trade fair. The *villages perchés* within easy access of the coast have turned into artsy-craftsy bazaars that reek of Disneyland. New people keep pouring in, while long-time residents have been forced to sell up, either expropriated or unable to afford the prices. The glamour and lustre of flaunted wealth that made the coast sparkle in the past is now concentrated on security and seclusion in private yachts and hideyhole villas. California has long been the Côte d'Azur's role model, and in the summer it seems to have as many cars but a lot fewer roads.

And yet, and yet, the tantalizing, hedonistic vision of a fantasy escape under the palms and mimosas remains as seductive as ever. Fashion and fame are still served by enough celebrities to support a battalion of paparazzi, and for every sin committed on the Côte d'Azur you can easily find forgiveness: in a radiant morning in Antibes' market or wandering the higgeldy-piggeldy lanes of old Nice, or by taking a lazy drive up to Peillon or Gorbio or Tourrettes-sur-Loup, or making an escape from the traffic on the islets off Hyères or along the wild beaches of Cap Sicié, or visiting the dazzling Fauves in the Annonciade museum in St-Tropez or Matisse's Chapelle de la Rosaire in Vence, or spending all afternoon over a portside drink at St-Jean-Cap-Ferrat.

Most of all, take the time to linger and remember what Sara Murphy, one of the summer pioneers on the Côte d'Azur back in the 1920s, wrote when she reflected on her many years in Antibes: 'We ourselves did nothing notable except enjoy ourselves.' Amen.

A Guide to the Guide

This **Introduction** contains an overview of the **Côte d'Azur**. The **Historical Outline** provides a historical context to the development of the region, and **Art on the Côte d'Azur** explores why this region has played a key role in the evolution of modern art. Following this is **Creating the Côte d'Azur**, a run-down of the writers, celebrities and foreigners who have been attracted to and had an influence on the French Riviera. Then comes **Food and Drink**, introducing the gastronomic specialities of the region and its wines, along with a list of vocabulary to help you make sense of the menu. There is a comprehensive **Travel** section which includes details of special-interest holidays, followed by the **Practical A–Z**, which covers everything you are likely to need, on subjects ranging from climate, insurance and health to tourist offices.

This book then follows the coast from east to west, starting at the Italian border and ending at Bandol, with forays inland when the local transport makes trips practicable. It travels along **The Three Corniches** from Menton to Nice. The city of **Nice** has a chapter devoted entirely to it. The book's journey continues **West of Nice** from Cagnes to Cannes, and completes its trip along the coast from **The Esterel to Bandol**.

The book concludes with a **Language** chapter supplying some essential basic vocabulary for travelling around; and a quick-reference **Glossary** of artistic, architectural and historical terms. To enrich your appreciation of the area, there are also some suggestions for **Further Reading**.

Historical Outline

02

The Côte d'Azur, a part of Provence since Roman times, does not have much of a history of its own. The difficult, rocky coastline has kept big cities and dense populations away since antiquity, when this coast was little more than an rocky obstacle to mariners between Italy and the heartland of Provence. Nevertheless, tools and traces of habitation around Monaco go back as far as 1,000,000 BC, and someone was in the neighbourhood for most of the millennia that followed – southern France is one of the most ancient stomping grounds of mankind.

Milestone Events

c. **60,000 BC** Neanderthal man turns up in the region.

c. **40,000 BC** That quarrelsome and unlovable species *Homo sapiens* appears and squeezes the poor Neanderthals out or kills them off.

c. **3500 BC** Neolithic civilization arrives, with settled agriculture, stock-raising, dolmens and astronomy.

c. **1000 BC** Native Ligurian peoples of the coast begin to build fortified villages, including Nice.

c. **600 BC** Arrival of the Celts and Greeks in Provence.

The Greeks were interested mainly in founding trading colonies, of which the first was Massalia (Marseille). Soon Massalia was founding colonies of its own: Nice and Hyères were among the most important. Greek influence over the indigenous peoples was strong from the start; as with everywhere else they went, they brought the vine (wild stocks were already present, but no one had worked out what to do with them) and the olive, and also their art. The Greeks on the coast and the Celts in the hinterlands sometimes fought each other, and sometimes got on well enough.

218 BC Hannibal's army and the elephants march through Liguria on their way to Italy. Caught in the middle of the Punic Wars, Ligurians, Greeks and Celts alike discover that there are much bigger fish in the pond waiting to gobble them up.

125 BC The Romans save Marseille from a Celtic attack.

It rapidly became clear that the aggressive republic wanted to keep Liguria and the Rhône valley for itself. The Romans reorganized the terrritory into their first 'provence' (the origin of 'Provence'), their first conquest outside Italy. Over the next century, Provence became thoroughly integrated into the Roman world.

121 BC First Roman road in the region, the Via Domitia, built by Domitius Ahenobarbus, the vanquisher of the Celts. The Celts were not through yet, though. Resistance continued intermittently until 14 BC; the great monument at La Turbie (*see* pp.84–5), on the border of Gaul, commemorates the defeat of the last hold-outs in the Alps.

49 BC Massalia punished by Caesar for supporting Pompey in the Roman civil wars. Thereafter, the influence of the Greek city gives way to newer, more Romanized towns, including Fréjus on the Côte.

AD 476 With the end of the Roman Empire, Provence and the Côte become part of the Visigothic Kingdom of Italy. In 535 the Franks snatch them away from the Visigoths, though they are never able to assert much control; the region drifts into *de facto* independence.

c. 700 The Arabs begin their invasions of southern Gaul from Spain. After the Franks defeat them at Poitiers (732), Charles Martel comes down south to wreak havoc in Provence. In this dark age, the Côte d'Azur remains one of the most backward and inaccessible parts of the Mediterranean – a perfect place for pirates. Arab corsairs hold parts of the coast, including St-Tropez and the Massif des Maures, until the 970s.

879 The Kingdom of Provence is proclaimed by a great-grandson of Charlemagne, though it is little more than a façade for feudal anarchy. The kingdom is united with the Kingdom of Burgundy in 949, and formally passes to the Holy Roman Empire in 1032, but the tapestry of battling barons and shifting local alliances continues without effective interference from the overlords.

1002 The first written document in the Provençal language appears.

1095 Beginning of the Crusades.

1125 The Counts of Barcelona control most of Provence south of the Durance river.

1297 Francesco Grimaldi seizes Monaco for Genoa; in 1308, the Grimaldis purchase Monaco outright from Genoa (they've held on to it ever since).

1309 The 'Babylonian Captivity' begins when the Papacy installs itself in Avignon.

1388 Nice throws out its Angevin rulers and pledges allegiance to the County of Savoy.

c. 1450 The Côte attains its first artistic distinction with the Nice school of painters, creating fine altarpieces in the Renaissance manner in many of the region's churches.

1481 Upon the death of Good King René, Provence is annexed by France.

From the start, the French pursued a policy of eradicating Provence's rights and institutions, along with its language and culture. Royal guarantees of the Provençal laws and parliament were soon exposed as lies, and the region gradually came under stricter control from Paris. The 1539 Edict of Villars-Cotterêts decreed French as the official language throughout the kingdom, and the work of replacing Provençal – Europe's first literary language, the language of the troubadours – was only completed by the Paris-controlled public schools in the 19th and 20th centuries.

1542 First massacres of Protestants in Provence, beginning the Wars of Religion.

1598 Henri IV decrees religious tolerance with the Edict of Nantes.

1696 The French briefly occupy Nice (and do it again in 1705, during the War of the Spanish Succession). The Niçois fear them: they think the French are cannibals.

1766 Cranky old Tobias Smollett's *Travels through France and Italy* puts the Côte on the map for British grand tourists.

1789 The French Revolution begins.

Provence and the south played only a small role in what was essentially a Parisian drama. In 1792 volunteers from Marseille had brought the Marseillaise *to Paris, while local mobs wrecked and looted hundreds of southern churches and châteaux. Soon, however, the betrayed south became violently counter-revolutionary. The royalists and the English occupied Toulon after a popular revolt, and were only dislodged by the brilliant tactics of a young commander named Bonaparte in 1793.*

1815 Napoleon lands at Golfe-Juan from Elba to start the 'Hundred Days'. Today the tourist offices promote the 'Route Napoléon', where Napoleon passed through – but at the time he had to sneak along those roads in an Austrian uniform, to protect himself from the Provençaux. The south never managed much enthusiasm for Napoleon or his wars. The Emperor called the Provençaux cowards, and said theirs was the only part of France that never gave him a decent regiment.

1834 Ex-Chancellor Lord Brougham 'discovers' Cannes.

1848 In Europe's year of revolutions, Menton and Roquebrune successfully revolt against the rule of the Grimaldis of Monaco.

1860 Nice and its hinterlands (now the *département* of Alpes-Maritimes) join France after a Stalinesque plebiscite. This was the price exacted by Napoléon III in 1860 for French aid to Vittorio Emanuele II in Italy's War of Independence.

1887 Minor poet and journalist Stephen Liégeard gives the Côte d'Azur its name.

1902 First Monte Carlo Rally held.

After 1910, economic factors conspired against all of southern France: rural depopulation, caused by the breakup of the pre-industrial agricultural society, drained the life out of the villages – and out of the dying Provençal culture. The First World War decimated a generation – go into any village church in the south and look at the war memorial plaques; from a total population of a few hundred, you'll see maybe 30 names of villagers who died for the 'Glory of France'. By 1950, most inland villages had lost at least half their population; some died out altogether. While all this was happening, the towns and villages along the coast found new life as tourist preserves, beginning when the Côte became the centre of the international high life in the 1920s.

1920 Moyenne Corniche road built.

1931 The first year the hotels on the Côte d'Azur stay open in summer.

1942 French fleet scuttled at Toulon.

1943–4 *Les Enfants du Paradis* filmed in Nice, in the midst of the German occupation of France.

1944 In August, American and French troops hit the beaches around St Tropez, and in a remarkably successful (and little-noticed) operation they have most of Provence liberated in two weeks. In the rugged mountains behind Nice, some bypassed German outposts hold out until the end of the war.

1946 Cannes Film Festival gets under way in earnest.

1982 Graham Greene publishes a pamphlet on organized crime on the Côte d'Azur called *J'Accuse: The Dark Side of Nice*.

1989 The TGV high-speed train network is extended to the Côte d'Azur.

1990 Under indictment for misuse of public funds, Nice mayor Jacques Médecin flees to Uruguay, advising his constituents to vote for the National Front.

1995 Establishment of new Euro-Mediterranean free-trade zone anounced in Barcelona, designed to create long term benefits for industrial ports like Toulon and Marseille.

1998 Jacques Médecin is extradited from Uruguay and dies in France.

The Côte d'Azur Today

The post-war era was all sweetness and ice-cream and reinforced concrete, a series of increasingly passionless snapshots: the Côte d'Azur become a myth of the masses – Grace Kelly with Cary Grant in *To Catch a Thief*, later with Rainier the Third in *Monaco*, and Brigitte Bardot showing her knickers to the paparazzi.

The arrival of mass tourism put plenty of dosh in everyone's pockets while coating the fabled coast with a thick layer of villas and mimosa. The changes have in fact been momentous. The overdeveloped, often corrupt and ever more schizophrenic Côte d'Azur has become the heart of Provence – the tail that wags the dog. Besides its resorts it has the likes of IBM and the techno-paradise of Sophia-Antipolis (*see* p.150), mythologized recently in J.G. Ballard's *Super-Cannes*. Above all, the self-proclaimed 'California of Europe' has money, and will acquire more; in two or three decades it will be the first province in centuries to start telling Paris where to get off. Waves of Parisians and foreigners, mostly British, still come looking for the good life and a stone house to fix up (though there are no longer any of these left). They have brought life to many areas, though the traditional rural atmosphere suffers a bit. Many of the big villas that go on the market these days are purchased by wealthy Arabs.

The greatest political event of recent decades was the election of the Socialist Mitterrand government in 1981, followed by the creation of regional governments across France. Though their powers and budgets are extremely limited, this represents a major turning point, the first reversal of a thousand years of increasing Parisian centralism. Its lasting effects will not be known for decades, perhaps centuries; already the revival of the Provençal language and culture is resuming in the hinterland, though English threatens to become the *lingua franca* on the coast. Politics, quietly Socialist in much of the Midi, can still be primeval on the Med. e Pen's National Front still commands a big vote, though to keep up appearances voters usually prefer to elect fellow-travellers in the mainstream right-wing parties, such as Nice's ex-mayor Jacques Médecin. Médecin, leader of the criminal dynasty that had ruled the city for almost a half-century, was finally caught out in 1990; when the courts started looking into his books, he fled to exile in Uruguay, avoiding extradition there for years before his return and conviction. Overtly fascist ideas, and fascist talk, still find a warmer reception on Provence's coasts than almost anywhere in Europe. The region's defenders offer a historical explanation: traditional hatred of Paris and its bureaucrats, the influx of bitter French *pieds-noirs* displaced from Algeria in the 60s, and the unwelcome wave of North African immigrants that came after. It isn't much of an excuse, but things may be slowly changing. The large numbers of newcomers are immune to old Provençal passions, and even some of the natives seem to be wearying of an extreme right most distinguished for lining its own pockets. The Côte d'Azur aspires to be a glittering showcase of Europe, and, if its politics ever climb out of the gutter, it will be when enough of its people finally decide that fascism is bad for business.

Art on the Côte d'Azur

03

A lady once came to look at Matisse's paintings and was horrified to see a woman with a green face. 'Wouldn't it be horrible to see a woman walking down the street with a green face?' she asked him. 'It certainly would!' Matisse agreed. 'Thank God it's only a painting!'

The Côte d'Azur, thanks to its clear Mediterranean light, vibrant colour and sheer popularity as a place to live and paint in the 20th century, has played a key role in the evolution of modern art. Pablo Picasso, Henri Matisse and a score of other major figures were inspired to create some of their most important works here, and a fair selection of paintings, sculpture and ceramics remain in the outstanding museums and foundations which grace the coast. There's also something magical about seeing art in situ, especially art so overwhelmingly sundrenched and sensuous and full of joy – the 'realer than real' French Riviera of our collective dreams and desires.

The first blows for modern art, however, were struck back in Paris, precisely when three large canvases of everyday, contemporary scenes by Gustave Courbet got past the judges into the 1850 Paris Salon to hang among rooms of stilted, academic historical, religious and mythological subjects. Today it's hard to imagine how audacious his contemporaries found Courbet's new style, which came to be called Realism – almost as if it took the invention of photography by Louis Daguerre (1837) to make the eye see what was 'really' there. 'Do what you see, what you want, what you feel,' was Courbet's advice to his pupils. One thing Courbet felt like doing in 1854 was painting in the south, a pioneering move. The canvases he brought back to Paris startled with their bright colour and light; he anticipated all the Moderns with his emphasis on the artist's methods and techniques over subject matter.

If photography played midwife to Realism, optics had an equal part in the invention of Impressionism. In the 1860s, the revolutionary discovery that colour derives from light, not form, fired the spirits of Camille Pissarro, Claude Monet and company, who made it their goal to strip Courbet's new-found visual reality of all subjectivity and simply record on canvas the atmosphere, light and colour the eye saw, all according to the latest scientific theories. Although many of the great Impressionists spent time in the south, only Renoir was to permanently relocate there (to Cagnes-sur-Mer, in 1895) and then only on doctor's orders for his rheumatic arthritis.

Meanwhile, elsewhere in Provence, a Dutch admirer of the Impressionists named Vincent Van Gogh had arrived in Arles seeking the landscapes he saw in Japanese prints (one wonders a bit about his sanity from the start). The big sun of Arles had the effect of a mystic revelation on his art in 1888, and he responded to the heightened colour and light on such an intense, personal level that colour came less and less to represent form in his art (as it did for the Impressionists), but instead took on a symbolic, emotional value, as the only medium Van Gogh found powerful enough to express his extraordinary moods and visions. As he wrote to his brother Theo: 'Instead of attempting to reproduce exactly what I have in front of my eyes, I use colour in a more arbitrary way, to express myself more forcibly.'

Van Gogh's liberation of colour from form was taken to an extreme by a group of painters that the critic Louis Vauxcelles nicknamed the Fauves ('wild beasts') for the violence of their colours. The Fauves used colour to express moods and rhythms, to the detriment of detail and recognizable subject matter. As art movements go, the Fauves were a red-hot flash in the pan, lasting only from 1904 until 1908, but in those few years they revolutionized centuries of European art. 'Fauve painting is not everything,' Matisse explained. 'But it is the foundation of everything.' Nearly all the Fauves – Matisse himself, André Derain, Maurice Vlaminck, Raoul Dufy and Kees Van Dongen – painted in St-Tropez as guests of the hospitable painter Paul Signac. Their efforts paved the way for Expressionism, Cubism and Abstraction – avenues few of the Fauvists themselves ever explored. For after 1908 the new vision these young men had shared in the south of France vanished as if they had awoken from a mass hypnosis; the group splintered, leaving others to carry their ideas on to their logical conclusions. The Musée de l'Annonciade in St-Tropez has the best collection of Fauvist painting on the Côte d'Azur, although two-thirds of the greatest Fauves are hidden in various private collections.

After the Fauves, individual artists went their own way. One of the leaders of the movement, Matisse, settled on the Côte d'Azur after 1917, where he was generally proclaimed, with Picasso, as the greatest painter of his age. Although he was never again associated with a school, he took Fauvism to the limit, expressing himself in pure abstract colour, brimful of the luxuriant sensuality of the south. His acquaintance with Picasso dated back to 1906 (both shared a fascination with African art and masks), and when Picasso moved permanently to the Côte d'Azur in 1946 the two kept up a friendly rivalry; the Spaniard, to whom modesty was a stranger, graciously acknowledged Matisse as his equal, and in many ways his master.

The reputation of Van Gogh, Paul Cézanne and the Fauves, and the presence of the two giants of modern art, drew scores of artists and would-be artists to the Côte d'Azur, among them Pierre Bonnard, Fernand Léger, Marc Chagall and Nicolas de Staël. From the late 1950s, the Neo-Realist reaction to both Abstract Expressionism and the precious, humourless art world was reflected in the 'second' School of Nice (the first was in the Renaissance) led by multi-media iconoclasts such as Arman, César and Ben, whose works are the highlights of the Musée d'Art Contemporain in Nice. Since then, the torch of contemporary art on the Riviera has been kept alight by the Fondation Maeght in St-Paul-de-Vence, with its excellent, ever-changing exhibits of contemporary art in an idyllic setting – a place to return to again and again.

Artists' Directory

Arman (1928–): sculptor best known for his witty combinations of junk and musical instruments, who snubbed the major exhibition of his works that inaugurated the new contemporary art museum in **Nice** to protest against anti-semitic remarks by mayor Jacques Médecin (Musée Picasso, **Antibes**, pp.143–6; Fondation Maeght, **St-Paul-de-Vence**, pp.132–3.

Bonnard, Pierre (1867–1947): although his early career is closely associated with the Nabis (a group of painters who, following Gauguin, rejected naturalism and natural colour), Bonnard changed gear in 1900 to become one of the 20th century's purest Impressionists, painting luscious, radiant, colour-saturated landscapes and domestic scenes, especially after 1925 when he moved to Le Cannet, near Cannes. Always experimenting with colour and form but uninterested in the avant-garde, Bonnard has forever been popular with collectors and is one of very few foreigners admitted to the British Royal Academy (1940) (Musée de l'Annonciade, **St-Tropez**, p.190).

Brea, Ludovico (active 1475–1544): leader of the International Gothic Nice school, influenced by the Renaissance in his later career; although commissioned to do hieratic medieval-style subjects, his precise line and beautiful sense of light and shadow stand out – still, to call him the 'Fra Angelico of Provence', as some French critics do, is going too far. He invented a shade of wine-red that French artists still call *rouge bréa* (Franciscan church in Cimiez, **Nice**, p.121; Palais Carnolès, **Menton**,p.68; and **Monaco** cathedral, p.83).

Chagall, Marc (1887–1985): highly individualistic Russian-Jewish painter and illustrator who drew his main themes from Jewish-Russian folklore and the Old Testament. Influenced by Cubism and Orphism (the pre-First World War movement that gave intellectual Cubism a lyrical quality with colour), his art is imbued with a distinctive fairytale, imaginative quality. After spending the war years in the USA, he moved permanently to St-Paul-de-Vence in 1950, where he became interested in stained glass (Musée National Message Biblique Marc Chagall, **Nice**, pp.119–20; Fondation Maeght, **St-Paul-de-Vence**, pp.132–3; Ancienne Cathédrale, **Vence**, p.134).

Cocteau, Jean (1889–1963): poet, surrealist film director, illustrator and leader of the gay 'Villefranche band' between the wars, Cocteau was long Riviera society's arbiter of avant-garde taste. A frequent collaborator with Diaghilev, Stravinsky and Satie, his flowing draughtsmanship was inspired by his friend Picasso; when the Côte d'Azur was down on its luck in the early 1950s, he decorated the walls of the Mairie and Museum in **Menton** (p.65) and the Chapelle de St-Pierre, **Villefranche-sur-Mer** (p.92) to re-create an interest in the arts and lend a new tone to the resorts. The Greek-inspired outdoor youth theatre in **Cap d'Ail** was one of his last projects, and the flamboyant Chapelle Notre-Dame-de-Jerusalem in **Fréjus** (p.180) was completed posthumously.

Derain, André (1880–1954): along with Vlaminck, he was a key Fauvist painter of extraordinary innovation and originality, who took Fauvism and Expressionism to the limit before the First World War, then lapsed into more conventional academism. He designed sets and costumes for the Ballets Russes in Monaco, and is credited as the first artist in the west to take a keen interest in primitive art (Musée de l'Annonciade, **St-Tropez**, p.190).

Dufy, Raoul (1877–1953): Dufy's most original and energetic painting was as a Fauve. After flirting with Cubism with Georges Braque in L'Estaque, his style took on its characteristic graphic quality, and he spent much of his remaining life in Nice, painting pleasing lightweight decorative interiors (Musée des Beaux Arts (Jules Chéret), **Nice**, pp.117–18).

Fragonard, Jean-Honoré (1732–1806): native of Grasse and student of Boucher, Fragonard painted frivolous rococo scenes in anaemic pastels, but with a verve and erotic wit that found favour with France's spiritually bankrupt nobility, who longed to escape into his canvases (Villa-Musée Fragonard, **Grasse**, pp.151–4).

Granet, François Marius (1775–1849): native of Aix and a pupil of David; although his canvases are run-of-the-mill academic, his watercolours and sketches reveal a poetic observation of nature that became the hallmark of the Provençal school (Musée d'Art et d'Histoire, **Grasse**, p.154).

Kisling, Moïse (1891–1953): always known as Kiki; a Polish-born Jew whose painting caused a sensation in Montparnasse in 1910. Influenced by Cubism and his friends Modigliani and Chagall, he fought in the Foreign Legion in the First World War and was severely wounded, and sent to the south to die in peace. Instead he married and thrived in Villa La Baie over Bandol, becoming a feature of the Côte d'Azur, where he was famous for his high spirits. Admired by Picasso and Braque, Kisling probably would be better known if he hadn't accepted so many commissions to paint portraits of society women, which he did with a highly personal flair, elegance and polish (Musée d'Art Moderne Méditerranéen, **Haut-de-Cagnes**, p.128).

Léger, Fernand (1881–1955): went from an early figurative manner to Cubism. Wounded in the First World War, Léger attempted to create an art that interpreted the experiences of ordinary people in war, work and play, culminating in his colourful, geometric, highly stylized figures of workers and factories. He worked in many media, especially mosaics and ceramics (Musée National Fernand Léger, **Biot**, pp.139–40; Fondation Maeght, **St-Paul-de-Vence**, pp.132–3).

Matisse, Henri (1869–1954): a trip to the south in the 1890s converted Matisse to luminous colours, while his first major painting and Fauve masterpiece, *Luxe, calme et volupté*, painted in St-Tropez in 1904–5, set out the main themes of his life's work: luxury, calmness and voluptuousness. After 1917 he settled in Nice, where the hot colours of the south continued to saturate his ever-sensuous, serene and boldly drawn works, qualities apparent even in the joyous paper cut-outs of dancing figures he made in his last bedridden years – his doctor, worried that the vivid intensity of the colours he chose would harm his vision, tried to make him wear dark glasses. Many art historians rate his Chapel of the Rosary in **Vence** (pp.135–6) as one of the most moving religious buildings of the 20th century (also see the Musée Matisse, **Nice**, pp.120–21 and the Musée de l'Annonciade, **St-Tropez**, p.190).

Picasso, Pablo (1881–1973): born in Málaga, Spain, the 20th century's most endlessly inventive artist is especially celebrated for his mastery of line and his great expressive power. In 1948, his blue, rose and Cubist days behind him, Picasso abandoned Paris and moved to the south of France, settling first in Vallauris, then Cannes, and finally at Mougins, where he died. His conviction was that 'painting is not done to decorate apartments; it is an instrument of war against brutality and darkness.' Living on the Côte d'Azur heightened the sensuous Mediterranean and mythological aspects of his extraordinarily wide-ranging work, and, although he never stopped drawing and painting, the greatest innovations of the latter half of his career were three-dimensional, in ceramics and sculpture (Musée Picasso, **Antibes**, pp.143–6; castle chapel at **Vallauris**, p.149; Musée des Beaux Arts (Jules Chéret), **Nice**, pp.117–18).

Renoir, Pierre-Auguste (1841–1919): as serene as Van Gogh was tormented, Renoir combined Impressionism with the traditional 'gallant' themes of Fragonard, updated to the 19th century: pretty girls, dances, fêtes, children, nudes, bathers, pastorals. Racked by rheumatism, he spent his last years in Cagnes, where his career was given a new lease of life, painting warm, voluptuous nudes and landscapes (Musée Renoir, **Cagnes-sur-Mer**, pp.126–7).

Seurat, Georges (1859–91): theorist and founder of neo-Impressionism, with his technique of *pointillisme* (juxtaposing dots of pure colour to achieve a greater luminosity); although he was highly influential, none of his disciples could match his precision and vision (Musée de l'Annonciade, **St-Tropez**, p.190).

Signac, Paul (1863–1935): Georges Seurat's most faithful follower down the path of *pointillisme*. When Seurat died, Signac left Paris and discovered St-Tropez in 1892, where, influenced by the Fauves, he gradually abandoned his scientific dot theory for a freer, more attractive style that charmed and influenced the young Matisse (Musée de l'Annonciade, **St-Tropez**, p.190).

Staël, Nicolas de (1914–55): highly influential abstract painter born in St Petersburg of noble Russian parents. He attended Fernand Léger's academy in Paris, but later destroyed all his pre-war paintings in favour of his new style, a visual and sensual rather than emotive abstraction, based on nature, that made him one of the more appealing young leaders of the post-war movement. He moved to the Côte d'Azur in 1953, where he complained that the light was 'as nerve-racking as a ping-pong ball' and committed suicide two years later (Musée Picasso, **Antibes**, pp.143–6).

Van Dongen, Kees (1877–1968): a Fauve painter of verve and elegance, who after Fauvism became the chief chronicler of Riviera society and mores of the 1920s and '30s (Musée des Beaux Arts (Jules Chéret), **Nice**, pp.117–18; Musée de l'Annonciade, **St-Tropez**, p.190).

Van Loo, Carle (1705–65): native of Nice and younger brother of the less successful Jean-Baptiste Van Loo, Carle was a rococo painter in the 'grand style' and a keen rival of Boucher, painting hunting scenes and religious paintings, and designing Gobelin tapestries for the kings of France and Savoy (Musée des Beaux Arts (Jules Chéret), **Nice**, pp.117–18).

Vuillard, Edouard (1868–1940): like his good friend Bonnard, Vuillard began as a Nabi and later became better known for his Impressionistic, intimate, domestic scenes (Musée de l'Annonciade, **St-Tropez**, p.190).

Ziem, Félix (1821–1911): started off illuminating canvases with a sense of light audacious for the period. Having found a successful formula, he repeated himself from then on. Much admired by Van Gogh, Ziem's favourite subjects were Venice and Martigues, near Marseille (Musée des Beaux Arts (Jules Chéret), **Nice**, pp.117–18).

Creating the Côte d'Azur

04

There was no one at Antibes this summer except me, Zelda, the Valentinos, the Murphys, Mistinguett, Rex Ingram, Dos Passos, Alice Terry, the Mackleishes, Charlie Brackett, Maude Kahn, Esther Murphy, Maquerite Namara, E. Philips Oppenheim, Mannes the violinist, Floyd Dell, May and Crystal Eastman, ex-Premier Orlando, Etienne de Beaumont – just a real place to rough it, and escape from all the world.
F. Scott Fitzgerald, in a letter to a friend

Even though in retrospect it seems inevitable that the Côte d'Azur was destined to become a hedonistic fantasyland, it owes a good deal to the personalities, desires and imagination of its colonizers. Statistics are coy, but many invalids who came here for a cure never went home. 'They check in, but they don't check out,' as a disgruntled resident in Nice once put it. The other striking fact about the Riviera's ascent to fame and fortune is that the locals had next to nothing to do with its creation myths: the fantasy was spun by the collective desires of strangers. Not a single person in the *dramatis personae* listed below is from the Côte d'Azur, and even the most famous native is really 'from' somewhere else: a certain Giuseppe Garibaldi.

The Cast

The story begins 200 years ago, when the French Riviera was a beautiful, isolated, impoverished place, a rather awkward corridor to Italy a traveller had to tackle after sailing down the Rhône. Two Englishmen who stopped on the way changed all that.

Tobias Smollett (1721–71): doctor and novelist unforgettably nicknamed 'Smelfungus' by Lawrence Sterne for his grumpiness, Smollett spent 1763 in Nice and three years later published his best selling *Travels through France and Italy* (with prices). He occasionally deigned to put in a good word for Nice – 'the plain presents nothing but gardens...blowing in full glory, with such beauty, vigour, and perfumes, as no flower in England ever exhibited' – while at the same time dismissing the locals as slovenly and slothful, poor and withered, or cheats, thieves and bankrupts who upped prices 30 per cent for foreigners. Seeking a cure for consumption, he shocked the Niçois by indulging in the then extraordinary practice of sea bathing, which he highly recommended, although warning, prophetically it turns out, that it would be difficult for women 'unless they laid aside all regards for decorum'. Typically, the more Smollett sniped at the Riviera, the more the British wanted to go there.

Henry Lord Brougham (1778–1868): ex-Lord Chancellor and the man who gave his name to a kind of carriage, Lord Brougham added an essential touch of class to the Riviera. It all happened through chance: because of a cholera quarantine on the Italian frontier (then just west of Nice), he was forced to spend a night in Cannes in 1834, where he found the climate he thought to find in Naples in La Napoule there. Soon after he bought an estate in Cannes, and returned every winter, encouraging his friends to do the same so he'd have someone to talk to. He amazed the locals by planting a grass lawn. Within 50 years of his arrival, Cannes had 50 hotels and the most aristocratic reputation on the coast.

The die was cast. Tubercular Brits and elderly aristocrats poured down to the Riviera to die in the winter sun. The next chapter began in 1864, when the railway was extended from Marseille to Nice, putting the coast within reach of a new kind of visitor.

Stephen Liégeard (1830–1925): a lawyer and minor poet born into a wealthy wine-growing family in Burgundy, Liégeard married a woman who owned Les Violettes, the villa adjacent to Lord Brougham's estate. He was by all accounts a most affable and charming toady of the members of the Académie Française, but they still wouldn't elect him in, and Liégeard would have been forgotten if he hadn't given the coast its name in his glowing, idolizing 1887 guidebook *La Côte d'Azur.*

Queen Victoria (1819–1901): wintered on the Riviera seven times beginning in 1887, following a trail blazed back in 1875 by her frisky son the Prince of Wales. As the mightiest monarch of the day, Victoria's diminutive presence was the best advert that the Côte d'Azur could wish for (in gratitude Nice erected her statue in Cimiez, where she stayed; the Germans knocked it over, but it was re-erected after the war). Accompanied by her Indian servants, she was popular for passing out coins to the crowds; unlike her son she studiously avoided Monaco (in London in the 1880s there was already a society for the abolition of the Casino). Her grandson who abdicated as Edward VIII was to spend much of his life as the Duke of Windsor on the coast, pursuing a rigorous social schedule with his American duchess.

James Gordon Bennett (1841–1918): black sheep heir to the founder of the *New York Herald*, Bennett founded the *Paris Herald* (ancestor of today's *International Herald Tribune*) in 1887 and ran it from his villa in Beaulieu, using it to advertise the coast and its visitors ('Monarchs Galore!'). Bennett was one of the millionaire rogues who set the brash tone of the Riviera in the 1880s and 1890s; if his food arrived late at a restaurant, he would buy the restaurant.

La Belle Otero (1877–1964): like Bennett, the famous *grande horizontale* Caroline Otero profited from the presence of royalty on the coast, with a list of lovers that included Tsar Nicholas II, Edward VII and Reza Shah. A stunning Andalusian gypsy dancer and child bride of an Italian nobleman, she made her fortune in Monte-Carlo in 1901 by staking her last two louis on red at *trente-et-quarante*. Knowing nothing of the game, she thought she had lost and walked away; by the time she returned red had come up 28 times. La Belle Otero was notorious for her rivalry with the courtesan Liane de Pougy (once in Monte-Carlo, Otero plotted to outshine Liane by making a grand entrance, blazing with every diamond she owned; Liane got word of it and followed in a simple white gown, accompanied by her dog wearing all her fabulous carats). The shape of her breasts immortalized in the cupolas of the Carlton hotel in Cannes, Otero retired in 1922 at age 45 worth 45 million francs, but gambled it away in a few years and died impoverished in a small furnished room in Nice.

The Roaring Twenties brought the first summer visitors to the Côte d'Azur. The Americans had the most money to spend and many made fools of themselves. After 1930, however, the Great Depression forced many to stay home, and in 1936 they began to be displaced by a new kind of visitor, when the French Parliament granted all workers a two-week paid holiday and cheap train tickets to the seaside.

Frank Jay Gould (1836–1892): America's most famous scoundrel, robber baron and stock market manipulator was, like James Gordon Bennett, excluded from respectable society in New York, but he left his son Frank Jay a cool $22 million when he died in 1892. Frank Jay was a drunk and a lout, and made his mark on the Côte d'Azur by acquiring even more money, by buying up the Casino and building the Hôtel Provençal at Juan-les-Pins in the 1920s and by constructing the enormous Palais de la Méditerranée casino in Nice to foil his rivals. His third wife, Florence Gould, redeemed him somewhat by spending his money to become one of the most beloved and generous hostesses on the coast.

Somerset Maugham (1874–1965): the British novelist was a solid fixture of the Riviera, presiding imperially at his Villa Mauresque in St-Jean-Cap-Ferrat, where he 'lived simply' to a strict routine with 13 servants, writing in the morning and using the Riviera as a background for many of his novels. He entertained a constant stream of celebrities – Kenneth Clark, Noel Coward and Cyril Connolly were regulars – and presided over very formal dinner parties in black tie and velvet slippers, treating his guests to his cook's secret recipe for avocado ice-cream.

Colette (1873–1954): a founding figure in St-Tropez, the only big resort on the Riviera 'discovered' by the French. (Guy de Maupassant was there first, and wrote about his boat trip around the coast in *Sur l'eau*, in 1887.) Colette bought a little house called La Treille Muscate in 1926, met the love of her life, Maurice Goudeket, and wrote *La Naissance du jour*, the ultimate St-Trop idyll. In 1937, a victim of her own success and tired of finding her garden full of strangers, she moved to Brittany.

Isadora Duncan (1878–1927): one of the founding mothers of modern dance, Duncan sought refuge in Nice after her children were tragically drowned in the Seine and she had separated from poet Sergei Esenin, the husband she had wed during the Russian Revolution. She opened a dance studio in Nice and was one of the most popular people on the coast. No one knew what she would say or do next, and although roly-poly, she could still enchant her audience with her unique impromptu dancing in her flowing, billowing clothes. '*Adieu, mes amis, je vais à la gloire!*' were her last words before she was driven off in a Bugatti down the Promenade des Anglais; her swirling scarf got entangled in the wheel and she died instantly of a broken neck. Although Isadora had raised funds for France during the First World War, Americans were very unpopular in France in 1927 because of the Sacco and Vanzetti case, and no one attended her funeral in Paris.

Coco Chanel (1883–1971): Isadora Duncan would have lived longer had she been dressed by Chanel. Raised in rural poverty, Gabrielle Chanel was a svelte dark beauty who got her start when her aristocratic English lover Boy Capel set her up in millinery. She soon displayed her gift as a designer in touch with the trends as well as her astute canniness as a businesswoman. In 1916, inspired by Cubism, she changed the course of fashion by making austerity and simplicity elegant, '*le luxe dans la simplicité*' as she put it, creating well cut and understated fashions and 'little black dresses' to appeal to both her *haute couture* clients and the newly emancipated working woman. A fixture of the Riviera in the 1920s, with pockets full of dukes – among them Grand Duke Dimitri of Russia and the Duke of Westminster –

she not only confirmed the new fad for sunbathing but also popularized a whole new style of clothing: sportswear, invented for Cocteau's ballet *Le Train bleu*. Chanel set the fashion for short hair and sailors' caps, and became one of the first designers to put her name to a scent when she discovered a perfumer in Grasse to produce a formula for an intriguing, long-lasting fragrance, packaged in the classic No.5 bottle.

Aldous Huxley (1894–1963): satirical novelist Huxley spent much of his life in Sanary near Toulon. His classic *Brave New World* (1932) was in response to the rosy ideas of H.G. Wells who lived nearby; he moved to California during the Second World War.

F. Scott Fitzgerald (1896–1940): charter members of the Lost Generation, Scott and talented wife Zelda personified the madcap recklessness and escapades that people associated with the Côte d'Azur, both devoted – doomed almost – to maintaining a continual high of hedonism. When drunk, which was nearly always, Scott would be sawing bartenders in half, tossing full ashtrays at people in restaurants or shot-putting ice-cream down the backs of ladies; Zelda liked to lie in front of cars or dance an impromptu pirouette half-naked in the ball room at Monte-Carlo. In 1929 Zelda suffered a nervous breakdown and was diagnosed as suffering from acute schizophrenia; she never recovered.

Jean Cocteau (1889–1963): a long-time resident of Villefranche-sur-Mer, gregarious painter, poet and *cinéaste*, promoter of avant-garde musicians and artists, and a close friend of the rich and famous, Cocteau did much to define the spirit of the Côte d'Azur in its heyday, especially in *Le Train bleu*, a work evoking the carefree sporting life by the sea (named after the legendary streamlined luxury train that linked Paris to the coast), which he wrote for Diaghilev's *Ballets Russes*, with music by Darius Milhaud, costumes by Chanel, and sets by Picasso. He would later play no small role in making sure Cannes was chosen as the venue for France's film festival, and was a frequent member of its jury.

Cole Porter (1893–1964): Porter began his career as America's best loved composer of subtle melodies and sophisticated lyrics before the First World War, when he enlisted in the French Foreign Legion and later served in the French army. In Paris in the 1920s, he was commissioned by Winnaretta, Princesse de Polignac and daughter of Isaac 'Sewing Machine' Singer to write a jazz ballet called *Within the Quota*; he hung around Paris, longing to study with Stravinsky. In the summer of 1922 he rented the Château de la Garoupe in Cap d'Antibes, invited his friends down from Paris, and convinced them that summer on the Riviera was the place to be.

Katherine Mansfield (1888–1923): master of the ironic, sensitive short story and married to John Middleton Murry, Mansfield spent the last five years of her life trying to find a cure for her tuberculosis, spending a good deal of time in Menton. Her letters to her husband and short stories offer an evocative view of the coast.

D.H. Lawrence (1885–1930): another victim of tuberculosis and friend of Mansfield, Lawrence was only 45 when after a life of wanderings he died in Vence, dismayed by what the 'vileness of man' had wrecked on the lovely coast, but commenting on the Mediterranean in a letter shortly before he died: 'It still seems as young as Odysseus, in the morning.' Another towering figure of English literature to topple on the coast was **W.B. Yeats**, who died at Cap Martin in 1939 and was buried at Roquebrune, where rumour has it part or all of him still remains – when his relics were transferred to Ireland they got the wrong stiff. Other Irishmen who found muses on the Côte d'Azur included **James Joyce**, who claimed Nice was the first inspiration for *Finnegans Wake*, and film director Rex Ingram, who shot *The Four Horsemen of the Apocalypse* in Nice, based on the novel by Blasco Ibáñez.

After the war, French glumness infected even the coast, although (with the exception of Toulon) it had escaped relatively intact. Even property prices were depressed. But it wasn't long before a new transfusion of glitter arrived and the joint was jumping all over again. Much of what seemed glamorous and carefree was now more calculated, however; the new movers and shakers included the likes of Greek shipping tycoon Aristotle Onassis and arms dealer Adnan Kashoggi.

Grace Kelly (1929–82): Monaco Inc. was approaching bankruptcy in 1955 and Aristotle Onassis, the majority stockholder in the Societé des Bains de Mer, was manoeuvring to pull all the Principality's purse strings. Prince Rainier III thwarted him by issuing more stock and marrying a glamorous American movie actress. Rita Hayworth was already spoken for: she had been living in the Château de l'Horizon in Vallauris in 1947 when she married Aly Khan, son of the Aga Khan. Rainier auditioned Marilyn Monroe, but Grace Kelly won the role, and the society marriage that made the daughter of a Philadelphia brick magnate into a Riviera princess took place in 1956. Perhaps appropriately enough for the star of *To Catch a Thief*, the bride's mother was robbed of her jewels after the ceremony. Monaco hasn't been in the red since.

Graham Greene (1904–91): in 1966 Greene moved to Antibes, where he wrote his autobiographical *A Sort of Life* and *Ways of Escape*. In 1982, in righteous anger, he published a booklet called *J'Accuse: The Dark Side of Nice*, lambasting the organized crime and corruption that mayor Jacques Médecin's political machine turned a blind eye to or abetted; it was, and still is, banned in Nice. Other writers who lived in Antibes after the war include Nikos Kazantzakis and Roland Barthes; Monaco was long the address of the English-born poet of the Yukon, Robert Service (who wrote an ode in honour of Princess Grace's wedding) and Anthony Burgess; French novelist Patrick Modiano favours Nice (his *Les Dimanches d'été* is about Nice, and *Voyages de noces* is about Jews taking refuge in the south during the war).

Dirk Bogarde (1920–1999): British screen star and respected writer, Bogarde lived for many years in a villa near Grasse. His films include the at-the-time controversial *The Servant* (1963) and *Death in Venice* (1970).

Brigitte Bardot (1934–): ever since she came down with Roger Vadim to St-Tropez to film *Et Dieu...créa la femme* in 1956, Bardot has personified the myth of its free, sensuous spirit. A longtime resident of the village, married in the '80s to an extreme right-wing politician, she devotes her publicity machine to animal rights.

What new kind of Côte d'Azur, if any, may be wrought by its new glitterati – such famous names as Elton John, Luciano Pavarotti, Claudia Schiffer, Boris Becker and Joan Collins – still waits to be seen. One thing is certain, at least: property prices won't go down any time soon. Buy that dream villa now – if you can afford it.

Food and Drink

05

...and south of Valence, Provincia Romana, the Roman Provence, lies beneath the sun.
There there is no more any evil, for there the apple will not flourish and the Brussels
sprout will not grow at all.

Ford Madox Ford, *Provence*

Eating is a pleasure in the south, where seafood, herbs, fruit and vegetables are often within plucking distance of the kitchen and table. The high quality of these fresh native ingredients demands minimal preparation – Provençal cooking is perhaps the least fussy of any regional French cuisine, and as an added plus neatly fits the modern definition of a healthy diet. For not only is the south a Brussels-sprout-free zone, but the artery-hardening delights of the north – the rich creamy sauces, butter, cheese and egg dishes, and mega-calorie desserts – are rare birds in the land of olives, fresh vegetables, apricots and almonds.

Some of the most celebrated restaurants in the world grace the south of France, but there are plenty of stinkers, too. The most tolerable are humble in their mediocrity while others are oily with pretensions, staffed by folks posing as Grand Dukes and Duchesses fallen on hard times, whose exalted airs are somehow supposed to make their clients feel better about paying an obscene amount of money for the eight *petits pois à la graisse de yak* that the chef has so beautifully arranged on a plate.

Just as intimidating for the hungry traveller are France's much ballyhooed gourmet bibles, whose annual awarding or removing of a star here, a chef's hat there, grade food the way a French teacher grades a *dictée* in school. Woe to the chef who leaves a lump in the sauce when those incognito pedants of the perfect palate are dining, and whose guillotine pens will ruthlessly chop off percentage points from the restaurant's final score. The less attention you pay them, the more you'll enjoy your dinner.

The Cuisine of Provence and the Côte d'Azur

Thanks to the trail-blazing work of writers and chefs like Elizabeth David and Roger Vergé, Provençal cooking no longer sends the average Anglo-Saxon into paroxysms of garlic paranoia as it did a hundred years ago. Many traditional dishes actually presage *nouvelle cuisine*, and their success hangs on the quality of the ingredients and fragrant olive oil, like the well-known *ratatouille* – aubergines (eggplant), tomatoes, garlic and courgettes (zucchini) which are cooked separately to preserve their individual flavour, before being mixed together in olive oil – or *bagna cauda*, a dish of the southern Alps, consisting of raw vegetables dipped in a hot fondue of garlic, anchovies and olive oil.

Between November and March the olives are crushed to make the fragrant olive oil which lies at the heart of the local cuisine: during this period, a number of olive mills are open to the public (usually just in the afternoons), among them the Alziari mill in Nice (318 Bd de la Madeleine), or the mills at Grasse (Moulin à Huile Ste-Anne, 138

Aïoli Recipe

This typical Provençal mayonnaise is best served with white fish such as bourride, or with snails, potatoes or soup.

Ingredients (per person)
1 egg yolk
1 clove of garlic (more if you're a garlic fiend)
extra-virgin olive oil

Using a mortar and pestle, crush the garlic to a paste and add the egg yolks. Begin whipping the mixture with a fork or small whisk while adding good quality (extra-virgin) olive oil, first drop by drop, then in a thin stream as the mayonnaise begins to set. Add salt only once all the oil has been integrated and the mayonnaise has formed.

Should the *aïoli* lack substance or the oil separate from the mixture, you can still 'save' your mayonnaise: remove the mixture and add another egg yolk to the clean mortar. Whipping constantly, reintegrate the old *aïoli* mixture and any remaining oil. This operation is called 'reconstituting' the *aïoli*.

Route de Draguignan), Opio (Moulins de la Brague, 2 Route de Châteauneuf), and Menton (Moulin à Huile Lottier, 102 Av des Acacias).

A favourite hors-d'œuvre is *tapenade*, a purée of olives, anchovies, olive oil and capers served on toast. The best known starter must be *salade niçoise*, interpreted in a hundred different ways even in Nice, but in general containing most of the following: tomatoes, cucumbers, hard-boiled eggs, black olives, onions, anchovies, artichokes, green peppers, croutons, green beans, tuna and even potatoes. Another lighter speciality is *omelette de putine*, an omelette with tiny fish. In Nice pasta dishes come in all sorts of shapes, but the favourites are *ravioli* and *gnocchi* (potato dumplings), two forms served throughout Italy and invented here when Nice was still *Nizza* (the city has many other special dishes: *see* p.103). Another dish that tastes best in the summer, *soupe au pistou*, is a thick *minestrone* served with a fresh basil, garlic and pine-nut sauce similar to Italian *pesto*.

Aïoli, a mayonnaise made from garlic, olive oil, lemon juice and egg yolks, served with codfish, snails, potatoes or soup, is for many the essence of Provence; Mistral even named his nationalist Provençal magazine after it. In the same spirit Marseille named its magazine *Bouillabaisse*, for its world-famous soup of five to twelve kinds of Mediterranean fish, flavoured with saffron; the fish is removed and served with *aïoli* or *rouille*, a sauce of fresh red chilli peppers crushed with garlic, olive oil, and the soup broth. Because good saffron costs money and the fish, especially the gruesome *rascasse* (scorpion fish) are rare, a proper *bouillabaisse* will cost at least €30. A less expensive but delicious alternative is *bourride*, a soup made from white-fleshed fish served with *aïoli*, or down a gastronomical notch is *baudroie*, a fish soup with vegetables and garlic. A very different kettle of fish is the indigestible Niçoise favourite (which the Monégasques also claim as their own), *estocaficada* – salt cod (and salt cod guts) stewed with tomatoes, olives, garlic and *eau-de-vie*. Less adventurous yet an absolutely delicious dish is *loup au fenouil*, sea bass grilled over fennel stalks.

Lamb is the most common meat dish; real Provençal lamb (becoming increasingly rare) grazes on herbs and on special salt-marsh grasses from the Camargue and Crau. Beef usually comes in the form of a *daube*, slowly stewed in red wine and often served with ravioli. A Provençal cook's prize possession is the *daube* pan, which is never washed, but wiped clean and baked to form a crust that flavours all subsequent stews. Rabbit, or *lapin à la provençale*, is simmered in white wine with garlic, mustard, tomatoes and herbs. The more daunting *pieds et paquets* are tripe packages stuffed with garlic, onions and salt pork, traditionally (although rarely in practice) served with calf's or sheep's trotters. Also look for *capoun fassum*, cabbage stuffed with sausage and rice, and *artichauts à la barigoule*, artichokes filled with pork and mushrooms.

Purely vegetable dishes, besides ratatouille, include *tian*, a casserole of rice, spring vegetables (usually courgettes) and grated cheese baked in the oven; *tourta de blea*, a sweet-savoury Swiss chard pie; stuffed courgette (zucchini) flowers; grilled tomatoes with garlic and breadcrumbs (*à la provençale*); and *mesclum*, a salad of dandelion and other green leaves. There aren't many Provençal cheeses: *banon*, nutty discs made from goat, sheep or cow's milk, wrapped in chestnut leaves, is perhaps the best known; *poivre d'Ain* is *banon* flavoured with savory; thyme and bay add a nuance to creamy sheep's milk *tomme arlésienne*.

Markets, Picnic Food and Snacks

The food markets in the south of France are justly celebrated for the colour and perfumes of their produce and flowers. They are fun to visit, and become even more interesting if you're cooking or gathering the ingredients for a picnic. In the larger cities food markets take place every day, while smaller towns and villages have markets on one day a week (we've listed all the ones we know in the text), which double as a social occasion for the locals. Most markets finish around noon.

Other good sources for picnic food are the *charcuteries* or *traiteurs*, both of which sell prepared dishes sold by weight in cartons or tubs. Many of the local specialities lend themselves well to picnics: *pissaladière*, a cross between an onion tart and a pizza, is good hot or cold, or *socca*, a kind of pancake made with chick-pea flour, or the delicious *pan bagna* filled with all kinds of delicious fillings. You can also find counters at larger supermarkets. Cities are snack-food wonderlands, with outdoor counters selling pastries, crêpes, pizza slices, *frites*, *croque-monsieur* (toasted ham and cheese sandwiches) and a wide variety of sandwiches made from *baguettes* (long thin loaves of bread).

Drink

You can order any kind of drink at any bar or café – except cocktails, unless it has a certain cosmopolitan *savoir-faire* or stays open into the night. Cafés are also a home from home, places to read the papers, play cards, meet friends and just unwind, sit back and watch the world go by. You can spend hours over one coffee and no one will try to hurry you along. Prices are listed on the *Tarif des Consommations*: note they are progressively more expensive depending on whether you're served at the bar (*comptoir*), at a table (*la salle*) or outside (*la terrasse*).

French coffee is strong and black, but lacklustre next to the aromatic brews of Italy or Spain (you'll notice an improvement in the coffee near their respective frontiers). If you order *un café* or *un express* you'll get a small black espresso; if you want milk, order *un crème*. If you want more than a few drops of caffeine, ask them to make it *grand*. For decaffeinated, the word is *déca*. Some bars offer *cappuccinos*, but again they're only really good near the Italian border; in the summer try a *frappé* (iced coffee). The French only order *café au lait* (a small coffee topped off with lots of hot milk) when they stop in for breakfast, and if what your hotel offers is expensive or boring, consider joining them. There are baskets of croissants and pastries, and some bars will make you a *tartine beurrée* (*baguette* with butter, jam or honey).

If you want to go native, try the Frenchman's Breakfast of Champions: a *pastis* or two, and five non-filter *Gauloises*. *Chocolat chaud* (hot chocolate) is usually good; if you order *thé* (tea), you'll get a nasty ordinary bag and the water will be hot rather than boiling. An *infusion* is a herbal tea – for example *camomille*, *menthe* (mint), *tilleul* (lime or linden blossom), or *verveine* (verbena). These are kind to the all-precious *foie*, or liver, after you've over-indulged at the table.

Mineral water (*eau minérale*) can be addictive, and comes either sparkling (*gazeuse* or *pétillante*) or still (*non-gazeuse* or *plate*). If you feel run down, Badoit has lots of peppy magnesium in it. The usual international corporate soft drinks are available, and all kinds of bottled fruit juices (*jus de fruits*). Some bars also do fresh lemon and orange juices (*citron pressé* or *orange pressée*). The French are also fond of fruit syrups – red *grenadine* and ghastly green *menthe*, which are mixed with lemonade to form a *diabolo* (e.g. *diabolo menthe*).

Beer (*bière*) in most bars and cafés is run-of-the-mill big brands from Alsace, Germany and Belgium. Draft (*à la pression*) is cheaper than bottled beer. Nearly all resorts have bars or pubs offering wider selections of drafts, lagers and bottles.

The strong spirit of the Midi comes in a liquid form called *pastis*, first made popular in Marseille as a plague remedy; its name comes from the Latin *passe-sitis*, or thirst quencher. A pale yellow 90 per cent nectar flavoured with anise, vanilla and cinnamon, pastis is drunk as an apéritif before lunch and in rounds after work. The three major brands, Ricard, Pernod and Pastis 51, all taste slightly different; most people drink their '*pastaga*' with lots of water and ice (*glaçons*), which makes it almost palatable. A thimble-sized *pastis* is a *momie*; mixed with grenadine it becomes a *tomate*; with *orgeat* (almond and orange flower syrup) it's a *mauresque*, and a *perroquet* is mint.

Other popular apéritifs come from Languedoc-Roussillon, including *Byrrh* 'from the world's largest barrel', a sweet wine mixed with quinine and orange peel, similar to Dubonnet. Spirits include the familiar Cognac and Armagnac brandies, liqueurs and *digestifs* made from walnuts, cherries, pears and herbs (these are a speciality of the Alps), and fiery *marc*, the grape spirit that is the same as Italian *grappa* (but usually better). Many Provençal villages have a special *marc* of their own; the *marc des orangers*, made in spring with orange flowers, is one of the nicest.

Wine

One of the pleasures of travelling in France is drinking great wines for a fraction of what you pay at home, and discovering new ones you've never seen in your local shop. The south holds a special place in the saga of French wines, with a tradition dating back to the Greeks, who are said to have introduced an essential Côtes-du-Rhône grape variety called syrah, originally grown in Shiraz, Persia. Nurtured in the Dark and Middle Ages by popes and kings, the vineyards of Provence and Languedoc-Roussillon still produce most of France's wine – certainly most of its plonk, graded only by its alcohol content.

Some of Provence's best-known wines grow in the ancient places near the coast, especially its quartet of tiny AOC districts Bellet, Bandol, Cassis and Palette. But the best-known wines of the region come from the Rhône valley, under the general heading of Côtes-du-Rhône, including Châteauneuf-du-Pape, Gigondas, the famous rosé Tavel and the sweet muscat apéritif wine, Beaumes-de-Venise. Elsewhere, wine-makers have made great strides in boosting quality in the past 30 years, recognized in new AOC districts.

'If rules inhibit your enjoyment of wines, there should be no rules,' Alexis Lichine wrote in the 1950s, and it still holds true today. The innocent drinker has to put up with even more words and snootery than the beleaguered eater. Confronting a wine list makes a lot of people nervous, while an oily, obsequious *sommelier* can ruin their entire meal. Note that restaurants, as in Britain, make a good portion of their income from marking up wines to triple or quadruple the retail price. Save money by buying it direct from the producers, or *vignerons*.

If a wine is labelled AOC (*Appellation d'Origine Contrôlée*), it means that the wine comes from a certain defined area and is made from certain varieties of grapes, guaranteeing a standard of quality. *Cru* on the label means vintage; a *grand cru* is a great, noble vintage. Down the list in the vinous hierarchy are those labelled VDQS (*vin de qualité supérieure*), followed by *vin de pays* (guaranteed at least to originate in a certain region), with *vin ordinaire* (or *vin de table*) at the bottom, which may not send you to seventh heaven but is usually drinkable and cheap. In a restaurant if you order a *rouge* (red), *blanc* (white) or *rosé* (pink), this is what you'll get, either by the glass (*un verre*), by the quarter-litre (*un pichet*) or bottle (*une bouteille*). Brut is very dry, *sec* dry, *demi-sec* and *moelleux* are sweetish, *doux* sweet, and *méthode champenoise* sparkling.

If you're buying direct from the producer (or a wine co-operative, or *syndicat*, a group of producers), you'll be offered glasses to taste, each wine older than the previous one until you are feeling quite jolly and ready to buy the oldest (and most expensive) vintage. On the other hand, some sell loose wine *à la* petrol pump, *en vrac*; many *caves* even sell the little plastic barrels to put it in.

Restaurant Basics

Restaurants generally serve between 12 noon and 2pm and in the evening from 7 to 10pm, with later summer hours; *brasseries* in the cities generally stay open continuously. Most post menus outside the door so you know what to expect and offer a

French Menu Reader

Hors-d'œuvre et Soupes (Starters and Soups)
amuse-gueule appetizers
assiette assortie plate of mixed cold *hors-d'œuvre*
bisque shellfish soup
bouchées mini *vol-au-vents*
bouillabaisse famous fish soup of Marseille
bouillon broth
charcuterie mixed cold meats, salami, ham, etc.
consommé clear soup
coulis thick sieved sauce
crudités raw vegetable platter
potage thick vegetable soup
tourrain garlic and bread soup
velouté thick smooth soup, often fish or chicken
vol-au-vent puff-pastry case with savoury filling

Poissons et Coquillages (Crustacés) (Fish and Shellfish)
aiglefin little haddock
alose shad
anchois anchovies
anguille eel
bar sea bass
barbue brill
baudroie angler fish
belons flat oysters
bigorneau winkle
blanchailles whitebait
brème bream
brochet pike
bulot whelk
cabillaud cod
calmar squid

carrelet plaice
colin hake
congre conger eel
coques cockles
coquillages shellfish
coquilles St-Jacques scallops
crabe crab
crevettes grises shrimp
crevettes roses prawns
cuisses de grenouilles frogs' legs
darne slice or steak of fish
daurade sea bream
écrevisse freshwater crayfish
éperlan smelt
escabèche fish fried, marinated and served cold
escargots snails
espadon swordfish
esturgeon sturgeon
flétan halibut
friture deep-fried fish
fruits de mer seafood
gambas giant prawns
gigot de mer a large fish cooked whole
grondin red gurnard
hareng herring
homard Atlantic (Norway) lobster
huîtres oysters
lamproie lamprey
langouste spiny Mediterranean lobster
langoustines Norway lobster (often called Dublin Bay prawns or scampi)
limande lemon sole
lotte monkfish
loup (de mer) sea bass
louvine sea bass (in Aquitaine)
maquereau mackerel
merlan whiting
morue salt cod
moules mussels

choice of set-price menus; if prices aren't listed, you can bet it's not because they're a bargain. If you summon up the appetite to eat the biggest meal of the day at noon, you'll spend a lot less money, as many restaurants offer special lunch menus – an economical way to experience some of the finer gourmet temples. Some of these offer a set-price gourmet *menu dégustation* – a selection of chef's specialities, which can be a great treat. At the humbler end of the scale, bars and brasseries often serve a simple *plat du jour* (daily special) and the no-choice *formule*, which is more often than not steak and *frites*. Eating *à la carte* anywhere will always be more expensive, in many cases twice as much.

oursin sea urchin
pagel sea bream
palourdes clams
petit gris little grey snail
poulpe octopus
praires small clams
raie skate
rascasse scorpion fish
rouget red mullet
saumon salmon
St-Pierre John Dory
sole (meunière) sole (with butter, lemon and parsley)
stockfisch stockfish (wind-dried cod)
telline tiny clam
thon tuna
truite trout
truite saumonée salmon trout

Viandes et Volailles (Meat and Poultry)
agneau (de pré-salé) lamb (grazed in fields by the sea)
ailerons chicken wings
aloyau sirloin
andouillette chitterling (tripe) sausage
autruche ostrich
biftek beefsteak
blanc breast or white meat
blanquette stew of white meat, thickened with egg yolk
bœuf beef
boudin blanc sausage of white meat
boudin noir black pudding
brochette meat (or fish) on a skewer
caille quail
canard, caneton duck, duckling
carré the best end of a cutlet or chop
cassoulet haricot bean stew with sausage, duck, goose, etc.
cervelle brains
chair flesh, meat
chapon capon
châteaubriand porterhouse steak
cheval horsemeat
chevreau kid
chorizo spicy Spanish sausage
civet meat (usually game) stew, in wine and blood sauce
cœur heart
confit meat cooked and preserved in its own fat
côte, côtelette chop, cutlet
cou d'oie farci goose neck stuffed with pork, foie gras and truffles
crépinette small sausage
cuisse thigh or leg
dinde, dindon turkey
entrecôte ribsteak
épaule shoulder
estouffade a meat stew marinated, fried and then braised
faisan pheasant
faux-filet sirloin
foie liver
frais de veau veal testicles
fricadelle meatball
gésier gizzard
gibier game
gigot leg of lamb
graisse or *gras* fat
grillade grilled meat, often a mixed grill
grive thrush
jambon ham
jarret knuckle
langue tongue
lapereau young rabbit
lapin rabbit
lard (lardons) bacon (diced bacon)
lièvre hare
maigret/magret, (de canard) breast (of duck)

Menus sometimes include the house wine (*vin compris*). If you choose a better wine anywhere, expect a scandalous mark-up; the French wouldn't dream of a meal without wine, and the arrangement is a simple device to make food prices seem lower. If service is included it will say *service compris* or s.c., if not, *service non compris* or s.n.c.

French restaurants, especially the cheaper ones, presume everyone has the appetite of Gargantua. A full meal consists of: an apéritif (*pastis*, the national drink of the south, is famous for its hunger-inducing qualities), *hors-d'œuvre* or a starter (typically, soup, pâté or *charcuterie*), an *entrée* (usually fish, or an omelette), a main course

manchons duck or goose wings	*tournedos* thick round slices of beef fillet
marcassin young wild boar	*travers de porc* spare ribs
merguez spicy red sausage	*tripes* tripe
moelle bone marrow	*veau* veal
mouton mutton	*venaison* venison
museau muzzle	
navarin lamb stew with root vegetables	**Légumes, Herbes, etc.**
noix de veau (agneau) topside of veal (lamb)	**(Vegetables, herbs, etc.)**
oie goose	*ail* garlic
os bone	*aïoli* garlic mayonnaise
perdreau (or *perdrix*) partridge	*algue* seaweed
petit salé salt pork	*aneth* dill
pieds trotters	*anis* anise
pintade guinea fowl	*artichaut* artichoke
plat-de-côtes short ribs or rib chops	*asperges* asparagus
porc pork	*aubergine* aubergine (eggplant)
pot au feu meat and vegetables cooked in stock	*avocat* avocado
poulet chicken	*basilic* basil
poussin baby chicken	*betterave* beetroot
quenelle poached dumplings made of fish, fowl or meat	*blette* Swiss chard
queue de bœuf oxtail	*bouquet garni* mixed herbs in a little bag
ris (de veau) sweetbreads (veal)	*cannelle* cinnamon
rognons kidneys	*céleri (-rave)* celery (celeriac)
rosbif roast beef	*cèpes* ceps, wild boletus mushrooms
rôti roast	*champignons* mushrooms
sanglier wild boar	*chanterelles* wild yellow mushrooms
saucisses sausages	*chicorée* curly endive
saucisson dry sausage, like salami	*chou* cabbage
selle (d'agneau) saddle (of lamb)	*chou-fleur* cauliflower
steak tartare raw minced beef, often topped with a raw egg yolk	*choucroute* sauerkraut
suprême de volaille fillet of chicken breast and wing	*choux de bruxelles* Brussels sprouts
taureau bull's meat	*ciboulette* chives
tête (de veau) head (calf's), fatty and usually served with a mustardy vinaigrette	*citrouille* pumpkin
tortue turtle	*clou de girofle* clove
	cœur de palmier heart of palm
	concombre cucumber
	cornichons gherkins
	courgettes courgettes (zucchini)
	cresson watercress
	échalote shallot

(usually meat, poultry, game or offal, *garni* with vegetables, rice or potatoes), often followed by a green salad (to 'lighten' the stomach), then cheese, dessert, coffee, chocolates and *mignardises* (or petits fours) and perhaps a *digestif* to round things off. Most people only devour the whole whack on Sunday afternoons, and at other times condense this feast to a starter, *entrée* or main course, and cheese or dessert. Vegetarians usually have a hard time in France, especially if they don't eat fish or eggs, but most establishments will try to accommodate them. This is easier in the Côte d'Azur than elsewhere in France, as many of the local specialities are meat-free (*see* pp.24–6).

endive chicory (endive)
épinards spinach
estragon tarragon
fenouil fennel
fèves broad (fava) beans
flageolets white beans
fleurs de courgette courgette blossoms
frites chips (French fries)
genièvre juniper
gingembre ginger
haricots (rouges, blancs) beans (kidney, white)
haricot verts green (French) beans
jardinière with diced garden vegetables
laitue lettuce
laurier bay leaf
lentilles lentils
maïs (épis de) sweetcorn (on the cob)
marjolaine marjoram
menthe mint
mesclun salad of various leaves
morilles morel mushrooms
moutarde mustard
navet turnip
oignons onions
oseille sorrel
panais parsnip
persil parsley
petits pois peas
piment pimento
pissenlits dandelion greens
poireaux leeks
pois chiches chickpeas
pois mange-tout sugar peas or mangetout
poivron sweet pepper (capsicum)
pomme de terre potato
potiron pumpkin
primeurs young vegetables
radis radishes
raifort horseradish

riz rice
romarin rosemary
roquette rocket
safran saffron
salade verte green salad
salsifis salsify
sarriette savoury
sarrasin buckwheat
sauge sage
seigle rye
serpolet wild thyme
thym thyme
truffes truffles

Fruits et Noix (Fruit and Nuts)

abricot apricot
amandes almonds
ananas pineapple
banane banana
bigarreau black cherries
brugnon nectarine
cacahouètes peanuts
cassis blackcurrant
cerise cherry
citron lemon
citron vert lime
coco (noix de) coconut
coing quince
dattes dates
figues (de Barbarie) figs (prickly pear)
fraises (des bois) strawberries (wild)
framboises raspberries
fruit de la passion passion fruit
grenade pomegranate
groseilles redcurrants
lavande lavender
mandarine tangerine
mangue mango
marrons chestnuts
mirabelles mirabelle plums

When looking for a restaurant, homing in on the one place crowded with locals is as sound a policy in France as anywhere. Don't overlook hotel restaurants, some of which are absolutely top notch even if a certain red book refuses on some obscure principle to give them more than two stars. To avoid disappointment, call ahead in the morning to reserve a table, especially at the smarter restaurants, and especially in the summer. One thing you'll soon notice is that there's a wide choice of ethnic restaurants, mostly North African (a favourite for their economical couscous – spicy meat and vegetables served on a bed of steamed semolina with a side dish of *harissa*, a hot red pepper sauce); Asian (usually Vietnamese, sometimes Chinese, Cambodian

mûre (sauvage) mulberry, blackberry
myrtilles bilberries
noisette hazelnut
noix walnuts
noix de cajou cashews
pamplemousse grapefruit
pastèque watermelon
pêche (blanche) peach (white)
pignons pinenuts
pistache pistachio
poire pear
pomme apple
prune plum
pruneau prune
raisins (secs) grapes (raisins)
reine-claude greengage plums

Desserts
bavarois mousse or custard in a mould
biscuit biscuit, cracker, cake
bombe ice-cream dessert in a round mould
bonbons sweets, candy
brioche light sweet yeast bread
charlotte sponge fingers and custard cream dessert
chausson turnover
clafoutis batter fruit cake
compote stewed fruit
corbeille de fruits basket of fruit
coulis thick fruit sauce
coupe ice cream: a scoop or in cup
crème anglaise egg custard
crème caramel vanilla custard with caramel sauce
crème Chantilly sweet whipped cream
crème fraîche slightly sour cream
crème pâtissière thick pastry cream filling made with eggs
gâteau cake
gaufre waffle

génoise rich sponge cake
glace ice cream
macarons macaroons
madeleine small sponge cake
miel honey
mignardises same as *petits fours*
mousse 'foam': frothy dessert
œufs à la neige floating islands/meringues on a bed of custard
pain d'épice gingerbread
parfait frozen mousse
petits fours sweetmeats; tiny cakes and pastries
profiteroles choux pastry balls, often filled with chocolate or ice cream
sablé shortbread
savarin a filled cake, shaped like a ring
tarte, tartelette tart, little tart
tarte tropézienne sponge cake filled with custard and topped with nuts
truffes chocolate truffles
yaourt yoghurt

Fromage (Cheese)
brebis (fromage de) sheep's cheese
cabécou sharp local goat's cheese
chèvre goat's cheese
doux mild
fromage (plateau de) cheese (board)
fromage blanc yoghurty cream cheese
fromage frais a bit like sour cream
fromage sec general name for solid cheeses
fort strong

Cooking Terms and Sauces
à point medium steak
bien cuit well-done steak
bleu very rare steak
aigre-doux sweet and sour

or Thai); and Italian, the latter sometimes combined with a pizzeria, although beware, quality very much depends on geographical proximity to Italy – the pasta and pizza are superb in Nice.

Don't expect to find many ethnic restaurants outside the big cities; country cooking is French only (though often very inventive). But in the cosmopolitan centres, you'll find not only foreign cuisine, but specialities from all over France. There are Breton *crêperies* or *galetteries* (with whole-wheat pancakes), restaurants from Alsace serving *choucroute* (sauerkraut) and sausage, Périgord restaurants featuring *foie gras* and truffles, Lyonnaise *haute cuisine* and *les fast foods* offering *basse cuisine* of chips, hot

aiguillette thin slice	*frais, fraîche* fresh
à l'anglaise boiled	*frappé* with crushed ice
à la bordelaise cooked in wine and diced vegetables (usually)	*frit* fried
à la châtelaine with chestnut purée and artichoke hearts	*froid* cold
à la diable in spicy mustard sauce	*fumé* smoked
à la grecque cooked in olive oil and lemon	*galantine* cooked food served in cold jelly
à la jardinière with garden vegetables	*galette* flaky pastry case or pancake
à la périgourdine in a truffle and foie gras sauce	*garni* with vegetables
à la provençale cooked with tomatoes, garlic and olive oil	*(au) gratin* topped with browned cheese and breadcrumbs
allumettes strips of puff pastry	*grillé* grilled
au feu de bois cooked over a wood fire	*haché* minced
au four baked	*hollandaise* a sauce of egg yolks, butter and vinegar
auvergnat with sausage, bacon and cabbage	*marmite* casserole
barquette pastry boat	*médaillon* round piece
beignets fritters	*mijoté* simmered
béarnaise sauce of egg yolks, shallots and white wine	*Mornay* cheese sauce
bordelaise red wine, bone marrow and shallot sauce	*pané* breaded
broche roasted on a spit	*pâte* pastry, pasta
chasseur mushrooms and shallots in white wine	*pâte brisée* shortcrust pastry
chaud hot	*pâte à chou* choux pastry
cru raw	*pâte feuilletée* flaky or puff pastry
cuit cooked	*paupiette* rolled and filled thin slices of fish or meat
diable spicy mustard or green pepper sauce	*Parmentier* with potatoes
émincé thinly sliced	*pavé* slab
en croûte cooked in a pastry crust	*piquant* spicy hot
en papillote baked in buttered paper	*poché* poached
épices spices	*pommes allumettes* thin chips (fries)
farci stuffed	*raclette* melted cheese with potatoes, onions and pickles
feuilleté flaky pastry	*sanglant* rare steak
flambé set aflame with alcohol	*salé* salted, spicy
forestière with bacon and mushrooms	*sucré* sweet
fourré stuffed	*timbale* pie cooked in a dome-shaped mould
	tranche slice
	vapeur steamed
	Véronique grape, wine and cream sauce
	vinaigrette oil and vinegar dressing

dogs and cheese sandwiches. There are still a few traditional French restaurants that would meet the approval of Auguste Escoffier, the legendary chef whose birthplace has become a place of pilgrimage in Villeneuve Loubet (*see* p.128); quite a few serve regional specialities and many feature *nouvelle cuisine*, which isn't so *nouvelle* any more, and has come under attack by devoted foodies for its expense (only the finest, freshest and rarest ingredients are used), portions (minute compared to usual restaurant helpings, because the object is to feel good, not full), and sheer quackery. *Nouvelle cuisine* is a subtle art, seeking to emphasize the natural flavour and goodness of a carrot, for example, by contrasting or complementing it with other flavours

Miscellaneous

addition bill (or check)
baguette long loaf of bread
beurre butter
carte non-set menu
confiture jam
couteau knife
crème cream
cuillère spoon
formule à €12 €12 set menu
fourchette fork
fromage cheese
huile (d'olive) oil (olive)
lait milk
menu set menu
nouilles noodles
pain bread
œufs eggs
poivre pepper
sel salt
service compris/non compris service included/not included
sucre sugar
vinaigre vinegar

Snacks

chips crisps
crêpe thin pancake
croque-madame toasted ham and cheese sandwich with fried egg
croque-monsieur toasted ham and cheese sandwich
croustade small savoury pastry
frites chips (French fries)
gaufre waffle
jambon ham
pissaladière a kind of pizza with onions, anchovies, etc.
sandwich canapé open sandwich

Boissons (Drinks)

bière (pression) beer (draught)
bouteille (demi) bottle (half)
brut very dry
chocolat chaud hot chocolate
café coffee
café au lait white coffee
café express espresso coffee
café filtre filter coffee
café turc Turkish coffee
demi a third of a litre
doux sweet (wine)
eau (minérale, plate ou gazeuse) water (mineral, still or sparkling)
eau-de-vie brandy
eau potable drinking water
gazeuse sparkling
glaçons ice cubes
infusion, tisane (verveine, tilleul, menthe) herbal tea, (usually either verbena, lime flower or mint)
jus juice
lait milk
menthe à l'eau peppermint cordial
moelleux semi-dry
mousseux sparkling (wine)
pastis anis liqueur
pichet pitcher
citron pressé/orange pressée fresh lemon/orange juice
pression draught
ratafia home-made liqueur made by steeping fruit or green walnuts in alcohol or wine
sec dry
sirop d'orange/de citron orange/lemon squash
thé tea
verre glass
vin blanc/rosé/rouge white/rosé/red wine

and scents; disappointments are inevitable when a chef is more concerned with appearance than taste, or takes a walk on the wild side, combining oysters, kiwis and cashews or some other abomination. But *nouvelle cuisine* has had a strong influence on attitudes towards food in France, and it's hard to imagine anyone going back to smothering everything in a *béchamel* sauce.

Travel

06

Before You Go

A little preparation will help you get more out of your holiday on the Côte d'Azur. Check the Calendar of Events (*see* pp.52–3) to help you decide where you want to be and when, and book accommodation early. If you plan to base yourself in one area, write ahead to the local tourist offices listed in the text for complete lists of self-catering accommodation, hotels, and campsites in their areas, or else contact one of the many companies in the UK or USA (*see* p.59). For more general information and a complete list of tour operators, get in touch with a tourist office.

French Government Tourist Offices

UK 178 Piccadilly, London W1J 9AL, t 09068 244123 (*6op per min*), *info@mdf.co.uk*.
Ireland 10 Suffolk St, Dublin 1, t (1) 560 235 235, *frenchtouristoffice@eircom.net*.
Australia Level 22, 25 Bligh St, Sydney, NSW 2000, t (02) 9231 5244, *france@bigpond.net.au*.
USA 444 Madison Avenue, New York, NY 10022, t (410) 286 8310, f (212) 838 7855, *info@francetourism.com*, *www.fgtoegte.net*.
676 N. Michigan Ave, Chicago, IL 60611, t (312) 751 7800, f (312) 337 6339.
9454 Wilshire Blvd, Suite 715, Beverly Hills, CA 90212, t (310) 271 6665, f (310) 276 2835.
1 Biscayne Tower, Suite 1750-2, South Biscayne Blvd, Miami, FL 33131, t (305) 373 8177, f (305) 737 5828
Canada, Maison de la France, 1981 Ave McGill College, No. 490, Montreal, Quebec H3A 2W9, t (514) 288 4264, f (514) 845 4868, *mfrance@attcanada.net*.
Maison de la France, 30 St Patrick St, Suite 700, Toronto M5T 3A3, t (416) 593 6427, f (416) 979 7587.

Useful Web Addresses

www.franceguide.com
www.francetourism.com
www.provencebeyond.fr
www.france.com
www.angloinfo.com
www.provenceweb.fr
www.visit-riviera.com
www.hotelstravel.com
www.francekeys.com
www.frenchconnections.co.uk

Getting There

By Air

The main international airports on the Côte d'Azur are at Nice and Marseille. Thanks to deregulation and the disintegration of state monopolies, prices are hugely competitive; to ensure a seat and save money, be sure to shop around and book ahead – especially during the summer and Easter holidays. Check with your travel agent or your major Sunday newspaper for bargains or packages.

There are lots of low-cost budget carriers operating from the UK to Nice, but from most other points of departure – Ireland, North America, Australia, etc. – it could be cheaper to fly to Paris and from there catch a cheap flight or train to the south.

British Airways serves Nice with four flights a day from Heathrow and Marseille with three flights a day from Gatwick. The BA reservations and general information number in France is t 0825 825 400.

Air France has three-four flights daily from London Heathrow to Nice from £92 return, and serves Marseille via Paris. **British Midland** also flies from other UK airports including Manchester, Edinburgh, Glasgow and Belfast, with bargain fares from as little as £24 return.

No-frills airline **easyJet** flies six times daily to Nice, from Gatwick, Stansted, Luton and Liverpool airports, with fares starting as low as £6.99 single if you book well in advance, and discounts for booking on the internet. **Ryanair** flies from London Stansted to Nîmes; off-peak fares are sometimes even advertised as 'free' but don't forget they'll include airport taxes of approximately £15 each way.

There are **domestic flights** on Air France from Orly Airport in Paris to Marseille (every half hour) and Nice (every hour); sizeable discounts exist if you fly off-peak.

All services may be less frequent in winter.

Students who equip themselves with the relevant ID cards are eligible for considerable reductions, not only on flights, but also on trains and admission fees to museums, concerts, and more. Agencies (*see* box, p.39) specializing in student and youth travel can help in applying for the cards, as well as filling you in on the best deals.

Airline Carriers

UK and Ireland

Air France, t 0845 359 1009, *www.airfrance.co.uk*.

BMI, t 0870 607 0555, *www.flybmi.com*.

BMIbaby, flights from East Midlands to Nice, **t** 0870 264 2229, *www.bmibaby.com*.

British Airways, UK **t** 0870 850 9850, *www.ba.com*; France **t** 0825 825 400 for bookings and general information.

Easyjet, t 0871 750 0100 (10p/min), *www.easyjet.com*.

Ryanair, t 0871 246 0000 (10p/min), *www.ryanair.com*.

Jet 2, flights from Leeds to Nice, **t** 0870 737 8383, *www.jet2.com*.

USA and Canada

Air France, USA, **t** 800 237 2747, *www.airfrance.us*; Canada **t** 800 667 2747, *www.airfrance.ca*.

American Airlines, t 800 433 7300, *www.aa.com*.

British Airways, t 800 AIRWAYS, *www.ba.com*.

Continental, USA & Canada, **t** 800 231 0856, **t** 800 343 9195 (hearing impaired); *www.continental.com*.

Delta, t 800 241 4141, *www.delta.com*.

Northwest Airlines, t 800 225 2525, *www.nwa.com*.

New Frontiers, 5757 West Century Blvd, Suite 650, Los Angeles, CA 90045, **t** (310) 670 7318, toll free **t** 1 800 677 0720; *www.newfrontiers.com* (US) or *www.newfrontiers.ca* (Canada). Low-cost transatlantic flights (from $429), package holidays, hotels, discount rail passes, low cost car rental, etc.

United Airlines, t 800 538 2929, *www.ual.com*.

Charters, Discounts, Students and Special Deals

UK and Ireland

Budget Travel, 134 Lower Baggot St, Dublin 2, **t** (01) 661 1866, **f** (01) 662 9249, *www.budgettravel.ie*.

Club Travel, 30 Lower Abbey St, Dublin 1, **t** (01) 435 0016 within Eire, *www.clubtravel.ie*.

STA Travel, t 08701 600 599, 6 Wrights Lane, London W8 6TA, with 65 branches in the UK including 86 Old Brompton Rd, SW7 3LQ,

117 Euston Rd NW1 2SX, plus Bristol, Leeds, Manchester, Oxford, Cambridge, Edinburgh, Southampton, Birmingham, Liverpool and Nottingham; *www.statravel.co.uk*.

Europe Student Travel, 6 Campden St, London W8, **t** (020) 7727 764; catering to students and non-students.

Trailfinders, 215 Kensington High St, London W8 6BD, **t** (020) 7937 1234, *www.trailfinders.co.uk*.

United Travel, 2 Old Dublin Road, Stillorgan, County Dublin, **t** (01) 283 2555, *www.unitedtravel.ie*

USIT *www.usitnow.ie*. 19 Aston Quay, Dublin 2, **t** 0818 200 0200; Cork, **t** (021) 427 0900 Belfast, **t** (028) 90327 111; Galway, **t** (091) 565 177; Limerick. **t** (061) 415 064; Waterford, **t** (051) 872 601.

Check websites including:
www.cheapflights.co.uk
www.lastminute.com
www.expedia.co.uk
www.majortravel.co.uk.

USA and Canada

Last Minute Travel Club, USA, **t** (416) 449 5400 or toll free **t** 1 877 970 3500; Canada, **t** 877 970 3500, *www.lastminuteclub.com*. Annual membership fee entitles you to cheap standby deals and special rates for major car rental companies in Europe and Europass train tickets.

New Frontiers, USA, **t** (310) 670 7318 or toll free **t** 1 800 677 0720, 5757 West Century Blvd, Suite 650, Los Angeles, CA 90045, *www.newfrontiers.com*.

STA Travel, t 800 781 4040, *www.statravel.com*.

Travel Avenue USA **t** 800 333 3335, *www.travelavenue.com*. The oldest rebate travel agency in the US; you arrange your tour, they book it and share the commission.

Travel Cuts, with 14 US branches including Portland, San Francisco, Stanford, LA, San Diego, New York and Seattle WA, **t** 1 800 592 CUTS, or in Canada at 187 College St, Toronto, Ontario M5T 1P7, **t** (416) 979 2406, or toll free **t** 1 888 FLY CUTS, *www.travelcuts.com*. Canada's largest student travel specialists; branches in most provinces.

www.traveldiscounts.com. Members get special rates on flights, hotels and tours.

By Train

Airport awfulness makes France's **high-speed TGVs** (*trains à grande vitesse*) an attractive (though not necessarily cheaper) alternative. **Eurostar** trains, t 08705 186 186, *www.eurostar.com*, leave from London Waterloo or Ashford International in Kent, and there are direct connections to Paris Gare du Nord (2hrs 35mins; from £50 single) and Lille (1hr 40mins; from £30 single). Fares are cheaper if booked 7 days in advance and you include a Saturday night away. Check in 20 minutes before departure, or you will not be allowed on to the train.

In Paris, go to the Gare de Lyon for a **TGV** to the south. TGVs zip along at average speeds of 180mph (when they're not breaking world records), and the journey from Gare de Lyon to Marseille takes a sleek 3hrs; to Nice 5½hrs. Some weekday departures require a very small supplement; all require a seat reservation, which you can make when you buy your ticket or at the station before departure.

Another pleasant, if slower, way of getting there is by overnight sleeper after dinner in Paris (SNCF have recently been cracking down on robberies in compartments at night by introducing security patrols). People under 26 are eligible for a substantial discount on fares (*see* the youth travel agencies listed on p.39), and there are other discounts if you're 60 or over, available from major travel agents.

If you're planning on taking some long train journeys, it may be worth investing in a rail pass. The excellent-value **Euro Domino** pass entitles EU citizens to unlimited rail travel through France for 3–8 days in a month for £127–£317, or £91–£179 for under 26's.

Passes for North Americans include the **France Railpass**, which gives four days of unlimited travel throughout the country in a one-month period for $218–$252. The equivalent **France Youthpass** gives under-26s four days' unlimited travel through France over a two-month period, including reduced rates on Eurostar, for $164–$189. There's also the six-day **Rail 'n' Drive** pass, giving four days' unlimited rail travel through France and two days' car rental from $245.

Other alternatives include the well-known **Inter-Rail** pass for European residents (of at least 6 months), which offers 12 or 22 days' or one month's unlimited travel in Europe (countries are grouped into zones), plus discounts on trains to cross-Channel ferry terminals and returns on Eurostar from £125. Inter-Rail cards are not valid on trains in the UK. For non-Europeans there are various **Eurail** passes valid for 15 days to three months.

Rail Europe handles bookings for all services, including Eurostar and Motorail and sells rail passes.

Rail Europe (UK), 178 Piccadilly, London W1V OBA, t 08705 848 848, *www.raileurope.co.uk*.

Rail Europe (USA/Canada), t 877 257 2887 (USA) or t 1 800 361 RAIL (Canada), *www.raileurope.com*.

You can also check out the independent train travel website: *www.seat61.com*.

By Coach

Bargain plane tickets have made this a less attractive option, but another cheap way to get from London to the south of France is by **National Express Eurolines** coach, t 08705 80 80 80, *www.nationalexpress.com*; tickets from any National Express office. There are up to four journeys a week to Marseille (20½ hours); tickets start at £108 return.

By Car

A car entering France must have its registration and insurance papers. If you're coming from the UK or Ireland, the dip of the headlights must be adjusted to the right. Carrying a warning triangle is not mandatory, but is advisable, and this should be placed 50m behind the car if you have a breakdown.

Drivers with a valid licence from an EU country, Canada, the USA or Australia no longer need an international licence. If you're driving down from the UK, you can either go through or around Paris, a task best tackled on either side of the rush hour, or take the A26 via Reims and Troyes. The various *autoroutes* will get you south the fastest, but be prepared to pay some €77 in tolls (for costs and route information see *www.autoroutes.fr*); the N7 south of Paris takes much longer, but costs nothing and offers great scenery.

A fairly comfortable option is to put your car on the train. It can be costly, but there is a sleeper service that is well priced if bought in advance and in conjunction with Eurotunnel. Motorail accommodation is compulsory, in a 4-berth (1st-class) or 6-berth (2nd-class) carriage. Linen is provided, and washing facilities. Compartments are not segregated by sex. Services run weekly from mid-May–Sept to Avignon, Nice and Narbonne. Contact Rail Europe or **French Motorail** (UK **t** 08702 415 415), *www.raileurope.co.uk/frenchmotorail*.

Taking the **Eurotunnel** train, **t** 08705 35 35 35, *www.eurotunnelcom*, is the most convenient way to get your car to France. It takes only 35 minutes from Folkestone to Calais on the train; you remain in your car, although you can get up to stretch your legs. Trains through the Channel Tunnel start from around £125 in the low season and rise substantially in the summer and high seasons. The price includes a car less than 6.5m in length and 1.85m high, the driver and all passengers.

If you prefer a dose of bracing sea air, you've plenty of choice, though changes and mergers may be on the horizon. Short ferry and catamaran crossings currently include: Dover–Calais with **P&O Stena, t** 0870 242 4999, *www.posl.com*; **SeaFrance, t** 08705 711 711, *www.seafrance.co.uk*; and **Hoverspeed, t** 0870 240 8070, *www.hoverspeed.com*. P&O Stena and Hoverspeed also operate Newhaven–Dieppe. **P&O Portsmouth, t** 0870 242 4999, *www.poportsmouth.com*, has crossings from Portsmouth to Cherbourg and Le Havre; Hoverspeed has a Folkestone–Bologne crossing, and **Brittany Ferries, t** 08703 665 333 *www.brittanyferries.co.uk*, operates Plymouth –Roscoff in Brittany, Portsmouth–Caen and St Malo, Poole–Cherbourg and Cork–Roscoff. **P&O North Sea Ferries, t** 08705 20 20 20, *www.mycruiseferries.com*, operates a Hull–Zeebrugge route, which entails about a

---

Car Hire

Europcar, *www.europcar.com*, **t** (877) 940 6900 (USA), **t** 0870 607 5000 (UK), **t** 0825 352 352 (France).
Europe by Car,*www.europebycar.com*, **t** (212) 581 3040 (USA), **t** 800 223 1516 (USA toll free).
Hertz, t 800 654 3131 (USA) or **t** 08708 448844 (UK), *www.hertz.com*.
Autos Abroad, *www.autosabroad.com*. For an instant price comparison online.

45min drive to France. Prices vary considerably according to season and demand, so it pays to shop around for the best deal.

If you plan to hire a car, look into air and holiday package deals as well as combination 'Train and Auto' rates to save money, or consider leasing a car if you mean to stay three weeks or more. Prices vary widely from firm to firm; make sure you read the small print about service charges and taxes.

Entry Formalities

Passports and Visas

Holders of EU, US, Canadian, Australian, New Zealand and Israeli passports do not need a visa to enter France for stays of up to three months, but everyone else still does. Apply at your nearest French consulate or embassy. In the USA, contact *www.ambafrance-us.org*, **t** (202) 944 6000, for a list of your consulates; in the UK contact the French Embassy at 58 Knightsbridge, London SW1X 7JT, **t** (020) 7073 1000, *www.ambafrance-uk.org*.

The most convenient visa is the *visa de circulation*, allowing for multiple stays of three months over a three-year period. If you intend to stay longer, the law says you need a *carte de séjour*, a requirement EU citizens can easily get around as passports are rarely stamped. Non-EU citizens often can as well, but the creeping rise of xenophobic legislation in France as a sop to the extreme right-wing National Front – which has its powerbase in the south – suggests that non-EU citizens had best apply for an extended visa before leaving home, a complicated procedure requiring proof of income, etc. You can't get a *carte de séjour* without the visa, and obtaining it is a trial run in the *ennuis* you'll undergo in applying for a *carte de séjour* at your local *mairie*.

Health and Travel Insurance

Citizens of the EU who bring along their E111 forms are entitled to the same health services as French citizens. This means paying up front for medical care and prescriptions, of which costs 75–80% are reimbursed a week to 10 days later. As an alternative, consider a travel insurance policy, covering theft and losses and offering 100% medical refund; check to see if it covers your extra expenses in case you get bogged down in airport or train strikes. Beware that accidents resulting from sports are rarely covered by ordinary insurance. Canadians may or may not be covered in France by their provincial health coverage; Americans and others should check their individual policies.

Getting Around

By Train

Call the SNCF nationwide information number, t 08 92 35 35 35 (€0.50 a minute), or go to www.sncf.com.

The SNCF runs a decent and efficient network of trains through the major cities of the south, with an added service called the Métrazur that links all the resorts of the Côte d'Azur from Menton to St-Raphaël as often as every half-hour in the peak summer season. The narrow-gauge *Train des Pignes* operated by the Chemin de Fer de Provence (French rail

passes are valid, other passes are granted a 50% discount) from Nice to Digne is well worth taking for the mountain scenery.

If you plan on making only a few long hauls the **France Railpass** (*see* p.40) will save you money. Other possible discounts hinge on the exact time of your departure. The SNCF has divided the year into blue (off-peak) and white (peak) periods, based on demand: white periods run from Friday noon to midnight Saturday, and from Sunday 3pm to Monday 10am and during holidays (all stations give out little calendars; see below for more on the complicated system of discounts).

Tickets must be stamped in the little orange machines by the entrance to the lines that say *Compostez votre billet* (this puts the date on the ticket). Any time you interrupt a journey until another day, you have to re-compost your ticket. Long-distance trains (*trains Corail*) have snack trolleys and bar/cafeteria cars; some have play areas.

Nearly every station has large computerized lockers (*consigne automatique*) which take

---

Discount Rail Fares

Découverte discounts are free; the *cartes* must be paid for. Ask about extra perks with the *cartes*, such as Avis car hire, hotel discounts, and discounts on Corsica ferries.

Découverte Séjour If you book a return ticket in advance, depart in a *période bleue* and travel at least 200km and stay away a Saturday night, you get a 25% discount.

Découverte à Deux If up to nine people (related or not) book a return trip together in advance, they are eligible for a 25% discount in first or second class for journeys begun in blue periods.

Découverte Enfant+ This is free, issued in the name of a child aged 4–12, and allows a 25% discount for the child and up to four others on trains departing in a *période bleue* as long as the tickets are booked in advance, subject to limited availability.

Découverte 12–25 Young people are eligible for a 25% discount if they buy their ticket in advance and begin travel in a *période bleue*.

Découverte Senior 25% off the journey for those over 60, travelling in *période bleue*; tickets must be booked in advance.

Carte Enfant+ This is bought in the name of a child aged 4–12, and allows the child and up to four people 50% discount on daytime TGVs and night berths on *trains Corail* (subject to limited availablity), plus also 50% discount on seats on daytime *trains Corail*, sleeping cars and TERs departing in a *période bleue* and booked in advance; or 25% when the 50% seats are gone, or when departing in a *période blanche*, or when tickets are bought on the train.

Carte 12–25 Young people aged 12–25 can buy this annual card giving 50% discount on daytime TGVs and night berths on *trains Corail* (subject to limited availablity), plus also 50% discount on seats on daytime *trains Corail*, sleeping cars and TERs departing in a *période bleue* and booked in advance; or 25% when the 50% seats are gone, or when departing in a *période blanche*, or when tickets are bought on the train. This card offers 25% off train journeys from France to 27 countries in Europe, plus other perks.

Carte Senior People over 60 can purchase a senior citizens' card, valid for a year, offering the same discounts as the Carte 12–25.

about half an hour to puzzle out the first time you use them, so plan accordingly; also note that any threat of terrorist activity in France tends to close them down across the board.

By Bus

Buses are essential for seeing small towns and villages that are not accessible on the rail network, but inland they can be tied to school and market schedules. Along the coast, and from towns like Nice up to Vence and Grasse, the services are quite efficient for travellers. They are less convenient and less economical in the western end of the Côte d'Azur.

Buses are run either by the SNCF (replacing discontinued rail routes) or private firms. Rail passes are valid on SNCF lines and they generally coincide with trains. Private bus firms, especially when they have a monopoly, tend to be a bit more expensive than trains; some towns have a *gare routière* (coach station), though many lines start from any place that catches their fancy.

By Car

Driving along the Côte d'Azur has its drawbacks: expensive petrol and car-hire rates, and an **accident rate** double that of the UK (and much higher than the USA).

Roads are generally excellently maintained, but anything of less status than a departmental route (D-road) may be uncomfortably narrow. Mountain roads are reasonable except in the vertical department of Alpes-Maritimes, where they inevitably follow old mule tracks. Shrines to St Eloi, patron of muleteers, are common here, and a quick prayer is a wise precaution. Traffic in the Côte d'Azur, the 'California of Europe', can be diabolically Californian and **parking** a nightmare. Many towns now have pricey guarded car parks underneath their very heart, spectacularly so in Nice, and even in smaller towns such as Vence. Everywhere else, the blue 'P' signs will infallibly direct you to a village or town's already full car park. Watch out for the tiny signs that indicate which streets are meant for pedestrians only (with complicated schedules in even tinier print); and for Byzantine street parking rules (which would take pages

to explain – do as the natives do, and be careful about village centres on market days).

Unless sweetened in an air or holiday package deal, **car hire** in France is an expensive proposition. The cheapest place to buy petrol is at the big supermarkets. Petrol stations keep shop hours (most close Sunday and/or Monday) and are rare in rural areas, so consider your fuel supply while planning any forays into the mountains – especially if you use unleaded. If you come across a garage with petrol-pump attendants, they will expect a tip for oil, windscreen-cleaning or air.

Speed limits are 130km/80mph on the autoroutes (toll motorways); 110km/69mph on dual carriageways (divided highways); 90km/55mph on other roads; 50km/30mph in an 'urbanized area' – as soon as you pass a white sign with a town's name on it and until you pass another sign with the town's name barred. **Fines** for speeding, payable on the spot, begin at €200 and can be astronomical if you fail the breathalyser. If you wind up in an accident, the procedure is to fill out and sign a *constat amiable*. If your French isn't sufficient to deal with this, hold off until you find someone to translate for you so you don't accidentally incriminate yourself. If you have a breakdown and are a member of a motoring club affiliated with the Touring Club de France, ring the latter; if not, ring the police. The French have one civilized custom of the road; if oncoming drivers unaccountably flash their headlights at you, it means that the *gendarmes* are lurking just up the way.

France used to have a rule of giving priority to the right at every intersection. This has somewhat disappeared. Watch out for the *Cédez le passage* (give way) signs and be careful. As you'd expect, give priority to the main road, and to the left on roundabouts. When you (inevitably) get lost in a town or city, the *toutes directions* or *autres directions* signs are like Get Out of Jail Free cards.

By Boat

The major towns, as well as the islands, along the Côte d'Azur, are linked by regular boat services. These come in handy, especially in the summer, when travelling by road is hot purgatory. This is particularly true around

Special-interest Holidays

There are various ways to combine a holiday with study or a special interest. For more information, contact the **French Centre** in London, 164-168 Westminster Bridge Road, London SE1 7RW, **t** (020) 7960 2600; or the **Cultural Services of the French Embassy**, 23 Cromwell Road, London SW7 2EL, **t** (020) 7073 1300, www.ambafrance-uk.org or 972 Fifth Ave, New York, NY 10021, **t** (212) 439 1400, www.ambafrance-us.org.

For language courses, see the **Worldwide Classroom** site at www.world wide.edu. French universities are easy to enter if you're already enrolled in a similar institution at home; tuition fees are nominal, but room and board are up to you. The Cultural Services can send a prospectus and tell you what paperwork is required.

In France

Alliance Française, 2 Rue de Paris, 06000 Nice, **t** 04 93 62 67 66, **f** 04 93 85 28 06, www.alliance-francaise-nice.com. French classes on all levels. Courses last a month, but they can and will tailor to your needs. *Closed between Christmas and New Year*.

Atelier du Safranier, 2 bis Rue du Cannet, 06600 Vieil Antibes, **t** 04 93 34 53 72, www.chez.com/ateliersafranier/. Year-round courses in painting, engraving, lithography, etc., and watercolour on a boat.

L'Ecole du Moulin, Restaurant L'Amandier, Place Cdt. Lamy, Mougins 06250, **t** 04 93 75 78 24. www.moulin-mougins.com. Week-long Cuisine du Soleil cookery courses under the auspices of Roger Vergé Inc.

From the UK

ACE Study Tours, Babraham, Cambs CB2 4AP, **t** (01223) 835 055, www.study-tours.co.uk. Tours include 'Art in the Côte d'Azur', taking in the legacy of Monet, Matisse, Bonnard and Picasso, and the July Aix opera festival.

Alternative Travel Group, 69–71 Banbury Road, Oxford OX2 6PT, **t** (01865) 315 678, **f** (01865) 315 697, www.atg-oxford.co.uk. Independent and escorted tours tracking down the painters and gardens of the south.

Andante, Grange Cottage, Winterbourne Dauntsey, Salisbury, Wiltshire SP4 6ER, **t** (01722) 713 800, **f** (01722) 711 966, www.andantetravels.co.uk. Archaeological and historical study tours of lesser-known sights led by experts in archaeology and ancient and modern history.

Arblaster & Clarke, Farnham Rd, West Liss, Petersfield, Hants, **t** (01730) 893 344, www.arblasterandclarke.com. Gourmet wine tours visiting top estates and led by experts.

CEI The French Centre, Devonshire House, 164–168 Westminster Bridge Road, London SE1 7RW, **t** (020) 7960 2600, **f** (020) 7960 2601; in France, 1 Rue Gozlin, 75006 Paris, **t** (33) 1 4329 1734, www.cei-frenchcentre.com. Language and themed programmes for young foreigners with choice of home stay or residental accommodation.

Cesa Languages Abroad, **t** (01209) 211 800, www.cesalanguages.com. Week-long college-based language courses with cultural programmes on the Riviera.

Chalfont Line Holidays, **t** (01895) 459 540 **f** (01895) 459 549 www.chalfont-line.co.uk. Slow-paced escorted coach or individual holidays for disabled and elderly people.

St-Tropez. Most are included in the text; just look for signs for the *gare maritime*.

Yacht, motorboat and sailing-boat charters are big business along the Riviera. Companies and individual owners hire them out by the hour or day, or in the case of yachts, by the week or fortnight. Average cost per week for a 16m yacht that sleeps six, including food, drink and all expenses is €15,000 – about what six people would pay for a week in a luxury hotel. If the boat business is slow you may haggle the price down. Contact individual tourist offices for lists of firms or try Camper &

Nicholsons, 25 Bruton Street, London W1X 7DB, **t** (020) 7491 2950, www.cnconnect.com.

Books on sailing in the area include *Reeds' Mediterranean Navigator* (Thomas Reed Publications) and *South France Pilot* by Robin Brandon (Imray Laurie). For canal-boats, *see* 'Special-interest Holidays' box, above.

By Bicycle

Cycling spells more pain than pleasure in most French minds, and one of the hazards of

Destination Provence, The Travel Centre, 5 Bishopthorpe Road, York YO23 INA, t (01904) 622 220, f (01904) 651 991, *www.destination provence.co.uk*. Self-catering villas and hotels: special interest golf, walking, cycling, cooking and self-drive discovery tours.

Elegant Resorts, The Old Palace, Chester, CH1 1RB, t (01244) 897 777, f (01244) 897 021, *www.elegantresorts.co.uk*. Deluxe hotels in St-Tropez and Cap Ferrat.

Equity Total Travel, 47 Middle St, Brighton BN1 1AL, t (01273) 277 377, *www.equity.co.uk*. Group tours by coach, also tailor-made individual holidays.

Euro Academy, 67–71 Lewisham High St, London SE13 5JX, t (020) 8297 0505 f (020) 8297 0984 *www.euroacademy.co.uk*. French language courses in Nice and Antibes from one-week: also business French, politics, art and literature, culture and civilization.

French Golf Holidays, The Green, Blackmore, Essex CM4 0RT, t (01277) 824100, f (01277) 824222, *www.frenchgolfholidays.com*. Fly-drive golfing holidays.

Headwater Holidays, The Old Schoolhouse, Chester Road, Northwhich, Cheshire CW8 1LE, t (01606) 720 099, f (01606) 720 034, *www.headwater.com*. Off the beaten track weekly/fortnightly cycling, walking and canoeing holidays, staying in hotels with pools.

JMB Travel Consultants Limited, High Tree House, 4 Cromwell Rd, Powick, Worcester WR2 4QJ, t (01905) 830 099, f (01905) 830 191, *www.jmb-travel.co.uk*.

Martin Randall, 10 Barley Mow Passage, London W4 4GF, t (020) 8742 3355, f (020) 8742 7766, *www.martinrandall.com*. Meticulously organized, escorted 'Art on the Côte d'Azur' tour, following hot on the coat-tails of Monet, Signac, Remoir, Bonnard, etc. for groups of 12–22 accompanied by specialist lecturers and staying in characterful 4-star hotels:

Page & Moy, 136–40 London Road, Leicester LE2 1EN, t 08700 106 212, f 08700 106 211, *www.page-moy.com*. Escorted, expert-led tours, e.g. 'The Camargue and the French Riviera' and 'Christmas in the Côte d'Azur'.

Travel for the Arts, t (020) 8799 8350, f (020) 8998 7965, *www.travelforthearts.co.uk*.

VFB Classic Interludes, t (01242) 240 340, *www.vfbholidays.co.uk*. Coach tours of the 'real' Côte d'Azur.

From the USA

Abercrombie & Kent, 1520 Kensington Road, Oakbrook, IL 60523, t 800 554 7016, f (630) 954 3324, *www.abercrombiekent.com*. From Paris to the Côte d'Azur, taking in Arles, Nice and Monte-Carlo for groups of up to 32.

Adventure Center, 1311 63rd Street, Suite 200, Emeryville, CA 94608, t 800 228 8747, t (510) 654 1879, f (510) 654 4200, *www.adventure center.com, tripinfo@adventurecenter.com*. Eight-day hiking trips for moderate walkers starting from Nice and taking in some rocky terrain: luggage transported ahead.

Dailey-Thorp Travel, 330 West 58th Street, Suite 610, New York, NY 10019, t (212) 307 1555, t 800 998 467. Music and opera tours: festivals and the opera house at Nice.

International Curtain Call, 3313 Patricia Avenue, Los Angeles, CA 90064, t (310) 204 4934 or toll free 800 669 9070, f (310) 204 4935, *www.iccoperatours.com*. Opera and music tours.

---

driving in France is suddenly coming upon bands of cyclists pumping up the kinds of inclines that most people require escalators for. Worse, most of them seem to be twice as old as you. If you mean to cycle in the summer, start early and stop early to avoid heatstroke. French drivers, not always courteous to fellow motorists, usually give cyclists a wide berth; and yet on any given summer day, half the patients in a French hospital are from accidents on two-wheeled transport. Consider a helmet. Also beware that bike thefts are fairly common along the Côte d'Azur, so make sure your insurance covers your bike – or the one you hire.

Getting your own bike to France is fairly easy: Air France and British Airways carry them free from Britain. From the USA or Australia most airlines will carry them as long as they're boxed and are included in your total baggage weight. In all cases, telephone ahead. Certain French trains (called Autotrains, with a bicycle symbol in the timetable) carry bikes for free; otherwise you have to send it as registered luggage and pay a fee, with delivery guaranteed within five days.

You can **hire** bikes of varying quality (most of them 10-speed) at most SNCF stations and in major towns. The advantage of hiring from a station means that you can drop it off at another, as long as you specify where at the time you hire it. Rates run at around €9 a day, with a deposit of €80 or credit card number. Private firms hire mountain-bikes (*VTT* in French) and racing bikes.

On Foot

A network of long-distance paths or **Grandes Randonnées**, GRs for short (marked by distinctive red and white signs), take in some of the most beautiful scenery in the south of France. Each GR is described in a *Topoguide*, with maps and details about camping sites and refuges, available in area bookshops. An English translation covering several GRs in the region, *Walks in Provence*, is available from Stanford's, Long Acre, London WC2, **t** (020) 7836 1321. Otherwise, the best maps for local excursions, based on Ordnance Surveys, are by the Institut Géographique National (1:50,000 or 1:100,000), available in most French bookshops.

There are 5,000km of marked paths in the Alpes Maritimes alone. Of special interest are: GR 5 from Nice to Aspremont; GR 52 from Menton up to Sospel, the Vallée des Merveilles to St-Dalmas-Valdeblore; GR 52a and GR 5 through Mercantour National Park, both of which are open only from the end of June to the beginning of October. The stunning GR 51, nicknamed 'the balcony of the Côte d'Azur', from Castellar (near Menton) takes in the Esterel and Maures before ending at Bormes-les-Mimosas.

In Provence, GR 9 begins in St-Tropez and crosses over the region's most famous mountains: Ste-Baume, Ste-Victoire, the Lubéron and Ventoux. GR 4 crosses the Dentelles de Montmirail and Mont Ventoux en route to Grasse, GR 6 crosses from the Alps through the Vaucluse and Alpilles to Beaucaire and the Pont du Gard, before veering north up the river Gard on to its final destination by the Atlantic. GR 42 descends the west bank of the Rhône from near Bagnols-sur-Cèze to Beaucaire.

Most tourist information centres have maps and leaflets on walks in the area.

Practical A–Z

Climate

The delicious, mild Mediterranean climate of the Côte d'Azur has been drawing aristocrats, dilettantes, consumptives, artists, literati and glitterati, post-war hedonists, hippies and poodle-toting retirees for more than two centuries. Most of the coastal towns claim a 'unique micro-climate' which virtually guarantees year-round sun and balmy temperatures. This is usually, but not always, true; although the coast began its career as a winter resort, and it can be brilliant in December and January, you can also get thoroughly wet and chilled. The sea breeze can sometimes mean it is chilly at night, even in the height of summer.

If you have the luxury of choosing when to visit the Côte d'Azur, May and June are the best months on the Riviera – nearly always bright and sunny, and not intolerably hot and crowded as in July and August. The flowers add a blaze of colour wherever you look; the flower markets in Nice and Antibes are stunning.

But each season has its pros and cons. In January all the tourists are in the Alps; in February the mimosas and almonds bloom and the branches of the citrus trees are weighed down with fruit. In April and May you can sit outside at restaurants and it's often warm enough for the first swim of the year. July and August are bad months, when everything is crowded, temperatures and prices soar and tempers flare, but it's also the season of the great festivals in Juan-les-Pins and Nice.

Things quieten down considerably once French school holidays end in mid-September. In October the weather is traditionally mild on the coast, although torrential downpours have been known to happen; the first snows fall in the Alps. November is another bad month; it rains and many museums, hotels and restaurants close down. December brings Christmas holiday tourists and the first skiers.

For regional weather reports call t 08 36 68 00 00, and for coastal reports call t 08 36 68 08 06.

Consulates and Embassies

UK: 26 Avenue Notre-Dame, 06000 Nice, t 04 93 62 13 56.
USA: 7 Avenue Gustave V, 06000 Nice, t 04 93 88 89 55.
Canada: 10 Rue Lamartine, 06000 Nice, t 04 93 92 93 22.
Ireland: 'Les Chênes Verts', 152 Bd J-F Kennedy, 06160 Antibes, t 04 93 61 50 63; Monaco: t 07 93 15 70 00.
New Zealand: 7 Rue Léonard de Vinci, 75116 Paris, t 01 45 01 43 43, *www.nzembassy.com*.
Australia: 4 Rue Jean Rey, 75724 Paris Cedex 15, t 01 40 59 33 00, *www.austgov.fr*.

Crime and the Police

Everyone in Marseille seemed most dishonest. They all tried to swindle me, mostly with complete success.
Evelyn Waugh

There is a fair chance that you will be had in the south of France; thieves and pickpockets go for the flashy fish on the Côte d'Azur. Road pirates prey on motorists blocked in traffic, train pirates prowl the overnight compartments looking for handbags and cameras, car bandits just love the ripe pickings in cars parked in isolated scenic areas or tourist car parks (they go for expensive or rental cars, the latter discernible by their number plates, as most are registered in *département* 51). In the cities, beware the bands of children who push notes on sheets of cardboard in the faces of their victims to distract them as they go through their pockets. Although violence is rare, the moral of the story is to leave anything you'd really miss at home, carry travellers' cheques and insure your property, especially if you're driving. Report thefts to the nearest *gendarmerie*, not a pleasant task but the reward is the bit of paper you need for an insurance claim. If your passport is stolen, contact the police and your nearest consulate for emergency travel documents. If your credit cards are stolen, call the emergency numbers

Average temperatures in °C (°F)

Jan	Feb	Mar	April	May	June	July	Aug	Sept	Oct	Nov	Dec
11 (52)	12 (54)	14 (56)	17 (62)	20 (69)	22 (72)	24 (75)	26 (79)	25 (77)	20 (69)	16 (61)	13 (55)

given on p.54. Carry photocopies of your pass-port, driver's licence, etc; it makes it easier when reporting a loss. By law, the police in France can stop anyone anywhere and demand an ID; in practice, they only tend to do it to harass minorities, the homeless, and scruffy hippy types.

The drug situation is the same in France as anywhere in the West: soft and hard drugs are widely available, and the police only make an issue of victimless crime when it suits them (your being a foreigner just may rouse them to action). Smuggling any amount of mari-juana into the country can mean prison.

Disabled Travellers

When it comes to providing access for all, France is not exactly in the vanguard of nations; many Americans who come over are appalled. But things are beginning to change,

especially in newer buildings, and national organizations are becoming more helpful too. The SNCF, for instance, now publishes a pamphlet, *Guide pratique du voyageur à mobilité réduite*, covering travel by train for the disabled. All TGVs are equipped for wheel-chair passengers – contact Rail Europe in the UK or USA (*see* p.40) or SNCF in France (*see* p.42) for details.

The Channel Tunnel is also a good way to travel: on Eurotunnel trains, car passengers stay in their vehicles, while Eurostar gives wheelchair passengers first-class travel for second-class fares. Most ferry companies will offer special facilities if contacted beforehand. Vehicles modified for disabled people are charged reduced tolls on *autoroutes*. An *autoroute* guide for disabled travellers (*Guides des autoroutes à l'usage des personnes à mobilité réduite*) is available free from the **Ministère des Transports**, Direction des Routes,

Other Useful Contacts

Access Ability, *www.access-ability.co.uk*. Information on travel agencies catering specifically for disabled people.

Access Travel, 6 The Hillock, Astley, Lancashire M29 7GW, t (01942) 888844, *info@access-travel.co.uk, www.access-travel.co.uk*. Travel agent for disabled people: special air fares, car hire and wheelchair-accessible *gîtes*.

Alternative Leisure Co, 165 Middlesex Turnpike, Suite 206, Bedford, MA 01730, t (718) 275 0023, f 275 2305, *www.alctrips.com*. Vacations abroad for disabled people.

Association des Paralysés de France is a national organization with an office in each *département*, with in-depth local informa-tion; headquarters are in Paris, t 01 40 78 69 00, f 01 45 89 40 57, *www.apf.ass.fr*.

Australian Council for Rehabilitation of the Disabled (ACRODS), PO Box 60, Curtin, ACT 2605, Australia, t/TTY (02) 6682 4333, *www.acrod.org.au*. Information and contact numbers for specialist travel agents.

Comité National Français de Liaison pour la Réadaptation des Handicapés, 236 bis Rue Tolbiac, 75013 Paris, t 01 53 80 66 66. Information on access and useful guides to various regions in France.

Disabled Persons Assembly, PO Box 27-254, Wellington 6035, New Zealand, t (6404) 801 9011, *www.dpa.org.nz*. All-round source for travel information.

Emerging Horizons, *www.emerginghorizons.com*. International on-line travel newsletter for people with disabilities.

Holiday Care Service, Imperial Building, Victoria Rd, Horley, Surrey, RH6 7PZ, t (01293) 774 535, f 784647, Minicom t (01293) 776943, *holiday.care@virgin.net, www.holidaycare.org.uk*. Publishes an information sheet on holidays in France (£2.50).

Mobility International USA, PO Box 10767, Eugene, OR 97440, USA, t/TTY (541) 343 1284, f 343 6812, *www.miusa.org*. Information on international educational exchange programmes and volunteer service overseas.

RADAR (Royal Association for Disability and Rehabilitation), 12 City Forum, 250 City Road, London EC1V 8AF, t (020) 7250 3222, f 7250 0212, Minicom t (020) 7250 4119, *www.radar.org.uk; radar@radar.org.uk*. Information and books on travel.

SATH (Society for Accessible Travel and Hospitality), 347 5th Avenue, Suite 610, New York, NY 10016, t (212) 447 7284, f 725 8253, *www.sath.org, sathtravel@aol.com*. Travel and access information; also details other access resources on the web.

Service du Contrôle des Autoroutes, La
Défense, Paris Cedex 92055, t 01 40 81 21 22.

Access and facilities in 90 towns in France
are covered in *Touristes Quand Même!
Promenades en France pour les voyageurs
handicapés*, a booklet usually available in the
tourist offices of large cities, or from the
**Comité National Français de Liaison pour la
Réhabilitation des Handicapés (CNRH)**, 236bis
Rue de Tolbiac, 75013 Paris, t 01 53 80 66 66.

Hotels with facilities for the disabled are
listed in Michelin's *Red Guide to France*.
A new book, *Gîtes accessibles aux personnes
handicapées*, published by Gîtes de France,
lists self-catering accommodation possibili-
ties. It is available from **Gîtes de France**, 59 Rue
Saint-Lazare, 75009 Paris Cedex 09, t 01 49 70
75 75, f 01 42 81 28 53, *www.gites-de-france.fr*.

E-mail and Internet

E-mail cafés haven't quite taken off in
France: there are fewer than you might
expect, and those that exist are mainly pared-
down computer posts in very basic offices,
often new enough to smell of plaster, without
any of the comforts of a café. Still, this is
changing all the time, even if relatively slowly,
and bigger cities like Nice have plenty of
places to get on-line (*see* p.99 for addresses).

Environment

'Come to the Côte d'Azur for a change of
pollution,' they say. Constantly threatened by
frequent oil spills, a suffocating algae mistak-
enly released into the sea at the Monte-Carlo
Oceanographic Institute, too many cars and
too many people, the well-named 'California
of Europe', from Marseille to Menton, may be
the first place in southern Europe to achieve
total ecological breakdown.

As elsewhere in the Mediterranean, a sad
litany of forest fires heads the television news
in summer. Especially in Provence, most of the
herbs and trees are xerophytes, able to thrive
in dry, hot conditions on poor, rocky soils. Most
forests are pine – Aleppo pines in limestone,
maritime pines in the Maures and Esterel.
Here they often close roads in summer to
decrease the chance of fires. Most are caused
by twits with matches (you'll be more careful,

won't you?), though many fires are deliber-
ately instigated by speculators who burn off
protected forests to build more holiday villas.

Fires often lead to erosion and flooding,
though the local governments now do a good
job of reforestation. The weird wasteland of
Blausasc, in a valley north of Nice (caused by
greedy logging in the 1800s), shows what
Provence would soon look like if they didn't.

The most spectacular environmental non-
issue continues to be the overbuilding of the
Côte d'Azur. The damage is done; one of the
most exceptional parts of the Mediterranean
coast has been thoroughly, thoughtlessly,
irreparably ruined. Since the war there has
simply been too much money involved for
governments to act responsibly; most of the
buildings you'll see were put up illegally – but
there they are. Though this is changing – a
politically connected developer near St-Tropez
was recently forced to demolish an illegal,
half-built project – local governments
continue to promote industrial and tourist
growth in areas where there is absolutely
no room to grow.

Paris bureaucrats are as responsible as local
politicians; in public transport, for example,
they insist on pushing a new TGV route
around the coast, bringing down even more
people, instead of improving local transport
that might cut down on the ferocious traffic
they already have. Citizens' groups in the
south fought it tooth and nail, but the
monstrous new route now cuts across scores
of scenic areas and wine regions.

Other enemies of the Midi include: the army,
which has commandeered enormous sections
of wilderness (including the Ile du Levant) and
regularly blows them to smithereens in
manoeuvres and target practice; the nuclear
industry, with France's nuclear research centre
at Cadarache and most of its nuclear missiles
hidden away on the Plateau du Vaucluse; the
chancre coloré, a fungus that, like phylloxera,
came from the USA (on wooden crates during
the Second World War) and now threatens the
lovely plane trees of Provence; and finally the
truly villainous national electric company, EDF,
which once tried to flood the Grand Canyon
du Verdon. The one genuine contemporary
ecological disaster is the Etang de Berre, now
entirely surrounded by the industrial and
suburban sprawl of Marseille, a ghastly horror

of power pylons, pollution and speculative development. In August, ecological dysfunction reaches its apogee on the sands of St-Tropez's crowded beaches, laced with trash, condoms and human excrement.

Festivals

The Côte d'Azur offers everything from the Cannes Film Festival to the local *fêtes* in the *villages perchés*, with a pilgrimage or religious procession, bumper cars, a *pétanque* tournament, a feast (anything from sardines to *bouillabaisse* to *socca*) and an all-night dance, sometimes to a local band but often to a travelling troupe playing 'Hot Music' or some other electrified cacophony.

A *bravade* (as in St-Tropez) entails pistol or musket-shots; a *corso* is a parade with carts or floats. St John's Day (24 June) and the *Fête de la St-Sylvestre* (New Year's Eve) are big favourites and usually feature bonfires and fireworks.

Overleaf is a calendar of events. Note that dates change every year; for complete listings and precise dates of events, pick up a copy of the annual lists, available in most tourist offices, or consult the tourist office website, *www.crt-riviera.fr* (go to 'Events'). You can also look on:

www.francefestivals.com
www.whatsonwhen.com
www.franceguide.com
www.guideriviera.com

Food and Drink

The French tend to eat quite early, often at 12 or 12.30 for lunch, and generally between 7 and 9pm in the evening, with slightly later summer hours for dinner. Brasseries and cafés are flexible and open long hours, but restaurants don't often like serving late. Most restaurants recommended in this book offer a choice of set-price menus, especially at lunchtime; these are often posted outside the door so you know what to expect. If service is included it will say *service compris* or s.c.; if not, *service non compris* or s.n.c.

For further information about eating in the Côte d'Azur, including local specialities, wines and a menu decoder, *see* the **Food and Drink** chapter, pp.23–36.

Health and Emergencies

Ambulance (SAMU), **t** 15
Police and ambulance, **t** 17
Fire, **t** 18

Local hospitals are the place to go in an emergency (*urgence*). Doctors take turns going on duty at night and on holidays even in rural areas: ring one to listen to the recorded message to find out what to do. To be on the safe side, always carry a phone card (*see* 'Post Offices and Telephones', p.55). If it's not an emergency, pharmacists are trained to administer first aid, and can dispense free advice for minor problems. In rural areas there is always someone on duty if you ring the bell; in cities pharmacies are open on a rotating basis and addresses are posted in their windows and in the local newspaper.

Doctors will give you a brown and white *feuille de soins* with your prescription; take both to the pharmacy and keep the *feuille* for insurance purposes at home. British subjects who are hospitalized and can produce their E111 forms (*see also* p.41) will be billed later at home for 25–30% of the costs that French social insurance doesn't cover. All EU citizens should bring an E111 with them (available from post offices). All nationalities should consider taking out a more comprehensive travel insurance policy before leaving home.

Money and Banks

On 1 January 1999 the **euro** became the official currency of France (and 10 other nations of the European Union) and franc notes and coins were no longer accepted after 17 February 2002. The euro is divided into 100 cents. Notes come in denominations of 5, 10,

---

....
Restaurant Price Ranges

Ranges are for the set menu or an average two-course meal for one without wine.

luxury over €60
expensive €30–60
moderate €15–30
cheap under €15
....

Calendar of Events

Festivals in the list below that do not have specific dates tend to move about within the month from year to year. Check with the local tourist office or on the websites listed on p.51.

January
27 *Fête de Ste Dévote*, **Monaco**
End of month Monte Carlo rally
Throughout month Festival of Sacred Music, **Antibes**
Throughout month *Fête de l'Olive*, **Le Cannet**

February
Corso du Mimosa, **Bormes-les-Mimosas** and **St-Raphaël**
Fête du Mimosa, **Mandelieu-La Napoule**
3 *Fête de St Blaise*, festival of olives and late golden Servan grapes, **Valbonne**
15 days at Carnival *Fête du Citron*, **Menton**; *Feria du Carnaval*, at **Nîmes**
Carnival Nice (*see* p.99)

March
4–5 Reconstruction of the landing of Napoleon, **Golfe-Juan**
5 *Fête de la Violette*, **Tourrettes-sur-Loup**
6 *Sea Bataille des Fleurs*, **Villefranche-sur-Mer**
26 *Festin des Cougourdons*, folklore and dried sculpted gourds, **Nice**

April
International show-jumping, **Monaco**
Flower show, **Cagnes-sur Mer**
Throughout month International tennis tournaments, **Monaco** and **Nice**
Throughout month New-Orleans-les-Pins Jazz Festival, **Juan-les-Pins** and **Antibes**
Mid-month Parade of vintage cars, **Menton**
Mid-month *Fête du Miel* and parade of decorated floats, **Mouans-Sartoux**
24 *Fête de l'Oranger*, **Le-Bar-Sur-Loup**

Last week Final leg of **Princess Rally** (women racing vintage cars) from Paris to **St-Raphaël**

May
Les Jardins dans la Cité, **Vence**
Jousting contest, **St-Raphaël**
Every Sunday *Les Fêtes Traditionnelles de Mai*, tastings and folklore, **Nice**
7 *Fête de Ste Baume*, traditional festival in the **Esterel**
Third Sunday after Easter *Bravade St François*, **Fréjus**
Second week Cannes Film Festival
Second weekend *Fête de la Rose*, **Grasse**
14 *Fête du Terroir*, food and wine tastings, **Tourettes-sur-Loup**
15 *Fête de Ste Maxime*
16–17 *Bravade de St Torpes*, **St-Tropez**
21 *Fête de St-Honorat*, traditional village festival with mass, parade and a dance, **Agay**
Ascension weekend Monaco International Grand Prix
Late May–mid-July International music festival, **Toulon**

June
Throughout month *Fête des Fleurs*, **Le Cannet**
Throughout month Festival of local artists, **St-Paul-de-Vence**
Throughout month *Fête de l'Eté*, **Gassin**
15 *Bravade des Espagnols*, **St-Tropez**
Corpus Christi *Procession dai limaça*, **Gorbio**
21 *Fête des Gênets* (broom), **Roquebrune-Cap-Martin**; *Fête de la Musique*, with outdoor concerts, celebrated all over France.

July
July–August Fireworks Festival, **Monaco**; modern music festival, **St-Paul-de-Vence**
Throughout month Traditional Music Festival, **Vence**
Throughout month Music festival at Monastère de l'Annonciade, **Menton**

20, 50, 100, 200 and 500 euros; coins come in denominations of 1, 2, 5, 10, 20 and 50 cents, and 1 and 2 euros. At the time of writing, the euro was worth UK£0.68, US$1.24 and C$1.66. (check the current rate on *www.xe.com/ucc*).

Traveller's cheques or **Eurocheques** are the safest way of carrying money. If you plan to spend a lot of time in rural areas, where banks are few and far between, you may want to opt for International Giro Cheques, exchangeable at any post office.

Major **credit and debit cards** are widely used in France. Visa (*Carte Bleue*) is the most readily accepted; American Express is often not accepted, however. French-issued credit cards have a special security microchip (*puce*) in

First week Baroque festival in many towns and villages

2 Medieval festival, **Roquebrune-Cap-Martin**

4–14 *Festival Américain*, **Cannes**

Second Sunday *Fête de St Pierre*, with water jousts, etc., **Cap d'Antibes** and **Villefranche-sur-Mer**; *Fête de St Pierre*, choral mass and boat-burning, **Nice**

Mid-July Jazz festivals in **Nice** and **Toulon**

11 International athletics, Nikaïa, **Nice**

10–23 *Nuits de la Danse*; festival of ballet in **Monte Carlo**

14 Fireworks, parties, *batailles des fleurs* and big celebrations in many places for Bastille Day. **Nice** has a Grand Banquet serving stockfish that runs along the Promenade des Anglais

Third weekend *Fête de Sainte Madeleine*, village festival with Provençal mass held in ancient chapel, **La Môle**

Last two weeks International Jazz Festival, **Juan-les-Pins**; Festival of the Ancient Salt Route, **Villefranche-sur-Mer**

22–23 *Fête de la Lavande*, **Ste-Agnès**

23–24 Historic Festival, **Eze**

Music and Dance Festival, at Henry Clews' folly, **Mandelieu-La Napoule**

August

Fête médiévale, medieval crafts and costumes, **Cagnes-sur-Mer**

Jasmine festival, **Grasse**

All month Chamber Music Festival, **Menton**

All month International Firework Festival, **Cannes** and **Monte Carlo**

1 *Fête du Pain*, **Saint-Martin-Vésubie**

5–6 *Fête de la Saint-Sauveur et du Terroir*, music, tastings and folklore, **Vallauris** and **Golfe-Juan**

5 Passion procession, **Roquebrune village**

9 and 11 *Les Fêtes Gourmandes*, gastronomic festival in Auguste Escoffier's home town, **Villeneuve-Loubet**

Mid-month *Fête de St Eloi* (patron saint of muleteers), village festival and parade, **Ollioules** and **Ramatuelle**

September

Vintage car rally, **Monte Carlo**

All month World *pétanque* championships, **Bormes-les-Mimosas**

First Sunday *Festin des baguettes*, **Peille**

3–5 *Fête du Bois*, **Saint-Martin-Vésubie**

12–16 Vintage car tour, **Nice**

16–22 Royal Yacht Regatta, **Cannes**

Third weekend *Journées du Patrimoine*, special events across the region to showcase national treasures and free entry to museums

Last week–first week Oct *Nioulargue*, yacht race in **St-Tropez**

October

First week Festival of regional food and wine, **Valbonne**

Oct and Nov *Verriales*, festival of glass, **Biot**

Throughout month *Fête de l'Automne*, **Ste-Agnès**

Throughout month *Fête de la Châtaigne*, **Collobrières** and other villages in the Massif des Maures

Thoughout month *Fête de la Châtaigne*, **St-Paul-de-Vence**

Thoughout month *Fête des Vendanges*, wine harvest festival, **Le Cannet**

December

All month Festival of Italian Cinema, **Nice**; traditional festivals in all the towns and villages

All month International Painting Festival, **Haut-de-Cagnes**

All month *Foire des Santons*, **Mouans-Sartoux**

Last two weeks *Fête des Lumières*, **St-Raphaël**

---

each card. The card is slotted into a card reader and the holder keys in a PIN number to authorize the transaction. UK cards are different, because the information is held on a magnetic strip, and this sometimes causes problems when the French machines can't read them. Your card is valid, however, and the French Government Tourist Office suggests

you use the following phrase to explain the problem: '*Les cartes étrangères ne sont pas des cartes à puce, mais à bande magnétique. Ma carte est valable et je vous serais reconnaisant d'en demander la confirmation auprès de votre banque ou de votre centre de traitement.*'

Under the Cirrus system, withdrawals in euros can be made from bank and post office

Lost Cards

In case of credit card loss or theft, call the following 24-hour services, which have English-speaking staff:

American Express, t 01 47 77 72 00/**t** 01 47 77 77 00.

Barclaycard, t (00 44) 1604 230 230 (UK).

Diner's Club, t 01 49 06 17 50/**t** 01 47 62 75 00 or 0810 314 159.

Mastercard, t 0800 90 13 87/**t** 01 45 67 84 84.

Visa, t 01 42 77 11 90.

automatic cash machines using your usual PIN number. The specific cards accepted are marked on each machine, and most give instructions in English. Credit card companies charge a fee for cash advances, but rates are often better than bank rates.

Banks are generally open from 8.30am–12.30pm and 1.30–4.30pm; they close on Sunday, and most close either on Saturday or Monday as well. Exchange rates vary, and nearly all take a commission.

Bureaux de change that do nothing but exchange money (and exchanges in hotels and train stations) usually have the worst rates or take out the heftiest commissions, so be careful. It's always a good bet to purchase some euros before you go, especially if you arrive during the weekend.

Opening Hours, Museums and National Holidays

While many **shops** and supermarkets in Nice and other large cities are now open continuously Tuesday–Saturday from 9 or 10am to 7 or 7.30pm, businesses in smaller towns still close down for lunch from 12 or 12.30pm to 2 or 3pm, or in the summer 4pm. There are local exceptions, but nearly everything shuts down on Mondays, except for grocers and *supermarchés* that open in the afternoon. In many towns Sunday morning is a big shopping period.

Markets (daily in the cities, weekly in villages) are usually open mornings only, although clothes, flea and antique markets run into the afternoon.

Most **museums** close for lunch as well, and often all day on Mondays or Tuesdays, and sometimes for all of November or the entire winter. Hours change with the season: longer summer hours begin in May or June and last until the end of September – usually. Some change their hours every darn month. We've done our best to include them in the text, but don't sue us if they're not exactly right. Most close on national holidays and give discounts if you have a student ID card, or are an EU citizen under 18 or over 65 years old; most charge admissions ranging from €1–€10.

Churches are usually open all day, or closed all day and only open for mass. Sometimes notes on the door direct you to the *mairie* or priest's house (*presbytère*) where you can pick up the key. There are often admission fees for cloisters, crypts and special chapels.

The third weekend of September is usually reserved for the *Journées du Patrimoine*, when state-owned museums throw open their doors to the public for free. The free (or at least reduced) entry is intended to give everyone a taste of France's national heritage and the weekend's events are very well publicized to ensure a good turn out. Even though queues can spiral around the museums and the hordes have to shuffle past the national treasures, everyone is very cheerful at the thought of a freebie, and nobody seems to mind not seeing very much.

On French **national holidays**, banks, shops and businesses close; some museums do, but most restaurants stay open. The French have a healthy approach to holidays: sometimes, if there is a holiday on a Wednesday, they 'make a bridge' (*faire le pont*) to the weekend and make Thursday and Friday holidays, too.

National Holidays

1 January New Year's Day
Easter Sunday March or April
Easter Monday March or April
1 May Fête du Travail
8 May VE Day, Armistice 1945
Ascension Day usually end of May
Pentecost and the following Monday beginning of June
14 July Bastille Day
15 August Assumption of the Virgin Mary
1 November All Saints' Day
11 November First World War Armistice
25 December Christmas Day

Post Offices and Telephones

Operator and directory enquiries, t 12

Known as the *La Poste*, easily discernible by a blue bird on a yellow background, **post offices** are open in the cities Monday–Friday 8am–7pm and Saturdays 8am until noon. Larger post offices are now equipped with special machines for you to weigh and stamp your package, letter or postcard without having to even see a real person. They are surprisingly simple to use, and have an English-language option. In villages, offices may not open until 9am, break for lunch and close at 4.30 or 5pm. You can receive letters *poste restante* at any of them; the postal codes in this book should help your mail get there in a timely fashion. To collect it, bring some ID. You can purchase stamps in tobacconists as well as post offices. Nearly all **public telephones** have switched over from coins to *télécartes*, which you can purchase at any post office or news stand for €7.40 for 50 *unités* or €14.75 for 120 *unités*. You can also purchase the US-style phonecards which use a PIN-number system. The French have eliminated area codes, giving everyone a ten-digit number.

If **ringing France from abroad**, the international dialling code is 33, and drop the first '0' of the number. For **international calls from France** dial 00, wait for the change in the dial tone, then dial the country code (UK 44; US and Canada 1; Ireland 353; Australia 61; New Zealand 64), and then the local code (minus the 0 for UK numbers) and number. The easiest way to **reverse the charges** is to spend a few cents ringing the number you want to call and giving them your number in France, which is always posted in the box; alternatively ring your national operator and tell him or her that you want to call reverse charges (for the UK, dial **t** 00 33 44; for the USA, **t** 00 33 11). For directory enquiries, dial **t** 12, or try your luck on the free, inefficient Minitel electronic directory in every post office.

Racism

Unfortunately in the south of France the forces of bigotry and reaction are strong enough to make racism a serious concern. We've heard some horror stories, especially about Marseille, Nice and Toulon, where campsites and restaurants suddenly have no places if the colour of your skin doesn't suit the proprietor; the bouncers at clubs will inevitably say it's really the cut of your hair or trousers they find offensive. If any place recommended in this book is guilty of such behaviour, please write and let us know; we will not only remove it in the next edition, but forward your letter to the regional tourist office and relevant authorities in Paris.

Shopping

Some villages have more boutiques than year-round residents but their wares are rarely compelling. Traditional handicrafts have all but died out, and attempts to revive them have resulted in little model houses and *santons*, terracotta Christmas crib figures dressed in 18th-century Provençal costumes, usually as artful as the concrete studies of the Seven Dwarfs sold at your neighbourhood garden centre. Every town east of the Rhône has at least one boutique specializing in Provençal skirts, bags, pillows and scarves, printed in intense colours (madder red, sunflower yellow, pine green) with floral, paisley or geometric designs. Block-print fabrics were first made in Provence after Louis XIV, wanting to protect the French silk industry, banned the import of popular Indian prints. Clever entrepreneurs in the papal-owned Comtat Venaissin responded by producing cheap imitations still known today as *indiennes*. The same shops usually sell the other essential bric-a-brac of the south – dried lavender pot-pourris, sachets of *herbes de Provence* (nothing but thyme and bay leaves) and perfumed soaps.

Big name French and Italian designers and purveyors of luxury goods have boutiques at Cannes, Monaco and Nice. Moustiers, Vallauris and Biot have hand-made ceramics, and in the *villages perchés* from Eze to St-Paul-de-Vence at least a million artists wait to sell you their works. Cogolin specializes in pipes and saxophone-reeds; Grasse sells perfumes and oils.

The sweet of tooth will find the Côte d'Azur heaven. Nearly every town has its own speciality: candied fruits in Nice, *nougats* in Vence, *marrons glacés* in Collobrières, orange-flavoured chocolates called *grimaldines* in Cagnes, and creamy *tartes tropéziennes* in St-Tropez.

Sports and Leisure

Bicycling
See 'Getting Around', pp.44–6.

Fishing
You can fish in the sea without a permit as long as your catch is for local consumption; along the Riviera captains offer expeditions for tuna and other denizens of the deep. Freshwater fishing requires an easily obtained permit from a local club; tourist offices can tell you where to find them.

Football
Professional football in the south is dominated by the three Ms: Marseille Olympique, Monaco, which is almost as wealthy, and Montpellier, the bright star in Languedoc – other first-division teams are in Toulon and Cannes.

Gambling
If you're over 21, every big resort along the coast comes equipped with a **casino** ready to take your hard-earned money. Scandals have plagued a few – Nice, especially (*see* p.116). Even if you aren't a gambler, a few are worth a visit: Monte Carlo, for its cynical mix of the voluptuous and the crass; or Cannes, for high-fashion vice. Or you can do as the locals do and play for a side of beef, a lamb or a VCR in a **Loto**, in a local café or municipal *salle des fêtes*. Everybody plays the horses, at the local bar with the *PMU* (off-track betting) outlet.

Golf
Increasingly popular in France, there are courses near most of the major resorts on the Côte d'Azur, and literally a hundred more planned or under construction. Cannes offers golfers the most choice, with three courses in Mandelieu and three in Le Cannet. The most spectacular course is Monaco's, which was laid out around the turn of the century.

Pétanque
Like *pastis* and olive oil, *pétanque* is one of the essential ingredients of the Midi, and even the smallest village has a rough, hard court under the plane trees for its practitioners – nearly all male, although women are welcome to join in. Similar to *boules*, the special rules of *pétanque* were, according to tradition, developed in La Ciotat, near Marseille, but the World Championships take place in Bormes-les-Mimosas in September. The object is to get your metal ball closest to the marker (*bouchon* or *cochonnet*). Tournaments are frequent and well attended.

Rugby Union
Although the southwest is the cradle of most of the players on the national team (movements to change one of the Five Nations from France to Occitania have so far fallen flat), you can still see fiery matches in Nice and Toulon.

Skiing
Ideally, if the weather ever decides to settle down, you can do as in California: ski in the morning and bake on the beach in the afternoon. The biggest resorts in the Alpes Maritimes are Isola 2000, Auron and Valberg and, closest to Nice, Gréolières-les-Neiges (northeast of Vence).

Comité Régional du Tourisme Provence-Alpes Côte d'Azur, CMCI, Espace Colbert, 2 Rue Henri Barbusse, 13001 Marseille, t 04 91 56 23 63, *crtprov.info@wanadoo.fr*, *www.crt-paca.fr*.

Fédération Française de Ski, 50 Rue des Marquisats, 74001 Annecy Cedex, t 04 50 51 40 34, *www.ffs.fr*.

Association Nationale des Maires des Stations de Montagne, 61 Bd Haussmann, 75008 Paris, t 01 47 42 23 32, *www.skifrance.fr*.

Water Sports and Beaches
In 1763, the consumptive English writer and doctor, Tobias 'Smelfungus' Smollett tried something for his health that shocked the doctors in Nice: he went bathing in the sea. Most extraordinary of all, it made him feel better, and he recommended that people follow his example, though it would be difficult for women 'unless they laid aside all

regards to decorum' – as they so often do in the most fashionable resorts. There are scores of fine, sandy beaches along the coast (*see* 'best beaches' selections in every chapter), although *not* on the Riviera east of Juan-les-Pins. Anyone who arrives with any ideas about access to the sea being a natural God-given right will be appalled to learn that paying concessions occupy most of the Côte; free, quiet beaches require more effort (the coves below the Esterel and the Maures, the Hyères islands). Areas are always set aside for *les naturistes*, or nudists: the Ile du Levant is one of Europe's biggest nudist resorts.

Every town on the coast hires out equipment for **water sports**, often for hefty prices. Juan-les-Pins claims to have invented waterskiing. Experienced **windsurfers** head for Brutal Beach off Cap Sicié, west of Toulon. The best **diving** is off Ile Port-Cros National Park. For a list of diving clubs, contact the **Fédération Française d'Etudes et de Sports Sous-Marins**, 24 Quai de Rive-Neuve, 13284 Marseille, t 04 91 33 99 31, f 04 91 54 77 43, *www.ffessm*.

If you're genuinely jaded and have a weakness for medical-psychobabble, you can even indulge in *thalassothérapie* to help make you thin, fit, stress-free, or even turn you into a laid-back non-smoker.

Tourist Information

Every city and town, and most villages, have a tourist information office, called (slightly confusingly) a *Syndicat d'Initiative* or more often an *Office du Tourisme* or even a *Maison du Tourisme*. In smaller villages this service is provided by the town hall (*mairie*). In most cases this extends to a website nowadays. They distribute free maps and town plans, hotel, camping and self-catering accommodation lists for their area, and can inform you on sporting events, leisure activities, wine estates open for visits and festivals.

Addresses, telephone numbers and websites are listed in the text, and if you write to them they'll post you their booklets to help you plan your holiday before you leave.

For general information before you go, *see* the main tourist information addresses and websites listed on p.38.

Regional tourist offices known as CRTs (*Comités du Tourisme*) offer useful information: *www.guideriviera.com*, *www.crt-paca.fr*.

Where to Stay

Hotels

In the south of France you can find some of the most splendid hotels in Europe and some genuine scruffy fleabags of dubious clientele, with the majority of establishments falling somewhere between. Like most countries in Europe, the tourist authorities grade them by their facilities (not by charm or location) with stars from four (or four with an L for luxury – a bit confusing) to one, and there are even some cheap but adequate places undignified by any stars at all.

We would have liked to put the exact prices in the text, but almost every establishment has a wide range of rooms and prices – a very useful and logical way of doing things, once you're used to it. In some hotels, every single room has its own personality and the difference in quality and price can be enormous; a large room with antique furniture, a television or a balcony over the sea and a complete bathroom will cost much more than a poky back room in the same hotel, with a window overlooking a car park, no antiques, and the WC down the hall. Most two-star hotel rooms have their own showers and WCs; most one-stars offer a wider range of rooms with or without. Hotels with no stars are not necessarily dives; their owners probably never bothered filling out a form for the tourist authorities. Their prices are usually the same as one-star places.

Standards vary so widely that it's impossible to be more precise, but we can add a few more generalizations. **Single rooms** are relatively rare, and usually two-thirds the price of a

Hotel Price Ranges
Note: all prices listed here and elsewhere in this book are for a double room.
luxury over €230
very expensive €150–230
expensive €100–150
moderate €60–100
inexpensive under €60

double, and rarely will a hotelier give you a discount if only doubles are available (again, because each room has its own price); on the other hand, if there are three or four of you, **triples** or **quads** or adding beds to a double room is usually cheaper than staying in two rooms. Flowered wallpaper, usually beige, comes in all rooms with no extra charge – it's an essential part of the French experience. **Breakfast** (usually coffee, a croissant, bread and jam for €5 or €6) is nearly always optional: you'll do as well for less in a bar. As usual rates rise in the busy season (holidays and summer, and in the winter around ski resorts), when many hotels with restaurants will require that you take **half-board** (*demi-pension* – breakfast and a set lunch or dinner). Many **hotel restaurants** are superb and described in the text, and non-residents are welcome. At worst the food will be boring, and it can be monotonous eating in the same place every night when there are so many tempting restaurants around. In the off-season, board requirements vanish into thin air.

Your holiday will be much sweeter if you **book ahead**, especially if you are looking for accommodation between May and October. The few reasonably priced rooms are snapped up very early across the board. At any time of year, phoning a day or two ahead is always a good policy, although beware that hotels will only confirm a room with the receipt of a cheque covering the first night, or a credit card number). Tourist offices have complete lists of accommodation in their given areas or even *département*, which come in handy during the peak season; many will even call around and book a room for you on the spot for free or a nominal fee.

Chain hotels (Sofitel, Formula One, etc.) are in most cities, but always dreary and geared to the business traveller more than the tourist, so you won't find them in this book. Don't confuse chains with the various **umbrella organizations** like *Logis et Auberges de France*, *Relais du Silence* or the prestigious *Relais et Châteaux*, which promote and guarantee the quality of independently owned hotels and their restaurants. Many are recommended in the text. Larger tourist offices usually stock their booklets, or you can pick them up before you leave from the French National Tourist Office. If you plan to do a lot of driving, you

may want to take the English translation of the French truckers' bible, *Les Routiers*, an annual guide (£14.99) with maps listing reasonably priced lodgings and food along the highways and byways of France.

Routiers Limited, 188–90 Earl's Court Rd, London SW5 9QT, **t** (020) 7370 5113).

Bed and breakfast: In rural areas, there are plenty of opportunities for a stay in a private home or farm. *Chambres d'hôtes*, in the tourist office brochures, are listed separately from hotels with the various *gîtes* (*see* p.60). Some are connected to restaurants, others to wine estates or a château; prices tend to be moderate to inexpensive.

B&B France, 94–96 Bell Street, Henley-on-Thames, Oxon RG9 1XS, **t** (01491) 578803, toll-free from the USA, **t** 800 454 87 04, **f** (01491) 410806, *bookings@bedbreak.com*, *www.bedbreak.com* (catalogue £15.25)

Association Française BAB France, 9 Rue Jacques Louvel Tessier, 75010 Paris, **t** 01 42 01 34 34, **f** 01 42 01 34 35, *bab@bedbreak.com* (catalogue £17.99).

Youth Hostels, *Gîtes d'Etape* and Refuges

Most cities and resort areas have youth hostels (*auberges de jeunesse*) which offer simple dormitory accommodation and breakfast to people of any age for around €7–12 a night. Most offer kitchen facilities as well, or inexpensive meals. They are the best deal going for people travelling on their own; for people travelling together a one-star hotel can be just as cheap. Another down-side is that many are in the most ungodly locations – in the suburbs where the last bus goes by at 7pm, or miles from any transport at all in the country. In the summer the only way to be sure of a room is to arrive early in the day. Most require a Hostelling International (HI) membership card, which you can usually purchase on the spot, although regulations say you should buy them at home.

Hostelling International, 14 Southampton Street, London WC2, **t** (0870) 870 8808, *www.hihostels.com.*

AYH, 1009 11th Street Northwest, Washington DC 20001, **t** (202) 783 49 43.

CHA, 75 Nicholas Street, Ottawa, Ontario K1N 7B9, **t** (613) 235 2595.

Self-catering Operators

In the UK

Allez France, 27a West St, Storrington, West
Sussex RH20 4DZ, t 0870 160 5743, f (01903)
745 044, *www.allezfrance.com*. Self-catering
apartments, cottages and villas in Antibes,
Juan-les-Pins, Gorges du Verdon and the
whole of the Côte d'Azur.

The Apartment Service, 5–6 Francis Grove,
London SW19 4DT, t (020) 8944 1444,
www.apartmentservice.com. Selected
apartment accommodation in cities for long
or short stays.

Chez Nous, Spring Mill, Earby, Barnoldswick,
Lancashire BB94 0AA, t 08700 781 400,
www.cheznous.com. Over 3,000 privately
owned holiday cottages and B&Bs.

CV Travel, 43 Cadogan Street, London SW3 2PR,
t (020) 7591 2800, *www.cvtravel.net*,
enquiries@cvtravel.net. Attentive personal
service from a company with years of experience and a great range of lovely upmarket
villas across France.

Dominique's Villas, 25 Thames House, 140
Battersea Park Rd, London SW11 4NB, t (020)
7738 8772, *www.dominiquesvillas.co.uk*. Large
villas and châteaux with pools.

Destination Provence, The Travel Centre,
5 Bishopthorpe Road, York YO23 INA,
t (01904) 622 220, f (01904) 651 991,
www.destinationprovence.co.uk. Self-
catering villas and hotels.

Fleur Holidays, t 0870 750 2121, f (01253) 595
151, *www.fleur-holidays.co.uk*. Camping.

French Affair, 5/7 Humbolt Road, London W6
8QH t (020)7381 8519, f (020) 7381 5423,
www.frenchaffair.com. Large selection of
rental properties.

Meon Villas, Meon House, College St,
Petersfield GU32 3JN, t (01730) 230 200 or
t 0870 850 8551, *www.meontravel.co.uk*.
Villas with pools.

Palmer and Parker Villa Holidays, Bank Rd,
Penn, Bucks HP10 8LA, t (01494) 815 411,
www.palmerparker.com. Upmarket villas
with pools on the Riviera.

VFB Holidays, Normandy House, High St,
Cheltenham GL50 3FB, t (01242) 240 340,
www.vfbholidays.co.uk. From rustic *gîtes* to
luxurious farmhouses and hotels; also
provides river cruises.

In the USA

At Home in France, PO Box 643, Ashland,
OR 97520, t (541) 488 9467, *www.athomein
france.com*. Apartments, cottages, farmhouses, manor houses and villas; moderate
to deluxe.

Doorways Ltd., PO Box 151, Bryn Mawr, PA
19010 2502, t 800 261 4460, t (610) 520
0806, *www.villavacations.com*. Villas and
apartments all over France.

Families Abroad, 194 Riverside Drive, New York,
NY 10025, t (212) 787 2434, t (718) 768 6185,
www.familiesabroad.com. Sabbatical and
vacation rentals, in apartments, villas and
châteaux on the Riviera.

France by Heart, PO Box 614, Mill Valley,
CA 94942, t (415) 388 3075, *www.franceby-
heart.com*. Hundreds of properties.

Global Home Network, Bridge Street
Corporate Housing Worldwide, t 800 528
3549, *www. globalhomenetwork.com*.
Apartments, hotels and corporate lodging in
major cities.

Heaven on Earth, 39 Radcliffe Rd, Rochester,
NY 14617, t 800 466 5605, t (585) 342 5550,
www.heavenlyvillas.com. Moderate to
luxury.

Hideaways International, 767 Islington St,
Portsmouth, NH 03801, t 800 843 4433,
t (603) 430 4433, f (603) 430 4444,
www.hideaways.com. Apartments in Paris,
plus villas, farmhouses and châteaux
throughout France.

New York Habitat, 307 7th Av, Suite 306,
New York, NY 10001, t (212) 255 8018, *www.
nyhabitat.com*. Over a thousand apartments
throughout Paris and the South of France.

Overseas Connection, PO Box 1800, Sag
Harbor, New York 11963, t (631) 725 9308,
www.overseasvillas.com. Villas and apartments in Provence and the Côte d'Azur.

Vacances Provencales, 1425 Bayview Av, Suite
204, Toronto, Ontario M4G 3A9, t 800 263
7152, t (416) 322 5565, *www.europeanhome
rentals.com*. Moderate to luxury villas,
country homes, châlets and apartments in
Provence and Côte d'Azur.

Villas of Distinction, PO Box 55, Armonk,
NY 10504, t 800 289 0900, t (914) 273 3331,
www.villasofdistinction.com. Private villas,
cottages and châteaux mainly in Provence
and the Côte d'Azur.

AYHA, 11 Rawson Place, opposite Central
Station, Sydney, New South Wales 2000,
t (02) 9281 9444, *www.yha.com.au*.

Another option in cities is the single-sex
dormitories for young workers (*Foyers de
jeunes travailleurs et de jeunes travailleuses*)
which will rent out individual rooms if any are
available, for slightly more than a hostel.

A *gîte d'étape* is a simple shelter with bunk
beds and a rudimentary kitchen set up by a
village along GR walking paths or a scenic bike
route. Again, lists are available for each
département; the detailed maps listed under
'On Foot' (*see* p.46), mark them as well. In the
mountains similar rough shelters along the
GR paths are called *refuges*, most of them
open summer only. Both charge around €6 or
€8 a night. *www.gites-de-france.fr/eng*.

Camping

Camping is a very popular way to travel,
especially among the French themselves, and
there's at least one campsite in every town,
often an inexpensive, no-frills place run by the
town itself (*camping municipal*). Other campsites are graded with stars like hotels from
four to one: at the top of the line you can
expect lots of trees and grass, hot showers, a
pool or beach, sports facilities and a grocer's,
bar and/or restaurant, and on the coast, prices
rather similar to one-star hotels (although
these, of course, never have all the extras). But
beware that July and August are terrible
months to camp on the Côte d'Azur, when
sites become so overcrowded (St-Tropez is
notorious) that the authorities have begun to
worry about health problems. If you want to
camp outside official sites, it's imperative to
ask permission from the landowner first, or
risk a furious farmer, his dog and perhaps even
the police.

Tourist offices have complete lists of campsites in their regions, or, if you plan to move

around a lot, pick up a *Guide officiel
camping/caravanning*, available in French
bookshops.

A number of UK holiday firms book
camping holidays and offer discounts on
Channel ferries:
Canvas Holidays, t (01383) 629 000,
www.canvasholidays.co.uk
Eurocamp Travel, t (01606) 787000,
www.eurocamp.co.uk
Keycamp Holidays, t 0870 7000 123,
www.keycamp.co.uk.

Gîtes de France and Other Self-catering Accommodation

The south of France offers a vast range of
self-catering: inexpensive farm cottages,
history-laden châteaux with gourmet frills,
sprawling villas on the Riviera, flats in modern
beach resorts or even on board canal boats.
The *Fédération Nationale des Gîtes de France* is
a French government service offering inexpensive accommodation by the week in rural
areas. Lists with photos arranged by *département* are available from the **Maison des Gîtes
de France et du Tourisme Vert**, 59 Rue Saint-
Lazare, 75439 Paris Cedex 09, **t** 01 49 70 75 75,
f 01 42 81 28 53, *www.gîtes-de-france.fr*,
info@gites-de-france.fr, or in the UK from the
official official Gîtes de France rep: **Brittany
Ferries**, The Brittany Centre, Wharf Road,
Portsmouth PO2 8RU, **t** 08705 360 360 or
t 08703 665 333, *www.brittany-ferries.co.uk*.
Prices range from €150–400 a week. Other
options are advertised in the Sunday papers or
contact one of the firms listed on p.59. The
accommodation they offer will nearly always
be more comfortable and costly than a *gîte*,
but the discounts holiday firms can offer on
the ferries, plane tickets or car rental can make
up for the price difference.

The Three Corniches:
Menton to Nice

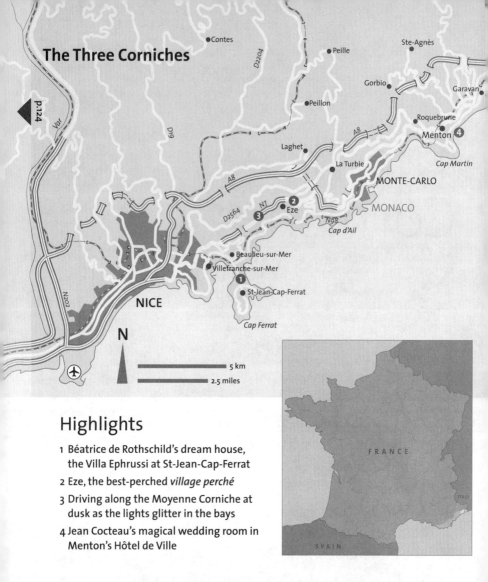

The Three Corniches

Contes
Peille
Ste-Agnès
Gorbio
Garavan
Peillon
Roquebrune
Menton **4**
Laghet
La Turbie
Cap Martin
MONTE-CARLO
Eze **2**
3
MONACO
Cap d'Ail
Beaulieu-sur-Mer
Villefranche-sur-Mer
1
St-Jean-Cap-Ferrat
NICE
Cap Ferrat

p.124

Var

D2204

D19

A8

D2564

N7

N98

N202

N

5 km
2.5 miles

FRANCE
ITALY
SPAIN

Highlights

1 Béatrice de Rothschild's dream house, the Villa Ephrussi at St-Jean-Cap-Ferrat
2 Eze, the best-perched *village perché*
3 Driving along the Moyenne Corniche at dusk as the lights glitter in the bays
4 Jean Cocteau's magical wedding room in Menton's Hôtel de Ville

A calcined, scalped, rasped, scraped, flayed, broiled, powdered, leprous, blotched, mangy, grimy, parboiled country, without trees, water, grass, fields – blank, beastly, senseless olives and orange-trees like a mad cabbage gone indigestible.

Swinburne

Just west of Italy begins that 20km swathe of Mediterranean hyperbole that represents the favourite mental image of the French Riviera, where the landscapes are at their most vertical and oranges and lemons ripen against a backdrop of snow-topped Alps. Menton, where Swinburne's senseless olives grow, is a perfect little sun-trap, rivalled only by Beaulieu a bit further along, the only place in France where bananas ripen naturally. Superb villas and gardens, that once belonged to dukes and kings, are

Beaches

The beaches of the eastern Riviera are not renowned for their beauty. The shore is rocky – beaches are shingle, or in some cases artificial pebble. Lack of sand is more than compensated for by the spectacular settings of many beaches, backed by 650ft cliffs, palm trees and some of the world's most expensive real estate. Nonetheless, prepare to be underwhelmed by the tiny sandpits which characterize many of the 'private beaches'.

Best Beaches

Monaco: chic and sharp; safe swimming.
Beaulieu (Plage des Fourmis): backed by palms, with a view across to Cap Ferrat.
Villefranche-sur-Mer: the trendiest beach in the region, and also one of the best for children as it's shallow, right by the train station and has very fine shingle that's almost sand.
St-Jean-Cap-Ferrat (Plage du Passable): popular, sloping beach with views to Villefranche.

scattered along the shores of St-Jean-Cap-Ferrat, Roquebrune and Cap Martin. High in the mountains hang spectacular medieval villages, including La Turbie, where the Romans erected a 'trophy' to celebrate their final victory over the Ligurian tribes who until then had effectively kept the Empire from the sweet delights of Provence.

Although first tamed by the Romans, this easternmost and tastiest morsel of the Côte d'Azur long remained a world apart, ruled until the mid-19th century by the Grimaldis of Monaco, and noted above all for its lemons and poverty. Bad relations with the French over Napoleon brought the first English and Russians, with their titles and weak lungs, to winter here, just outside France, in spite of the difficult roads. They built hotels, villas and casinos in the grand, fulsome, rococo-spa style of the period, and to this day the spirit lingers, a slightly musty violet perfume in a semi-tropical climate. Ian Fleming summed up the bygone spirit in writing about the fate of Monaco, where high class has gone high rise: 'Part of the trouble with the Monte-Carlo rooms is that they were built in an age of elegance for elegant people, and the gambling nowadays has the drabness of a Strauss operetta played in modern dress...what used to be a pastime has now become a rather deadly business of amassing tax-free capital gains.'

Even if most of the old glamour has faded, the scenery is as breathtaking as ever, one mighty mountain after another plummeting drunkenly into the sea, traced by hairpinning corniche roads that zigzag on ledges over vertiginous drops. Here, Continental hormones traditionally go into overdrive as the rich and famous in dark glasses and sporty convertibles race down to 'Monte', although not so much to gamble these days as to visit their bank managers. And the only racing that really happens is the Monaco Grand Prix; the traffic is nearly always slow and heavy – a fact that doesn't prevent some would-be James Bonds from contributing to an appalling accident rate. The worst traffic jams inch along the lowest road, the **Basse Corniche** (N98), through the seaside resorts; most of the frequent buses that ply the coast use this road, which runs parallel to the railway. To relieve the traffic, already choking in the 1920s, the most dramatic of the roads, the **Moyenne Corniche** (N7), was drilled through the rock and hung sheerly through the hills, making it the favourite for car-chase scenes. Higher up, along the route of the Roman Via Aurelia (also called Via Julia Appia), Napoleon built the **Grande Corniche** (D2564), with the most panoramic views of all.

Menton

The Côte d'Azur starts halfway between the fleshpots of Paris and Rome at Menton, right on the Italian frontier. Its history starts here as well, with the earliest traces of Riviera humans – folk who a million years ago already had the good sense to settle where a wall of mountains, still crowned with snow in April, blocks out the cold so that lemon trees can blossom all year.

Despite this early start, the Menton area wasn't inhabited again until the 10th century, when settlers clustered around the Annonciade hill, where they felt safe from Saracen pirates. The town first belonged to the counts of Ventimiglia – little better than pirates themselves – then briefly joined Provence before it was sold to Charles Grimaldi of Monaco in 1346.

The Grimaldis became rich from taxing Menton's citrus fruit and continued to enjoy the fruits of this wealth until 1848, when the town and its neighbour, Roquebrune, declared their independence. Unlike most of the revolts in Europe that fateful year, this puny one succeeded, and the Free Towns of Menton and Roquebrune endured until 1861, when the people voted to unite with France, and Charles III of Monaco sold his claim on the towns to Napoléon III for four million gold francs.

The following year, a Dr J. Henry Bennet wrote *Menton and the Riviera as a Winter Climate*, a book that soon attracted a community of 5,000 Brits to the town, led by Queen Victoria herself in 1883. (Her bust glowers regally from a fountain tiled like a municipal swimming pool on the Quai Bonaparte.) During the Second World War the Germans wrecked Menton's port and, when they were chased out, lobbed bombs on to it from the Italian side of the border. The damage wasn't repaired until 1956.

Nattering nabobs of negativism claim that Menton has a poor beach and as much atmosphere as your grandmother's antimacassar, a town where 30 per cent of the population are retirees (the highest percentage in France) and most of the rest are poodles. Yet Menton is magnificently situated, sprinkled with some of the coast's finest gardens, and has a healthy attitude to relaxation compared with the hardened glamour-pusses to the west. A recent influx of families and young people, mainly from nearby Italy, have begun to liven up the beaches and main streets.

Jean Cocteau, Love and Lemons

Menton is squeezed between the mountains and a pair of shingle-beached bays: the **Baie de Garavan**, on the Italian side, where villas and gardens overlook the yacht harbour, and the **Baie du Soleil** (the Roman *Pacis Sinus* or Gulf of Peace), stretching 3km west to Cap Martin.

In between these two bays stands a little 17th-century harbour bastion looking out to sea that Jean Cocteau converted into the **Musée Cocteau** (*t 04 93 57 72 30; open 10–12 and 2–6; closed Tues; adm*) in the late 1950s, and which is decorated with grey and white mosaics made from seaside pebbles. The hallway is dominated by an enormous bloodthirsty tapestry, Cocteau's first, *Judith et Holopherne*, in which Judith seduces Holofernes, general of the enemy forces, in order to save her city, and then decapitates him in his sleep and slinks out looking vicious. Niches on the upper level,

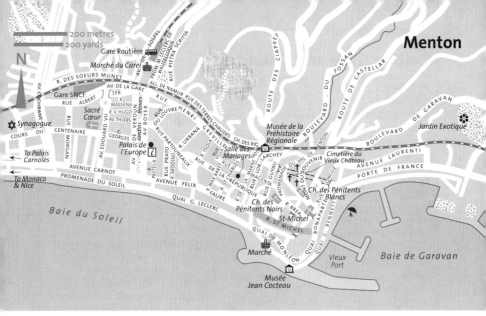

each with their own pebble-mosaic floor and a Cocteau-designed display case, hold the playful *Animaux fantastiques*, which Cocteau created in a burst of admiration for the colourful ceramics that Picasso was making in Vallauris in the late 1950s. Picasso's work also inspired the series of coloured pencil drawings, *Les Innamorati*, portraying the happier love affairs of the Mentonnais.

This theme of Menton's lovers was first explored by Cocteau in his decorations for the 1957 **Salle des Mariages** (*t 04 92 10 50 00; open 8.30–12.30 and 2–5; closed Sat and Sun; adm*), in the Hôtel de Ville, 5 minutes' walk northwest on Rue de la République. At the entrance, gilt mirrors are painted with a blowsy Marianne, symbol of the Republic, whom French law insists makes it to every French wedding. The interior resembles a louche nightclub: carpeted with leopard-skin, upholstered with plush red velvet and lit with sinuous tulip-shaped lamps. A lemon-picker weds a fisherman amid rather discouraging mythological allusions: on the right wall there's a wedding party in Saracen costume, referring to the Mentonnais' Saracen blood, although among the company we see the bride's frowning mother, the groom's jilted girlfriend and her armed brother. The other wall shows Orpheus turning back to see if his beloved Eurydice is following him out of Hell, condemning her to return there forever, while, on the ceiling, Love, Poetry (on Pegasus) and Science (juggling planets) look on.

Love was also a favourite theme of the original Riviera inhabitants, who carved the little Cro-Magnon Venuses now housed in the **Musée de la Préhistoire Régionale**, a couple of blocks north on Rue Loredan Larchey (*t 04 93 35 84 64; open 10–12 and 2–6; closed Tues*). An earnest series of dioramas recreates the area's cave interiors from the time when the furry animals people lived alongside were mammoths rather than poodles, but the star exhibit is the 30,000-year-old skeleton of Menton Man (found just over the border in Grimaldi), buried in a bonnet of seashells and deer teeth long since calcified into the bone; note, too, rock carvings from the Vallée des Merveilles, high above Menton in the Roya valley of the Alpes-Maritimes.

Getting There and Around

By Train

Métrazur (St-Raphaël–Ventimiglia) and all other Nice–Italy trains stop in Menton (Menton-Centre), Rue de la Gare.

There's another station – Menton-Garavan – behind the port. **SNCF, t** 08 92 35 35 35.

By Bus

Buses for Nice (via Roquebrune-Cap-Martin and Monte-Carlo) depart frequently from the *gare routière* on Esplanade du Careï, northeast of the train station. Tickets from Monte-Carlo with the Broch and RCA bus companies, **t** 04 93 28 43 27, are valid on both.

Other bus services go to Ventimiglia, Castillon and Sospel and to Ste-Agnès, Gorbio and Castellar, often in *navettes* (minibuses).

All local Menton bus lines pass by Esplanade du Careï.

Tourist Information

Menton: Palais de l'Europe, 8 Av Boyer B.P. 239, 06506 Menton Cedex, **t** 04 92 41 76 76, **f** 04 92 41 76 58, *ot@villedementon.com*, *www.villedementon.com*. Open July–Aug Mon–Sat 9–7, Sun 9–1; Sept–June Mon–Fri 8.30–12.30 and 2–6, Sat 9–12, 2–6. Has details on 'passports' with reduced entrance fees for local attractions.

Post office: Corner of Cours George V and Rue Edouard VII, **t** 04 93 28 64 70.

Taxis: Taxi rank outside the Menton-Centre SNCF station, or call **t** 04 92 10 47 00/01/02/03/04.

Internet: **Le Café des Arts**, 16 Rue de la République, **t** 04 93 35 78 67.

Market Days

Food market every morning at the Halles; Sat am at Vieux Port (clothes, accessories). Flea market, on the Place aux Herbes, Friday.

Festivals

Fête du Citron, Feb–Mar: floats, processions, special entrance to the gardens; call the tourist office for details.

Music Festival at Monastère de l'Annonciade, July–Aug at St-Michel. Call **t** 04 92 41 76 95 or **t** 08 92 70 52 05 for reservations.

Where to Stay

Menton ✉ 06500

All but one of Menton's old grand hotels have been converted into flats, and no new ones have risen to take up the slack. If all the below are full, you could try *www.hotel menton.com*.

★★★★Hôtel des Ambassadeurs, 3 Rue Partouneaux, **t** 04 93 28 75 75, **f** 04 93 35 62 32, *www.ambassadeurs-menton.com* (*luxury*). Though now a Clarion hotel, this is the last *grande dame* – gracious, spacious, pink and balconied, and slap bang in the middle of town. There's nearly every luxury, but no pool. *See also* 'Eating Out', opposite.

★★★Hôtel l'Aiglon, 7 Av de la Madone, **t** 04 93 57 55 55, **f** 04 93 35 92 39, *www.hotelaiglon. net* (*very expensive–expensive*). Tucked into a drowsy corner of the Parc de la Madone, this independent Belle Epoque hotel is light, stylish and very chic, with spindly antiques and high ceilings. By the pool there is a lovely arbour with wooden beams. *See also* 'Eating Out'.

★★★Napoléon, 29 Porte de France, **t** 04 93 35 89 50, **f** 04 93 35 49 22, *www.napoleon-menton.com* (*expensive*). This is a delight; the rooms may be decorated in comfortable dark brown like a favourite great aunt's, but it has a pool, soundproofed, air-conditioned rooms, a private beach, and friendly, obliging staff. *Closed mid-Nov–mid-Dec.*

★★★Royal Westminster, 28 Av Félix Faure, **t** 04 93 28 69 69, **f** 04 93 28 60 81, *westminster@wanadoo.fr*, *www.hotel-menton.com/hotel-royal-westminster* (*expensive*). This upmarket chain hotel is aimed mostly at retirees; however, it is on the seafront, with quiet rooms furnished in cool sea colours, views over the bay, huddles of elderly ladies on the terrace playing poker, and a *pétanque* court on the gravel drive. *Closed Nov.*

★★Hôtel de Londres, 15 Av Carnot, **t** 04 93 35 74 62, **f** 04 93 41 77 78, *www.hotel-de-*

londres.com (*moderate*). Nothing is too much trouble for this hotel's cheerful host, who will even lend you a cushioned mattress for the stony beach. Rooms are simple but attractive, with air-conditioning, and some overlook the shady, flower-filled garden with its little bar and games area. *Closed end Oct–Dec.*

Claridge's, 39 Av de Verdun, **t 04 93 35 72 53, **f** 04 93 35 42 90, *www.claridges-menton.com* (*moderate–inexpensive*). A slightly old-fashioned, quiet hotel on the flowery, clipped Jardin Biovès, a good 10 minutes from the sea, but very near one of Menton's local food markets.

*Hôtel Beauregard, 10 Rue Albert Iᵉʳ, **t** 04 93 28 63 63, **f** 04 93 28 63 79, *beauregard.menton@ wanadoo.fr* (*inexpensive*). A sweet place with a quiet garden below the station, this is also a good bargain. *Closed Nov.*

Youth hostel, Plateau St-Michel, **t** 04 93 35 93 14, **f** 04 93 35 93 07, *menton@fuaj.org* (bus no.6 from the train station). *Closed Dec–Jan.*

Eating Out

Fiori, Hôtel des Ambassadeurs (*see* opposite; *expensive*). Posh nosh. *Closed Sun, Mon lunch, Sat lunch and mid-Nov–mid-Dec.*

Le Nautic, 27 Quai de Monléon, **t** 04 93 35 78 74 (*expensive*). Between the market and the sea, opposite the Musée Cocteau, this bright blue eatery serves up every possible fish dish, including *bouillabaisse.*

Le Riaumont, Hôtel l'Aiglon (*see* left). This hotel's restaurant (*expensive–moderate*) serves traditional regional cuisine overlooking its swimming pool in the summer. *Closed Nov–mid-Dec.*

La Coquille d'Or, on the corner of Quai Bonaparte, **t** 04 93 35 80 67 (*expensive–moderate*). This may be a tourist trap, complete with Gypsy strummers. but, surprisingly, it also packs in crowds of locals for the *bouillabaisse* and *paella. Closed Wed and Nov.*

Pierrot-Pierrette, Place de l'Eglise, Rte de Sospel, **t** 04 93 35 79 76 (*moderate*). Up at Monti, this restaurant complements its views with delicious fresh blue trout. *Closed Mon, Christmas and most of Jan.*

All along Rue St-Michel, in the old town, masses of restaurants vie for your attention, spilling out into the street at lunchtime with tempting displays of hot pastries and baguettes. Try the following:

Crêperie St-Michel, 5 Rue Piéta, **t** 04 93 28 44 64 (*inexpensive*). Tucked away off the main street, the alarmingly brisk service and odd mixture of decoration (on the mantelpiece are a sailing ship, a pair of men's shoes and a photo of Eric Cantona) make this a good lunch stop if you've a bus to catch.

Rikiki, 7 Square Victoria, **t** 04 93 28 27 88. (*moderate*). Away from the fray, this atmospheric and popular place serves authentic Italian dishes.

A Braijade Meridiounale, 66 Rue Longue, **t** 04 93 35 65 65 (*moderate*). Tucked away in the maze of alleyways near St-Michel, serving Provençal favourites. *Closed Wed.*

L'Amandine, 24 Rue St-Michel (*inexpensive*). A tempting array of nougat and all kinds of locally produced *confiserie* and *fruits confits.*

Entertainment and Nightlife

Menton isn't exactly a hopping place, but check the Menton page in *Nice-Matin* or the brochure published by the tourist office.

Clubs and Bars

The young grumble that there's nothing to do, and head west to Monaco for nightlife; **Le Casino** and its disco **Le Brummell** (both **t** 04 92 10 16 16) are disdained as tourist ghettos.

Theatre

Théâtre Francis-Palmero, **t** 04 92 41 76 95, in the Palais de l'Europe, has a varied programme in French only.

Leisure

Koaland, Av de la Madone, **t/f** 04 92 10 00 40. Activities to keep children entertained, such as mini-golf, go-karting, etc. *Open Sept–June 10–12 and 2–7; July–Aug 10–12 and 3pm–12am; closed Tues out of season.*

The 1909 **Palais de l'Europe**, west of the Salle des Mariages, on Av Boyer, was once the casino, but is now an exhibition hall (*open 10–12 and 2–6; closed Tues*) and the tourist office. In front of it is the exotic **Jardins Biovès**, the most tidied, kempt, combed and swept bit of green space you're ever likely to come across, where the elderly sit in sunshine in beige and grey to match their poodles, watching life pass by. Here the fantastical lemon-studded floats of Menton's *Fête du Citron* are parked at carnival time.

A kilometre west of the town centre, the frothy pink and white summer home of the princes of Monaco, the Palais Carnolès (1717), is now an art museum, the **Musée des Beaux-Arts du Palais Carnolès** (*3 Av de la Madone, t 04 93 35 49 71, bus no.3 and no.7; open 10–12 and 2–6; closed Tues; adm*). It holds a Byzantine-inspired *Virgin and Child* from 13th-century Tuscany, Ludovico Brea's luminous *Madonna and Child with St Francis*, several oils attributed to Leonardo da Vinci, and all the previous winners from Menton's very own Biennale of painting, some of which are so awful that you can only wonder what the losers were like. Other works were donated by the English landscape and portrait artist Graham Sutherland, who lived part of every year in Menton from 1947 until he died in 1980. In the grounds, a piercingly fragrant citrus fruit orchard (try to make it in the spring) doubles up as a contemporary sculpture garden; among the mixed bag of 40 pieces are Max Siffredi's languorous *Aegina* and Guy Fage's dreamy marble *Rêverie*.

Just north of here, on the route to Gorbio, is one of Menton's most romantic gardens. The **Jardin de la Serre de la Madone** (*t 04 93 57 73 90, f 06 86 37 91 49; ring for details about guided tours; closed Mon; closed 5 Nov–5 Feb; adm*) covers 15 hectares with spectacular terraces. Grottoes and nymphs sprouting from ponds with fronds of trailing ivy lend an air of enchantment and secrecy. The garden was created between 1919 and 1939 by Sir Lawrence Johnstone, another of the fervent English botanists who seemed to overrun this corner of the world in the early part of the 20th century; he was also responsible for the famous English garden at Hidcote Manor.

The Vieille Ville

The tall, narrow 17th-century houses of Menton's Vieille Ville, overlooking the Vieux Port east of the Musée Cocteau, are reminiscent of the old quarter of Genoa, knitted together by anti-earthquake arches that span stepped lanes named after old pirate captains and saints. It's hard to believe that the quiet main street, **Rue Longue** (the Roman Via Julia Augusta), was until the 19th century the main route between France and Italy. According to legend, the lady at the Palais Princier (at No.123) received a secret nocturnal visit from Casanova, who crept in through the sewers.

From Rue Longue, the shallow stairs of the Rampes St-Michel lead up to the *parvis* of the ice-cream-coloured church of **St-Michel** (1675), the largest and one of the most ornate Baroque churches of the region, decked out and made fit for the princes of Monaco by two Mentonnais artists, Puppo and Vento. A gloomy late 17th-century painting depicts Sainte Dévote looking suitably martyrish in front of the Rock of Monaco. Honoré III of Monaco tied the knot in the church in 1757 and presented the damask hangings, which are still brought out on special occasions as a celebratory gift. St-Michel's Baroque neighbour, the pert little **Chapelle des Pénitents Blancs**, was headquarters of one of the old Riviera's many religious confraternities (*see* **Nice**, p.109), and was feverishly restored in the 19th century with elaborate festooning and stucco. The three Theological Virtues glower uneasily among all the frills. The *parvis* (square in front of the church) has a pebble mosaic of the Grimaldi arms. It is used as the setting for Menton's megastar chamber music festival in August.

The Montée du Souvenir leads to the top of the Vieille Ville, where the citadel was replaced in the 19th century by the romantic, panoramic **Cimetière du Vieux Château** (*open summer 7am–8pm, winter 7–6*), windy and pine-scented. Curiously, it is not marked on the tourist map, but is just a quick steep haul up from those sitting out their last years below; as if a foretaste of death, it's the one place in Menton where they can't bring their poodles. Guy de Maupassant called it the most aristocratic cemetery in Europe – the venerable names inscribed on the hierarchical array of ornate tombs and little pavilions include William Webb-Ellis, the 'inventor of rugby', and a handful of Russian Grand Princes. Many immigrants, like Aubrey Beardsley, were consumptives in their teens and twenties and only came to Menton to die.

The Gardens of Garavan

From the cemetery, Boulevard de Garavan leads into the neighbourhood where this dead élite would reside if they were alive today, dotted with elegant villas amid some of the most beautiful gardens on the coast. The **Jardin Exotique du Val Rahmeh** (*entrance on Av St-Jacques, t 04 93 35 86 72; open April–Sept 10–12.30 and 3–6; Oct–Mar 10–12.30 and 2–5; closed Tues; adm; guided tours sometimes available*) was planted around the ivy-covered Villa Val Rahmeh by enthusiastic English botanists in the 1930s and has since been substantially expanded by the Natural History Museum in Paris. Now more than 700 tropical and subtropical species from around the world bloom contentedly on the garden's sloping terraces. Nearby, the drowsy **Parc du Pian** (*open daily*), an old olive orchard, is dotted with shady wooden benches perfect for afternoon siestas and secret assignations.

Beyond the gardens, a road off the boulevard, Av Blasco Ibañez, was named after the author of *The Four Horsemen of the Apocalypse* (1867–1928), who lived here in the **Villa Fontana Rosa** (*contact the Service du Patrimoine, t 04 92 10 33 66, for details of guided tours*). He decorated his fantastical **Jardin des Romanciers** with colourful *azulejo* tiles from his native Valencia in the 1920s in homage to the great storytellers. Brightly tiled columns, wide shallow fountains and flower-covered walkways give way to outdoor 'reading rooms'.

Villa Isola Bella, on the other side of the Garavan station, was the home of another victim of tuberculosis, Katherine Mansfield (1888–1923); although ailing, she was happy here, and fictionalized her experiences in a number of short stories. To the north of Boulevard de Garavan, the romantic red-ochre villa and gardens of the **Domaine des Colombières** (*open one day a year in June, contact the Service du Patrimoine, t 04 92 10 97 10, for details*) was the 40-year project of French artist and writer Ferdinand Bac (1859–1952), the flamboyant and indefatigable illegitimate son of Napoléon III. As well as designing the botanical gardens, with secret leafy passageways dotted with statues, ponds and fountains, he painted all the paintings and frescoes in the house himself and designed the elegant Modernist furniture. Out almost at the town's eastern limits, on the Promenade Reine Astrid, the **Villa Maria Serena** (*t 04 92 10 33 66; guided tours Tues 10am*) is enclosed by another lush garden, this one devoted to an extensive collection of rare palm trees, soaking up the sunshine in what is reputedly the most temperate garden in France.

North of Menton

Four narrow mountain valleys converge at Menton, with villages hanging over their slopes; they are linked by bus from Menton and to each other by mule tracks. Above the easternmost valley is **Castellar** (7km from Menton), laid out on a grid plan in 1435 to replace the original 1258 village, built by the counts of Ventimiglia high on a rocky crag. An hour's hike will take you to the ghostly ruins of old Castellar, or take the less strenuous walk up the Sospel road as far as the waterfall at the **Gourg de l'Oura**. Up the second valley, the Val du Careï, sailors have made the little monastery of **L'Annonciade** (5.5km from Menton) the focus of their May pilgrimage since the 11th century. It has gone through countless transformations over the years and the current building dates from the 17th century. Best of all are its grand views, from a terrace which looks over the whole valley and out to the sea, and its *ex votos,* dating back to the 17th century and including an unusual more recent one – a piece of a zeppelin. Further up the Val du Careï, amid the viaducts of the old Menton–Sospel railway, you can wander through the scented **Forêt de Menton**, then up to **Castillon**, awaft with the scent of fresh concrete and artisan shops, and well into its third incarnation as 'the most beautiful new village in France' after being flattened by an earthquake in 1887 and bombed in 1944.

From Menton the narrow, winding D22 noodles up to **Ste-Agnès**, at almost 2,625ft the loftiest village on the entire coast, which huddles on the northern side of the peak with its back to the sea. Mornings can be chilly before the sun makes its way around,

Where to Stay and Eat

Castellar ✉ 06500

*Hôtel des Alpes, Place Clemenceau, t 04 93 35 82 83, f 04 93 28 24 25, *www.hotelmenton. com/hotel-des-alpes* (*inexpensive*). Tidy little rooms and good food (*cheap*). *Closed mid Nov–mid Dec.*

Castillon ✉ 06500

***Bergerie, Castillon, t 04 93 04 00 39, f 04 93 28 02 91 (*moderate*). More upmarket, with a pool, rustic but very comfortable rooms and elaborate food. *Closed mid-Oct–mid-Nov.*

Le Saint-Yves, Rue des Sarrasins, t 04 93 35 91 45, f 04 93 35 65 85 (*inexpensive*). For sweet dreams, dreamy views and, most notably, courtesy. The restaurant (*moderate*), which looks out over a dramatic view of mountains and sea, serves up regional dishes such as *lapin aux herbes. Closed mid-Nov–mid Dec.*

Le Logis Sarrasin, 40 Av des Sarrasins, t 04 93 35 86 89, f 04 93 35 65 85 (*moderate– cheap*). A restaurant offering a warm welcome and more panoramic views, as well as six courses, including delicious *raviolis maison. Closed Mon and mid-Nov–mid-Dec.*

even in the height of summer. There are three buses a day from Menton, or drive up, passing under and over the mighty viaducts of the A8, which look as insubstantial as spider's legs once you reach Ste-Agnès. The village was founded in the 10th century, some say, by a Saracen who fell in love with a local girl and converted to Christianity for her sake. It certainly looks old enough – a patchwork quilt of vaulted passageways and tiny squares that have succumbed to a mild attack of trinketshopitis. When you can't look at another smirking *santon*, head up Rue Longue for a view that stretches to Corsica on a clear day, or scramble up to the ruins of the 12th-century château, which dominate the peak. It was destroyed by Louis XIV and has mouldered away ever since. The villagers have now taken over and are attempting to shore it up, but are not above putting it to practical use – in the miniature medieval garden is a patch of crazy paving and a whirling clothesline.

Ste-Agnès, perched at such a dizzying height, has always been on the defensive front line; a **fort** (*open July–Sept daily 3–6, Oct–June Sat and Sun only, 2.30–5.30; call town hall on t 04 93 35 84 58 for information about guided tours*) was gouged into the rock here in the 1930s as part of the infamous Maginot Line. Despite containing the most powerful concentration of artillery of the entire length of the Line, the fort couldn't hold out against the Germans in the Second World War; its bleak living quarters and grim cannons and mortar are still on view.

Come down the mountain at dusk if you can – it's the only safe way to see if anything's coming round those cliff-face bends, and there's the added bonus of watching Menton light up for the evening, far, far below. On foot – make sure it is a comfortably shod foot – a narrow stony path descends from Ste-Agnès to Menton in 2 hours or, better still, take the 1-hour shortcut which forms part of the Balcon de la Côte d'Azur (the GR51) to **Gorbio** (from Menton it's 8km), passing by the tiny 17th-century Chapelle Saint-Lazare, abandoned and forlorn at the entrance to the village. Gorbio is just as picturesquely medieval as Ste-Agnès, with ivy-covered houses of pale honey-coloured stone and twisting vaulted streets, but has somehow been spared the trinkets. In the Place de la République, more commonly known as the Place du Village, there are a couple of terraced restaurants, a plain fountain for the gossips to collect around and an olive tree planted in 1713 (which does double service as the bus stop for Menton). The best time to visit is at Fête Dieu (Corpus Christi) in June, for the medieval Procession dai Limaça, when the village lanes are lit by thousands of flickering lamps made from snail shells filled with olive oil, set in beds of sand.

A Dip into Italy

Just over the border from Menton, in the village of Grimaldi, the beachside **Balzi Rossi** (red caves) were the centre of a sophisticated Neanderthal society that flourished *c.* 100,000 to 40,000 BC and produced some of Europe's earliest art, displayed in the **Museo Preistorico** (*t (00 39 for Italy, if calling from France) 0184 38113; museum open Tues–Sun 8.30–7.30; closed Mon; adm*).

The town of **Ventimiglia** has a huge market which completely takes over the town every Friday; a number of bus tours go there from Menton. Outside Ventimiglia, at Mortola Inferiore, you can visit the extraordinary **Hanbury Gardens** (*t (0039) 0184 22 95 07; open 10–6 in summer, 10–4 in winter, closed Wed; adm*), a botanical paradise of acclimatized plants from around the world, founded in 1867 by Sir Thomas Hanbury and his brother Daniel. Sir Thomas was a wealthy dealer in silks and spices from China, who fell in love with the spot during a holiday on the Côte d'Azur in 1867. The gardens fell into decay during the Second World War, but are now back in shape and managed by the University of Genoa: highlights include the Australian forest, the Garden of Scents and the Japanese garden.

If you plan to go deeper into Italy, you can save money by filling up with petrol in Menton (that's what all those Italians are doing). If you plan to feast on an excellent Italian meal, it's only 12km to **Bordighera**,where you can spend your petrol savings and your children's inheritance at the lovely, very expensive Art Nouveau **La Via Romana** (*Via Romana 57, t (0039) 0184 26 66 81; www.viaromana.it; closed Wed all day, and Thurs lunch*).

The Grande Corniche

Roquebrune-Cap-Martin

Nearly every potential building site on the lush mountain shore between Menton and Monaco is occupied by Roquebrune-Cap-Martin – from old Roquebrune just beside the Grande Corniche down to the exclusive garden cape of Cap Martin. Purchased by the Grimaldis in 1355 for 1,000 florins, Roquebrune (like Menton) later revolted against Monaco and became a Free Town until joining France in 1861.

The medieval village is all steep, winding, arcaded streets with a fair number of over-restored houses, galleries and *ateliers*, culminating at the top in the **château** (*t 04 93 35 07 22; open Nov–Jan daily 10–12 and 2–5; Feb–Mar and Oct 10–12 and 2–6; April–June and Sept 10–12 and 2–6.30; July–Aug 10–12 and 3–7.30; adm*), with the oldest surviving *donjon* in France, erected in the 10th century by the counts of Ventimiglia against the Saracen threat. In the 15th century, Lambert of Monaco built much of what stands today, including the keep; in 1911, Sir William Ingram purchased the castle, planted the mock medieval *tour anglaise* by the gate, and donated it all to the town in 1921. The rooms between the ravaged 11ft-thick walls are surprisingly poky – most people have bathrooms bigger than this lordling's reception hall, which lost its roof to cannonballs in 1597. An uninspired audiovisual exhibition animates the prison, the archers' room and the kitchens, but the view from the top floor, huge enough for any ego, is by far the best of the castle's attractions. The castle guards lived below in picturesque **Rue Moncollet**, tunnelled out of the living rock, which leads down into Rue Grimaldi and the Place des Deux-Frères, a pretty square with a fat, attractive old olive tree, the little village *lavoir*, a sprinkling of cafés and restaurants, and a vertiginous view across the red-tiled rooftops and over the bay.

Tourist Information

Roquebrune: 218 Av Aristide Briand, **t** 04 93 35 62 87, **f** 04 93 28 57 00, *office-du-tourisme. rcm@wanadoo.fr, www.roquebrune-cap-martin.com*. Offers tours of the old town and château as well as Le Corbusier's cabin. Detailed walking maps also available. *Open Mon–Sat 9–1, 3–7, Sun 10–1, 3–7.*

Markets

Provençal market, Parking du Marché de Carnolès. *Open daily 8–1, larger on Wed.*
Roquebrune village, flea market. *Mid-Sept.*

Where to Stay and Eat

Along the Corniches ✉ 06190

****Vista Palace Hôtel, t 04 92 10 40 00, **f** 04 93 35 18 94, *info@vistapalace.com, www.vistapalace.com* (*luxury*). If money's no object, this is the ultimate in luxury, hanging on a 1,000ft cliff on the Grande Corniche, with a God's-eye view over Monaco; it also has a heated pool, squash, gym, sauna and famous restaurant (*see below*). *Closed Feb.*

Westminster, 14 Av L. Laurens, **t 04 93 35 00 68, **f** 04 93 28 88 50, *hotel@westminster o6.com, www.westminstero6.com* (*moderate–inexpensive*). With a pretty garden terrace near the junction of the lower two Corniches. *Closed end Nov–end Dec.*

Le Vistaero, Vista Palace Hôtel (*see above*). This cliff-hanging restaurant (*very expensive*) offers some of the Côte's most talked-about cuisine under the auspices of chef Jean-Pierre Pestre. *Closed Feb.*

Roquebrune

Hôtel des Deux Frères, Place des Deux-Frères, **t** 04 93 28 99 00, **f** 04 93 28 99 10, *info@ lesdeuxfreres.com, www.lesdeuxfreres. com* (*moderate*). Looking out over Monaco, this hotel has been refurbished and is ethereally light and airy with a graceful curved stone staircase. The rooms are small, but white muslin canopies draped over the beds, whitewashed walls and endless views make up for the lack of space. Friendly, knowledge-able staff serve excellent regional dishes in the flower-edged terrace restaurant (*expensive–moderate*). *Closed mid-Nov–mid-Dec. Restaurant closed Sun night and Mon.*

Au Grand Inquisiteur, 18 Rue du Château, **t/f** 04 93 35 05 37 (*expensive–moderate*). In a former sheepfold cut into the rock, this restaurant has well-prepared Provençal dishes such as *fleurs de courgette farcies. Closed Mon and Tues lunch, and mid-Nov–mid-Dec.*

La Grotte, Place des Deux-Frères, **t/f** 04 93 35 00 04 (*moderate–cheap*). A cheaper troglodyte choice, La Grotte also has tables outside at the entrance to the Vieille Ville, and offers pizzas, pasta and a good value *plat du jour. Closed Wed and end Oct–Nov.*

Back on Rue du Château is the pink and orange church of **Ste-Marguerite**, originally built in the 12th century but well and truly Baroqued since, which contains a *Resurrection* and *Pietà* by 17th-century Roquebrunois artist Marc-Antoine Otto. A formidable gang of village ladies maintains its current gleaming splendour. Nearby Rue de la Fontaine (turn off Rue du Château just after the post office) leads to a remarkable contemporary of the castle: a 1,000-year-old olive tree measuring 33ft in circumference, with a tangle of roots bursting out of the soil.

In 1467, as plague decimated the coastal population, the Roquebrunois vowed to the Virgin that if they were spared they would, in thanksgiving, annually re-enact tableaux of the Passion. The Virgin apparently thought it was a good deal, and the villagers have faithfully kept their side of the pact every year on 5 August, illuminating the procession with little lamps made from sea shells and snail shells. The best and most coveted of the 500 roles involved in the colourful processions are jealously 'owned' by the oldest families, who pass them down like heirlooms.

Cap Martin

In the 1890s a pair of empresses, Eugénie of France (widow of Napoléon III) and Elisabeth ('Sissi') of Austria, made Roquebrune's little peninsula of Cap Martin an aristocratic enclave, 'whispering of old kings come here to dine or die', as F. Scott Fitzgerald wrote. Churchill did the dining and Yeats, King Nikola of Montenegro and Le Corbusier the dying, the last succumbing to a heart attack in 1965 while swimming off the white rocks beside what is now the **Promenade Le Corbusier** – a lovely walk around the cape, down a succession of little ramps and stairways and past villas immersed in luxuriant pines, olives, cypresses and mimosas. Corby had been staying in one of the villas, one of the most beautiful on the Côte d'Azur, built in 1929 by furniture designer Eileen Gray; the story goes that he loved the house so much that he got a wealthy friend to buy it at auction, helping him defeat the higher bids of Aristotle Onassis by dragging the auctioneer off at a crucial moment. In a garden down by the sea, he built himself a tiny **cabin** (*guided tours Tues and Fri at 10 am from the tourist office; register the previous day at the tourist office; adm*) just 12ft square, which comprised a frescoed corridor and one simple room, and wrote rapturously to a friend of the comforts of his seaside 'château'. It was built as a model of minimal accommodation based on the 'modulor', his patented system of architectural proportions, and encompassed, in his opinion at least, all a man needed to live a comfortable existence. Although unprepossessing on the exterior, each of the carefully crafted interior fittings has several ingenious functions. Le Corbusier is buried in Roquebrune churchyard, along with his wife, in a tomb he designed himself.

The spectacular path leads from Cap Martin to Monte-Carlo beach. If you walk it (about a four-hour walk), look back towards the Cap to see the ruined tower of the long-gone **convent of St-Martin**. When it was built, the men of Roquebrune vowed to protect the nuns from pirates, and one night in the late 14th century the tower's bell sounded the alarm; the Roquebrunois piled out of bed and ran down the hill to defend the good sisters, who laughingly confessed that they were just testing the bell's efficiency. A few nights later, pirates really did appear, and although the nuns rang like mad, their defenders only rolled over in bed. Next morning, in the smouldering ruins, the older nuns were found with their throats slit, while the younger, prettier ones had been carted off to the slave markets of Barbary.

Monaco

Big-time tax-dodgers agree: it's hard to beat Monaco for comfort and convenience when the time comes to snuggle down with your piggy chips. Unlike most other tax havens, the Principality is not an island, so you can purr over to France or Italy in the Lamborghini in just a few minutes. The grub is good, you can safely flaunt your jewels and there's enough culture to keep you from feeling a total Philistine; the homeless and other riffraff who might trouble your conscience are kept at bay. Security, understandably, is the prime concern: closed-circuit cameras spy over every corner; every traffic signal records every passing car. In emergencies, the whole Principality can be closed off in a few minutes.

Rainier III, chairman of the board of Monaco Inc., will probably go down in history as the Principality's greatest benefactor. Through landfill and burrowing he has added a fifth to his realm and on it built more (but certainly not better) structures than any of his predecessors, creating a Lilliputian Manhattan. Of the Principality's some 32,000 residents, only 4–5,000 are actually his subjects. To obtain one of the precious resident's permits, you have to own or rent a flat in one of these grey towers and watch your ass. Residents who still choose to work, the Luciano Pavarottis and Claudia Schiffers, are hardly ever home. Money is the main topic of conversation no matter where you go in this perfectly sanitized bolthole on the Med, where a calendar of car races, circuses, fireworks, First Division football and operas puts a glittering mask over its ghoulish, acquisitive face.

History Starts with a Stinker

Seven hundred years ago, in 1297, an ambitious member of Genoa's Guelph party, Francesco Grimaldi the Spiteful, dressed up like a friar and knocked at the door of the Ghibelline fortress at Monaco, asking for hospitality. The soldiers sleepily admitted him, whereupon the phoney friar pulled a knife from his robe, killed the soldiers and let in his men. Although Francesco was the first Grimaldi to get into Monaco, the family became lords of their rock only when they purchased it from Genoa in 1308.

Once they were rulers of a mini-empire including Antibes and Menton; today the Grimaldis' sovereign Ruritania has been reduced by the ambitions of others to a sea-hugging 194 hectares (slightly larger than half of Central Park) under the looming mountain, Tête de Chien. Here Rainier III presides as the living representative of the oldest ruling family in Europe, and Europe's last constitutional autocrat.

For centuries the Grimaldis' main income came from a tax levied on Menton's lemons and olives, and when Menton revolted in 1848 they faced bankruptcy; Monaco was the poorest state in all Europe. In desperation, Prince Charles III looked for inspiration to the Duke of Baden-Baden, whose casino lured Europe's big-spending aristocrats every summer. Monaco, Charles decided, would be the winter Baden-Baden, and he founded the **Société des Bains de Mer** (SBM) to operate a casino and tourist industry, with the Principality as the chief shareholder. The casino was built on a rock which the prince named Monte-Carlo after himself, and he hired François Blanc, the talented French manager of the Homburg Baden casino, to create a gambling city to order, 10 per cent of all profits going to the crown. Blanc was one of the most successful financiers of the day and he proved his worth. He loaned the French Government nearly 5 million francs for the completion of Napoléon III's centrepiece, the Paris Opéra, and in return assured that the French built a new railway from Nice in 1868. With transport to bring in the punters, the money poured in by the bushel; in 1870 the coffers were so full that Charles abolished direct taxation in Monaco, a state of affairs that endures to this day.

But gone are those fond days when the Monégasques could live entirely off the folly of others. France and Italy legalized gaming in 1933, ending the Principality's

Monaco

MONEGHETTI

ROUTE DE LA MOYENNE CORNICHE

BOULEVARD DU JARDIN EXOTIQUE

BOULEVARD DE BELGIQUE

BD PRINCESSE CHARLOTTE

BOULEVARD DE SUISSE

AV PASTEUR

Musée d'Anthropologie Préhistorique

BOULEVARD DE BELGIQUE

RUE AUGUSTIN VENETO

BRETELLE AUREGLIA

Grottes de l'Observatoire

RUE GRIMALDI

PLACE STE-DEVOTE

AV DE LA COSTA

Jardin Exotique

AV PASTEUR

Gare

RUE DE LA TURBIE

RUE GRIMALDI

RUE FLORESTINE

RUE PRINCESSE

RUE SUFFREN REYMOND

AV D'OSTENDE

BOULEVARD CHARLES III

BOULEVARD RAINIER III

Jardin Animalier

R. PRINCESSE CAROLINE

QUAI ALBERT 1ER

LA CONDAMINE

AVENUE

BOULEVARD CHARLES III DE FONTVIEILLE

Collection des Voitures Anciennes

Zoological Terraces

AVENUE DU PORT

Musée Naval

Musée des Timbres

R. DE L'INDUSTRIE   AV PRINCE HÉRÉDITAIRE

AV DES PAPALINS

Palais Princier

Musée des Souvenirs Napoléoniens

Musée du Vieux Monaco

AV DE LA PORTE NEUVE

QUAI ANTOINE 1ER

Stade Louis II

PLACE DU CAMPANILE ST-NICHOLAS

Historial des Princes de Monaco

R. COMTE FELIX-GASTALDI

FONTVIEILLE

Espace Fontvieille

QUAI DES SANBARBANI

Chapel of Mercy

Cathedral

Musée de la Chapelle de la Visitation

Princesse Grace Rose Garden

AVENUE   SAINT   MARTIN

Musée Océanographique

Monte Carlo Story

MONACO-VILLE

monopoly, and the proportion of its revenue that Monaco gleans from the tables has declined from 95 per cent to a mere 4 per cent. In the dark, bankrupt 1950s, Rainier III gave his little realm a fairytale cachet by wedding a luminous American film actress named Grace Kelly, bringing in a much-needed injection of socialites and their fat bankrolls. Since then, the Prince and the omnipresent SBM have found new ways to keep Monaco's residents from paying income tax, especially in 'offshore' banking (some 50 banks do business here), in the media (Télé and Radio Monte-Carlo), in 'business tourism' (there's a new, ultra-modern congress hall) and tourism, with no little interest fuelled by the media's scrutiny of the sadly tarnished fairytale lives of Princesses Caroline and Stéphanie.

Monte-Carlo

Set back in the sculpture-filled gardens of Place du Casino is the most famous building on the whole Côte d'Azur: the 1863 **Casino de Monte-Carlo** (*t 92 16 20 00, www.casino-monte-carlo.com*), a fascinating piece of Old World kitsch known in its heyday as the 'cathedral of hell'. Anyone over 21 in civilian clothes (no military uniforms) with a passport can visit the *machines à sous* section just inside the door, with one-armed bandits and other mechanized games. To get past the mastodons at

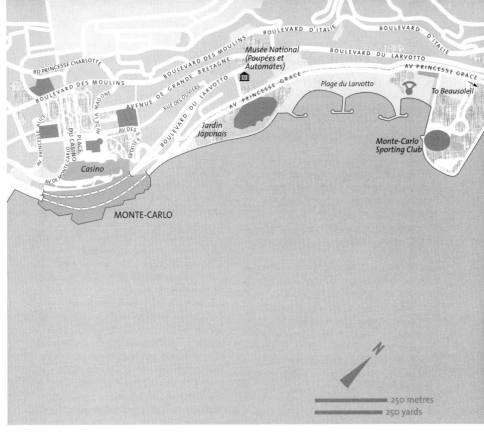

the doorway to the glittering Salon of Europe you have to fork out €10; here, American roulette, craps and blackjack tables click and clatter away just as in Las Vegas or Atlantic City. €20 gets you into the *salons privés* (*open June–Oct, Mon–Fri from 4pm, Sat and Sun from 3pm; Nov–May daily from 3pm*), quieter and more intense, where oily croupiers, under gilt, over-the-top rococo ceilings, accept limitless bets on roulette and *chemin de fer*. In the Pink Salon Bar, where naked, cigar-chomping nymphs float on the ceiling, Charles Deville Wells celebrated his three-day gambling spree in 1891 that turned $400 into $40,000 and inspired the popular tune 'The Man who Broke the Bank at Monte-Carlo'. (Later, he spent eight years in prison after being convicted of fraud in England, but no one ever discovered the secret of his success in Monte-Carlo.)

Superstitious gamblers have used a variety of means to ensure the same success: some believed that rubbing the knee of the bronze horse bearing Louis XIV in the lobby of the Hôtel de Paris next door brought luck. The Prince of Nepal, whose religion only let him gamble for five days a year, had private rooms here so that he wouldn't lose a single precious second, and Cornelius Vanderbilt insisted that his entire family was present before betting a franc. Whatever you do, don't miss the thrill of flushing one of the Casino's loos.

The Casino's bijou opera-theatre, the red and gold **Salle Garnier** (*open only for performances*), was designed by Charles Garnier, his part of the payback for François

Getting There and Around

There are no customs formalities; you can just **drive** into Monaco along the Basse Corniche, or take the **helicopter** from Nice airport if you're in a hurry (7mins, return €145, Héli Air Monaco t 92 05 00 50; Monacair t 97 97 39 00).

Buses leave hourly from Nice airport (terminal 2, 9am–9pm), or you can get a **taxi** (45mins). Buses every 15mins between Menton and Nice stop at several points along the Corniche.

The Monaco/Monte-Carlo **train** station is in Av Prince Pierre, t 08 92 35 35 35 and t 377 93 10 60 15.

Small as it is, Monaco is divided into several towns: Monte-Carlo to the east, Fontvieille by the port, Monaco-Ville on the rock and La Condamine below; there's a **public bus** network to save you some legwork. More importantly, free **public lifts** and **escalators** operate between the tiers of streets. These are all marked on the free map from the tourist office. **Taxis** run 24 hours, t 93 15 01 01 or 93 30 71 63. For **bike hire**, try Auto-Moto Garage, 7 Rue de Millo, t 93 50 10 80.

Tourist Information

Note: If the telephone number has only eight digits, you must dial t 00 377 before calling from anywhere outside Monaco, even from France. If the number has 10 digits, it operates like a French number.

Monaco: 2a Bd des Moulins, Monaco, t 92 16 61 16, f 92 16 60 00, *dtc@monaco-tourisme.com, www.monaco-tourisme.com. Open Mon–Sat 9–7, Sun 10–12.*

Markets

Marché de la Condamine, Place d'Armes, daily 6–2pm; food market, near Eglise St-Charles, *Mon–Sat, 7–1, Mon, Tues, Thurs, Fri also 4–7.30.*
Port de Fontieille, flea market. *Sat 9.30–5.30.*

Money

Monaco's unit of currency is the euro; Monégasque coins are in circulation but are rarely accepted outside the Principality.

Sports and Activities

Thanks to the SBM, there's always something to do in Monaco: a mountain-top 18-hole **golf course** high above the town at La Turbie; **tennis** and every imaginable **water sport**; one **free beach** (Plage du Larvotto, near the Japanese garden) among the exclusive paying ones, such as the beach at the eastern tip of town belonging to the **Monte-Carlo Sporting Club**; deep-sea tuna fishing and cruises; and **helicopter tours** of the coast (Héli Air Monaco or Monacair, *see* 'Getting Around'). In January there's the **Monte-Carlo Rally** – the first one in 1902 occasioned the world's first tarmac road, designed to keep the spectators from being sprayed with dust. In April you can watch the tennis championship; the second week of May sees the famous **Monte-Carlo Grand Prix** (when even the pavements charge a hefty admission price). For **football** tickets at the Louis II stadium, call t 92 05 40 00.

Where to Stay

Monaco ✉ 98030, t (00 377–)

Monaco's hotels have nearly as many stars as the Milky Way, so if you'd like one of the few more reasonably priced rooms in the summer, you can't reserve early enough.

Luxury
★★★★★**Hôtel de Paris**, Place du Casino, t 92 16 30 00, f 92 16 38 49, *hp@sbm.mc, www.montecarloresort.com.* A palatial residence where the tycoons check in. Opened in 1865 by the SBM for gambling tsars and duchesses, it now has direct access to the

Blanc's loan that completed his even more elaborate Paris Opéra. Inaugurated by Sarah Bernhardt in 1879 and backed by pots of SBM money, it became one of the most exciting theatres in Europe, especially under Raoul Gunsberg, who had been director of the Tsar Nicholas II Theatre. He commissioned operas from composers like Saint-Saëns and Massenet and, in 1911, invited Diaghilev's Ballets Russes, who became the

modern-day Riviera prerequisite, a thalas-sotherapy centre. Also houses the famous Café de Paris, t 92 16 20 20.

*****Hermitage, Square Beaumarchais, t 92 16 40 00, f 92 16 38 52, hh@sbm.mc, www.montecarloresort.com. Also owned by the SBM, this Belle Epoque hotel perched high on its rock, overlooking the Port d'Hercule, has an Italian loggia and a sumptuous 'Winter Garden' designed by Gustave Eiffel.

Hôtel Columbus Monaco, 23 Av des Papalins, t 92 05 90 00, f 92 05 91 67, www.columbus hotels.com. Stylish boutique hotel with all the amenities, a favourite with glittering young celebs. Bar open to non-guests.

Very Expensive

***Terminus, 9 Av Prince Pierre, t 92 05 63 00, f 92 05 20 10, www.terminus.monte-carlo.mc. This may be yet another concrete high-rise block, but it has been refurbished recently and to spend a night here still doesn't quite require a king's ransom.

Expensive

***Balmoral, 12 Av de la Costa, t 93 50 62 37, f 93 15 08 69, resa@hotel-balmoral.mc, www.hotel-balmoral.mc. Next door to the Hermitage, for a fraction of the price and with a view of the sea, the old Balmoral is a top choice.

***Hôtel Alexandra, 35 Bd Princesse Charlotte, t 93 50 63 13, f 92 16 06 48, hotel-alexandra@monaco377.com. More turn-of-the-last-century opulence is to be had at this gilded hotel.

**Le Versailles, 4 Av Prince Pierre, t 93 50 79 34, f 93 25 53 64, hotel-versailles@monte-carlo.mc. A cheaper choice near the station, with a reasonable French–Italian restaurant.

Moderate

**Hôtel de France, 6 Rue de la Turbie, t 93 30 24 64, f 92 16 13 34, hotel-france@monte-

carlo.mc. A peachy building in a street full of art galleries.

**Helvetia, 1 bis Rue Grimaldi, t 93 30 21 71, f 92 16 70 51, hotel-helvetia@monte-carlo.mc, www.monte-carlo.mc/helvetia. An old-fashioned place overlooking a pedestrianized shopping street lined with orange trees.

Eating Out

Very Expensive

Louis XV, Hôtel de Paris (see above), t 92 16 29 76. In Monte-Carlo, those who make it big at the tables, or have simply made it big at life in general, dine in the incredible golden setting of the Louis XV. This was a favourite of Edward VII when he was Prince of Wales; once, while dining here with his mistress, he was served a crêpe smothered in kirsch, curaçao and maraschino that its 14-year-old maker, Henri Charpentier (who went on to fame as a chef in America), accidentally set alight, only to discover that the flambéeing improved it a hundredfold. The Prince himself suggested that they name the new dessert after his companion, hence crêpes Suzette. Under Alain Ducasse, the youngest chef ever to earn three Michelin stars, the cuisine is once again kingly – and is as sumptuous and spectacular as the setting. Closed Tues, and Wed, also Dec and mid-Feb–mid-Mar.

Expensive

Le Vistamar, in the Hermitage hotel (see above). A riotous pink and silver period piece, and a historical monument to boot, the famous Belle Epoque is now reserved for groups; in its stead, Le Vistamar, t 92 16 27 72, offers fresh fish dishes like the pescadou à pesca du matin, which brings the fish from the sea to your plate in under an hour at lunchtime.

Ballets de Monte-Carlo in 1926. Since the Second World War it's gone bland and mostly serves as an excuse for residents to put on the dog. But in the old days its gods – Diaghilev, Nijinsky, Stravinsky, and set designers Picasso, Derain and Cocteau – held court among the dukes and flukes in the café of SBM's frothy **Hôtel de Paris**, next to the Casino (see 'Where to Stay', above). Or as Katherine Mansfield put it: 'the famous

L'Hirondelle, 2 Av Monte-Carlo, **t** 92 16 49 30. Gourmets on a diet can take solace here, with lovely, light dishes accompanied by views over the sea. *Lunch only.*

Moderate–Cheap

Le St Benoît, 10 ter Av de la Costa (enter the car park and take the lift up), **t** 93 25 02 34. Just below the Hermitage, Le St Benoît offers superb seafood to go with the views from the terrace, high above the port. Some dishes *expensive. Closed Mon lunch and Sat lunch, and Dec.*

Loga Café, 25 Bd des Moulins, **t** 93 30 87 72. Sit out on the terrace and dine sumptuously on *barbagiuan* (a kind of fried cheese- and leek-filled pie) or *stocafi* (stockfish stewed with tomatoes, herbs, wine and olives), and other Monégasque specialities. *Closed Sun and Aug.*

Le Périgordin, 5 Rue des Oliviers, **t** 93 30 06 02. For rich duck dishes straight out of the Dordogne. *Closed Sat lunch and Sun and last 2 weeks Aug.*

Tony, 6 Rue Comte Félix Gastaldi, **t** 93 30 81 37. Another good choice, near the palace, with generous menus. *Lunch only. Closed Sat and Nov–Dec.*

Le Texan, 4 Rue Suffren Reymond, La Condamine, **t** 93 30 34 54. Come to this vivacious, rowdy, Tex-Mex joint just up from the port for the possibility of brushing shoulders with Crown Prince Albert and Boris Becker over a pizza. One of the best value places for beer. *Lunch only. Closed Sun.*

Entertainment and Nightlife

Nightlife in Monaco is a glitzy, bejewelled fashion parade catered for by the omnipresent SBM at the **Monte-Carlo Sporting Club**, Av Princesse Grace, with its summer discotheque, Las Vegas-style floor shows, dancing, restaurants and casino. There are similar offerings at **SBM/Loews Monte-Carlo**, 12 Av des Spélugues, and at the **American Bar** at the Hôtel de Paris.

Jimmy'z, 26 Av Princesse Grace, **t** 92 16 22 77. Entrance is free, but the drinks require a small bank loan at Monte-Carlo's number one dance club, favourite of U2, Sting and other rich old men. Now has a Cuban cigar bar. Upstairs is the **Bar et Bœuf**, **t** 92 16 60 60, the Philippe Starck-designed Alain Ducasse restaurant. Open til the small hours. *Closed Nov–May.*

Le Stars n' Bars, 6 Quai Antoine 1ᵉʳ, **t** 97 97 95 95, *www.starsnbars.com*. Young people from all along the coast drive to this sports bar and club. *Closed Mon in winter.*

Flashman's, 7 Av Princesse Alice, **t** 93 30 09 03. A Brit-run imitation pub, open until the wee hours.

Ship and Castle, 42 Quai Jean-Charles Rey, **t** 92 05 76 72. Another late-running Brit-pub (which also serves food).

Opera, Circus and Fireworks

In January the **opera**, **theatre** and **ballet** season begins (**t** 92 16 22 99 or **t** 99 99 30 30 for info).

In January or February there is an excellent **Circus Festival** (**t** 92 05 23 45); in March, join or at least gawp at the queues of the high and mighty for the annual **Rose Ball**.

Sign up for well-attended **Concerts at the Palace** in July, August, October and December. The Monégasque **National Holiday** is 18–19 Nov.

Cinema

Cinéma d'été, **t** 08 36 68 00 72, 26 Terrasses du Parking des Pêcheurs. Open-air and showing a different film in its original language every evening at 9.30 from 25 June to 10 Sept.

Cinéma Le Sporting, Place du Casino, **t** 08 36 68 00 72, *www.cinemasporting.com*. Three screens.

Café de Paris with *real* devils with tails under their aprons cursing each other as they hand out the drinks. There at those tables sit the damned.'

If smug displays of wealth give you the misanthropic jitters, you can take comfort in the porcelain, metal, wood and plastic people in the **Musée National (Poupées et Automates)** (*17 Av Princesse Grace, **t** 93 30 91 26, www.monte-carlo.mc/musee-national;*

open daily Easter–Sept, 10–6.30; Oct–Easter 10–12.15 and 2.30–6.30; adm), in a luscious campanile villa designed by Charles Garnier, surrounded by rose gardens. Jolliest among the exhibits is an enormous 18th-century Neapolitan *presepio*, or Christmas crib, with 250 figurines from Virgin to sausage-vendor. A smaller room holds a Josephine Baker automaton in a grass skirt and Princess Caroline's Barbie doll.

Just west of here, along Av Princesse Grace, you can unfray your nerves for free with a dose of Côte d'Azur Shintoism at the **Jardin Japonais** (*open daily 9am–nightfall*), with waterfalls, ponds and a cedar-wood Tea House. It has been blessed by a Shinto priest and the gardeners have even been taught special Eastern methods of pruning the pine and olive trees, but the calm is ruffled by the posse of boiler-suited men who ensure the rules (no picnicking, no games, no balls) are kept. Further east are beaches of imported sand, resort hotels and the élite **Monte-Carlo Sporting Club**.

La Condamine and Fontvieille

The natural amphitheatre of La Condamine, the port quarter between Monte-Carlo and Monaco-Ville, has suffered the most from the speculators, their big cement brutes dwarfing the 11th-century votive chapel dedicated to Monaco's patron saint, **Ste-Dévote**. After her martyrdom in Corsica in 305, Dévote's body was put in a boat that sailed by itself, guided by a dove that flew out of her mouth, to Monaco (still known then as *Portus Herculis Monoeci*, after Hercules). In the 11th century some relic pirates snatched her bones, only to be foiled when the Monégasques set their boat on fire, an event re-enacted every 26 January amidst the armada of yachts, with a big celebratory procession the next day.

From Place Ste-Dévote, Rue Grimaldi leads west to Place du Canton and the **Zoological Terraces** (*t 93 25 18 31; open daily June–Oct 9–12 and 2–7; Mar–May 10–12 and 2–6; Oct–Feb 10–12 and 2–5; adm*), used to acclimatize animals imported from the tropics, including a black panther, a white tiger and some disgruntled rhinos.

Or there's the Prince's very own **Collection de Voitures Anciennes** (*t 92 05 28 56; open 10–6; adm*), which displays over 100 vintage cars, including the 1929 Bugatti which won the first Grand Prix. At the **Musée des Timbres et des Monnaies** (*t 93 15 41 50; open daily 10–5, in summer until 6; adm*) visitors can admire the fruits of Prince Rainier III's other hobby, probably kept for rainy days: coins, bank notes, commemorative medals and a 60-year-old copper stamp press are on display with a gift of 'a free stamp for paying guests' at the end of the tour. Nearby, the **Musée Naval** (*t 92 05 28 48, www.musee-naval.mc; open daily 10–6; adm*) has more examples of earnest princely passions, this time models of famous ships from the *Titanic* to the battleship *Missouri*. The earliest were constructed by Prince Albert Ier (the 'Scientist Prince') at the end of the 19th century.

More unusual are the prickly contents of a garden near the Moyenne Corniche, the **Jardin Exotique** (*t 93 15 29 80, bus no.2; www.monte-carlo.mc/jardinexotique; open daily mid-May–mid-Sept 9–7; winter 9– 6 or nightfall; adm*), where 6,000 succulents planted in the rock face of the Tête de Chien in 1933 range from the absurd to the obscene. Footbridges dangle over 33ft African 'candelabra' cacti that seem to be holding out their arms to catch the less-than-nimble

The same ticket admits you to the adjacent **Grottes de l'Observatoire**, one of the few places in Provence inhabited in the Palaeolithic era and, curiously, the only cave in Europe that gets warmer instead of cooler as you descend into its maw. Here, too, is the **Musée d'Anthropologie Préhistorique** (*t 93 15 80 06*), where the collection includes the bones of reindeer, mammoths and hippopotami, along with some from early editions of humankind.

To the south, between the sea and the ultra-modern **Stade Louis II** (*t 92 05 40 11, guided tours in English Mon, Tues, Thurs and Fri at 2.30 and 4pm, except during events; adm*), where AS Monaco regularly punish the rest of the French football league, stretches Fontvieille Park, where the charming **Princess Grace Rose Garden** (*open daily dawn–dusk*) is a memorial to Monaco's beloved princess, film actress and daughter of an Irish–American brick magnate in Philadelphia – the very same Kelly who supplied Ignatz mouse with ammo in George Herriman's classic comic strip *Krazy Kat*.

Near here, a **sculpture path** winds its immaculate way up from the Place du Campanile St-Nicholas. The whirling figures of Arman's *Cavalleria Eroica* and César's massive clenched fist look incongruously emotional against the fastidiously manicured lawns.

Up on the Rock: Monaco-Ville

In 1860 the Principality of Monaco consisted of 2,000 people living in this old Italian town, clinging spectacularly to a promontory 300m above the sea; they never dreamed it would turn into a shopping centre for Prince Rainier ashtrays and Princess Grace dolls. As scrubbed and cute as any town in Legoland, it offers devilries that in comparison make the Casino seem like an honest proposition: the **Historial des Princes de Monaco** (*27 Rue Basse, t 93 30 39 05; open daily Mar–Sept 9–6; Oct–Feb 11–5; adm*), with waxworks running the gamut from Francesco the Spiteful to Caroline and Stéphanie; the **Multi-vision Monte-Carlo Story** (*Terrasses du Parking du Chemin-des-Pêcheurs, t 93 25 32 33; showings hourly in summer 2–6, Jan–June and Sept–Oct 2–5; adm*), which presents 'Monaco le Film' and a mildly interesting collection of old film posters and magic lanterns; and the **Musée des Souvenirs Napoléoniens** (*Pl du Palais, t 93 25 18 31; open daily June–Sept 9.30–6; Oct 10–5; Dec–May Tues–Sun 10.30–12.30 and 2–5, closed Mon; adm*), with over 1,000 items connected to the little Corsican, including 'garments and toys belonging to the King of Rome!' – his ill-fated son.

Also along Rue Basse is the pink and yellow **Chapel of Mercy**, built in 1639 and disfigured in the 19th century by a sickly ceramic adoration scene above the door; inside is sculpted woodwork by Napoleon's official sculptor, François Josef-Bosio. It was the seat of the Brotherhood of the Black Penitents, whose first prior was Monaco's Prince Honoré II. In the **Musée de la Chapelle de la Visitation** (*t 93 50 07 00; open Tues–Sun 10–4; closed Mon; adm*), thanks to a sizeable private donation of sacred art, Rubens' podgy angels and Ribeira's bleeding martyrs float in the 17th-century Baroque chapel.

From June to October you can yawn your way through the plush **Palais Princier** itself (*t 93 25 18 31; open daily June–Sept 9.30–6; Oct 10–5; closed Nov–May; adm*) which, with its 19th-century 'medieval towers', is built around the Genoese fortress of 1215 (note the Grimaldi coat of arms, featuring two sword-wielding monks). At other times, when Rainier's at home, you'll have to be content with the rooty-toot-toot 11.55am **Changing of the Monégasque Guard**. Here, too, is Monaco's unattractive **cathedral**, built in 1875 using white stone from La Turbie, at the expense of a Romanesque chapel. From the chapel it inherited two lovely retables by Ludovico Brea from the early 16th century: *La Pietà*, over the sacristy door, and the grand *St Nicolas* with 18 panels, in the ambulatory. The more recent princes of Monaco are buried here, including Princess Grace, whose simple tomb inscribed *'Gratia Patricia Principis Rainerii III Uxor'* is often bedecked with nosegays from admirers, all waiting for the miracle that will sway the Vatican to beatify her.

Monaco's most compelling attraction is nearby: the **Musée Océanographique de Monaco** (*Av St-Martin*, *t* *93 15 36 00, www.oceano.mc; July–Aug daily 9–8; April–June and Sept 9–7; Oct–Mar 10–6; adm*), founded in 1910 by Prince Albert Ier, who sank all of his casino profits into a passion for deep-sea exploration. To house the treasures he accumulated in his 24 voyages, he built this museum in a cliff, filling it with instruments, shells, whale skeletons and, on the ground floor, a fascinating aquarium where 90 tanks hold some of the most surreal fish ever netted from the briny deep, including a mesmerizing cylindrical tank where thousands of identical fish swim in an endless circling shoal. The rest of the building is taken up with research laboratories, which used to be headed by Jacques Cousteau, specializing in the study of ocean pollution and radioactivity. You can park directly underneath and get a lift straight up into the museum, but don't neglect to go out and look back at this remarkable Belle Epoque building clinging to its cliff, with an 250ft sheer stone façade.

Besides the path east to Cap Martin (*see* p.74), there's another trail that begins on the D53 in Beausoleil, Monaco's French suburb, and ascends to the top of **Mont des Mules**. A third path, beginning at Fontvieille's Plage Marquet, heads west along the crashing sea to the train station at **Cap d'Ail** (Cape Garlic). It continues around the cape past more snooty Belle Epoque residences, including Greta Garbo's bolthole, and then drops down a wooded slope to the little cove of **Mala Plage**.

Also out here on Cap d'Ail is another jolly Cocteau creation: the **Mediterranean Centre for French Studies** (*t* *04 93 78 21 59*). A grassy path decorated with stones etched with cavorting fauns and surreal flowers leads to the open-air theatre; based on a classical Greek amphitheatre, it has bold black and white mosaic profiles in the centre of the circular stage, and a wonderful handrail formed by a sinuous gold and turquoise snake to guide the audience to their seats.

North of Monaco

From Monaco, the D53 ascends to the Grande Corniche, a road the Romans called Via Julia Augusta, built to link up the Urbs to its conquests in Gaul and Spain. Several hard campaigns had to be fought (25–14 BC) before the fierce Ligurians finally let the road builders through, and in 6 BC the Roman Senate voted to erect a mighty commemorative monument known as the Trophy of the Alps (the Romans called it

Getting Around

By Bus
There are buses daily from Nice (*gare routière*) to La Turbie, continuing up to Peille (not on Sundays), and several from Monaco. Buses leave less regularly from Nice to Peillon.

By Train
Both Peillon and Peille have train stations, but they lie several steep kilometres below their respective villages.

Tourist Information

La Turbie: at the *mairie*, **t** 04 92 41 51 61, **f** 04 93 41 13 99, *accueil@ville-la-turbie.fr. Open Mon and Wed–Fri 9–12 and 2–5, Tues and Sat 9–12; closed Sun.*
Peillon: 620 Av de l'Hôtel-de-Ville, **t** 04 93 91 98 34. *In the old village. Open winter Mon–Fri 1–5, summer Tues–Sat 1–5.*
Peille: at the *mairie*, **t** 04 93 91 71 71, **f** 04 93 79 89 37. *Open Mon–Fri 9–12.*

Markets
La Turbie: General market, Thursday morning.

Where to Stay and Eat

La Turbie ✉ 06320
Le Napoléon, 7 Av de la Victoire, **t 04 93 41 00 54, **f** 04 93 41 28 93 (*moderate*). Ask for a room on the top floor. You can eat good food here, too (*expensive*). *Restaurant closed Wed.*
Hostellerie Jérôme, 20 Rue Comte de Cessole, **t** 04 92 41 51 51 (*very expensive–expensive*). Simple, delicious dishes featuring regional produce. *Eves only; closed Mon and Tues.*

Peillon ✉ 06440
***Auberge de la Madone, **t** 04 93 79 91 17, **f** 04 93 79 99 36, *www.chateauxhotels.com/madone* (*expensive–moderate*). Just outside the walled village, this family-run inn has astonishing views over the valley. Dine out on its terrace (*expensive*). *Closed Jan, 20 Oct–20 Dec, and Wed.*
Auberge Lou Pourtail, **t** 04 93 79 94 58 (*inexpensive*). A cheaper but equally charming annexe to the Auberge de la Madone. *Closed Jan.*

Peille ✉ 06440
*Belvédère, Place Jean Miol, **t** 04 93 79 90 45, **f** 04 93 91 93 47 (*inexpensive*). The only hotel in the village, the Belvédère has five simple rooms with mountain views and a restaurant (*moderate–cheap;, book*). *Closed Dec.*

Tropea Augusti, or 'Augustus' Trophy') at the base of Mont Agel. The views are precipitous, and you can escape the crowds by venturing even further inland to Peille and Peillon, two of the most beautiful villages on the Côte d'Azur, or by following the ancient salt route up the Paillon valley to l'Escarène.

La Turbie and its Trophy

Though hemmed in by upstart mini-villas and second homes, La Turbie (a corruption of *Tropea*) still retains its old typical core of narrow vaulted alleys, built back in the days when it merited a mention by Dante in *The Divine Comedy*: see the relevant immortal lines proudly engraved on the tower. La Turbie also has an elliptical 18th-century church, **St-Michel-Archange**, with a sumptuous Baroque interior; the altar alone uses 17 different kinds of marble, the communion table glitters with onyx and agate and the paintings are attributed to, or by the schools of, Raphael (*Saint Mark writing the Gospel*), Veronese, Rembrandt, Ludovico Brea, Murillo and Ribera (a stark *Ste Dévote*) – not bad for a village of 2,000 or so souls!

The old Via Julia Augusta (Rue Comte-de-Cessole) passes through town on its way to the **Trophy of the Alps**. This monument originally stood 147ft high, supporting a series of Doric columns interspersed with statues of eminent generals, the whole surmounted by a colossal 20ft statue of Augustus flanked by two captives; on its wall were listed the 44 conquered Ligurian tribes, and stairs throughout allowed passers-by to enjoy the view. When St Honorat saw the local people worshipping this marvel in the 4th century, he vandalized it; in the dark ages it was converted into a fort; Louis XIV ordered it to be blown up in 1705, and the stone was quarried to build St-Michel-Archange. The still formidable pile of rubble that remained in the 1930s was resurrected to 114ft and its inscription replaced thanks to the patronage of a rich American, Edward Tuck. The only other such trophy to survive *in situ* is in Romania, although the base of an even older one has recently been found at Le Perthus on the Spanish border. A small **museum** (*t 04 93 41 20 84; open mid-May–mid-Sept daily 9.30–6; mid-Sept-mid-May Tues–Sun 10–1, 2.30–5; adm*) on the site has models and drawings which trace the Trophy's history, while the park behind offers magnificent views of Monaco and the coast below.

Peillon and Peille

The two villages are tiny and lovely; balanced atop adjacent hills, both require a wearying climb to reach them. But Peille and Peillon aren't quite the Tweedledee and Tweedledum of the Côte. **Peillon**, most easily reached on the D53 from Nice, is a bit posher, complete with a *foyer* – a cobbled square with fountain at the village entrance. Inside are peaceful medieval stairs and arches, which snake up through vaulted passageways to the summit and a theatrically restored Baroque parish church, the **Church of the Transfiguration**, built on the highest point of the village. But Peillon's big attraction is right at the entrance: the **Chapelle des Pénitents Blancs** (*ring the tourist office to arrange a visit, groups only*), adorned with a cycle of Renaissance frescoes on the *Passion of Christ* by the charming and vigorous Giovanni Canavesio (*c.* 1485), who would certainly be better known had he painted anything outside the valleys of the Maritime Alps. Look out for Judas, tormented by a malignant black devil who is ripping out his soul. From Peillon, there are trails that lead to country rambles.

One of those walks (*signposted near the parish church*) follows the Roman road in two hours to **Peille**, further up the D53. More isolated, Peille has more character, and its very own dialect, called *Pelhasc*. There's an ensemble of medieval streets like Peillon's and a church begun in the 12th century, with an interesting medieval portrait of Peille and its now ruined castle. Once, during a drought, Peille asked for help from a shepherd (in Provence, shepherds often moonlight as sorcerers), and he made it rain on condition that the lord of this castle give him his daughter to wed – an event remembered in a fête on the first Sunday in September. The Church may frown at such goings-on, but Peille often had its own ideas on religion, preferring twice in the Middle Ages to be excommunicated rather than pay the bishop's tithes.

The Paillon river flows up the valley to **L'Escarène**, a strategic pit stop in the days of the salt route, when salt from the marshes of Hyères and Toulon was loaded on to mules in Nice and taken across the mountains to Turin.

From the bridge, you can see the houses overhanging the river. The lovely 17th-century neoclassical church of **St-Pierre-aux-Liens** was designed by Jean-André Guibert, architect of the Cathedral Ste-Réparate in Vieux Nice. It was restored in the 19th century with admirable (and unusual) restraint, and now hosts a festival of ancient and Baroque music in the summer. Under its wings, tucked in on either side, are the twin chapels of the Pénitents Blancs, with spectacular rococo decoration, and the Pénitents Noirs.

The Moyenne Corniche

Between Monaco and Nice, the main reason for taking the middle road has long been the extraordinary village of Eze, the most perched, perhaps, of any *village perché* in France, squeezed on to a cone of a hill 1,400ft over the sea. It barely avoided being

Getting There and Around

By Train

Métrazur trains stop at Eze's coastal outpost; in summer a minibus (*navette*) will shuttle you up to the village.

By Bus

Some buses from Nice to Peille stop at Eze-Grande Corniche three times daily. There are several buses a day (no.112) from Nice directly for Eze-Village. All the frequent buses on the Nice–Menton line stop at Eze-Bord-de-Mer; in summer minibuses leave regularly from the Basse Corniche for Eze-Village and Eze-Grande Corniche.

Tourist Information

Eze: Place du Général de Gaulle,
t 04 93 41 26 00, f 04 93 41 04 80, *www.eze-riviera.com, eze@webstore.fr*. Walkers can pick up an excellent little guide to walks in the area here. *Open April–Oct daily 9–7; Nov–Mar daily 9–6.30. Closed hols, and Sun Nov–Mar.* There's also a small office on the Basse Corniche, near the station. *Open April–Oct Mon–Sat 10–1 and 3–6.30.*

Shopping

Every other doorway in Eze spills over with art or souvenirs, with the usual range of

quality. There are one or two more unusual places worth seeking out.

Terre de Provence, 20 Rue Principale, t 04 92 10 85 63, f 04 92 10 85 82. Whitewashed and wooden-beamed, with a selection of the best Provençal wines, regional delicacies and beautiful tableware and crystal.

La Salamandre, near the Jardin Exotique, t 04 93 41 19 06. A friendly shop offering soft cotton and linen clothes, mostly made in France and often dyed in sunny Provençal colours. *Closed Nov–Mar.*

Where to Stay and Eat

Eze ✉ 06360

A road links the three *corniches* at Eze, and there are hotels on each level.

Eze-Grande Corniche

★★★★**Les Terrasses d'Eze**, Rte de la Turbie, t 04 92 41 55 55, f 04 92 41 55 10, *info@ terrasses-eze.com, www.terrasses-eze.com* (*luxury–very expensive; half board compulsory in season*). Part of the Best Western chain. The rooms are not quite as big as you might hope for the price, but the restaurant (*expensive*) offers the best views along the coast to go with the rich Mediterranean cuisine.

★★**L'Hermitage**, Grande Corniche, 2km from Eze village, t 04 93 41 00 68, f 04 93 41 24 05 (*inexpensive*). Two kilometres from Eze, L'Hermitage offers priceless views,

poached as well as perched in a catastrophic fire in 1986 which ravaged the pine forest that once surrounded the village.

Eze

Eze, they say, is named after a temple to Isis that the Phoenicians built on this hill. The village then passed to the Romans, to the Saracens, and so on, although rarely did Eze change hands by force: even if an enemy penetrated its 14th-century gate and walls, the tight little maze of stairs and alleys would confuse the attackers, the better to ambush them or spill boiling oil on their heads.

These days, if intruders got far enough to assault what remains of the castle – 1,400ft above sea level – they would run into the needles of the South American cacti in the **Jardin Exotique** (*t 04 93 41 10 30; open daily Sept–June 9–12 and 2–6;*

traditional décor and monstrous portions of startlingly good, very *moderately* priced Provençal food. From the hotel a footpath leads along the ancient Voie Aurélienne on to Mont Leuze, with breathtaking views. *Closed Dec–Jan; restaurant closed Thurs and Fri lunch.*

Eze-Moyenne Corniche

In Eze-Village there are two luxurious inns with only a handful of rooms each to let, but superb kitchens.

****Château Eza**, Rue de la Pise, **t** 04 93 41 12 24, **f** 04 93 41 16 64, *www.chateza.com* (*luxury*). This former prince's residence is actually a collection of medieval houses linked together to form an eagle's nest, all sharing an extraordinary perched terrace restaurant (*very expensive–expensive*). *Closed Nov–Mar; restaurant closed Nov–Christmas, and Tues and Wed in winter.*

****Château de la Chèvre d'Or**, Rue du Barri, **t** 04 92 10 66 66, **f** 04 93 41 06 72, *reservation@chevredor.com, www.chevredor. com* (*luxury*). In a medieval castle rebuilt in the 1920s, this romantic Relais & Châteaux hotel has a small park rippling down the mountain-side, a pool and more ravishing views. Chef Jean-Marc Delacourt creates refined, light versions of the French classics (*very expensive*). *Reserve well in advance. Closed Dec–Feb.*

Le Troubadour, 4 Rue du Brec, **t** 04 93 41 19 03 (*expensive*). Turbot or *filet de bœuf aux cèpes*

go down nicely here, and the price is nice too. *Closed Sun and Mon lunch and mid-Nov–mid-Dec.*

Le Nid d'Aigle, Rue du Château, **t** 04 93 41 19 08 (*moderate*). Head to this place on the summit of the rock, next door to the Jardin Exotique, for lofty fish (*daurade au pistou*, salmon) and all kinds of Provençal staples, including *lapin à la provençale.*

Mas Provençal, Av de Verdun, **t** 04 93 41 19 53 (*expensive*). Just outside the tangle of medieval streets, this friendly *mas* is completely covered in flowers and ivy, and comfortably ensconced in the 19th century. Sink into plush red velvet chairs (with anti-macassars) and dine on milk-fed pig roasted on a spit, or *risotto aux cèpes*, before ordering the carriage home. *Closed Sun in winter and mid-Feb–Mar.*

Eze-Bord-de-Mer

*****Cap Estel**, **t** 04 93 01 50 44, **f** 04 93 01 55 20, (*luxury*). Set in a park, this luxurious, sparkling Riviera dream, which was originally built for a Russian princess, has two heated pools and a flight of movie-star steps down to the manicured gardens. *Ring for closing dates.*

Auberge Le Soleil, **t** 04 93 01 51 46, **f** 04 93 01 58 40, *www.auberge-le-soleil.cote.azur.fr* (*moderate*). A family-run place with well-priced rooms and gourmet dining (*expensive–moderate*). *Hotel closed Nov, restaurant closed Mon eve and Tues eve.*

July–Aug 9–8; adm), a spiky paradise created on municipal initiative in 1949 by *ingénieur agronome* Jean Gastauld.

Eze's other non-commercial attraction, the cream and yellow **Chapelle des Pénitents Blancs**, built in 1766, has gathered an eccentric collection of scraps: an old model of a sailing ship is suspended from the ceiling in place of a missing chandelier, and a disembodied arm brandishes a 13th-century Catalan crucifix, the *Christ of the Black Death* (as is typical in medieval Catalan art, the sculptor emphasized Christ's divine nature, and he smiles, even on the Cross). Here, too, is a 14th-century *Madone des Forêts*, where baby Jesus, rather unusually, holds a pine cone.

A scenic path descending to Eze-Bord-de-Mer is called the **Sentier Frédéric Nietzsche** after the philosopher. (It starts at the entrance to the old village, down a narrow, almost hidden, path on the left, which also leads to a small observation spot.) Nietzsche, however, walked up instead of down, an arduous trek that made his head spin and inspired the third part of his *Thus Spake Zarathustra*.

He might have cleared his head up in the park which curls around the **Grande Corniche**, a speleologists' delight with caves and chasms. Nature trails, bike trails and horse trails splinter off in all directions and an orientation table surmounts a Genoese-style tower, looking across the Plateau de la Justice, where the gibbet of the Lords of Eze once stood, and out to Corsica and St-Tropez.

The Basse Corniche

To the west of Eze-Bord-de-Mer another wooded promontory, Cap Ferrat, protrudes into the sea to form today's most fashionable address on the Côte d'Azur. The fascinating, wildly eclectic Villa Ephrussi de Rothschild and gardens crown the summit of Cap Ferrat, while the awful King Léopold II of the Belgians, Otto Preminger and Somerset Maugham had sanctuaries by the sea. To the east, the peninsula and steep mountain backdrop keep Beaulieu so sheltered that it shares with Menton the distinction of being the hottest town in France, while to the west the Corniche skirts the top of the fine old village of Villefranche-sur-Mer, with a port deep enough for battleships – grey tokens from the grey world beyond the Riviera.

Beaulieu

'*O qual bel luogo!*' exclaimed Napoleon in his Corsican mother tongue, and the bland name stuck to this lush, banana-growing town overlooking the Baie des Fourmis (Bay of Ants), so called for the black boulders in the sea. It was eccentric American millionaire and press baron James Gordon Bennett who put Beaulieu on the European tourist map; after his enforced exile from New York, he idled along the Riviera coast in his extravagant yacht and was smitten by the bay. The local fishermen refused to let him buy it and build a fabulously expensive new port, and he had to be content with establishing a coach service betweeen Nice and Beaulieu, drawn by four horses and sometimes accompanied by a brass band, to bring in the sun-seekers.

Getting Around

The most amusing way to visit is by way of the Côte d'Azur's equivalent of Hollywood's 'See the Homes of the Stars' bus tours: a 'little train' starts on the quay at Villefranche and chugs around the promontory with a guide calling out, in French and abominable English, the names of the famous who live(d) in the villas.

Tourist Information

Beaulieu: Place Clemenceau, t 04 93 01 02 21, f 04 93 01 44 04, *tourisme@ot-beaulieu-sur-mer.fr, www.ot-beaulieu-sur-mer.fr. Open Sept–June Mon–Sat 9–12.15 and 2–6; July–Aug Mon–Sat 9–12.30 and 2–7, Sun 9–12.30.*

Market Days

Beaulieu: Fruit and vegetable market on Place du Marché daily. Expands to include clothes and household goods on Saturdays. An antiques (and *brocante* – 'junk') market takes place by the port on the third Sunday of each month.

Where to Stay and Eat

Beaulieu-sur-Mer ✉ 06310

★★★★La Réserve, 5 Bd Général Leclerc, t 04 93 01 00 01, f 04 93 01 28 99, *reserve@wanadoo.fr, www.reservebeaulieu.com* (*luxury*). In the 1870s, when the wealthy James Gordon Bennett, owner of the *New York Herald* and the man who sent Stanley to find Livingstone, was booted out of New York society for his scandalous behaviour, he came to the Riviera and ran the Paris edition of his newspaper from here. It is now one of the most exclusive hotels on the Riviera and offers grand sea views, a beach and marina, heated pool and more delights, including an elegant neo-Renaissance restaurant (*very expensive*). *Closed mid-Nov–mid Dec.*

★★★Artemis, 3 Bd Maréchal Joffre, t 04 93 01 12 15, f 04 93 01 27 46, *www.hotel-artemis.com* (*expensive*). Near the station, this modern hotel has rooms with balconies and access to a pool at the back. *Closed Jan.*

★★Le Havre Bleu, 29 Bd Maréchal Joffre, t 04 93 01 01 40, f 04 93 01 29 92, *hotel.lehavrebleu@wanadoo.fr, www.hotel-lehavrebleu.fr* (*moderate–inexpensive*). Attractive hotel with pleasant rooms, many with terraces. *Closed Dec.*

★★Sélect, 1 Rue André Cane, t 04 93 01 05 42, f 04 93 01 34 30 (*inexpensive*). This small, simple place near the station is convenient, yet impersonal.

★Le Riviera, 6 Rue Paul Doumer, t 04 93 01 04 92, f 04 93 01 19 31 (*inexpensive*). With pretty wrought-iron balconies, just up from the Basse Corniche. *Closed Nov–after Xmas.*

Le Catalan, Bd Maréchal Leclerc, t 04 93 01 02 78 (*moderate–cheap*). Wood-fired pizzas and delicious pasta abound round the corner from the Riviera hotel (*à la carte*). *Closed Sun.*

Le Salon des Ambassadeurs, 4 Av Fernand Dunan, t 04 93 76 48 00 (*moderate–cheap*). To dance all night with the ageing but still game local retirees, head for the Casino's piano-bar and restaurant. Friday 9pm–3am.

Beaulieu admits to a mere four days of frost a year and calls its steamy easternmost suburb La Petite Afrique; most of its affluent population are trying to imitate Gustave Eiffel, who retired here and lived to be 90. Beaulieu's vintage casino (*open daily 11am–4am, 5am at weekends*) has been renovated after years of dilapidation and is back to its former sparkling grandeur, with all the usual means of squandering fortunes, along with restaurants and a salon for *dîners-spectacles*. The *thés dansants* held in **La Rotonde** are a further retro attraction, but the *real* magnet is a place so retro that even Socrates would feel at home there: the **Villa Kerylos** (*t 04 93 01 01 44, www.villa-kerylos.com; open Feb–Oct daily 10–6; July–Aug until 7; Nov–Jan Mon–Fri 2–6, Sat, Sun and school hols 10.30–6; adm; bus stop Hôtel Métropole then a 5min walk*), a striking reproduction of a wealthy 5th-century BC Athenian's abode, furnishings and garden, built in 1908 by archaeologist Théodore Reinach. The marble bathroom is fantastically opulent, with a submerged throne and a playful mosaic of bizarre sea creatures. The library beats most poky studies; built over two storeys, the lofty ceilings and high windows let in long shafts of natural light, along with the gentle rushing sound of the sea. Outside, the sea breeze ruffles the aromatic herbs and plants, which draw droves of giant dragonflies, buzzing like mini-helicopters. Reinach spared no expense on the marble, ivory, bronze, mosaic and fresco reproductions to help his genuine antiquities feel at home; glass windows, plumbing and a hidden piano which unfolds like a Chinese puzzle box are the only modern anachronisms. And here, on a shore that reminded him of the Aegean, this ultimate philhellene lived himself like an Athenian, holding symposia, exercising and bathing with his male buddies, and keeping the womenfolk well out of the way.

St-Jean-Cap-Ferrat

Another retro-repro fantasy, the **Villa Ephrussi de Rothschild** (*t 04 93 01 33 09, www.villa-ephrussi.com, a 10min walk from the Basse Corniche, or catch the St-Jean bus which passes its entrance; open daily Feb–Oct 10–6; July–Aug until 7; Nov–Jan Sat, Sun and school holidays 10–6, weekdays 2–6 state rooms and gardens only; adm*) crowns the narrow isthmus of bucolic Cap Ferrat, enjoying spectacular views over both the Baie des Fourmis and the harbour of Villefranche. The flamboyant Béatrice de Rothschild, who never went anywhere without her trunk of 50 wigs and greeted guests to her parties dressed as Marie-Antoinette, was a compulsive art collector and lover of the 18th century and, after marrying the banker Baron Ephrussi, had this Italianate villa specially built to house her treasures – a Venetian rococo room was designed for Béatrice's Tiepolo ceiling, while other rooms set off her Renaissance furniture, Florentine bridal chests, paintings by Boucher, rare Chinese screens and furniture, Flemish and Beauvais tapestries, Sèvres and Meissen porcelain, Louis-Quinze and Louis-Seize furniture, covered Andalucían patio (a favourite location shot for films), hidden bathroom and collection of porcelain chamber pots.

To create the equally eclectic gardens, the isthmus was given a crew cut and terraced into different levels, all linked together by little pathways and stone steps. There's a French garden with a copy of the *Amour* fountain from the Petit Trianon; a Florentine garden with a white marble ephebe; a Spanish garden, with papyrus, dates and pomegranates; exotic, Japanese, English and Provençal gardens; and a lapidary garden decorated with Romanesque capitals, arches and gargoyles.

For all the trouble she took to build this glorious pile, Béatrice actually spent very little time here, preferring her villa in Monte-Carlo as it was closer to the gambling tables. In the summer you can take luncheon, tea or cakes in the elegant former *salon d'hiver*.

Cap Ferrat, with its lush greenery, secret villas and little azure coves, is ripe territory for strolls or swims – there are a dozen small beaches, albeit of fine gravel. **Plage de Passable** along Chemin du Roy, west of Villa Ephrussi, is popular with families and

Tourist Information

St-Jean-Cap-Ferrat: 59 Av Denis Séméria, **t** 04 93 76 08 90, **f** 04 93 76 16 67, *ot.saintjeancapferrat@tiscali.fr*. Can provide lists of local *chambres d'hôtes*.

Where to Stay and Eat

St-Jean-Cap-Ferrat ✉ 06230

Even though its villas are the most exclusive on the Riviera, Cap Ferrat has hotels in all price ranges, beginning with one of the most beautiful small hotels on the entire Côte:

★★★★La Voile d'Or, Av Jean Mermoz, **t** 04 93 01 13 13, **f** 04 93 76 11 17, *reservation@ lavoiledor.fr, www.lavoiledor.fr* (*luxury*). A charming Italian villa, overlooking the marina and once owned by film director Michael Powell, who inherited it from his father (and sold it because no one ever paid their bar bills), the Voile d'Or is an ideal honeymoon hotel, with a garden hanging over the port, a heated pool and rooms with every luxury a hotel could provide. Its equally exceptional restaurant is favoured by the tanned and languid yachting set. *Closed Nov–Mar, and during Grand Prix.*

★★★★Grand Hôtel du Cap Ferrat, 71 Bd Général de Gaulle, **t** 04 93 76 50 50, **f** 04 93 76 04 52, *reserv@grand-hotel-cap-ferrat.com, www. grand-hotel-cap-ferrat.com* (*luxury*). At the very fashionable Belle Epoque Grand Hôtel the already luxurious rooms have been restored in a more airy, comfortable Riviera style, all set in acres of gardens, lawns and palms. A funicular railway lowers guests down to an Olympic-size seawater swimming pool just over the Mediterranean. Its restaurant, **Le Cap**, on a palatial terrace shaded by parasol pines, serves delicious meals (*very expensive*) decidedly unhealthy for your wallet. *Closed Jan–Feb.*

★★★★Royal Riviera, 3 Av Jean Monnet, **t** 04 93 76 31 00, **f** 04 93 01 23 07, *www.royal-riviera.com* (*luxury*). A sumptuous hotel in a pale pink Belle Epoque villa set, again, in acres of elegantly landscaped gardens, with the usual Riviera paraphernalia: a sandy, private beach offering a wide variety of watersports; an airy, terraced restaurant serving classic French and Provençal cuisine (*expensive*); and a nearby helipad to park the runaround. *Closed Dec–19 Jan.*

More down-to-earth choices include:

★★★Brise-Marine, Av Jean Mermoz, **t** 04 93 76 04 36, **f** 04 93 76 11 49, *info@hotel-brise marine.com, www.hotel-brisemarine.com* (*expensive*). With a garden, terrace and large rooms, half with sea views. *Closed Nov–Jan.*

★★Clair Logis, 12 Av Centrale, **t** 04 93 76 04 57, **f** 04 93 76 11 85 (*expensive*). Near the centre of the Cap, this wonderful and very reasonable hotel is in a welcoming villa set back in a lush enclosed garden (*no restaurant*). *Closed Dec–Feb.*

Le Cap, Grand Hôtel du Cap Ferrat (*very expensive, see above*). Nice but pricey restaurant.

Le Provençal, Place Clemenceau, **t** 04 93 76 03 97 (*very expensive–expensive*). For a frisson of south-coast *hauteur*.

Around the Port de Plaisance (marina) you'll find several nautically named beaneries:

Le Pirate, **t** 04 93 76 12 97 (*moderate*).

Le Sloop, **t** 04 93 01 48 63 (*moderate*).

Skipper, **t** 04 93 76 01 00 (*moderate*). Best for the fish on its well-priced menus.

scuba divers. The 'Roy' in question was bad old King Léopold II of the Belgians, whose ruthless exploitation of the Congo (see Conrad's *Heart of Darkness*) helped to pay for his luxurious life here, where he took a swim every day with his beard neatly folded into a rubber whisker-protector while his valet ironed his newspapers. His villa (Les Cèdres) is now more democratically used for a delightful **zoo** (*t 04 93 76 07 60, www.zoocapferrat.com; open daily 9.30–7 in summer; 9.30–5.30 in winter; adm*).

The former-fishing-now-yacht-port of **St-Jean-Cap-Ferrat** has the distinction of a *Salle des Mariages* painted by Jean Cocteau (without the same vigour as in Menton). A walking path circles around the dewclaw of land south of the port called **Pointe St-Hospice** where, in the 6th century, the Niçois saint Hospice had a hermitage (now marked by a 19th-century chapel). With one arm chained to the wall, Hospice lived off algae brought to him by pious souls, and uttered dire prophecies about barbarian invasions that came true, recorded by Merovingian historian Gregory of Tours.

Modern-day invasions take place at nearby **Plage de Paloma**, favourite of Italian day-trippers and millionaire pensioners, and **Plage des Fosses**. Another path, the **Promenade Maurice Rouvier**, leads from St-Jean's beach to Beaulieu, passing **Villa Scoglietto** and its sea-defying garden, where Charlie Chaplin spent his summer holidays and actor David Niven lived the last years of his life.

Villefranche-sur-Mer

In the 14th century the deep, wooded bay between Cap Ferrat and Nice was a duty-free port, hence Villefranche's name. It became an important military port for the Savoys in the 18th century, a period that saw Villefranche take on the appearance it has today: tall, brightly coloured, piled-up houses; and narrow lanes and stairs, some so overhung with houses that they're actually tunnels. An example is **Rue Obscure**, 'a good place for a knifing,' as William Sansom described it, which Cocteau used as an underworldly setting for his film *Orphée*. It also came in handy as a bomb shelter in the Second World War. In the heart of the old town is the church of **St-Michel**, Baroqued with unusual restraint and containing a recumbent Christ which was carved from a fig tree by a 17th-century slave.

The streets open up to the wide quay, given over to bars and restaurants, and a fine beach with a shallow slope and calm bay that is ideal for children. The charm of the place, and the presence of so many brawny sailors from around the world on shore-leave, made Villefranche a popular intello-gay resort in the 1920s, with Jean Cocteau weaving his personal mythologies with opium, 'fluids' and his friends in the little Hotel Welcome: 'Poets of all kinds, speaking every language, lived there and by a simple contact of fluids transformed the extraordinary little town, whose steep chaos ends at the water's edge, into a veritable Lourdes, a centre of legends and inventions.'

Villefranche's fishermen once stored their nets in the portside Romanesque **Chapelle St-Pierre** (*Quai Courbet, t 04 93 76 90 70; open summer 10–12 and 4–8.30; winter 9.30–12 and 2–6; adm*), and in 1957, after a protracted battle with the local municipal authorities, Cocteau, who had become fascinated by the little church three decades earlier, won permission to restore and renovate it. The fishermen resisted at first, disgruntled at the loss of a convenient storage place, and even stole his ladders when the project finally got under way. They only came round when Cocteau offered to give the proceeds of visits to the chapel to the Fishermen's Benevolent Fund. Finally let loose on the 500-year-old chapel, he began to fresco it in 'ghosts of colours' with scenes from the Life of St Peter (walking on the water with an angel's help, which astounds the fish but makes Christ smile), plus images of the fish-eyed fishergirls of Villefranche, the Gypsies at Saintes-Maries-de-la-Mer, and angels from Cocteau's private heaven.

Tourist Information

Villefranche-sur-Mer: Jardin François Binon, t 04 93 01 73 68, f 04 93 76 63 65, ot@ville-franche-sur-mer.com, www.villefranche-sur-mer.com. Open July–Aug daily 9–7, June and Sept Mon–Sat 9–12 and 2–6.30, Oct–May Mon–Sat 9–12 and 2–6. Offers guided tours of the town.

Market Days

Villefranche: Flea market in the Jardin François Binon and Av Amélie Pollonnais all day Sunday.
Provençal market in the Jardin François Binon and Promenade de l'Octroi on Saturday morning.

Where to Stay and Eat

Villefranche-sur-Mer ✉ 06230

★★★Welcome, Quai Amiral Courbet, t 04 93 76 27 62, f 04 93 76 27 66, resa@welcome-hotel.fr, www.welcomehotel.fr (luxury–expensive). Just beside the port, this legendary hotel is ideally situated, although its wild days are over. The newly refurbished and finely decorated rooms are air-conditioned; those on the 5th floor are ravishing. Closed mid-Nov–22 Dec.

★★Provençal, 4 Av du Maréchal Joffre, t 04 93 76 53 53, f 04 93 76 96 00, provencal@riviera.fr, www.hotelprovencal.com (moderate–inexpensive). Unpretentious and family-run. Closed Nov–Christmas.

L'Echalote, 7 Rue de l'Eglise, t 04 93 01 71 11 (expensive–moderate). This charming restaurant has a minuscule terrace and serves excellent, and rich, Provençal dishes (themed menus change every 3 weeks). Open evenings only; closed Sun except in summer.

Le Carpaccio, Promenade des Marinières, t 04 93 01 72 97, www.restaurant-carpaccio.com (moderate). This has long been a favourite of the Rolls-Royce crowd, who travel from Monaco, yet remains affordable for the rest of us, either for a splurge or for a modest pizza.

La Belle Epoque, Place de la Paix, t 04 93 01 96 22 (moderate). As you wind your way downhill towards the sea from the Corniche, you will pass this pleasant restaurant full of locals, which serves daily lunch specials on a large covered terrace.

La Grignotière, 3 Rue du Poilu, t 04 93 76 79 83 (moderate). Local Niçois specialities in the old town. Open evenings only, plus all day Sun; closed Wed in winter.

Michel's, Place Amélie Pollonnais, t 04 93 76 73 24, www.michel-s.net (moderate). Michel's has a startling frieze (they are very proud of it) depicting Villefranche, a lovely terrace looking out over the bay and very friendly staff. Light, local specialities; the melt-in-the-mouth house pâté and the red pepper and aubergine terrine are especially good. A la carte only. Closed Tues.

Le Versailles, 7 Bd Princesse Grace de Monaco, t 04 93 76 52 52, www.hotelversailles.com (moderate). With suitably commanding views and kingly cuisine; the delicately prepared cod is served with the most delicious aïoli on the coast. Closed Mon except July–Aug.

Joïa, 18 Rue du Poilu, t 04 93 76 62 40 (moderate). Trendy bar/restaurant specializing in fish dishes.

The Duke of Savoy's 16th-century **Citadelle St-Elme** has been put back to work as the Hôtel de Ville, with a few more paintings by Jean Cocteau (upstairs) and three free museums (t 04 93 76 33 27 for general enquiries, all open June and Sept 10–12 and 2.30–6; July–Aug 10–12 and 2.30–7; Oct–May 10–12 and 2–5.30; closed Sun am, Tues and Nov). The first, the **Fondation Musée Volti**, has voluptuous bronze, copper and terracotta female figures sculpted by Antoniucci Volti, set in an idiosyncratic series of small chambers, patios and niches. During the Second World War, Marcel Carné used them to film Les Visiteurs du soir and Les Enfants du Paradis. The **Musée Goetz Boumeester** has paintings and engravings by the American artists and collectors Henri Goetz and his wife, Christine Boumeester, along with a sprinkling of gifts to the couple from their celebrity friends, a constant parade of big stars and writers. Finally, there is the little **Collection Roux**, with ceramic figurines inspired by medieval and Renaissance manuscripts.

Nice

History **106**
Vieux Nice 109
Cours Saleya **113**
The Port, Terra Amata, and Hilltop Follies 113
Up the Paillon 114
West of Place Masséna and the Promenade des Anglais 116
Fine and Naïf Arts, and a Russian Cathedral 117
Cimiez: Chagall, Matisse and Roman Ruins 119

09

Nice

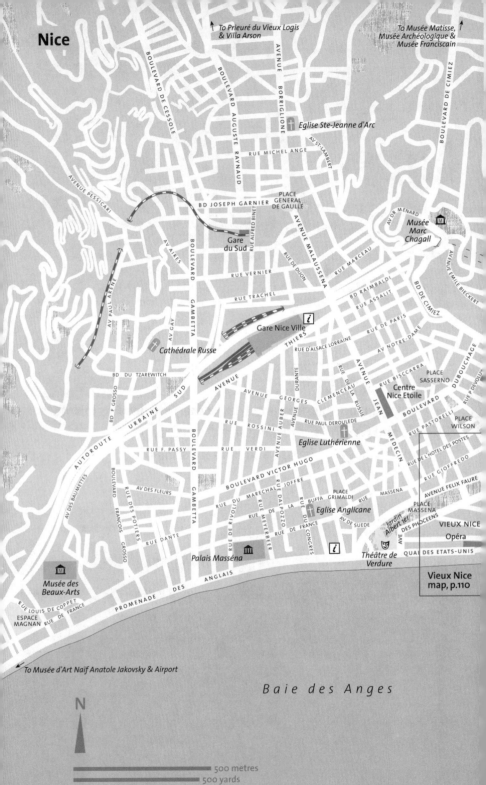

To Prieuré du Vieux Logis & Villa Arson

To Musée Matisse, Musée Archéologique & Musée Franciscain

AVENUE BORRIGLIONE

Eglise Ste-Jeanne d'Arc

RUE MICHEL ANGE

AV ST-LAMBERT

BOULEVARD AUGUSTE RAYNAUD

BOULEVARD DE CESSOLE

AVENUE PESSICART

BD JOSEPH GARNIER

PLACE GENERAL DE GAULLE

RUE ALFRED BINET

AVENUE MALAUSSENA

AV DR MENARD

Musée Marc Chagall

AV AIRES

BOULEVARD GAMBETTA

Gare du Sud

RUE DE DIJON

RUE VERNIER

RUE MARCEAU

BOULEVARD DE CIMIEZ

AVENUE EMILE BIECKERT

AV PAUL ARENE

AV GAY

RUE TRACHEL

BD RAIMBALDI

RUE ASSALIT

BD DE CIMIEZ

Cathédrale Russe

Gare Nice Ville

THIERS

RUE DE PARIS

AV NOTRE-DAME

BD DU TZAREWITCH

AVENUE

RUE D'ALSACE LORRAINE

RUE DE LA RUSSIE

PLACE SASSERNO

DUBOUCHAGE

RUE DEVOLUI

BD F. GROSSO

BOULEVARD SUD

AVENUE GEORGES CLEMENCEAU

DURANTE

AVENUE JEAN MEDECIN

RUE BISCCARRA

BOULEVARD

PLACE WILSON

AUTOROUTE URBAINE

RUE ROSSINI

AVENUE AUBER

AVENUE

RUE PAUL DEROULEDE

Centre Nice Etoile

RUE PASTORELLI

RUE DE L'HOTEL DES POSTES

RUE F. PASSY

RUE VERDI

Eglise Luthérienne

RUE GIOFFREDO

BOULEVARD VICTOR HUGO

AV DES FLEURS

RUE DE RIVOLI

RUE DU MARECHAL JOFFRE

RUE DALPOZZO

RUE MEYERBEER

LA BUFFA

PLACE GRIMALDI

RUE

MASSENA

AVENUE FELIX FAURE

BOULEVARD FRANCOIS GROSSO

RUE DES POTIERS

RUE DANTE

RUE DE FRANCE

RUE DU CONGRES

Eglise Anglicane

AV DE SUEDE

PLACE MASSENA

AVE DES PHOCEENS

VIEUX NICE

Opéra

AV DES BAUMETTES

Palais Masséna

Jardin Albert 1er

Théâtre de Verdure

QUAI DES ETATS-UNIS

Vieux Nice map, p.110

Musée des Beaux-Arts

RUE LOUIS DE COPPET

ESPACE MAGNAN

RUE DE FRANCE

PROMENADE DES ANGLAIS

To Musée d'Art Naïf Anatole Jakovsky & Airport

Baie des Anges

N

500 metres
500 yards

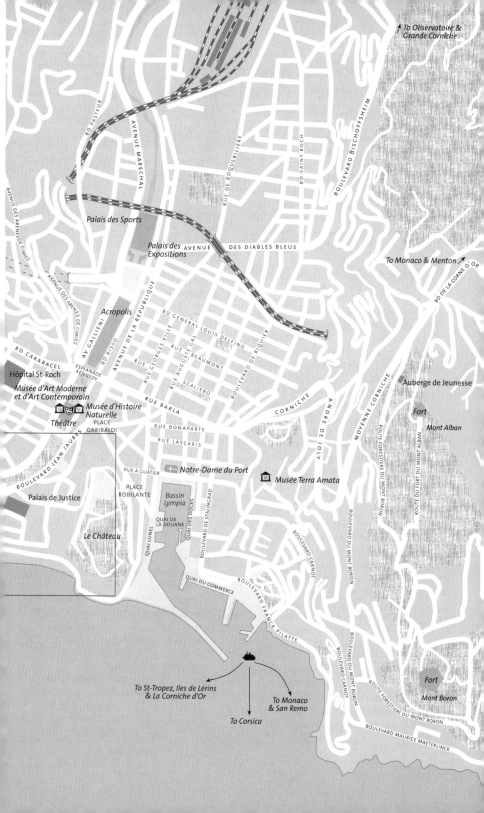

To Observatoire &
Grande Corniche

BD PASTEUR

AVENUE MARECHAL

RUE DE ROQUEBILLERE

RUE SAINT ROCH

BD SAINT ROCH

BOULEVARD BISCHOFFSHEIM

Palais des Sports

Palais des
Expositions

AVENUE   DES   DIABLES BLEUS

To Monaco & Menton

BD DE LA CORNE D'OR

AVENUE DES ARENES DE CIMIEZ

AVENUE DES ARENES DE CIMIEZ

Acropolis

BD GENERAL LOUIS DELFINO

AV GALLIENI

BD RISSO

AVENUE DE LA REPUBLIQUE

RUE GEORGES VILLE

RUE AUGUSTE GAL

RUE SCALIERO

RUE BEAUMONT

BOULEVARD DE RIQUIER

CORNICHE

MOYENNE CORNICHE

ROUTE FORESTIERE DU MONT BORON

ROUTE DU FORT DU MONT ALBAN

Auberge de Jeunesse

Fort
Mont Alban

BD CARABACEL

Hôpital St-Roch

Musée d'Art Moderne
et d'Art Contemporain

ESPLANADE
KENNEDY

RUE BARLA

ANDRE DE JOLY

Musée d'Histoire
Naturelle

Théâtre

PLACE
GARIBALDI

RUE BONAPARTE

RUE LASCARIS

BOULEVARD JEAN JAURES

RUE A GUATIER

Notre-Dame du Port

Musée Terra Amata

Palais de Justice

PLACE
ROBILANTE

Bassin
Lympia

QUAI DES DOCKS

BOULEVARD STALINGRAD

BOULEVARD CARNOT

BOULEVARD DU MONT BORON

BOULEVARD DU MONT BORON

Le Château

QUAI LUNEL

QUAI DE
LA DOUANE

QUAI DU COMMERCE

BOULEVARD FRANCK PILATTE

BOULEVARD CARNOT

ROUTE FORESTIERE DU MONT BORON

Fort
Mont Boron

To St-Tropez, Iles de Lérins
& La Corniche d'Or

To Monaco
& San Remo

To Corsica

BOULEVARD MAURICE MAETERLINCK

Getting There and Around

By Air

Nice's large, modern **Aéroport Nice-Côte d'Azur** is the second busiest airport in France, served by a wide variety of flights from around the world. For information on all the day's flights and changes for the next day, call **t** 08 36 69 55 55, *www.nice aeroport.fr.*

Flights to or from Paris go via Aérogare 2; all others go through Aérogare 1. Airline numbers include Air France, **t** 0 820 820 820; British Airways, **t** 0 825 825 400; Delta, **t** 0 800 354 080; EasyJet, **t** 0 825 082 508; and Virgin Express, **t** 0 821 230 202.

By **helicopter,** between Nice and St-Tropez, try Nice Hélicoptères, **t** 04 93 21 34 32; between Nice and Monaco, Héli Air Monaco, **t** (00 377) 92 05 00 50 or Héli France, **t** 04 89 98 51 51.

Buses run every 12mins between the airport and Nice coach station in the centre of town, stopping along the Promenade des Anglais and at Place Masséna, while bus no.23 provides links with the train station every 30mins. The bus ticket to town will also give you a free onward connection on another city bus (only valid for 1 hour). After 10pm the yellow airport bus will detour to the train station if you ask the driver, or else stops in Place Masséna, from where the night buses depart. Bus info: Aérogare 1, **t** 04 93 21 30 83, Aérogare 2, **t** 04 93 21 43 84.

There are also several buses daily from the airport to Antibes, Cannes, Grasse, Marseille, Menton, Monaco, St-Raphaël and St-Tropez.

By Train

Nice's **main train station**, **t** 08 92 35 35 35 for SNCF information, is in Av Thiers, not far from the centre of town, and has handy left-luggage lockers. Besides Métrazur trains between Ventimiglia and St-Raphaël, Nice has frequent connections to Marseille and is on the TGV route to Paris (6hrs).

The **Gare du Sud**, 4 bis Rue Alfred Binet, **t** 04 97 03 80 80, *www.trainprovence.com*, is served by the little **Train des Pignes** (so called for the pine cones that the crew used to stop to collect for pine nuts). You can take an excursion on this train to Provençal towns

high up the Var valley – a cool and refreshing relief when the beaches are blistering and the shopping malls pall, and you can go as far as Digne for €40 return (4 returns per day).

By Coach

The *gare routière* (coach station) is on the Promenade du Paillon, on the edge of Vieux Nice, **t** 04 93 85 61 81. There are frequent and inexpensive buses to Aix-en-Provence, Eze, Antibes, Cagnes, Cannes, Grasse, Marseille, Menton, Monte-Carlo, St-Raphaël and Vence. Bus no.17 links the coach and train stations.

By Bus

Buses run by the **Sunbus** company are more than nice. Pick up a free *Guide Horaire du Réseau Bus* with maps and schedules at the tourist office or from Sunbus' information centre, 10 Av Félix Faure, **t** 04 93 13 53 13.

Several tourist tickets, called 'Sun Pass', are available from the Sunbus office and at Allô Sunbus, 29 Av Malausséna, **t** 04 93 13 53 13, *www.sunbus.com*, offering limitless rides for one, five or seven days and including one trip to the airport; they save money if you plan to make three or more bus trips a day. A one-day Sun Pass is also on sale on buses.

Buses stop early, around 9pm, and are replaced by four **Noctambus** services, all leaving from Place Masséna, in Vieux Nice, until about 1am; 8pm Sun and hols.

By Taxi

You cannot stop taxis in the street; call at a rank or call **t** 04 93 13 78 78.

By Ferry

In the summer **SNCM Ferryterranée** has frequent sailings to Corsica. For information and reservations, contact the company at the **Gare Maritime**, Quai du Commerce, **t** 04 93 13 66 66 or **t** 04 93 13 66, or contact **Corsica Ferries**, Quai Amiral Infernet, **t** 0 825 09 50 95.

Car, Bicycle and Scooter Hire

Among the cheapest car-hire places is **Rent-a-Car**, opposite the train station on Av Thiers, **t** 04 93 88 69 69, **f** 04 93 88 43 36, or in the town centre, **t** 04 93 37 42 22, **f** 04 93 37 42 20, or just by the airport at 61 Route de Grenoble, **t** 04 93 19 07 07.

International car hire giant **Avis** is at the train station, **t** 04 93 87 90 11, **f** 04 93 87 32 82, or at the airport Aérogare 1, **t** 04 93 21 36 33, and Aérogare 2, **t** 04 93 21 42 80, **f** 04 93 21 43 81. **Hertz** is at the airport, **t** 0825 342 343. Both Avis and Hertz are more expensive.

For bike/moped/scooter hire, a few options include **JML**, 34 Av Auber, **t** 04 93 16 07 00, **f** 04 93 16 07 48; **Nicea Location Rent**,12 Rue de Belgique, **t** 04 93 82 42 71, **f** 04 93 87 76 36; or **Arnaud**, 5 Rue François I er, **t** 04 93 87 88 55.

Tourist Information

Nice: The main office is at 5 Promenade des Anglais, **t** 0892 707 407, **f** 04 92 14 46 49, *info@nicetourisme.com, www.nicetourisme.com; open daily 8–8 in summer, Mon–Sat 9–6 in winter.* There is also a large office on Av Thiers, next to the train station, *open summer daily 8am-8pm; winter daily 8–7.* Other offices include: airport Aérogare 1, *open summer daily 8am–10pm; winter closed Sun;* and Parking Ferber, *open summer daily 8–8 and at Carnival time daily 9–7, winter Mon–Sat 10–5.*

Museum card: A 1/3/7-day **Carte Musées Côte d'Azur** can be obtained for €8/15/25 from any museum ticket desk or the tourist office, or FNAC bookshop (Nice Etoile). There is also a 7-day **Museum Pass** (over a 15-day period) giving unlimited access to all Nice municipal museums only, for €6. On the first and third Sundays of every month, all museums in Nice are free – so everyone goes. Avoid this day unless you are hard up or it is low season.

Sightseeing: Le Grand Tour is a 1½-hour sight-seeing tour in an open-deck bus with commentary in five languages (individual handsets). It runs all year round; tickets available from the bus driver, **t** 04 92 29 17 00. In summer, a dinky little white tourist train leaves from the Promenade des Anglais hourly on a trip through the old town and up to the château.

Main post office: 23 Av Thiers, near the station, **t** 04 93 82 65 22, and at Place Wilson, **t** 04 93 13 64 10, with *poste restante. Open Mon–Fri 8–7, Sat 8–12.*

Internet cafés: These are few and far between on the Côte d'Azur, so make the most of the facilities in Nice, most of which are off Av Jean Médecin: **Thenetgate**, 40 Rue de la Buffa, **t** 04 97 03 27 97, *www.thenetgate.it*; **3.W.O.**, 32 Rue Assalit, **t** 04 93 80 51 12; **Webstore**, 12 Rue de Russie, **t** 04 93 87 87 99.

Medical: Casualty wards: **Hôpital St-Roch**, 5 Rue Pierre Dévoluy and Rue Delille (adults only), **t** 04 92 03 33 75; **Children's Emergency**: **Hôpital Lenval**, 57 Av de la Californie, **t** 04 92 03 03. All-night pharmacies: 7 Rue Masséna, **t** 04 93 87 78 94, and 66 Av Jean Médecin, **t** 04 93 62 54 44. Twenty-four-hour doctor service: **Nice-Médecins**, **t** 04 93 52 42 42, and **SOS Médecins**, **t** 08 01 85 01 01. Emergency dental care: **t** 04 93 80 77 77.

Market Days
See **Markets** below.

Festivals

Nice is famous for its **Carnival** in the two weeks before Lent, first mentioned in the 13th century. It died out in the 1800s, and subsequent attempts to revive it to amuse the tourists only succeeded in 1873, when the painters Alexis and Gustav-Adolf Mossa took over the show. They initiated a burlesque royal cortège to escort the figure of King Carnival, *Sa Majesté Carnaval*, down Av Jean Médecin, accompanied by comical *grosses têtes* – masqueraders with giant papier-mâché heads. During the subsequent parades, dances and battles of flowers and sweets, King Carnival reigns in Place Masséna, only to be immolated on the night of Mardi Gras to the explosive barrage of fireworks.

In spring there is the **Fête des Mai**, probably Nice's oldest festival, with balls, folk dancing and picnics, and stalls around town selling lily-of-the-valley, a traditional gift.

On **Fête de la Mer** (St Peter's Day) in June, fishermen burn a boat down on the Plage des Ponchettes (opposite the old town) in honour of their patron saint, and on 14th July **Bastille Day** is marked by a huge firework show on the

Promenade des Anglais and a Grand Ball on Place Masséna.

The third week of July sees the excellent **Festival de Jazz** in the Jardins Publics de Cimiez (*www.nicejazzfest.com*), and the **Nuits Musicales de Nice**, (t 04 93 81 01 23) in the cloisters of the monastery in Cimiez.

From the end of July through August there is **Musicalia**, a series of world music concerts and, every two years, in September, there is the **Nice Military Tattoo**, which brings over 1,000 military musicians to parade through the streets. Finally, on the Sunday after Christmas, revellers head off shivering for the **Bain de Noël** – a skinny-dip in the Med.

For information on all the festivals, call t 0892 707 407.

Shopping

The warren of streets that is **Vieux Nice** is the most attractive place to shop, and here you can browse for art, local crafts, clothes and glorious specialist foods (*fruits confits*, hand-made pasta) at the markets and local shops.

The **pedestrian zone** around Place Masséna has scores of designer clothes shops and cheap boutiques, while on **Av Jean Médecin** you'll find Nice's biggest department store, Galeries Lafayette, as well as Nice Etoile, a shopping centre with useful shops like the bookshop FNAC, t 04 92 17 77 77 (which also sells tickets to concerts and other events) and the Body Shop. Up near Av Thiers, Phox sells the cheapest camera film in Nice. The perfumery chain Sephora have a branch in Nice Etoile which sells its own range of stylish black-packaged toiletries.

Food and Drink

Auer, 7 Rue St-François-de-Paule, t 04 93 85 77 98. This Niçois landmark, in fabulously rococo premises, has been in the same family since 1820, making the region's most celebrated confectionery, jams and 'the only true' *fruits confits* for almost two centuries.

Confiserie Florian, 14 Quai Papacino, t 04 93 55 43 50. Offers free guided tours of the factory for its acclaimed sweets, with tastings.

Cave Bianchi, 7 Rue de la Terrasse, t 04 93 85 65 79. This 15th-century wine cellar benefits

from an ancient underground spring that humidifies it, and has been run by the same wine-growing family for generations. No plonk here, just the cream of France's finest wines, including the best of the Provençal region, and the charming owner will be delighted to share his extraordinary knowledge. The back room hosts modern art exhibitions.

Huilerie des Caracoles, 5 Rue St-François-de-Paule. Has a wide range of regional food products, gifts and toiletries.

Maison de l'Olive, 18 Rue Pairolière. Boasts a tempting display of olives and olive oil.

Boutique Alziari, 14 Rue St-François-de-Paule, t 04 93 85 76 92. Many Niçois gourmets swear that the olives and olive oil from this 70-year-old shop are the best in the world (there would doubtless be many prepared to contest this claim).

Souvenirs

Among the tack in the souvenir shops you may find the occasional gem, such as big straw shopping baskets with enough room for a small dog and several baguettes.

La Maïoun, 1 Rue du Marché. A good selection.

Aux Parfums de Grasse, 10 Rue Saint-Gaétan.

Santons

La Couquetou, 8 Rue St-François-de-Paule.

Les Poupées Yolande, 4 Rue A. Gautier. A fine selection of fabrics, too.

Provençal Fabrics

Les Olivades, 8 Av de Verdun.

Antiques

For antiques, try the shops around Rue Antoine-Gautier (by the port) or the antiques market, **Village Ségurane**, at 28 Rue Catherine-Ségurane. *Open daily except Sun*.

Other Shops

BaoBab, 10 Rue du Marché. For pretty wares made from wicker and straw – from bags to hats, furniture and table goods.

Papeterie Rontani, 5 Rue Alexandre Mari. An old-fashioned, wood-floored shop which sells delicious paper of every sort, and maps a-plenty.

The Cat's Whiskers, 30 Rue Lamartine, near the train station. English language books, including second-hand.

Markets

Cours Saleya: Food and flower market – a wonderful array of herbs and every fruit you can imagine crystallized and glowing – *open Tues–Sat 6am–5.30pm, Sun 8–12*. The fresh produce is replaced by stalls selling old books, clothes and bric-a-brac on Monday. Arts and crafts appear on Wednesday afternoon and paintings on Sunday afternoons. During the summer, there is also an evening craft market daily here until midnight.

Place du Général de Gaulle: Colourful and authentically local food market, north of the train station, daily.

Place Robilante: Flea market near the port, Tues–Sat 10–6.

Place St-François: Fish market, Tues–Sun mornings.

Sports and Activities

Beaches

Many of the **paying beaches** along the Baie des Anges offer some kind of sport, including parascending, volleyball, jet-skiing and even bouncy castles. The beaches charge by the day and work out expensive if you only want a few hours' escape from the pebbles and local teenagers hogging the water's edge.

Various companies around the port offer **diving** and **snorkelling**, including:

Club Nautique de Nice, 50 Boulevard Franck Pilatte, t 04 93 89 39 78.

Locaventure, t 04 93 56 14 67. For kayaks, canoes and inflatable boats.

Nausicaa, 45 Rue de Roquebillière, t 04 93 89 04 13.

Other Activities

Golf de Nice, 698 Route de Grenoble, t 04 93 29 82 00. Golf course. *Open summer 8am–9pm, winter 8.30–6.30.*

Visiobulle, Embarcadère Courbet, Juan-les-Pins, t 04 92 00 42 30. In summer, go out into the bay in a glass-bottomed boat to revel in the submarine coastal life. 4–7 trips a day.

Trans Côte d'Azur, t 04 92 00 42 30. Offers one-hour boat tours from the Promenade des Anglais to Villefranche-sur-Mer.

To find out about **skiing** in the mountains, visit the Comité Régional de Ski, 234 Route de Grenoble, t 04 93 18 17 18.

Where to Stay

Nice ☒ 06000

Nice is packed with hotels of all categories, and in the summer most are just as tightly packed inside.

If you arrive without a reservation, the tourist office next to the station will book rooms for free. Get there by 10am in the summer, or risk joining the nightly slumber parties on the beach or in front of the station, where you'll encounter giant cockroaches from hell. Come instead in the off season, when many of the best hotels offer the kind of rates the French would call *très intéressant*.

Luxury–Very Expensive

****Negresco, 37 Promenade des Anglais, t 04 93 16 64 00 f 04 93 88 35 68, *direction@hotel-negresco-nice.com, www. hotel-negresco-nice.com*. Nice has luxury grand hotels galore, but for panache none can top the fabulous green-domed Negresco. A national historic monument, it was designed for Romanian hotelier Henri Negresco (who started his career as a Gypsy violinist) by Edouard Niermans, architect of the Moulin Rouge and the Folies Bergères. The one hotel in Nice where a Grand Duke would still feel at home, and the last independent luxury hotel on the coast, its 150 chambers and apartments have all been redecorated with Edwardian furnishings and paintings by the likes of Picasso and Léger. Don't miss the Salon Royal, lit by a Baccarat chandelier made for the Tsar and recently topped off with a contemporary sculpture by Niki de Saint Phalle, *Nana Jaune*.

****Château des Ollières, 39 Av des Baumettes, t 04 92 15 77 99, f 04 92 15 77 98, *chateaudesollieres@chateaudesollieres.com, www.chateaudesollieres.com*. A flamboyant pink, orange and yellow crenellated folly which once belonged to a Russian prince. Now it has only eight heavenly rooms, including a suite in the tower, with antique furnishings, eccentric stained glass and four-poster beds.

****Palais Maeterlinck**, 30 Bd Maeterlink, t 04 92 00 72 00, f 04 92 04 18 10, info@palais-maeterlinck.com, www.palais-maeterlinck.com. A fastidiously refurbished pink and white palace set in beautiful gardens without so much as a pine needle out of place, with a highly acclaimed restaurant, **Le Mélisande** (*expensive*), which serves wonderfully creative Mediterranean dishes on a precipitous terrace.

****La Pérouse**, 11 Quai Rauba-Capeu, t 04 93 62 34 63, f 04 93 62 59 41, lp@hroy.com. Halfway up the Colline du Château, high above the hubbub, with a swimming pool and good restaurant (*moderate*). *Restaurant closed mid-Sept–mid-Mar.*

Expensive

***Windsor**, 11 Rue Dalpozzo, between the station and Promenade des Anglais, t 04 93 88 59 35, f 04 93 88 94 57, contact@hotelwindsornice.com. In the middle of a tropical garden, featuring a pool, an English-style pub, a Turkish-style hammam, a Thai-style sitting room and frescoes in the rooms.

***Vendôme**, 26 Rue Pastorelli, t 04 93 62 00 77, f 04 93 13 40 78, contact@vendome-hotel-nice.com. In the centre of town, with prettily renovated, air-conditioned rooms, a superb stairway and a refreshingly peaceful garden to escape the hubbub.

***Hôtel du Petit Palais**, 10 Av Emile Bieckert, t 04 93 62 19 11, f 04 93 62 53 60, petitpalais@provence-riviera.com. A handsome, white Belle Epoque and Relais du Silence mansion, connected with the Best Western chain, where you can enjoy a simple breakfast on the flower-filled terrace. Rooms vary in size, but the best (at the back) look out over the rooftops of the old town to the sea.

Expensive–Moderate

****Le Grimaldi**, 15 Rue Grimaldi, t 04 93 16 00 24, f 04 93 87 00 24, zedde@le-grimaldi.com, www.hotel-grimaldi-nice.cote.azur.fr. A delightful little hotel, which has had an expensive facelift to give it an agreeable charge of Provençal colour. *Closed 10–30 Jan.*

***Hôtel Suisse**, 15 Quai Rauba-Capeu, t 04 92 17 39 00, f 04 93 85 30 75. Beneath the Colline du Château, with fantastic sea views.

Moderate

**Nouvel Hôtel, 19 bis Bd Victor Hugo, t 04 93 87 15 00, f 04 93 16 00 67, info@nouvel-hotel.com, www.nouvel-hotel.com. More reasonable than some of above, this handsome Belle Epoque-style hotel has fairly bland, modern, but comfortable rooms.

For **long-term stays**, there are three comfortable apartment-hotels just off the Promenade des Anglais, run by the Citadines group: www.citadines.com.

Nice Buffa, 21 Rue Meyerbeer, t 0825 010 360, nicebuffa@citadines.com.

Nice Fleurs, 17 Av des Fleurs, t 0825 010 361, nicefleurs@citadines.com.

Nice Promenade, 3–5 Bd F. Grosso, t 0825 010 362, promenade@citadines.com.

Inexpensive

**Trianon, 15 Av Auber, t 04 93 88 30 69, f 04 93 88 11 35. Overlooking the Place Mozart in the musicians' quarter; a white grand piano serves as a reception desk, and the sweeping white staircase and little lift with a wrought-iron grille give it a comfortably old-fashioned feel.

**Comté de Nice, 29 Rue de Dijon, north of the station, t 04 93 88 94 56, f 04 93 87 67 40, hotel.comte.de.nice@wanadoo.fr. Good value rooms and apartments, if little charm and frosty staff. Avoid the noisy first-floor rooms.

**Floride, 52 Bd de Cimiez, t 04 93 53 11 02, f 04 93 81 57 46, info@hotel-floride.fr. In quiet Cimiez, this hotel has lost some of its former charm, but is still an attractive old villa with a shady garden; each blue room has a colour TV and bath. *Closed Jan.*

* **La Belle Meunière**, 21 Av Durante, t 04 93 88 66 15, f 04 93 82 51 76. A stone's throw from the station, this friendly place is a

long-time favourite of budget travellers in Nice, especially students. It even has parking and a little garden for breakfast. *Closed Dec–Jan.*

Les Orangers, 10 bis Av Durante, **t** 04 93 87 51 41, **f** 04 93 82 57 82. A slightly downmarket, though comfy, alternative to the Belle Meunière. Most rooms have a balcony.

Auberge de Jeunesse, Rte Forestière du Mont-Alban, **t** 04 93 89 23 64, **f** 04 92 04 03 10, *www.fuaj.org.* The youth hostel is 4km east of town (*bus no.14 to the auberge; beware that the last bus leaves at 7.45pm*). *Closed Dec–mid-Jan.*

Relais International de la Jeunesse Clairvallon, 26 Av Scudéri, **t** 04 93 81 27 63, **f** 04 93 53 35 88, *CLAJPACA@cote-dazur.com.* Even further afield (*bus no.15*), although it has the added plus of a pool.

Eating Out

Although now in a solidly French-speaking corner of the Hexagon, Nice's cuisine still has a heavy Ligurian accent, with a fondness for seafood, olive oil and tiny black olives, chickpeas, fresh basil and pine nuts.

A typical first course consists of pasta (ravioli filled with seafood or artichoke hearts, or served with a walnut sauce), gnocchi or, in the winter, *soupe au pistou*, a hearty soup of courgettes, tomatoes, beans, potatoes, onions and *vermicelli*, served with *pistou*, a sauce based on basil, pine nuts and garlic.

Other Niçois favourites are *bourride*, a fish soup served with *aïoli* that many prefer to the more elaborate Marseille *bouillabaisse*, and teeny-tiny fish called *poutines*, by law only fished out of the sea between Beaulieu and Cagnes, which local cooks fry in omelettes or pile on top of pasta.

Another popular first course is the world-famous *salade niçoise*, which even in Nice is made in as many 'true and genuine' ways as *bouillabaisse* in Marseille – with quartered tomatoes, capers, black olives, spring onions, anchovies or tuna, green beans, and with or without hard-boiled eggs and potatoes.

Main courses are often from the sea: grilled fish with herbs or, more of an acquired taste,

estocaficada, wind-dried cod and guts, stewed in *eau-de-vie*, with potatoes, garlic, onions and peppers. Favourite side dishes include ratatouille (another famous dish of Niçois origin) or boiled Swiss chard (*blette*) in vinaigrette. Snacks include *socca* (a sort of flat chickpea pancake), *pan bagnat*, *pissaladière* (onion tart) and stuffed vegetables or courgette flowers (*farcies*).

Very Expensive–Expensive

Le Chantecler, 37 Promenade des Anglais, **t** 04 93 16 64 00, *direction@hotel-negresco. com.* Gastronomic Nice is dominated by the Belle Epoque magnificence of this restaurant, which snuggles into the opulent arms of the Negresco. Here, chef Alain Llorca, successor to Dominique Le Stanc, has succeeded in seducing the Niçois with his own fabulous versions of Chantecler favourites, such as sea bass served with tomatoes and pesto, roast pigeon with *foie gras* ravioli, and desserts like the exotic liquorice-flavoured meringue with raspberry sorbet. *Closed mid-Nov–mid-Dec.*

Expensive

Chez Simon, above Nice in St-Antoine de Ginestière, 275 Rue St-Antoine de Ginestière, **t** 04 93 86 51 62. Chefs here have been serving up local specialities – *beignets* stuffed with fresh sardines or courgettes, a melting fricassée of wild *cèpe* mushrooms in parsley – for four generations. Rustic wood carvings, a profusion of flowers and a lovely terrace in summer. *Closed Mon except for pre-booked groups, and Mar.*

Auberge de Théo, 52 Av Cap de Croix, Cimiez, **t** 04 93 81 26 19. Genuine Italian pizzas, salads with *mesclun*, and Venetian *tiramisù* for dessert. Can be *moderate. Closed Sun eve in winter and Mon all year, Christmas, New Year, and three weeks from 20 Aug.*

Chez Fanny, 407 Rte de Bellet **t** 04 93 37 87 07. Worth a trip just outside the town centre for fresh and fun cuisine. *Closed Mon and Tues, two weeks in Aug and beginning of Jan.*

Moderate

The best restaurant-hunting territory in this price range is Vieux Nice and, especially for fresh fish, around Place Garibaldi and the port.

Don Camillo, 5 Rue des Ponchettes, t 04 93 85 67 95. *vianostephane@wanadoo.fr*. Opened by a former pupil of Maximin and Paul Ducasse, and already celebrated for its home-made ravioli filled with Swiss chard *en daube*, and for its desserts. *Closed Sun, and Mon lunch*.

La Mérenda, 4 Rue de la Terrasse, near the Opera House and the Cours Saleya. Join the glitterati enjoying Dominique le Stanc's celebrated idiosyncratic Niçois cuisine at this tiny bistro. *Closed weekends and school holidays. No credit cards*.

Villa d'Este, 6 Rue Masséna, t 04 93 82 47 77, www.*boccaccio.com*. The best Italian restaurant in Nice, over three floors with *trompe l'œil* Italianate décor in pretty pastel colours, attentive service and top-notch pasta. The plate of *antipasti* is a gastronomic feast. Get there early (12 noon) for lunch and watch it fill up!

Le Pizzaïolo, 4 bis Rue du Pont-Vieux, t 04 93 92 24 79. Specialities include beef *carpaccio*, *farcis niçois* and local seafood. The surroundings may be humble, but the food ain't bad and the staff are very good-natured. *Closed Tues*.

L'Indyana, 11 Rue Delaye, t 04 93 80 67 69. World cuisine in trendy, minimalist surroundings. *Closed Sun lunch and Mon lunch*.

La Zucca Magica, 4 bis Quai Papacino, t 04 93 56 25 27. By far the best and friendliest vegetarian restaurant in Nice, with imaginative dishes that draw customers from the entire Riviera coast. Book ahead. *Closed Sun and Mon*.

Le Safari, 1 Cours Saleya t 04 93 80 18 44. Enjoying a privileged spot overlooking the water, this is one of the few restaurants on this street where the waiters don't need to entice passers-by. With wood-fired oven and terrace.

Jo L'Ecailler-Café de Turin, 5 Place Garibaldi, t 04 93 85 30 37, *cafedeturin@club-internet.fr*. Try this 19th-century café for a drink or a snack or some of the best oysters in town. *Open until 11 in summer*.

Moderate–Cheap

Voyageur Nissart, 19 Rue d'Alsace-Lorraine, t 04 93 82 19 60, *www.voyageur-nissart,com*. This is the best place near the station, with two wide-ranging menus. *Closed Mon and part of Aug*.

Hippopotamus, on the corner of Avenue Félix Faure and Place Masséna,t 04 93 92 42 77. A very central restaurant, part of a chain, but it fills up reassuringly with locals at lunchtime. Choose from several set menus or a lunchtime special of *plat du jour* and coffee.

Cheap

Chez René Socca, 2 Rue Miralheti, t 04 93 92 05 73. A self-service café offering *socca*, *pissaladière*, pizza by the slice and much more. *Closed Mon and Nov*.

Spaghettissimo, 3 Cours Saleya, t 04 93 80 95 07. For Italian, try this small and cheap eatery.

Pâtisserie Cappa, 7–9 Place Garibaldi, t 04 93 62 30 83. An elegant and exclusive *pâtisserie* serving afternoon tea. *Closed mid-Sept–mid-Oct*.

Fenocchio, Place Rossetti, t 04 93 80 72 52, 6 Place de la Poissonerie, t 04 93 62 88 80, 36 Rue Centrale, t 04 93 62 88 82. It's hard to beat the 99 varieties of ice cream here: lavender cream, jasmine sorbet and the bitterest chocolate imaginable make a heavenly combination.

Entertainment and Nightlife

You can find out what's happening in Nice in the daily *Nice-Matin*, although it's not much good for anything else except lining the canary's cage.

Other sources covering the entire Côte are *7 jours/7 nuits*, distributed free in the tourist offices, the *Semaine des Spectacles*, which appears Wednesdays on the news-stands, and Riviera Radio, the coast's English-language station, which broadcasts out of Monaco on 106.3 and 106.5 FM.

Local news, hours of religious services in English and more are in the monthly English-language *Blue Coast Magazine*, a glossy look at life on the Riviera, distributed in newsagents and English bookshops.

If you need a **babysitter**, try the babysitting service **Allô Mary Poppins** at 35 Rue Pastorelli, t 04 93 62 61 30, or **Association Family Jeunesse**, 4 Rue Masséna, t 04 93 82 28 22.

Film

The movie-goer in Nice is spoilt for choice:

Pathé Paris, 54 Av J. Médecin, t 0892 68 22 88.

Pathé Masséna, 31 Av Jean Médecin, t 0892 68 22 88.

UGC Variétés, 7 Bd Victor Hugo, t 0836 68 68 32.

Rialto, 4 Rue de Rivoli, t 0836 68 08 41. For films in their original language.

Nouveau Mercury, 16 Place Garibaldi, t 0836 68 81 06.

Cinémathèque de Nice, 3 Esplanade Kennedy, t 04 92 04 06 66.

Theatre, Opera and Music

Opéra de Nice, 4–6 Rue St-François-de-Paule, information t 04 93 13 98 53, reservations t 04 92 17 40 00. Puts on operas, concerts and recitals at various locations.

Acropolis, 1 Esplanade Kennedy, t 04 93 92 83 00.

Fondation Sophia-Antipolis, at Hôtel Westminster, 27 Promenade des Anglais, t 04 92 14 86 86. Organizes morning classical music concerts.

Fondation Kosma, Conservatoire de Nice, 24 Bd de Cimiez, t 04 92 26 72 20. Free classical music on Mondays at 6pm.

Concerts are also held at:

Musée Chagall, Av du Docteur Ménard, west of Bd de Cimiez, t 04 93 53 87 20 (*Sept–May*).

Musée des Beaux-Arts, 33 Av des Baumettes, t 04 92 15 28 28 (*Oct–May, once a month; adm*).

Musée d'Art Moderne et d'Art Contemporain, t 04 93 62 61 62, *www.mamac-nice.org*. Music, from ancient to avant-garde, and art videos.

CEDAC de Cimiez, 49 Av de la Marne, t 04 93 53 85 95. Big-league musicians and dancers, and jazz musicians twice a month.

Forum Nice Nord, 10 Bd Comte de Falicon, just off the A8 at Nice-Nord, t 04 93 84 24 37. A major venue for modern dance in July, and world music.

Théâtre de Verdure, Jardin Albert Ier. From April onwards rock, jazz and other outdoor concerts.

There are several small theatres in Vieux Nice that stage imaginative productions and some concerts:

Théâtre du Cours, 5 Rue de la Poissonnerie, t 04 93 80 12 67.

Théâtre de La Semeuse, 21 Rue Saint-Joseph, t 04 93 92 85 08.

For Molière and other classics:

Théâtre de l'Alphabet, 10 Bd Carabacel, t 04 93 13 08 88.

Théâtre de Nice, by the Contemporary Art Museum, t 04 93 13 90 90.

Clubs and Bars

Nice's nightlife is divided between expensive clubs, bland hotel piano bars and the livelier bars and clubs of Vieux Nice, which come and go like ships in the night. Some of the most jumping joints are the expat havens in Vieux Nice.

Cherry's Café, 35 Quai des Etats-Unis, t 04 93 13 85 45. Well-known gay club/restaurant.

Wayne's, 15 Rue de la Préfecture, t 04 93 13 46 99, *www.waynes.fr*. A British-owned pub and restaurant with live music every night. *Open 12pm–12.30am, reservations obligatory at weekends*).

Scarlett O'Hara's, 6 Rue Rossetti, t 04 93 80 43 22. Fiddlers fiddle in this Irish pub till 2am.

De Klomp, 6 Rue Mascoïnat, near Place Rossetti, t 04 93 92 42 85. A Dutch joint with live jazz, single malt, and a hedonistic atmosphere (not for teetotallers or anti-smokers).

Jonathan's, Rue de la Loge, t 04 93 62 57 62 Food lit by candles, and 1970s-inspired 'live' music hosted by Jonathan himself: wait long enough and he might treat you to his Rolf Harris impersonation.

Plasma Café, 11 Rue Offenbach, t 04 93 16 17 32. Juice bar and sushi bar, with Internet access. *Open till 2am.*

Other places may be fun,
But when all is said and done,
It's so much nicer in Nice.
        Sandy Wilson, *The Boyfriend*

The funny thing is, it's true. Superbly set on nothing less than the Bay of Angels, Nice has a gleam and sparkle in its eye like no other city in France: only a sourpuss could resist its lively old town squeezed between promontory and sea, its markets blazing with colour, the glittering tiled domes and creamy *pâtisserie* of 19th-century hotels and villas, the immaculate exotic gardens, and the famous voluptuous curve of the beach and the palm-lined Promenade des Anglais. It is the one town on the Côte that doesn't seem to need tourists, the one that stays open through the winter. You could go for the food alone, a seductive mix of the best of France and Italy; you haven't really had ravioli until you tuck into a plate in Nice, where it was invented.

The capital of the *département* of Alpes-Maritimes and France's fifth largest city (pop. 400,000), Nice is also the most visited after Paris. The English have been coming for well over 200 years, back when 'Nizza la Bella' still belonged to Savoy, and Russian Tsarinas and Grand Dukes fleeing winter's blasts weren't far behind. The presence of so many rich, idle foreigners who stayed for months at a time formed a large part of the city's character: corruption, reactionary politics and organized crime are part of the famous *salade niçoise*, along with a high density of apricot poodles and frown-faced poodle ladies. But Nice also has a university, big culture (over 20 museums and counting), the brilliant light that Matisse loved, and a genuine identity as a city – rough, affable and informal.

History

Nice was a hot spot even 400,000 years ago, when the hunters who tracked mammoths and learned how to make fires to grill their prey frequented the caves of Terra Amata. The Ligurians, around 1000 BC, were the first to move in permanently, constructing their *oppida* at the mouth of the Paillon river and on the hill overlooking the valley. Greeks from Marseille founded a commercial colony near the seaside *oppidum* and named it Nikaïa after an obscure military victory, or perhaps after the nymph Nikaïa. Beset by Ligurian pirates, the Nikaïans asked the Romans for aid. The Romans duly came, and stayed, but preferred to live near the hilltop *oppidum* because it was closer to the Via Julia Augusta. They named this town Cemenelum (modern Cimiez) and made it the capital of the province of Alpes Maritimae. By the 3rd century AD, Cemenelum had 20,000 inhabitants, all quickly going soft amid swimming pools and central heating.

However, by the 6th century, luxury-loving Cemenelum had collapsed with the rest of the Roman Empire, while Greek Nikaïa struggled on and regrouped itself in the 10th century around a cathedral. By the 1340s, with a population of 13,000, Nice was the third city in Provence after Marseille and Arles. The city's coat of arms had an eagle's head on it, looking to the left, to France. The Black Death and civil wars of the period soon cut it down to size, and in 1388 the city's leaders voted to hitch their wagon to a brighter star than Louis d'Anjou and pledged allegiance to Amadeus, Count of Savoy. The eagle was redrawn to look right, towards Italy.

The Savoys fortified Nice and it grew rich trading with Italy. It had its own little Renaissance, thanks to Ludovico Brea and the other members of the mid 15th-century Ecole Niçoise – Antoine and François Bréa, Jean Mirailhet and Jacques Durandi – noted for their uncluttered, simple compositions and firm sense of line. The 17th century saw the expansion of Nice outside its medieval walls, and in 1696 and 1705 came the first of several French interludes that interrupted Savoy rule – interludes that Louis XIV took advantage of to blow up the city's fortifications.

Cold Brits and Absorption into the Mystic Hexagon

Although relations remained sour with France, the Savoys became firm allies with the English, and by 1755 the first trickle of milords had begun to discover the sunny charms of a Riviera winter. Doctor and novelist Tobias Smollett spent a year in Nice in 1763, and in his singularly grouchy *Travels through France and Italy* (1766) did what Peter Mayle has since done for Provence: made the Côte, because of, or in spite of, its quaint local characters, irresistible to the British. Even though it took at least two weeks to reach Nice from Calais, by 1787 there were enough Brits wintering here to support a casino (then a fashionable Venetian novelty), an English theatre, an estate agent and a newspaper. In 1830, when a frost killed all the orange trees, the English community raised funds to give the unemployed a job: building a seafront promenade along the Baie des Anges, known to this day as the Promenade des Anglais. Part of its purpose was to keep English girls away from the riffraff, or more particularly the

Vin de Bellet AOC

'The wine-merchants of Nice brew a balderdash, and even mix it with pigeon's dung and quick-lime,' wrote Tobias Smollett. But they never dared to mess with Vin de Bellet, the rare and costly elixir produced in the steep, sun-soaked hills west of Nice.

The vineyards owe their special quality to the alternating currents of sea and mountain air and to their original varieties of red grapes: braquet, folle noire and négrette de Nice, all of which combine to create a noble wine with a bouquet of wild cherry that can be aged up to 30 years. The rosés, from the same grapes, are one of the best accompaniments to *loup*, the most delicate of Mediterranean fish. Vin de Bellet blanc, reminiscent of Chablis, is a blend of rolle, spagnou, roussan and mayorquin. Only 1,200 hectolitres are produced each year, and most of it never gets much further than the cellars of the Riviera's top restaurants.

Alternatively, pick up a bottle of your own by ringing ahead and following the Route de Bellet north of Rue de France (parallel to the Promenade des Anglais) to St-Roman-de-Bellet and the 18th-century **Château de Bellet**, t 04 93 37 81 57. The second estate, **Château de Crémat**, at 442 Chemin de Crémat, t 04 92 15 12 15, is a fantasy castle, built in 1850 in a pseudo-medieval style called *style troubadour*.

Niçois – along with their money, the British brought attitudes so arrogant that, as early as the 1780s, sensitive locals left town each winter to avoid being humiliated by their visitors.

In 1860, as Napoléon III's reward for promising to help Vittorio Emanuele II of Savoy create the future kingdom of Italy, a secret treaty was signed ceding Nice and Savoy to France. To keep up appearances, a plebiscite was held. Vittorio Emanuele encouraged his subjects to vote for union with France, but even more encouraging was the presence of the French army marching through Nice, and French agents bullying the majority Italian-speaking population. The final result (24,449 pro-France to 160 against) stinks even to this day. But the railway arrived shortly after and Nice settled down to its chosen vocation as the winter haven for Europe's élite. Sumptuous neo-Moorish-Gothic-Baroque follies were built to house some 20,000 wintering Britons and Russians by 1890; 20 years later the numbers of foreigners had increased to over 150,000.

Queen Victoria preferred the suburb of Cimiez; her haemophiliac son, Prince Leopold, introduced croquet to Nice before dying after slipping on the marble floor in the casino. The city even made an early bid to become the Hollywood of France, when the Victorine film studios were founded in 1911 and later purchased in 1925 by Rex Ingram, who brought in a constant parade of big stars and writers. During the war, Marcel Carné used them to film *Les Visiteurs du soir* and *Les Enfants du Paradis*.

Nice Today

Since the 1930s, many of Nice's hotels and villas have been converted into furnished flats, while the concrete mixers of destiny march further and further west and up the valleys. The Victorine studios are still there, but plagued by noise from jets landing at Nice airport, and now used mostly for television commercials. Wealthy, politically conservative retirees help support an equally right-wing *rentier* population. All this money floating about has attracted the corruption and underworld activities of the *milieu*, previously associated only with Marseille.

For decades Nice was ruled as the personal fiefdom of the right-wing Médecin family, who pretend to be related to the Medicis, although it doesn't look as if their dynasty will endure quite as long. Jean Médecin reigned as mayor from 1928 until 1965, and was succeeded by his flamboyant son Jacques, cook, crook and anti-Semitic hoster of a National Front congress no other city would have, the man who twinned Nice with Cape Town when apartheid was still on the books. Jacques Médecin had an edifice-complex nearly the size of Mitterrand's in Paris, filling Nice with huge new public complexes, and his cronies had their fingers in all kinds of pies – most spectacularly Albert Spaggiari, who got hold of the plans of Nice's sewer system in order to steal 46 million francs from the Société Générale, and was captured by the police only to escape the courtroom by jumping out of the window on to a waiting motorcycle and making a clean getaway. In 1990 the slow, grinding wheels of French justice began to catch up with Médecin, when it was discovered, among other things, that money for the Nice Opéra was being diverted into the mayor's bank account. He took to his heels and hid out in Punta del Este, Uruguay, until 1995 when he was extradited to France, where he died in 1998. His sister Geneviève narrowly defeated the National Front candidate in local government elections and took his old seat on the Conseil Général of the Alpes-Maritimes *département*; his successor as mayor of Nice, Honoré Bailet, had some troubles of his own, especially in the form of a son-in-law accused of murdering a local restaurant owner. In 1995 he was ousted by Jacques Peyrat, a friend of Le Pen and former FN member who has found a home in President Chirac's UMP. Under Peyrat, many of the FN's ideas have been implemented into city policy. He gave Médecin a funeral in Nice's city hall when the old crook died, and now there is a proposal to name a boulevard after him. Médecin's critics, noting the billion euros of debt he left the city, along with the millions he stole for himself, have proposed Rue Mozart for the honour – the street that leads to the city's prison.

Vieux Nice

Dismissed as a dangerous slum in the 1970s, Nice's Vieille Ville, a piquant quarter east of Place Masséna, is easily the trendiest part of Nice, brimful of cafés, bistros, nightclubs, designer boutiques and galleries. And the population, once poor and ethnically mixed, is now more than half French and upwardly mobile. But the shock of the new is mitigated by the tenacity of the old grandmotherly underwear, paint and stationery shops, and no-name working-men's bars, which have so far refused to budge. Picasso liked to walk here because it reminded him of Barcelona's Barrì Chino.

'Vieux' in Vieux Nice means Genoese seaside Baroque – tall, steep *palazzi*, many with opulent 17th- and 18th-century portals and windows, turning the narrow streets and steps below into chasms that suddenly open up into tiny squares, each with its chapel. To this day, the old Niçois are among the most religious people on the coast, and still join the confraternities of Penitents: lay organizations dedicated to public demonstrations of penitence, founded in Italy in the 14th century during the great Franciscan and Dominican revivals. During the Baroque period, when a number of their chapels sprang up, the brotherhoods, distinguishable by the colours of their hooded cloaks, became increasingly involved in a kind of early social work: the White Penitents cared for the sick, the Black Penitents for the dying and the Blue Penitents looked after orphans. Of the city's original seven confraternities, four still survive, all of which reside in this neighbourhood.

At its eastern end, the Vieille Ville is closed by the **Colline du Château**, the ancient acropolis of Nikaïa and site of the 10th- to 12th-century town and the cathedral of Ste-Marie. Of the latter, a few ruins remain – the Savoyards demolished it to make way for their citadel, which was in turn blown up by the congenitally suspicious Sun King, Louis XIV. Greek and Ligurian remains have been discovered beneath it. The daily cannon blast, heard across Nice at noon, booms out from up here; the tradition was begun by an Englishman, Sir Thomas Coventry, who got fed up with eating his meals at irregular hours and put a stop to it with the precisely timed firing of the cannon. You can either walk up the steps to the château, take a mini-train (€6) from the

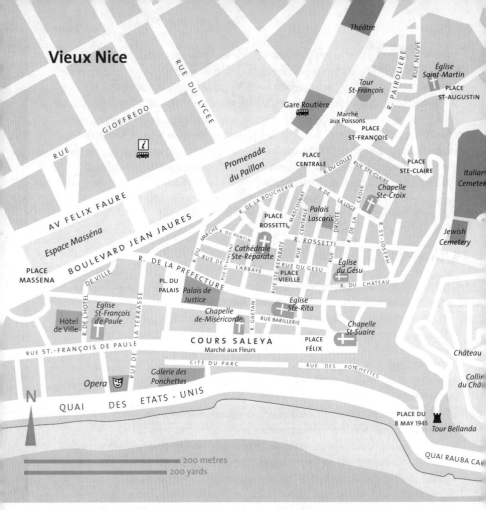

Promenade des Anglais which gives you a little tour through the flower market and around the Vieille Ville on the way, or pay a few *sous* to take the lift at the east end of the Quai des Etats-Unis, near **Tour Bellanda**, where Berlioz composed his *King Lear Overture*. From the belvedere by the artificial cascade, the real boats down below don't look much bigger than the models in the museum, and the shimmering, tiled, glazed rooftops of Nice curl into the distance around the Baie des Anges.

Among the gardens at the top of the hill are two cemeteries: in the grandiose Italian one you can find the tombs of Garibaldi's mother and of Mercedes Jellinek, who gained immortality in 1902 when her father chose her name for a new line of Daimlers. More sombrely, a reminder of the Holocaust stands just inside the gates of the Jewish cemetery: a pair of urns containing ashes from the incinerators of the concentration camps and a phial of human fat collected by the Nazis to make soap.

If you descend by way of the east flank of the hill, down Montée Eberlé and Rue Catherine-Ségurane (where Nietzsche lived between 1883 and 1888), you'll end up in the wide, yellow, arcaded 18th-century **Place Garibaldi,** named after its statue of the hero of Italy's unification, who was born near the port in 1806. Once named the 'Piazza Vittorio' by the war-weary Niçois in an attempt to curry favour with King Victor Amédée III of Sardinia, it was built to both cow and flatter Sardinian sovereigns arriving from Turin. The arcades on the eastern side are now full of buzzy, lively fish restaurants. The Blue Penitents have their sombre neoclassical chapel of **St-Sépulcre** (1782) on this square, while just around the corner, facing the esplanade at 60 bis Bd Risso, is the **Muséum Barla d'Histoire Naturelle** (*t 04 97 13 46 80, www.mhnn.org; open Tues–Sun 10–6; free guided tours Wed at 3pm*), where you can ponder, among other things, a rather unusual 19th-century collection of 7,000 painted plaster mushrooms.

South of Place Garibaldi off Rue Neuve is one of the city's oldest parish churches, **St-Martin-St-Augustin,** where a monk named Martin Luther said a mass during his momentous pilgrimage to Rome in 1514. The dim interior was Baroqued in the 17th century; its treasures include a fine *Pietà* (*c.* 1500) attributed to Ludovico Brea, a tatty photocopy of Garibaldi's baptismal certificate, and a cross marking the spot where the galleys of Aladin Barbarossa sent a Turkish cannonball through the walls in the siege of 1543. Opposite the entrance to the church is a plaque to Catherine Ségurane, Amazonian heroine of that same siege, wild-eyed and wielding her washing-paddle (*see p.114*).

Further west, Rue Pairolière leads into 'Babazouck', the curious nickname for the heart of Vieux Nice, and **Place St-François**, once the terminus for the '*courreras*' (stage coaches) and now the setting for a raucous and pungent fish market which takes place every morning except Monday around a pretty fountain of entwined fish. The sad-eyed building in the northeast corner is the once-grand Palais Communal, built in 1580, now the Job Centre. South of the square, another cannonball from the Turkish siege is lodged in the plaster of a house on the corner of Rue de la Loge and Rue Droite. Continuing southeast, the **Chapelle Sainte-Croix** in Rue de la Croix is the headquarters of the Pénitents Blancs, the oldest confraternity (founded in 1306) and the most popular, perhaps because they were still into public self-flagellation in the 1750s.

Back on Rue Droite, at No.15, the **Palais Lascaris** (*t 04 93 62 72 40; open Wed–Mon 10–12 and 2–6; closed Tues and hols*) is a grand 1648 Genoese-style mansion with wrought-iron and marble balconies, hard to pick out on this dim little street. It was built for Jean-Baptiste Lascaris-Vintimille, the Duke of Savoy's brigadier, and was later sold to the counts of Peille. But its aristocratic days were numbered and it became a military garrison during the Revolution, before succumbing to the fate of most of the town's palaces and being converted into flats. It sagged into sorry disrepair until 1942, when the town bought and handsomely restored it. The ground floor contains a reconstructed pharmacy of 1738, with some of the original Delftware fittings; a fantastically opulent staircase lined with classical statues leads up to the *étage noble*, where guests would be received with suitable pomp. It is saturated with elaborate Genoese 'quadratura' (architectural *trompe-l'œil*) frescoes, Flemish tapestries, ornate woodwork and a 1578 Italian precursor of the pianoforte. The ceremonial chamber is divided with an ornamental stucco wall, supported by caryatids and atlantes and liberally sprinkled with cherubs and gilt embellishments.

The museum also holds temporary exhibitions, usually with a local or regional flavour, and has recently taken on another role as the Centre du Patrimoine, dedicated to the upkeep and restoration of the city's treasures. Craftspeople are often invited to demonstrate their arts, and there are special events for children held between 2 and 4pm most days. Baroque concerts are sometimes held here in summer; ask at the tourist information office for details of these events and activities.

Contemporary exhibitions take place at several galleries on the Rue Droite and at the corner of Rue Droite and Rue de la Loge, at the **Galerie Renoir** (*t 04 93 13 40 46; open Tues–Sat 10.30–1 and 2–6; closed Sun and Mon*). Also down Rue Droite is the **Eglise de Gésu**, groaning with fake marble and oppressively ornate stucco and *putti*; it was once owned by the Jesuits, who revamped it between 1612 and 1642, producing a terrifying monument to the art of the Counter-Reformation, much envied and emulated by smaller regional chapels. The fishermen's festival (held in June) starts with a choral mass sung here, followed by a procession down to the Plage des Ponchettes (opposite the Cours Saleya), where a boat is burned in honour of St Pierre, patron saint of fishermen.

Take Rue Rossetti west to the cafés of pretty Place Rossetti, dominated by Nice's 17th-century **Cathédrale Ste-Réparate**, designed by Jean-André Guibert and crowned with a joyful dome and lantern of glazed tiles in emerald bands. The interior is extraordinary, even by the theatrical standards of Niçois Baroque: a plague of cherubim and seraphim infest the fanciful festoons around the cornice, and the chapels, each owned by an affluent family or corporation responsible for their decoration and upkeep, vie with each other in glitzy magnificence. The uncorrupted body of the young saint Réparate, a 15-year-old virgin martyred in Caesarea in the 4th century, arrived in Nice in a boat of flowers towed by a pair of angels (hence Baie des Anges).

This same Réparate was the first patron saint of Florence before the city adopted intermediaries with greater heavenly clout, and here, too, in Nice, the young virgin is currently losing a popularity contest with St Rita of Cascia, whose appeal is more contemporary. At the 17th-century **Chapelle de l'Annonciation**, which everyone calls Eglise de Sainte Rita, at 1 Rue de la Poissonnerie, her altar gets nearly all the business, possibly because her speciality is unhappy middle-aged housewives – Rita herself was burdened in the 14th century with a rotten husband, ungrateful children and a smelly sore on her forehead that just wouldn't heal.

Rita's compatriot, Paganini, who died nearby in 1840 at 23 Rue de la Préfecture, had his share of troubles too, but most of them were posthumous. Ste-Réparate's bishop was convinced that the sounds Paganini made on his violin could only have been produced by the devil incarnate (the maestro liked to startle the neighbours by making it howl like a tomcat) and refused him a Christian burial. He even wanted to toss Paganini's body into the Paillon. In the end, however, the poor dead fiddler was shunted to Cannes, and then on to Genoa and Parma, where he was finally buried in 1896. Since then he has received the acclaim he deserved.

Cours Saleya

After the dark lanes of Vieux Nice, the sun pops back into the sky over Cours Saleya, an elongated little gem of urban planning set back just a couple of blocks from the sea, where bars and restaurants line up along the famous outdoor market, overflowing with flowers and sumptuous food displays worthy of the Riviera's gourmet vortex. Matisse lived for 17 years amid all the vivid colours that he loved, just off the Cours Saleya at **No.1 Place Charles Félix**; the brightly painted house is still there, although there is no commemorative plaque. The Cours is closed at one end by the 17th-century **Ancien Sénat**, or the old Court of Appeal, and **St-Suaire**, home of the Red Penitents, who assisted pilgrims.

But the principal focal point of the Cours is the Black Penitents' **Chapelle de la Miséricorde**, designed in 1740 by Bernardo Vittone, a disciple of Turin's extraordinary Baroque architects Guarino Guarini and Juvarra. Inside (*unfortunately locked*), it's all virtuoso Baroque geometry, a gold and stucco confection with vertiginous *trompe-l'œil* paintings in the vault. A fine, early Renaissance *Polyptique de la Miséricorde* (1430) by Jean Mirailhet hangs in the sacristy, painted for the confraternity, whose mission was to assure the dead a dignified burial.

A double row of one-storey buildings separates Cours Saleya from the Quai des Etats-Unis, where you'll find, if you look very hard, the elusive **Galerie des Ponchettes** (*t 04 93 62 31 24; open Tues–Sun 10–6; closed Mon*). These used to contain the exuberant paintings of Raoul Dufy and the Niçois father-and-son team Alexis and Gustav-Adolf Mossa. Although, confusingly, their names are still over the door, the paintings have been moved to the Musée des Beaux-Arts (Jules Chéret) (*see pp.117–18*) to brighten up an otherwise wan collection, leaving the Galerie des Ponchettes with little to do but display lacklustre temporary exhibitions. Stairs lead up to the roofs of the slim row of 19th-century houses which edge the seafront, where gentlefolk used promenade before the construction of the Promenade des Anglais.

The Port, Terra Amata and Hilltop Follies

To the east, Quai des Etats-Unis circles around the wind-punched hill of the Château, where it's known as Quai Rauba-Capéu ('hat thief'), before it meets placid **Bassin Lympia**, the departure point for ferries to Corsica. The great columned edifice set into the flank of the hill is the **Monument aux Morts**, which commemorates the 4,000 Niçois who died during the First World War.

The **Place de l'Ile de Beauté**, lined with 18th- and 19th-century buildings, opens out onto the port and the imposing neoclassical **church of Notre-Dame**, topped with a statue of the Virgin Mary, where sailors still pray for full nets and a safe return.

Chekhov used to saunter along the jetty opposite, where old men still sit with their papers and pooches to muse away the mornings.

East of here is the **Musée de Terra Amata** (*25 Bd Carnot, t 04 93 55 59 93, www. musee-terra-amata.org, bus nos.32 and 14 from central Nice; open Tues–Sun 10–6; closed Mon and holidays*), rather improbably tucked into a typical Niçois *résidence*, complete with stripy blue and white awnings. Underneath, the museum comprises a cave holding one of the world's oldest 'households', a pebble-walled wind-shelter built by elephant-hunters 400 millennia ago, which was discovered in 1966. A fascinating set of models, bones and tools helps evoke life in Nice in theprehistoric era. Nor had things changed radically 200,000 years later, judging by the palaeolithic relics left in the nearby **Grotte du Lazaret** (*for information or to arrange visits, call t 04 92 00 17 37; you need to be a scholar or in a group of at least 10 people to visit, although there are also some open days every year*).

Boulevard Carnot (the Basse Corniche) continues east out of the port, up past some extravagant Belle Epoque villas gazing loftily out of the suburban sprawl, culminating in eccentricity in the **Château de l'Anglais** (*private residence, no entry*) – pink, turreted, and then crenellated for good measure. Built in 1858 by Colonel Robert Smith, a military engineer in India, the result weds English Perpendicular with mock-Mogul Palace to produce one of the best follies on the Riviera. Behind this rise the forested slopes of **Mont Boron**; off Route Forestière du Mont Boron, the magnificent **Sentier Bellevue** meanders to the top, which is capped by a fort of 1880.

A far more delightful piece of military architecture, **Fort Alban**, is just off the Moyenne Corniche, above the youth hostel (take bus no.14 to Chemin du Fort or, if you're driving, turn right off Rte Forestière du Mont Boron, on to Chemin du Fort du Mont Alban). Built in 1570, it bristles with four toy turrets roofed with glazed Niçois tiles. The guards could see all the way to Menton.

To the north, off the Grande Corniche, is an elegant **Observatoire** (*Boulevard de l'Observatoire, t 04 92 00 30 11, www.obs-nice.fr, bus no.74 from Boulevard Pierre Sola; tours Sat at 3pm; adm*), designed in part by Charles Garnier, with a dome by Gustave Eiffel. The 59ft lens was once one of the most powerful in the world: 2,000 stars have been discovered here, which visitors can see for themselves at the annual Festival of Space and Stars in August.

Up the Paillon

In the old days, Nice's laundresses plied their trade in the torrential waters of the Paillon, and were scrubbing away in 1543 when Ottoman pirates, under the dread admiral Barbarossa, attacked. Hearing the racket on the walls, an exceptionally beefy laundress named Catherine Ségurane rushed to the highest tower, and with her hollering, enthusiasm and skilful wielding of her washerwoman's paddle galvanized the defence. When she saw that Nice was about to fall in spite of her best efforts, she climbed a ladder, bent over and dropped her drawers. The historians write that the Turks took one look at the biggest backside they had ever seen and, fearing further revelations, retreated in complete confusion and raised anchor. The often dangerous Paillon was canalized and began to vanish under the pavements in the 1830s; today it secretly flows below some of Nice's proudest showcases and prettiest gardens.

Nearest the sea, Jardin Albert Iᵉʳ is the site of the open-air **Théâtre de Verdure**, and the garden also hosts free music concerts in the summer, while upstream, as it were, vast ochre-painted **Place Masséna** is generously endowed with flowerbeds and wisteria-shaded benches for Nice's sun-loving retirees. Marshal Masséna, the son of a humble Niçois wine merchant, was born in 1758, and ran away to sea. Canny and corrupt, he leapt on whichever bandwagon offered the highest price, managing to fight consecutively for Nation, Emperor and King, and scooping up a lucrative collection of titles from duke to prince during his perfidious career. Further up, the Promenade du Paillon is dominated by the dingy hanging gardens of the bus station/ multistorey car park, a mini-Babylon with an unsavoury reputation for small-time vice – vice that pales in the face of ex-Mayor Jacques Médecin's pair of dreadnoughts looming beyond.

The first of these, reached by sets of Aztec temple steps, is Nice's answer to the Pompidou Centre in Paris: the 282-million-franc **Théâtre de Nice** (*t 04 93 13 90 90*) and the marble-coated **Musée d'Art Moderne et d'Art Contemporain** (*t 04 93 62 61 62; open 10–6; closed Mon and hols; adm*). Inauspiciously inaugurated in June 1990, as the public revelations of Médecin's sins and fury over his anti-Semitism reached a pitch, the ceremony was boycotted by the Niçois art community, who convinced France's culture minister Jack Lang to stay away as well.

If you overlook the fact that the roof was already leaking four months after it was finished, or that the museum had to be closed for major repairs in December 1991 when large cracks were discovered in its foundations, the building – four concrete towers, linked by glass walkways that seem to smile and frown and afford pleasant views over the city – is an admirable setting for the works of Christo, Niki de Saint-Phalle, Warhol, Dine, Oldenburg, Rauschenberg, and other influential figures of the 1960s and '70s.

The first floor has been given over to temporary exhibitions, but the primary focus is on the artists of the 'Second School of Nice'. The most prominent of these, Yves Klein, gets a whole gallery to himself on the second floor, with paintings and sculptures like *Blue Victory of Samothrace* and *Blue Venus* electrified by his hallmark shade of 'IKB' blue. The epic *Wall of Fire* looms down from the museum's roof terraces. The New Realist concoctions of Martial Raysse, César, Arman and Swiss-born Jean Tinguely – plastic consumer junk, broken machinery, musical intruments and exploding suicide machines – and the irreverent neo-Dadaist works by the Fluxus artists like Ben, Serge III and Fillious, spoof not only society, but also the artificial, rarefied and wordy world of contemporary art – especially the push-button fun house called *Ben's Hut*. American Pop Art, which was unleashed on the other side of the Atlantic at about the same time as the New Realists were causing chaos on the French art scene, is fearsomely represented with a number of major works, from Tom Wesselman's tripartite *Still Life* – a rotary telephone, a light switch and a burning cigarette – to Jim Dine's *Hard Hearts* and Andy Warhol's serigraphed dollar signs.

The view up the Paillon is blocked by Médecin's 1985 congress and art centre and *cinémathèque* at no.1 Esplanade Kennedy, **Acropolis** (**t** 04 92 04 06 66) – a gruesome megalithic bunker of concrete slabs and smoked glass, with perfectly synchronized jet fountains spurting up soullessly at the entrance. No design could be more diametrically opposed (stylistically and philosophically) to the acropolis in Athens, and the mass of guitars in Arman's *Music Power* at the entrance hardly redeems it. Beyond this are more mastodons: a **Palais des Expositions**, which looks more like an enormous tractor shed, and the **Palais des Sports**.

West of Place Masséna and the Promenade des Anglais

The Paillon neatly divides Vieux Nice from the boom city of 19th-century tourism, full of ornate, debonair apartments, immaculate squares and hotels. Important streets fan out from Place Masséna and the adjacent Jardin Albert Ier: Nice's main shopping street, **Av Jean Médecin**, leads up to the train station (the shops become progressively shabbier and the pavement fills up with hawkers and traders selling fresh fish, meat and vegetables to crocodiles of hard-eyed old ladies); **Rue Masséna** is the centre of a lively pedestrian-only restaurant and shopping zone; and the fabled, palm-lined **Promenade des Anglais** is still aglitter through the fumes of the traffic, which is usually as strangled as poor Isadora Duncan was when her scarf caught in the wheel of her Bugatti here in 1927. The pebble beach is crowded day and night in summer, when parties spontaneously erupt among the illegal but tolerated campers.

Visitors from the opposite end of the economic spectrum check into the fabled pink Belle Epoque **Hôtel Negresco** at No.37 (*see* p.101), vintage 1906, and now they can again roll snake eyes in the 1929 **Palais de la Méditerranée**, a masterpiece of French Art Deco built by Frank Jay Gould. In 1960 it was the most profitable casino in France; by 1979 it was bankrupt, thanks to the machinations of Jacques Médecin and his cronies who favoured the rival **Casino Ruhl**, all brash ferro-concrete and neon. The Ruhl reopened next to the Negresco in spring 1995, in spite of the unsolved case of the disappearance and presumed murder of Agnès Le Roux, daughter of Renée Le Roux, at the time the main owner of the Palais de la Méditerranée. Five months before disappearing in 1977, Agnès had secretly sold her share in the family business to Jean-Dominique Fratoni, owner of the Ruhl and a man with mafia and Médecin links. Meanwhile the Palais de la Méditerranée was destined for the wrecking-ball, but the speculators gave in to the protests at the last minute, on condition that the building had all its original innards removed. For years it stood, a desolate façade, increasingly a blot on the landscape and a sad reminder of glory days long past; but now it has finally been redeveloped into a new luxury hotel with a car park beneath and business spaces, plus a revamped casino.

Another gem clinging to the Promenade among the new buildings is at No.139, a flowery Art Nouveau-style villa of 1910 built by a Finnish engineer.

On the other side of the Negresco is the garden of the **Palais Masséna** (*t 04 93 88 11 34; closed for restoration, expected to reopen 2006, gardens still open*). Built in the Empire style in 1901 for Prince Victor Masséna, the grandson of Napoleon's marshal, it was left to Nice on condition that it become a *musée d'art et d'histoire*. At the entrance, a solemn statue of Napoleon tarted up in a toga sets the tone for the ground-floor salons – heavy and pompous and stylistically co-ordinated from ceiling stucco to chair leg. The atmosphere lightens upstairs with a pair of fine retables from the 1450s by Jacques Durandi, panels from a polyptych attributed to Ludovico Brea, ceramics, armour, and a curious 16th-century Flemish painting, the *Vierge à la fleur* with a fly in the flower, 'a symbol of death and vanity'.

The top floor displays statues of the *Ten Incarnations of Vishnu*, Spanish earrings, views of Nice and rooms dedicated to home-town boys Garibaldi and the cruel and wicked Marshal Masséna, the military genius Napoleon called '*l'enfant gâté de la victoire*', whose appetite for atrocities was matched only by his greedy plundering. Then there's the obligatory Napoleana: a billiard-ball from St Helena and Josephine's bed, with a big 'N' on the coverlet.

Fine and Naïf Arts, and a Russian Cathedral

A brisk 10-minute walk from the Masséna museum, or bus no.38 from the bus station (right to the door), takes you to the handsome 1876 villa built by a Ukranian princess, enlarged by an American millionaire and now home of the **Musée des Beaux-Arts (Jules Chéret)** (*33 Av des Baumettes, t 04 92 15 28 28, www.musee-beaux-arts-nice.org; open 10–6; closed Mon; adm*).

With the Matisses and Chagalls in Nice's other museums, the Musée des Beaux Arts is left with little more than the 'old masters of the 19th century' – a euphemism for tired, flabby academic paintings and portraits of Madame This and Madame That, a *Portrait of an Old Man* by Fragonard and works by Carle Van Loo, a native of Nice.

There are a few other meaty paintings: a 1615 *David* attributed to Tanzio da Varallo, a Lombard follower of Caravaggio; a self-portrait by eccentric young Russian aristocrat Marie Bashkirtseff; and a roomful of her contemporary Kees Van Dongen, including his entertaining 1927 *Tango of the Archangel*, which perhaps more than any painting evokes the Roaring Twenties on the Riviera – even the archangel, in his dinner jacket, is wearing high heels.

Picasso also gets a look-in in this room with a small collection of the ceramic pieces he created while at Vallauris (*see p.149*). Recently, the works of a much cheerier soul, Raoul Dufy, who spent his latter years in Nice producing colourful 'cafe-society' art, have been brought in to brighten the place up a bit. The handful of his early Fauve works are the most compelling, especially the remarkable 1908 *Bateaux à l'Estaque*. One room is devoted to Félix Ziem, and another to the Belle Epoque's favourite lithographist, Jules Chéret, who introduced colour posters to France in 1866, most of them decorated with his most famous creation, a pert-nosed doll-woman who became known as 'La Chérette', caught in swirling pastel tornadoes of silly *putti*. His oil portraits decorate the walls of the upper staircase, among them portraits of Baron and Baroness Vitta, who collected Chéret's work and and then unloaded it onto the museum which now bears his name.

The florid output of Nice's carnival duo, father and son Alexis and Gustav-Adolf Mossa, has also found a home here. The collection features landscapes by Alexis, a native of Nice, who is better known for his fabulous designs for pageants and floats for the Nice Carnival, which he dragged out of obscurity in 1860. His son, Gustav-Adolf Mossa (1883–1971), painted exquisite mytho-morbid Symbolist works between 1903 and 1917, and then just stopped. He also followed in his father's footsteps and created several frothy, exuberant carnival floats.

To the west, the founder of the Monte-Carlo casino built the strawberry pink Château de Ste-Hélène, which had a succession of owners before being bought and redesigned by the perfume magnate, Coty, in 1922. It now houses the **Musée d'Art Naïf Anatole Jakovsky** (*Av de Fabron, t 04 93 71 78 33, bus nos.8, 9, 10, 11,11B, 12, 34, stop Fabron; open Wed–Mon 10–6; closed Tues; adm*), an offshoot of the Pompidou Centre in Paris, with a collection formed of around 600 paintings spanning the 18th to the 20th centuries, donated by Jakovsky, a tireless promoter of naïve art who became known as '*le Pape des Naïfs*'. Jakovsky met the American painter Gertrude O'Brady when they were both dabbling in Bohemianism in Paris's Latin Quarter; several of her stylized, nostalgic portraits figure here, among them one of Jakovsky himself, pipe in hand, in his plush Saint-Germain apartment. The Yugoslavs are especially well represented, with an enthusiasm for the genre that perhaps in some way counterbalances the unsolvable, nightmarish imbroglio of their politics. But even among the scenes of jolly village fêtes and fairs the surreal is never far, especially in *The Clock* by Jules Lefranc, and in the funny *Sodom and Gomorrah*, where the columns go flying every which way.

Near the airport you may already have noticed the mega-greenhouse of **Parc Floral Phœnix** (*405 Promenade des Anglais, t 04 92 29 77 00, bus nos.9, 10, 23, 24, 26; open daily 9–8; in winter only until 5; adm*), a Disneyland for botanists or garden-lovers: its diamond dome supports 2,500 different plants in seven tropical climates. Also in the park is the austere white marble **Musée des Arts Asiatiques**, designed by Japanese architect Kenzo Tange, 'a swan that floats on the water of a peaceful lake' (*t 04 92 29 37 00, www.arts-asiatiques.com; open May–mid-Oct Wed–Mon 10–6; mid-Oct–April Wed–Mon 10–5; closed Tues and hols; adm*). The central building is based on geometrical forms of the square and circle, symbolizing the earth and the sky, reflected in a shallow pool. Four cubes spread out over the lake contain the permanent collection: Chinese jade and bronze and Japanese lacquer and ceramics lead into Cambodian sculpture and Indian textiles. An elliptical glass staircase curves up inside to the rotunda, the 'spiritual sphere' where the up-to-the-minute multimedia displays and exhibitions with a spiritual theme round up an original collection in an original and beautiful building. Tea ceremonies – the meditative ritual of Japan or the earthier tastings of Chinese *Gong Fu Cha* (*call to reserve a place*) – take place on Thusdays and

Sundays in a Japanese pavilion decorated with delicate ceramics and reached by a small footbridge.

In 1865 the young Tsarevich Nicholas was brought south to Nice and, like so many consumptives who arrived in search of health, he met the grim reaper instead. The luxurious villa where he died was demolished to construct a Byzantine mortuary chapel and the great **Cathédrale Orthodoxe Russe St-Nicolas,** known as the Eglise Russe, located a few blocks west of the train station, just off Boulevard Gambetta (*Av Nicolas II,* **t** *04 93 96 88 02, bus nos.7 or 15; open daily except Sun am and services, summer 9–12 and 2.30–6; spring and autumn 9.15–12 and 2–5.30; winter 9.30–12 and 2.30–5; no shorts or sleeveless shirts; adm*), and modelled on the five-domed church of Jaroslav near Moscow.

Tsar Nicolas II was paying the bills, so the architects bought only the best – bricks from Germany, crosses from Italy and hand-finished Russian mosaics. The design may be strictly Russian, but the colours are sublimely Mediterranean: pink Italian granite, blue terracotta tiling from Florence and palest white stone from La Turbie, its five onion domes shining with a colourful coating of glazed Niçois tiles. It was completed only five years before the Bolshevik Revolution. The interior, splayed like a Greek cross, is a sparkling wonderland of gilded frescoes, woodwork and icons, many of which were donated by the immigrants fleeing Russia in 1917.

North of here (take bus no.5 – it is quite a hike) is the **Prieuré du Vieux Logis** (*59 Av Saint-Barthélémy,* **t** *04 93 84 44 74; open Wed, Thurs, Sat and first Sun of month 3–5*), an old Niçois villa which was remodelled in the 1930s to hold a collection of religious art from the 14th to the 17th centuries gathered by an obsessive forager and Dominican monk, Alfred Lemerre. The pride of the collection is a 15th-century Flemish *Pietà*, but the real delight is the mellow old building itself, with its balustraded balconies and terraces and its dreamy little garden.

The Ministry of Culture sponsors the activities in the nearby 18th-century **Villa Arson** (*20 Av Stephen Liégeard,* **t** *04 92 07 73 73, www.villa-arson.org; bus nos. 4, 7; open summer 2–7; winter 2–6; closed Tues*) – not the headquarters of a pyromaniac club, but a centre for contemporary art, with students, studios for working artists, exhibitions, a library and, thankfully, a café, surrounded by 'brutalistic' buildings designed in the late 1960s by Michel Marot, and concrete terraces decorated with pebbles.

Cimiez: Chagall, Matisse and Roman Ruins

On the low hills northwest of the Paillon, where wealthy Romans lived the good life in Cemenelum, modern Niçois do the same in Cimiez, a luxurious 19th-century suburb dotted with the grand hotels of yesteryear, now genteel apartment buildings.

Bus no.15 from the train station will take you to the main attractions, beginning with the **Musée National Message Biblique Marc Chagall**, at the foot of Cimiez hill (*Av du Docteur Ménard, west of Bd de Cimiez,* **t** *04 93 53 87 20; open Oct–June Wed–Mon 10–5; July–Sept Wed–Mon 10–6; closed Tues; adm*). While Picasso, Matisse and Cocteau were all busy painting and restoring chapels (*see* pp.149, 135 and 180 respectively) dotted along the Riviera, Chagall was embarking on an integrated cycle of 17 paintings based on stories from the Old Testament. He hoped to hang them in one of a cluster of small deconsecrated 17th-century chapels just outside Vence, but, despite a lot of municipal trumpeting, nothing came of the plan. Eventually, the writer André Malraux, a friend of Chagall and erstwhile Minister of Culture, suggested that a new museum be built to hold the series, and work began in Nice. The low, unassuming building is set among a suitably biblical garden of olives and cypresses. Constructed of pale stone from La Turbie, it was dedicated in 1973 on Chagall's 86th birthday.

Temporary exhibitions, usually with a spiritual or biblical theme, take place in the niched gallery to the left of the entrance hall; to the right is the zigzag central hall, designed to allow the paintings to be viewed both as a group and individually, where Chagall's *Biblical Message Cycle* begins. The paintings are divided into three sections: *Genesis, Exodus* and the *Songs of Solomon*. They have been hung, as Chagall requested, chromatically rather than chronologically, and are paired to complement each other's rich glowing emeralds, cobalts and magentas. They leap with Chagall's idiosyncratic symbolism – tumbling flowers, fish, angels and rabbits. Best of all, in an adjacent, octagonal gallery, is the rapturous red, red, red series of the *Song of Songs* – dedicated to Vava, Chagall's wife. A small room branches off for contemplation of an exterior mosaic of *The Prophet Elijah* (Elijah soaring across the sky in his chariot of fire, surrounded by signs of the zodiac), set over a pond in order to create a kaleido-scopic, shimmering reflection.

Cimiez owed much of its original cachet to Queen Victoria, and she's gratefully remembered with a statue in front of her favourite lodging, the **Hôtel Excelsior Regina Palace** on Av Regina, off Av Reine Victoria, an unbridled effusion of ballrooms, loggias and bowed galleries. After the Second World War, the same hotel became headquarters for Henri Matisse, who died here in 1954, leaving the city a priceless collection of his works, displayed in the nearby **Musée Matisse** (*164 Av des Arènes-de-Cimiez, t 04 93 81 08 08, www.musee-matisse-nice.org, take bus nos.15, 17, 20 or 22 from the Promenade des Anglais or Av Jean-Médecin; open Wed–Mon 10–6; closed Tues and some holidays; adm*), a late 17th-century Genoese villa with a *trompe l'œil* façade, set in the olive-studded Parc des Arènes. The archaeological museum also used to call the Villa d'Arènes home, but was shunted to the other side of the Roman ruins in 1993 when a new, glassy modern wing, designed by Jean-François Bodin, was constructed to cope with the burgeoning Matisse collection. The extension, with the main entrance, is partly underground to the right of the villa and can be difficult to find: head down the wide flight of white steps.

Matisse's last work, the gargantuan paper cut-out, *Flowers and Fruit 1952–3*, dominates one whole side of the entrance hall. He first used this technique when designing the costumes and sets for Diaghilev's ballet *Le Chant du rossignol* (*The Nightingale's Song*) in the 1920s and returned to it increasingly, particularly in later life when his hands could no longer comfortably hold a paintbrush. He covered the walls and ceilings of his rooms at the Regina with a multicoloured world of flowers and creatures, chuckling to himself at the reactions of critics: 'Old Matisse, nearing the end of his life, is having a lot of fun cutting up paper,' he imagined them saying. He preferred to think of it as 'drawing with scissors'.

The main collection begins with some of his early bronze sculptures – among them *Le Serf* (1900), the largest of his sculptures, and the deliciously brazen *La Serpentine* (1909). There is also a lyrical series of back studies (*Dos*), an obsession to which he returned again and again throughout his career. The museum has gathered most of his sculptures and drawings, although many of his most famous paintings had already been snapped up by foresighted foreign buyers by the time Matisse really hit the big time in France. Some of his earliest paintings from the 1890s are on view in the main house, accessed by an underground passage. Even in these early works, some colours sing out, especially in the sultry *Odalisque au coffret rouge* (*Odalisque with a Red Box*, 1926); others include the soft, dreamy *Figure endormie* (*Sleeping Figure*), and the most famous painting of the collection, *Nature morte aux grenades* (*Still Life with Pomegranates*, 1947). Among the comprehensive collection of his drawings are studies for book illustrations – Joyce's *Ulysses*, Baudelaire's *Fleurs du Mal* – and a delightful series entitled *Nadia*, with every fluttering shade of the sitter's countenance recorded. There are more cut-outs, including the bright bold *Nu bleu IV* (1952) and *La Vague* (*The Wave*, 1952), plus some amusing photographs of Matisse with his hulking classical statue and a pretty lithograph series of giggling mermaids.

Upstairs, in a room specially lit to recreate the chapel light, are photographs, models and studies for the Chapelle du Rosaire in Vence, which Matisse worked on – often from his wheelchair – until his death, designing everything from the lovely building itself to the wall frescoes, the stained glass windows and the priests' vestments.

Adjacent to the Matisse Museum is the new **Musée Archéologique** (*t 04 93 81 59 57; open Wed–Mon 10–6; closed Tues and some holidays; guided tours Wed and first Sun of every month; adm*), entered through the excavations of Cemenelum (*see* p.106). These include the baths (hot, medium and cold, with the remnants of the heating apparatus still visible), a marble summer pool and the amphitheatre, with seating for 4,000 (unusually small for a population of 20,000, but perhaps the Romans here were too couth for gladiators). In July, Nice's jazz festival takes place here. The museum houses vases, coins, statues, jewels and models of what Cimiez looked like 2,000 years ago, with a fittingly underground section devoted to funereal steles and sarcophagi.

From the archaeological museum, it's a short walk back past the Matisse museum and across the Jardin Public to the **Musée Franciscain, Eglise et Monastère de Cimiez** (*t 04 93 81 00 04; open Wed–Sat and Mon 10–12 and 3–6; closed Tues , Sun and holidays*). The Franciscans have resided here since the 16th century, but their church was heavily restored in 1850, although it still has two beautiful altarpieces by Ludovico Brea: the *Vierge de Piété*, one of his earliest works, and a *Crucifixion* on a gold background, painted later in his life. In the cloister are other, less explicable 17th-century paintings that some scholars think may have alchemical meanings.

There's a museum documenting Franciscan life in Nice from the 13th to the 18th centuries, with frescoes, engravings, sculptures and a reconstruction of the spartan cell of a poor Franciscan monk of the 17th century. Dufy and Matisse are buried in the adjacent cemetery, and there are fine views over the valley of the Paillon from the monastery garden.

West of Nice
Cagnes to Cannes

10

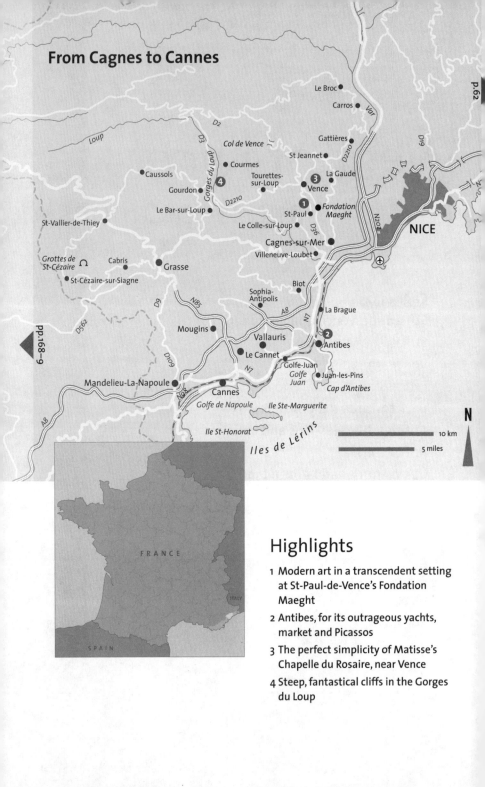

From Cagnes to Cannes

p.62

Le Broc
Carros
Var
Loup
D2
D3
Gorges du Loup
Col de Vence
Gattières
St Jeannet
D2210
D19
Courmes
4
Tourettes-sur-Loup
La Gaude
3
Caussols
Gourdon
D2210
Vence
Le Bar-sur-Loup
St-Paul
1 *Fondation Maeght*
N202
St-Vallier-de-Thiey
Le Colle-sur-Loup
D36
Cagnes-sur-Mer

NICE

Villeneuve-Loubet
Grottes de St-Cézaire
Cabris
Grasse
St-Cézaire-sur-Siagne
Biot
Sophia-Antipolis
D9
N85
A8
N7
La Brague

pp.168-9

D562
Mougins
Vallauris
2 Antibes
D109
Le Cannet
N7
Golfe-Juan
Golfe Juan
Juan-les-Pins
Cap d'Antibes
Mandelieu-La-Napoule
N98
Cannes
Golfe de Napoule
Ile Ste-Marguerite
A8
Ile St-Honorat
Iles de Lérins

N

10 km
5 miles

FRANCE
ITALY
SPAIN

Highlights

1 Modern art in a transcendent setting at St-Paul-de-Vence's Fondation Maeght

2 Antibes, for its outrageous yachts, market and Picassos

3 The perfect simplicity of Matisse's Chapelle du Rosaire, near Vence

4 Steep, fantastical cliffs in the Gorges du Loup

Beaches

Between Nice and Antibes the shore is as rocky as the eastern side of the Côte. Purists should make for Antibes, where the sand starts in earnest. There are two public beaches in Antibes: the best lies south of the town centre. Juan-les-Pins, blessed with fine sand, is also cursed with countless private beach clubs. Public beaches do exist here – try further west towards Golfe-Juan. Cannes has even more snooty beach clubs, but there is a public beach right in front of the Palais des Festivals. Further west towards Mandelieu, the beach is beautifully sandy – and free.

Best Beaches
Antibes: Port, and south of centre on D2559.
Cannes: Palais des Festivals and west to Mandelieu.

The deep Greek of the Mediterranean licked its chops over the edges of our febrile civilization.
Zelda Fitzgerald

The stretch of the Riviera between Nice and Cannes is just about as dense, febrile and excessive as old Europe ever gets – 'one vast honky-tonk,' declared Noel Coward back in 1960: too many cars, villas, theme parks and marinas full of yachts the size of tankers, too many gift shops in the lovely *villages perchés*, too many Parisians and movie stars in Cannes and too many technocrats in Sophia-Antipolis, the 'Silicon Valley of the Riviera'.

The scenery, especially up around the Gorges du Loup, is decidedly excessive, and you can be bedazzled by the perfumes at Grasse and the surplus of art that crowds the coast: Renoir in Cagnes, Léger in Biot, more Matisse in Vence, Picasso in Antibes and Vallauris, and all the contemporary greats up at the dazzling Fondation Maeght. There are so many good restaurants at Mougins that you hardly dare go out.

Cagnes

West of Nice runs the Var river, the wet but politically prickly border between France and Savoy, whose dukes were usually allied to France's rivals – England, Spain or Austria. As bridges over the Var were periodically blown up, for centuries people crossed the water sitting on the shoulders of two strong men. Nowadays, in the maelstrom of traffic and overbuilding, it's hard even to notice the Var at all.

Across the river lies the bloated amoeba of Cagnes, divided into three cells – over-built Cros-de-Cagnes by the sea, with a Hippodrome; Cagnes-sur-Mer, further up, site of Renoir's house, the happiest of all artists' shrines in the south; and medieval Haut-de-Cagnes on the hill, notorious in the 17th and 18th centuries for the indecorous pastimes and the brilliant parties held in its castle before the Revolution – beginning a long tradition of artsy decadence and futility chronicled in Cyril Connolly's *The Rock Pool* (1936), in which Zelda Fitzgerald's carnivorous Greek Mediterranean becomes merely 'the tideless cloaca of the ancient world'.

Cagnes-sur-Mer

Musée Renoir

Av des Colettes, t 04 93 20 61 07; open May–Sept 10–12 and 2–6; Oct and Dec–April 10–12 and 2–5; closed Tues and Nov; adm.

There is only one thing to do in sprawling Cagnes-sur-Mer: from central Place Général de Gaulle follow Av Auguste Renoir up to Chemin des Colettes, to

Getting There and Around

There are **train stations** in both Cagnes-sur-Mer and Cros-de-Cagnes (call the central number, t 08 92 35 35 35), and a continuous service of **minibuses** from Cagnes-sur-Mer station up the steep hill to Haut-de-Cagnes.

There's a massive **underground car park** just outside the village entrance, and restricted parking in the serpentine streets of the old village (beware of parking by the police station at the back of the château). **Buses** from Nice to Vence stop in Cagnes-sur-Mer, where you can also **hire a bike** at Cycles Marcel, 5 Rue Pasqualini, t 04 93 20 64 07.

There is a **free shuttle** from the bus station in Haut-de-Cagnes to the old town. For **taxis**, t 08 02 06 60 00.

Tourist Information

Cagnes-sur-Mer: 6 Bd Maréchal Juin, t 04 93 20 61 64, f 04 93 20 52 63, *info@cagnes-tourisme.com, www.cagnes-tourisme.com. Open July–Aug Mon–Sat 9–7, Sun 9–12 and 3–7; June and Sept Mon–Sat 9–12 and 2–7, Oct–May Mon–Sat 9–12, 2–6.* Also 20 Av des Oliviers, Cros-de-Cagnes, t 04 93 07 67 08, f 04 93 07 61 59. *Open July–Aug daily 9–1 and 3.30–6.30; Sept–June Mon–Sat 9–12.*
Haut-de-Cagnes: Espace Solidor, Place du Château, t 04 92 02 85 05. *Open July–Aug daily 10–1 and 3–6.30; April–June and Sept Wed–Sun 2–6; Oct–Mar Wed–Sun 2–5.*

Market Days

Cagnes-sur-Mer: Fruit and vegetables in the Cité Marchande every morning from Tuesday to Sunday, and in Bd Kennedy on Friday mornings. Bric-a-brac, clothes and almost everything else in the big car park opposite the bus station on Wednesday mornings.
Cros-de-Cagnes: General market on Tuesday and Thursday mornings, Rue des Oliviers.

Where to Stay and Eat

Cagnes-sur-Mer ✉ 06800

★★★★Le Cagnard, Rue Sous-Barri, t 04 93 20 73 21, f 04 93 22 06 39, *resa@le-cagnard.com, www.le-cagnard.com (luxury–very expensive).* The most luxurious choice on this stretch of the coast, with sumptuous comforts discreetly arranged to fit in with the 14th-century architecture. Nearly every room has a private terrace, but the largest and most magical belongs to the hotel's Michelin-starred restaurant (*expensive*), which also has a coffered Renaissance-style ceiling that opens up in summer. Among the delicacies served up beneath it are pigeon stuffed with morels and *foie gras*, and crispy red mullet with garlic and rosemary. *Restaurant closed Nov–mid-Dec, and all day Mon, Tues lunch and Thurs lunch.*
L'Oiseau d'Or, 2 Place du Général de Gaulle, t 04 93 20 80 54, *http://oiseau-d-or-chocolatier.com.* Few of the restaurants in Cagnes-sur-Mer stand out, but the 40 different kinds of fresh chocolates found here do, including *grimaldines*, flavoured with fresh orange juice. *Closed Sun and Mon.*

Villeneuve-Loubet ✉ 06270

Hôtel du Parc, 1 Av de la Libération, t 04 93 20 88 13, f 04 93 20 82 52, *www.hotelduparc villeneuve.com (inexpensive).* A simple place in the old village, with an adequate restaurant (*moderate*) and room for campers. *Restaurant closed Sun eve and Mon.*

Le Domaine des Colettes, where Renoir spent the last 12 years of his life. Stricken with rheumatoid arthritis, Renoir followed his doctor's advice to move to warmer climes and chose Cagnes, where 'one's nose is not stuck in the mountains'. He rented an apartment in the old Maison de la Poste (which has since become the Town Hall) for himself, his wife and the youngest of their three sons, and then, in 1907, purchased an ancient olive grove – originally destined for destruction – with an old stone farm-house. His wife had grander ideas and eventually Renoir built a sturdy bourgeois villa to compensate her for the years of wandering.

'The story of Cagnes and Renoir is a love story,' said his son, the film-maker Jean Renoir. Rejuvenated by the climate, Renoir produced paintings even more sensuous and voluptuous than before, and there's no contrast more poignant than that of the colour-saturated *Les Grandes Baigneuses* (in the Philadelphia Museum of Art) and the photograph in the museum of the painter's hands, so bent and crippled that they're painful even to look at. 'I pay dearly for the pleasure I get from this canvas,' he said of one portrait that he especially liked, painted with brushes strapped to his hands. It was also in Cagnes that Renoir first experimented with sculpture, by proxy, brand-ishing the long stick which he used as an extension of his twisted hands and dictating detailed instructions to a young sculptor, Richard Guino, a Spaniard who had been trained in Paris by Aristide Maillol. It was Maillol who urged Renoir to try sculpture when he first arrived in Cagnes, but he was only able to complete two pieces without aid before his hands failed him: *Buste de Coco* (a bust of his youngest son, Claude, nicknamed Coco) and a little medallion, *Médaillon de Claude*, both on display in the house.

In 1989 the museum's collection of portraits of Renoir by his friends was supple-mented with 10 canvases the master himself painted in Cagnes, among them a later red-hued version of *Les Grandes Baigneuses*, and an affectionate portrait of Claude, with long blond hair, reading. He looks as though butter wouldn't melt in his mouth, but it is thought that Claude was responsible for the naughty handpainted tile depicting a nude on a bidet which is tucked into a discreet corner of the bathroom. The north studio, with his wheelchair and easel, looks as if Renoir might return any minute – even the chicken wire he put over the window to keep out the children's tennis balls is in place. You can wander freely through the venerable olive grove; a quiet, serene and refreshingly unkempt spot with patches of clover and violets. The only drastic change from Renoir's day is the view down to the sea.

Haut-de-Cagnes

Spared the worst of the tourist shops, intricate, medieval Haut-de-Cagnes has become instead the fiefdom of contemporary artists, thanks to the UNESCO-sponsored Festival International de la Peinture. The crenellated **Château-Musée Grimaldi** (*t 04 92 02 47 30; open summer Wed–Mon 10–12 and 2–6, winter 10–12 and 2–5; closed Tues and three weeks Nov; enquire at tourist office for guided tours; adm*) was built by the first Rainier Grimaldi in the 14th century, at a time when there were a hundred excess male Grimaldis prowling the coast, looking for a castle to call home. This particular branch of the family held on to Cagnes until the Revolution; its most famous twig was Henri, a good friend of Louis XIII, who convinced his cousin in Monaco to put himself under the protection of France rather than Spain.

In sharp contrast with the château's dour feudal exterior, a handsome Renaissance inner courtyard is tiered with galleries to provide all the castle's light and air, shaded now by a 200-year-old pepper tree. In the vaulted halls on the ground floor there's a **Musée de l'Olivier**, where among the presses you may find a small machine for pressing coins, not olives, used by the marquis to counterfeit the king's coin (he was arrested in 1710, by Comte d'Artagnan of *Musketeers* fame). Upstairs are Henri Grimaldi's ornate reception rooms, topped by *The Fall of Phaeton* (1624) by the Genoese Giovanni Andrea Carlone, one of those hysterical *trompe-l'œil* ceiling paintings of floating horse stomachs and testicles that the Italians were so fond of. In another room, the **Donation Suzy Solidor** contains paintings donated by the free-living *chanteuse* and star of Parisian cabarets between the wars. Suzy spent the last 25 years of her life in Haut-de-Cagnes, hobnobbing with local artists and bumping up her portrait collection. There were 224 – all of herself. The 40 on display here are each by a different artist – Van Dongen, Dufy, Kisling, Friesz, Cocteau, and so on. On the next floor, the **Musée d'Art Moderne Méditerranéen** is dedicated to a rotating collection of works by the above and other painters who have worked along the coast.

Villeneuve-Loubet and Escoffier

To the southwest of Cagnes, on another hill dominated by another medieval castle, Villeneuve-Loubet is a small village known for its fishing, a visit from François Ier (where he signed a 10-year peace treaty with Charles V in 1538) and Marshal Pétain, hero of the First World War, who was working as a farmer and wine-grower before accepting the summons to govern France from Vichy. The event that really put it on the map, however, was the birth in 1846 of Auguste Escoffier, who went on to become 'the chef of kings and the king of chefs' – the king in question being Edward VII, who encouraged Escoffier and the hotelier César Ritz to move to London, thus making the Savoy and the Carlton citadels of class and cuisine. The Emperor William II gave Escoffier the title of 'Emperor of the World's Kitchens' after gorging on his creations on the imperial steamer, and France awarded him the Legion of Honour. Escoffier's birthplace is now the **Musée Escoffier de l'Art Culinaire** (*3 Rue A. Escoffier,* **t** *04 93 20 80 51, www.fondation-escoffier.org; open summer Tues–Sun 2–7; winter Tues–Sun 2–6; closed Mon, hols and Nov*), but don't come looking for nibbles or scratch-and-sniff exhibits of his creations. Instead there's a 19th-century Provençal kitchen; an auto-graphed photo of soprano Nellie Melba thanking Escoffier for calling his new peach dessert after her (though his asparagus ice-cream never took off); a collection of the chef's radical 'light menus', which seem incredibly elaborate nowadays; and the sugar sculptures Escoffier loved, still prepared by local *pâtissiers* for saccharine competitions that put the kitsch back into kitchen.

There's also a **Musée d'Histoire et d'Art** (*Place de Verdun, t 04 92 02 60 39; open Mon–Fri 10–12 and 2–6, Sat 9.30–12.30*), with a retrospective exhibition depicting life in Villeneuve over the last century; a modest collection of modern sculpture, painting and photographs; and a floor devoted to sobering displays covering the biggest conflicts of the 20th century, from the First World War to the Gulf War.

Villeneuve-Loubet-Plage is another kettle of fish, home of those concrete ziggurats you may have already noticed, looming over the Bay of Angels with all the charm of totalitarian Mesopotamia. They are part of the Marina Baie des Anges, built in the 1970s, before the French regulated building on the coast – too late, indeed, for the once beautiful stretch between here and Cannes.

St-Paul-de-Vence and Vence

Inland from Cagnes are two towns as bound up with contemporary art as any in the whole of France. St-Paul-de-Vence is the home of the wonderful Fondation Maeght, while Vence has a unique chapel painted by Matisse.

St-Paul-de-Vence

Between Cagnes and St-Paul the D6 winds above the Loup river, passing through **La Colle-sur-Loup**, a village once famous for its roses that now earns its keep from the overspill of tourists from St-Paul-de-Vence, its mother town. For La Colle was founded in 1540, when François Ier showed his gratitude to St-Paul-de-Vence for standing up to the assaults of his arch rival, Emperor Charles V, by financing a rampart around the town. Some 700 houses had to be demolished to make room for the king's gift, obliging the displaced populace to move elsewhere.

Reduced in size, **St-Paul-de-Vence** became a *ville fortifiée*, and still preserves a *donjon* watchtower dating from the 12th century, as well as François' costly ramparts. The ramparts have held up for almost five centuries and St-Paul remained a military outpost until 1868. A cannon captured from Charles V is embedded near the town gate, a gate much more accessible these days than the simple wooden door of the restaurant **La Colombe d'Or**, down in the square, which was built just after the First World War. Its first owner, an unschooled farmer named Paul Roux, fell in love with modern art and for 40 years accepted paintings in exchange for hospitality from the impoverished artists who flocked here after the First World War – including Picasso, Derain, Matisse, Braque, Vlaminck, Léger, Dufy and Bonnard. By the time he died he had accumulated one of France's greatest private collections (but strictly for viewing by those who can at least afford a meal). Just across the street, in front of the Café de la Place, is a shady *pétanque* court, dotted with moustachioed extras from a Pagnol film, where Yves Montand himself used to work off a little artistic steam.

If you're prone to claustrophobia, visit St-Paul early, before its little lanes are clogged with visitors and baskets of artsy trinkets. From its ramparts, to the north you can see

Getting There

There are frequent **buses** from Cagnes-sur-Mer to La Colle-sur-Loup, St-Paul-de-Vence and Vence, and connections nearly every hour from Nice. La Gaude can be reached by bus from St-Jeannet and Cagnes-sur-Mer (but not from Vence); Tourrettes-sur-Loup and Le Bar-sur-Loup are on the Vence–Grasse bus route. For bus times, call SAP on **t** 04 93 58 37 60.

Tourist Information

St-Paul-de-Vence: 2 Rue Grande, **t** 04 93 32 86 95, **f** 04 93 32 60 27, *artdevivre@wanadoo.fr. Open daily June–Sept 10–7; Oct–May 10–6.*
Vence: Pl du Grand-Jardin, **t** 04 93 58 06 38, **f** 04 93 58 91 81, *officedetourisme@ville-vence.fr, www.ville-vence.fr. Open July–Aug Mon–Sat 9–7, Sun 9–1; Sept–Oct, April–June Mon–Sat 9–6, Nov–Mar Mon–Sat 9–5.*

Market Days

Vence: Fruit, vegetables, flowers and clothes on Place du Grand-Jardin, every morning. Flea market on Place du Grand-Jardin, Wed. Market in the historical centre, Tues and Fri.

Festivals

St-Paul-de-Vence: **Fête des Châtaignes** in October.
Vence: **Fête de Pâques** in April, with parades, a *bataille des fleurs* and folk dancing. **Festival of Traditional Music** and a **garlic fair** in July.

Where to Stay and Eat

St-Paul-de-Vence ✉ 06570

To stay in St-Paul-de-Vence, you must have buckets of money and book well in advance.
★★★**La Colombe d'Or**, Place de Gaulle, **t** 04 93 32 80 02, **f** 04 93 32 77 78, *contact@la-colombe-dor.com, www.la-colombe-dor.com* (*luxury*). Earthy stone, low tiled roofs and rustic shutters; the rooms are full of character, the pool is heated, the stone-arcaded terrace lovely. The restaurant (*expensive*), where Yves Montand and Simone Signoret celebrated their wedding

and Arnold Schwarzenegger hosted his 1993 Cannes Film Festival bash, is more a feast for the eyes than for the stomach, but you won't go wrong with its traditional groaning platters of *hors-d'œuvre* and grilled meats. *Closed Dec–23 Jan.*
★★★★**Le St-Paul**, 86 Rue Grande, **t** 04 93 32 65 25, **f** 04 93 32 52 94, *stpaul@relaischateaux. com, www.lesaintpaul.com* (*luxury*). The interior designers let their hair down in this 16th-century building to create unusual but delightful juxtapositions of medieval, surreal, Egyptian and Art Deco elements. Its equally attractive restaurant (*very expensive–expensive*) is in an ancient vault, with a summer terrace settled around a stone fountain. *Closed Tues lunch and Wed lunch Nov–Mar.*
★★★**La Grande Bastide**, 1350 Route de la Colle, **t** 04 93 32 50 30, **f** 04 93 32 50 59, *www. la-grande-bastide.com* (*very expensive*). A stylishly renovated 16th-century manor on the hillside just outside St-Paul-de-Vence, with swimming pool, sun terrace and a very welcoming *patronne*. Hazy pastel colours brighten the rooms, some of which have private terraces leading into the gardens. No restaurant. *Closed 25 Nov–20 Dec and 12 Jan–15 Feb.*
★★★**Le Hameau**, 528 Rte de La Colle, **t** 04 93 32 80 24, **f** 04 93 32 55 75, *lehameau@wanadoo. fr, www.le-hameau.com* (*expensive*). One of the loveliest hotels in the area, with wide views over the orange groves from its low-beamed rooms decked out in cheery Provençal fabrics, and a small swimming pool. There is no restaurant, but two rooms have kitchenettes and there is home-made marmalade and jam for breakfast. *Closed mid-Nov–mid-Dec and early Jan–end Feb.*
★★★**Les Orangers**, Chemin des Fumerates, **t** 04 93 32 80 95, **f** 04 93 32 00 32, *www. stpaulweb.com/hlo* (*expensive*). Exposed beams and armfuls of flowers in a Provençal house tucked into the hillside.
★★**Hostellerie Les Remparts**, 72 Rue Grande, **t** 04 93 32 09 88, **f** 04 93 32 06 91, *www. stpaulweb.com/remparts* (*moderate*). Cheapest of all, with medieval nooks and crannies and antique furnishings; there's

also a good, affordable restaurant with a superb terrace.

Le Sainte Claire, Espace Ste-Claire, t 04 93 32 02 02, *http://aline.gerard.free.fr* (*moderate*). Sturdy Provençal décor to match the cuisine, which is well priced and served up on a panoramic terrace a couple of minutes by car from St-Paul. *Closed Tues out of season.*

Café de la Place, Place de Gaulle, t 04 93 32 80 03 (*cheap*). A good lunch or coffee stop, with its own *boules* court, large covered terrace and grand Parisian-style mirrored interior.

La Terrasse, t 04 93 32 02 05 (*cheap*). Crêpes, cider and home-made cakes on a tiny, flower-filled terrace off the Rue Grande. *Closed Wed.*

Vence ✉ 06140

Vence has more choice and lower prices than St-Paul.

****Château du Domaine St-Martin, 3km from Vence on Rte de Coursegoules (Av des Templiers), t 04 93 58 02 02, f 04 93 24 08 91, *www.chateau-st-martin.com* (*luxury*). A set of villa-*bastides* built around a ruined Templar fortress. The 12-hectare park has facilities for riding, fishing, tennis and a heart-shaped pool installed at the request of Harry Truman. The restaurant is equally august, with prices to match. *Closed Oct–end Feb.*

****Relais Cantemerle, 258 Chemin Cantemerle, t 04 93 58 08 18, f 04 93 58 32 89, *info@relais-cantemerle.com, www.relais-cantemerle.com* (*very expensive*). A member of the Relais du Silence group, decorated with Art Deco bits and pieces from the gutted Palais de la Méditerranée in Nice, and very tranquil. Set in a piney garden, with terraces and a pool, the Cantemerle's restaurant (*expensive*) serves some of the finest food in Vence. *Closed Nov–Mar.*

***Villa La Roseraie, 14 Av H. Giraud, t 04 93 58 02 20, f 04 93 58 99 31 (*expensive–moderate*). Offers a garden of magnolias and cedars, and enormous home-made breakfasts by an impeccable pool. There are antiques, Salernes tiles aplenty and lovely ironwork. Even the bicycle provided to pedal

off to the Matisse Chapel is picturesque. Beware the two topmost rooms. *Closed mid-Nov–mid-Feb.*

***Diana, Av des Poilus, t 04 93 58 28 56, f 04 93 24 64 06, *www.hotel-diana-vence.com* (*moderate*). Very reasonable single and double rooms (some with kitchenettes) in the historic centre of Vence. A tad dour on the outside, paintings and sculptures brighten up the inside and there's a library and a little breakfast terrace with a water garden.

**Le Mas de Vence, 539 Av Emile Hughes, t 04 93 58 06 16, f 04 93 24 04 21, *www.azurline.com* (*moderate*). Guests are treated like one of the family here; there is a decent pool and the restaurant is one of the best places to try real Niçois ravioli.

La Closerie des Genêts, 4 Impasse Marcellin Maurel, t 04 93 58 33 25, f 04 93 58 97 01 (*inexpensive*). Charming yet unpretentious, with quiet rooms and a shady garden where you can bring your own picnic.

Le Vieux Couvent, 37 Rue Alphonse Toreille, t/f 04 93 58 78 58 (*expensive*). Hearty helpings of locally produced, well-prepared regional dishes. *Closed Wed, Thurs lunch, and mid-Jan–mid-Mar.*

La Farigoule, 15 Av Henri Isnard, t 04 93 58 01 27 (*expensive*). Provençal cuisine and good fresh fish. *Closed Tues, Wed and Sat lunch in summer, Tues and Wed out of season.*

Auberge Les Templiers, 39 Av Joffre, t 04 93 58 06 05 (*expensive*). Elegant and traditional French – lamb, *foie gras* and fish. Rustic Provençal surroundings and warm service. *Closed Mon lunch, Tues lunch and Wed lunch in summer, Mon and Tues out of season.*

Le Pigeonnier, Place du Peyra, t 04 93 58 03 00 (*moderate*). In the Vieille Ville, this quaint place makes its own pasta and ravioli. *Closed Mon in season and Jan.*

Le Pêcheur du Soleil, Place Godeau (behind the church), t 04 93 58 32 56 (*cheap*). A dazzling choice of 500 different combinations of pizza toppings. You'll need fifteen minutes just to read the menu. *Closed Sun and Mon out of season and mid-Oct–mid-Jan.*

the odd, sphinx-shaped rock called the **Baou de St-Jeannet**, that was painted into the uncanny landscape of Nicolas Poussin's *Polyphème*. Just outside the tip of the ramparts is a tiny **cemetery**, shaded by 100-year-old cypress trees, where Chagall chose to be buried. There's a handsome urn-shaped fountain and an arcaded *lavoir* along the Rue Grande and, further up, the 12th-century *donjon* and the lovely pale stone **Chapelle des Pénitents Blancs**. Also here at the summit of the village and top of the Rue Grande is the Collegiate church of the **Conversion de St-Paul**, where you can press yourself a tin medal to commemorate your visit. It is sumptuously furnished with Baroque stuccos, woodwork and paintings – including one of *St Catherine of Alexandria* in the left aisle, attributed in part to Tintoretto. Some of its treasures are in the **Musée d'Histoire Locale** (*t 04 93 32 41 13; open daily 10–12.30 and 1.30–5.30; adm*), in the medieval residence around the corner, which tries to tempt unwary visitors with pop-eyed waxworks but actually redeems itself with a collection of celebrity photos: film stars in dark glasses and chiffon headscarves laughing over cocktails at the Colombe d'Or.

At the **Musée de St-Paul** (*t 04 93 32 86 95; open Oct–May daily 10–1 and 2–6, June–Sept daily 10–7*), next to the tourist office, artists from around the world exhibit their work, with a different artist featured each month.

Fondation Maeght

Here is an attempt at something never before undertaken: creating a world with which modern art can both find its place and that otherworldliness which used to be called supernatural.

The Foundation's inaugural speech by André Malraux, 1964

Set back in the woods up on Route Passe-Prest, the **Fondation Maeght** (*t 04 93 32 81 63, f 04 93 32 53 22, www.fondation-maeght.com; open daily July–Sept 10–7; Oct–June 10–12.30 and 2.30–6; adm*) is the best reason of all for visiting St-Paul – a vibrant and intelligently curated centre for contemporary art. Its fairy godparents, Aimé and Marguerite Maeght, art dealers and friends of Matisse and Bonnard, were struck by tragedy in 1953 when their youngest son, Bernard, died of leukaemia. When they discovered that a dilapidated chapel near their home was dedicated to St Bernard, their artist friends, among them Braque and Léger, suggested they restore it in memory of their son. The idea grew over several months and eventually the Maeghts decided they wanted to create an ideal environment for contemporary art, where they could bring together their collection and add some space for their artist friends to work and exchange ideas. They hired Catalan architect José-Luis Sert, a pupil of Le Corbusier and good buddy of Joan Miró, to design the setting – 'building' seems too confining a term for these walls that are 'a play between the rhythms of the interior and exterior spaces', as Sert himself described them. The various levels of the building follow the changes in ground level; the white 'sails' on top collect rainwater for the fountains; 'light traps' in the roof are designed to distribute natural light evenly, although the quality of light varies from room to room. The restored chapel of St Bernard has been discreetly incorporated into the grounds, with a simple statue of the saint at its entrance. Whitewashed walls offset a restrained mosaic by Léger and a dramatic wooden 15th-century Spanish crucifix. The interior is gently illuminated by Braque's stained-glass mauve and white dove and Raoul Ubac's glowing *Cross and the Rosary*.

The permanent collection, which includes around 6,000 pieces by nearly every major artist of the past century, is removed during the Fondation's frequent exhibitions of young artists and retrospectives of established ones. But you'll always be able to see the works that were incorporated into the walls and gardens from the outset: Chagall's first mosaic, *Les Amoureux*, sparkles on an exterior wall, and Miró was busy laying out the beginnings of his dreamy *Labyrinth* as the building was being raised. It has become a winding series of garden paths and terraces lined with delightful sculptures, whimsical creatures like the smooth white *Solar Bird*, gargoyle-faced fountains and a ceramic half-submerged *Egg*. Braque's blue-mosaiced fountain basin, *Les Poissons*, and Calder's *Humptulips*, with its feet in a pool, were also created specifically for the Fondation.

The works in the shady sculpture garden at the entrance to the Fondation rotate from time to time, but usually among them are Miró's great *Monument*, an airy *Stabile* by Calder, Jean Arp's *Large Seed*, and a wet and wobbling tubular steel fountain by Pol Bury. Around them, Tal-Coat's 'stone-painting' oozes earthily from the enclosing wall. On the other side of the museum, opposite the entrance hall, Giacometti's sculpture courtyard is inhabited by stick-figured animals and elongated people like his loping *Walking Man*, reminiscent of Etruscan bronzes at their quirkiest. He had to paint the bronzes in this courtyard with a wash in order to offset the blazing Mediterranean light and bring them into relief, and then, while in pragmatic mode, went on to design the quirky wrought-iron chairs and tables of the garden café. The Fondation also has a cinema and a studio for making films, plus art workshops, and one of the world's most extensive art libraries.

Vence

I live among rocks, which happy fate
Has sprinkled liberally with roses and with jasmine,
Trees carpet them from foothill to summit,
Rich orange groves blossom in the plains;
The emerald in their leaves reveals its hue,
On the fruit shines gold, and silver on the flower.
Antoine Godeau, on Vence

D. H. Lawrence and Marc Chagall died in Vence, a pleasant enough old town where real people still live among the writers, artists and perfectly tanned Martians with their lifted and stretched faces.

Twin city of Ouahigouya in Burkina Faso, Vence lies 3km from St-Paul and 10km from the coast, sufficiently far to seem more like a town in Provence than a Riviera fleshpot. Roman Vintium, it kept up its regional prestige in the Middle Ages as the seat of a bishopric (albeit the smallest in France) with a series of remarkable bishops. Two are now Vence's patron saints: Véran (449–81), an alumnus of the seminary of St-Honorat near Cannes, and Lambert (1114–54). Lambert had to confront the claims of the new baron of Vence, Romée de Villeneuve, knighted by Raymond Bérenger V of Provence after Romée arranged for Bérenger's daughters the four most strategic marriages of all time – to the kings of England, France (Saint-Louis) and Naples, and the German emperor. Although Romée earned a mention in Dante's *Paradiso* (an apocryphal story telling how he began and ended his career as an impoverished pilgrim), as baron he set a precedent of quarrelling with the bishop of Vence that lasted until the Revolution abolished both titles. Alessandro Farnese was head of Vence's see from 1508 to 1511 – one of the 16 absentee bishoprics he accumulated thanks to his beautiful sister Giulia, the mistress of Pope Alexander IV, who slept with enough cardinals to get her brother elected Paul III. But best loved of Vence's bishops was Antoine Godeau (1639–72), a dwarf famed for his ugliness, a gallant poet and 'the wittiest man in France'. Appointed the first member of the Académie Française by Cardinal Richelieu, Godeau tired of it all by the time he was 30, took holy orders and devoted himself to reforming his see.

Although a fair amount of villa sprawl extends on all sides, the **Vieille Ville** has kept most of its medieval integrity, partly because the citizens were granted permission to build their homes against the ramparts in the 15th century. Enter the walls by way of the west gate, the fortified **Porte du Peyra**. The solid, square watchtower dates from the 12th century and was annexed to the newly consucted château by the haughty Villeneuves in the 17th century, despite the heated objections of the townsfolk. It is now yet another art gallery, the **Château de Villeneuve–Fondation Emile Hughes** (*t 04 93 58 15 78; open July–Sept 10–6; Oct–June 10–12.30 and 2–6; closed Mon; adm*), which displays a comprehensive collection covering Hughes' fluttering career: after flirting with Abstraction, Dadaism and Realism, he finally settled on a hallucinatory mix of all three in a wide range of media. Temporary exhibitions showcase a selection of modern and contemporary paintings and sculptures, with regular retrospectives of major 20th-century artists who made the Cote d'Azur their home.

Just inside the walls, the **Place du Peyra** was the Roman forum and is still the site of the daily market. The grand, urn-shaped fountain once (with the help of the Basse Fontaine on Place Vieille at the opposite end of town) provided all the town's drinking water until the late 19th century, when the Riou river was canalized.

Roman tombstones are incorporated in the walls of the **Ancienne Cathédrale**, a rococo church full of little treasures – the pre-Christian sarcophagus of St Véran; the tomb of Bishop Godeau and St Lambert; Merovingian and Romanesque fragments of stones and birds, especially in the chapel under the belfry; a spluttery 1979 mosaic by Chagall with a flappy, beetling angel; reliquaries donated by Alessandro Farnese; and, best of all, the stalls with lace-fine carvings satirizing Renaissance customs and mores, sculpted by Jacques Bellot in the 1450s. The old cathedral had sagged into dusty decline when in 1988, in an astonishing display of collective enthusiasm, all the townsfolk got together to clean, polish and repaint it.

West, outside the walls, **Place du Frêne** is named in honour of a majestic ash tree planted here in 1538 to commemorate visits by François Ier and Pope Paul III. Vence's Saturday market spills beyond the confines of the city into the Place du Grand Jardin, and all that's home-grown, -crafted or -made is exhibited with worthy pride. Trawl the stalls and you may well find something way above the ordinary (Olivier de Celle hunts out his woods with the passion of a truffle-hunter, and carves them into fruits so beautiful they're hard not to touch). You'll be hurried by the crowds and the sweet stench of bakeries browning new wares, and pancakes hissing and crisping from trollies on the corners.

Matisse's Chapelle du Rosaire

t 04 93 58 03 26. From Vence, follow Av des Poilus to the route for St-Jeannet/ La Gaude. Open Tues and Thurs 10–11.30am and 2–5.30, Mon, Wed and Sat 2–5.30 (in school hols also Fri 2–5.30); closed mid-Nov–mid-Dec; adm.

During the war, Matisse refused to leave France, but his home in Nice was danger-ously near the city's arsenal and he was eventually persuaded to move to Vence in 1941 to escape the coastal bombing. Some years earlier, a young woman called Monique Bourgeois had answered an advertisement for a 'young and pretty night nurse for the painter Henri Matisse', who was recovering from a serious operation. Later, she became a Dominican nun and was sent, by an odd coincidence, to a convent opposite the villa which Matisse had taken in Vence to wait out the war. The sisters at the convent were using an old run-down garage as a chapel, but they used to daydream about the chapel they might have one day if they could get some money together. Monique, now Sœur Jacques-Marie, showed Matisse a design for a stained-glass window, which the painter promised to finance. An idea for a chapel began to develop, and with the help of a young novice priest, Frère Raysiguier, the simple **Chapelle du Rosaire**, built and designed by Matisse, came about.

Matisse worked on the project from 1946 to 1951, by now well into his 80s and using long poles to hold his brushes when he was forced to keep to his wheelchair. He insisted on designing every aspect of the chapel, from the soaring wrought-iron cross which surmounts the tiled roof, down to the priest's robes and candlesticks (chasuble designs and early models of the chapel can be seen at the Musée Matisse in Nice). He considered the result his masterpiece, an expression of the 'nearly reli-gious feeling I have for life', the fruit 'of a life consecrated to the search for truth'. The truth he sought, however, was not in Christianity but in the essentials of line and light.

Probably the most extraordinary thing about these decorations by the most sensual of Fauves is their lack of colour, except in the geometrically patterned stained-glass windows that occupy three walls and which give the interior an uncanny, kaleidoscopic glow – at its best, Matisse considered, at 11 o'clock on a winter morning when the light is less fierce. On the west wall is *The Tree of Life*, glowing with an intense blue, green and yellow leaf motif which the sun slants through and replicates across the plain stone altar. The altar-cloth, candelabra and crucifix are all also Matisse designs. The other walls are of white faïence from Vallauris (each tile was personally examined by Matisse for evenness and luminosity), on which Matisse drew sweeping black line drawings of *St Dominic holding a Bible*, the *Virgin and Child*, the *Crucifixion* and the *14 Stations of the Cross*. None of the figures has a face – except the face of Christ that appears on St Veronica's veil, which is exactly the same shape as the Tree of Life at the opposite end of the chapel – but they are powerfully drawn and compelling in their simplicity.

Excursions around Vence: the Gorges du Loup

Vence makes an excellent base for exploring the countryside, especially if you have your own car – otherwise the only connections are the once- or twice-daily buses from Nice to St-Jeannet and Gattières.

Ten kilometres beyond the Chapelle du Rosaire, the wine-making village of **St-Jeannet** balances on a terrace beneath the distinctive Baou, a sheer 1,312ft rock that dominates the surrounding countryside. The delicious local white wine is said to make the drinker hear angels. A two-hour path from the Auberge de St-Jeannet leads to the summit, with views stretching to the Alps. A narrow road continues south to the *village perché* of **La Gaude**, unspoiled and surrounded still by the vines and flowers that used to provide its livelihood, despite the giant Y-shaped IBM research centre along the way. Alternatively, continuing northeast on D2210, there are three *villages perchés* that have yet to sell their souls to Mammon: **Gattières**, surrounded by olive groves; **Carros**, on a 985ft rock over the Var crowned by a 13th-century château; and **Le Broc**, 4km up the Var on the D2209, with a Canavesio in its church.

Another excursion from Vence (take the D2 north) takes you through the austerely beautiful **Clues de Haute-Provence** by way of the **Col de Vence**, 3,200ft up and affording an incomparable, breathtaking view of the coast from Cap Ferrat to the Esterel. The D2 continues through dramatic, arid expanses of scrub and tiers of white stone to **Coursegoules**, a tiny village teetering on the brink of a ravine, popular with walkers and the perfect place to dry out after the hedonistic coast: the bar is closed on Friday and Saturday nights. The minuscule church used to hold a retable by Ludovico Brea but, to the outrage of the old lady who has become guardian of the chapel keys, it was recently stolen by some discerning art thieves.

The most popular excursion of all is to loop-the-Loup, so to speak, around the upper valley of the Loup river, starting on the D2210. On the way you can call at the **Château Notre-Dame des Fleurs**, 2.5km from Vence on Route de Grasse (*t 04 93 24 52 00; open by appointment only; adm*), a 19th-century castle built over the ruins of an 11th-century Benedictine abbey, which used to be home to the deliciously named Musée du Parfum et de la Liqueur, but is now sadly yet another contemporary art gallery. Still, as recompense, you can browse among works by Warhol, César and Arman, and the terraced gardens offer panoramic views over olive groves and flower plantations.

Some essential oils, especially of violets, originate in **Tourrettes-sur-Loup**, 2.5km further on. Its medieval core of rosy golden stone has often been compared to an Algerian town, the houses knitted together so that their backs form a wall defended

Tourist Information

Tourrettes-sur-Loup: 2 Place de la Libération, t 04 93 24 18 93, f 04 93 59 24 40, *ot@ tourrettessloup.com, www.tourrettessurloup. com*. Offers detailed walking guides in English, and lists of local violet oil producers. *Open summer daily 9.30–12.30 and 2.30–6.30, winter Tues–Sat only.*
Gourdon: Place de l'Eglise (in the *mairie*), t/f 04 93 09 68 25, *sygourdon@ wanadoo.fr, www.gourdon-france.fr. Open July–Aug daily 9–7; hours vary at other times.*

Festivals
Tourrettes-sur-Loup: Fête des Violettes in March.

Markets
Tourrettes-sur-Loup: Wed.

Where to Stay and Eat

Tourrettes-sur-Loup ✉ **06140**
★★Hôtel-Restaurant Les Belles Terrasses, Rte de Vence, t 04 93 59 30 03, f 04 93 59 31 27, *bellesterrasses@free.fr (low moderate)*. Basic but pleasant rooms, with views from the hotel's terraces and a good little restaurant. *Closed mid Nov–mid Dec; restaurant closed Mon–Sat lunch and all day Mon.*
★★Auberge de Tourrettes, 11 Route de Grasse, t 04 93 59 30 05, f 04 93 59 28 66, *www. aubergedetourrettes.fr (expensive)*. For comfortable, clean rooms and a view of orange trees and distant sea, head here. The restaurant offers *coq au vin* and *médaillon de lotte aux légumes. Restaurant closed Mon, Tues lunch in winter, and Jan.*

Le Bar-sur-Loup ✉ **06140**
L'Amiral, 8 Place Francis Paulet, t 04 93 09 44 00 *(moderate)*. Stop for lunch with local shopkeepers and *gendarmes* in this impressive 18th-century house that belonged to Amiral de Grasse. The dishes on the menu change daily, and are always spot on for freshness and value. Be sure to reserve for dinner in the summer. *Closed Sun eve and Mon, Mon lunch only July–Aug, closed Jan.*

Coursegoules ✉ **06140**
★★Auberge de l'Escaou, t 04 93 59 11 28, f 04 93 59 13 70, *escaou@wanadoo.fr, www.hotel-escaou.com (low moderate)*. Over 3,000ft up, in the heart of the tiny village. At the restaurant *(moderate)* – outdoors under the shade of plane trees, or inside in a vertigo-inducing glassed-in terrace – try the delicious ravioli stuffed with wild mushrooms. *Closed Dec.*

Gourdon ✉ **06620**
There are no hotels in Gourdon, only a few *gîtes*, but a couple of restaurants stand out.
Auberge de Gourdon, Route de Caussols, t 04 93 09 69 69 *(moderate)*. Offers good, fresh Provençal food at reasonable prices.
Taverne Provençale, Place de l'Eglise, t 04 93 09 68 22 *(moderate)*. Dine gazing out to the coast and as far away as Corsica on fine days. *Lunch only Sept–June; closed Jan and Mon eves in July–Aug.*

Courmes ✉ **06620**
Auberge de Courmes, 3 Rue des Platanes, t 04 93 77 64 70, f 04 93 77 65 90, *www. provenceweb.fr (inexpensive)*. Booking is recommended for this charming inn, with its twisty old vine, relaxing terrace and low-beamed whitewashed walls. There are just five simple rooms *(half-board compulsory for more than three nights)* and an excellent restaurant *(moderate)* serving duck with caramelized pears and other dishes from southwest France. *Closed Sun eve, Mon and Jan.*

by the three small towers that give the village its name. Tourrettes grows more violets than any town in France, and in March all the façades are covered with bouquets for the *Fête des Violettes,* a day that ends in a public 'flower battle'. But in the summer Tourrettes turns into a veritable *souk*, where you can purchase hand-made fabrics, jewellery, marionnettes, ceramics, household items and more. The 15th-century village church has a triptych by the school of Ludovico Brea, a handsome carved wooden retable and a Gallo-Roman altar dedicated to Mercury, while the Chapelle St-Jean, at the village entrance, has naïve frescoes mixing biblical tales with local life, painted by Ralph Souplaut in 1959.

Before heading into the Gorges du Loup, take a short detour south at Pont-du-Loup to **Le Bar-sur-Loup**, scented by its plantations of oranges, jasmine, roses and violets. The village surrounds the château of the lords of Bar, a branch office of the counts of Grasse (one of whom grew up here to become the Amiral de Grasse who chased the British out of Chesapeake Bay so that Washington could blockade Yorktown and win the American War of Independence). Legend has it that one of his 15th-century ances-tors held a wild party here in the middle of Lent, during which the guests all dropped dead. Mortified, the lord commissioned an itinerant artist from Nice to commemo-rate the event by painting a curious little *Danse Macabre*, now in the tribune of the church of St-Jacques: the elegant nobility dance to a drum, unaware that tiny demons of doom echo the dance on their heads. Death, grinning, mows them down, while busy devils extract their souls in the form of newborn babies and pop them into the mouth of Hell. The church also has a retable by Ludovico Brea and, on the door, beautiful Gothic and Renaissance panels representing St Jacques, carved by Jacques Bellot of Vence.

Not to be missed in **Pont-du-Loup** is the Confiserie Florian (*t 04 93 59 32 91; open daily 9–12 and 2–6*), where jams, jellied fruits, crystallized flowers, chocolates and sweets are made before your eyes, by men in white hats and blue aprons. The factory is quaint and full of antique kitchen furniture, but best is the free tasting at the end of each tour.

North of Pont-du-Loup, the D6 leads into the steep, fantastical cliffs of the **Gorges du Loup**, cooled by waterfalls (one, the Cascade de Courmes next to the road, falls a sheer 150ft) and pocked by giant *marmites*, or glacial potholes. The largest of these is up at **Saut-du-Loup**, and in spring the river broils through it like a witch's cauldron.

At Pont de Bramafan you can cross the gorge and head back south. Looming ahead is **Gourdon** (pop. 324), 'the Saracen', a brooding eagle's nest converted into yet another rural shopping-mall of crafts and goodies. Its massive, rectangular château was built in the 13th century over the Saracen citadel and restored in 1610. Inside are a pair of museums (*t 04 93 09 68 02, www.chateau-gourdon.com; open June–Sept 11–1 and 2–7; Oct–May 2–6 and closed Tues; adm*): the **Musée Historique**, with antique arms and armour, the odd torture instrument in the dungeon, a Rembrandt *Self-Portrait* and Marie-Antoinette's writing desk, and, upstairs, a **Musée de Peinture Naïve**, featuring a small portrait by the Douanier Rousseau and works by his French and Yugoslav imita-tors. The panoramic three-tiered castle gardens were laid out by André Le Nôtre.

You can take a spectacular two-hour walk on the **Sentier du Paradis** from Gourdon to Pont-du-Loup, or sneak a preview of lunar travel by driving up the D12 (or walking along the GR4 from Grasse) on to the desolate **Plateau de Caussols**, boasting the driest, clearest air in France – hence an important observatory. Now, clouds of multi-coloured hang-gliders float over it (*www.beyond.fr/sports/hangglider.html*). French film directors often use it for Western or desert scenes, the very kind used these days for selling French cars and blue jeans.

Back Towards the Coast: Biot

Between Cagnes and Cannes, the *résidences secondaires* battle for space with huge commercial greenhouses and fields of flowers destined for the scent distilleries of Grasse, a paroxysm of fragrance and colour powerful enough to make a sensitive soul swoon. Set inland a couple of miles from the sea, Biot (rhymes with yacht) is a handsome village endowed with first-rate clay – in Roman times it specialized in wine and oil jars large enough to contain Ali Baba's 40 thieves. In 1955, Fernand Léger purchased some land here in order to construct a sculpture garden of monumental ceramics – then died 15 days later. In 1960 his widow used the land to build a superb museum and garden to display the works he left her in his will. Come late in the day if you want to see more of Biot and less of the human race.

Musée National Fernand Léger

Chemin du Val-de-Pome, t 04 92 91 50 20; open July–Sept 10.30–6; Oct–June 10–12.30 and 2–5.30; closed Tues; tours by appt for groups; adm, free 1st Sun of the month.

To the right of the entrance to Biot, the museum is hard to miss behind its giant, sporty ceramic-mosaic designed for the Olympic stadium of Hanover. Opened in 1960, the museum was the first to be built exclusively for the work of a single artist. It was enlarged in 1989 to provide more space for the 348 paintings, tapestries, mosaics and ceramics that trace Léger's career from his first flirtations with Cubism in 1909 – although even back then Léger was nicknamed 'the tubist' for his preference for fat noodly forms. After being gassed in the First World War, he recovered to flirt with the

Getting There

Biot's **train station** is down by the sea at La Brague, and you will have a steep 5km walk from here up to the village. **Buses** approximately every hour from Antibes stop at the train station en route to Biot village.

Tourist Information

Biot: 46 Rue Saint-Sébastien, t 04 93 65 78 00, f 04 93 65 78 04, *tourisme.biot@ wanadoo.fr*, *www.biot-coteazur.com*. Has lists of *chambres d'hôte* and artists' studios. *Open summer Mon–Fri 10–7, Sat, Sun and hols 2.30–7; winter Mon–Fri 9–12 and 2–6, Sat, Sun and hols 2–6.*

Market Days

There's a fruit and vegetable market Tues and Fri am.

Where to Stay and Eat

Biot ✉ **06410**

*★**Hôtel des Arcades**, 16 Place des Arcades, t 04 93 65 01 04, f 04 93 65 01 05 (*moderate–inexpensive*). A delightful old hotel in a 15th-century building furnished with antiques. The popular artsy restaurant (*moderate*) below does a *soupe au pistou* and other Provençal favourites. *Closed Sun eve, and Mon.*

*★★**Auberge du Jarrier**, Passage de la Bourgade, t 04 93 65 11 68 (*expensive*). For a special feast, reserve a table at least a week in advance in this old jar-works. A magical terrace, friendly service and a superb four-course seasonal Provençal menu. *Closed Mon and Tues out of season; closed Mon, Tues, Wed and Thurs lunch in season.*

Purist movement founded by his buddies Le Corbusier and Amédée Ozenfant around 1918, a reaction to the 'decorative' tendencies of Cubism. Purism was to be the cool, dispassionate art of the machine age, emotionally limited to a 'mathematical lyricism', and Léger's scenes of soldiers and machines fitted the bill. After teaching at Yale during the Second World War, he returned to France with a keen interest in creating art for the working classes, using his trademark style of brightly coloured geometric forms to depict factories, workers and their pastimes.

The new wing of the museum contains Léger's ceramics, mosaics and other works – most notably the tapestries called *La Création* (1922) and *Liberté*, the latter illustrating the eponymous poem by his friend Paul Eluard. The surrounding garden holds the **Bonsai Arboretum** (*t 04 93 65 63 99; open Oct–April Wed–Mon 10–12 and 2–5.30; May–Sept 10–12 and 3–6.30; closed Tues; adm*), with a collection of bonsai from all over the world.

Crafts and Arts

The presence of the museum has boosted the local ceramics and glass industries; across from the museum at **Ecomusée du Verre** (*Chemin des Combes, t 04 93 65 03 00*) you can watch workers make glass suffused with tiny bubbles (*verre à bulles*). Small workshops dotted around the big main *verrerie*, below the town walls, all sell bubbly glassware more cheaply than the museum shop. More ceramics and glass can be seen in the charming, tiny **Musée d'Histoire et de Céramique Biotoises** back up in the walled town (*Rue Saint-Sébastien, t 04 93 65 54 54; open summer Wed–Sun 10–6; winter Wed–Sun 2–6; closed Tues; adm*); most of the pieces, and 400 photographs, were donated by the villagers. The town itself, and the roads leading down to the station, are crammed with art and pottery galleries, and workshops of individual artists, of widely varying quality. Even the town plan, on the wall near the bus stop, is made of glazed tiles.

Guarded by 16th-century gates, Biot itself has retained much of its character, especially around the central **Place des Arcades**. A hundred years ago, the accents in this charming square would have been Genoese – Biot's original population was almost wiped out by the Black Death and the village was only resettled in 1460, when the Bishop of Grasse invited in 50 families from Genoa.

The remains of a 13th-century Templars' chapel were demolished to create the present church, tucked among the arcades. It has two excellent 15th-century altarpieces: the red and gold *Retable du Rosaire* by Ludovico Brea, and the recently restored *Christ aux plaies* by Giovanni Canavesio, who was married to a Biotoise. The 17th-century gate depicts Mary Magdalene, Biot's feisty patron saint. The triangular, brightly tiled tower in the Place des Pénitents-Noirs once belonged to the chapel and now languishes picturesquely.

With his bright colours and often playful forms, Léger is one artist children usually like. Afterwards you can take them to **La Brague**, by the sea, to watch the performing dolphins and other sea creatures at **Marineland**, play on the slides at **Aquasplash** and see butterflies at **La Jungle des Papillons** (*for details of these attractions and others on the Route de Biot, see p.145*).

Antibes, Juan-les-Pins and Vallauris

Set on the largest of the Côte's peninsulas, Antibes started out as the Greek trading colony of Antipolis, the 'city opposite' Nice. But these days it's also the antithesis of the Nice of retired folks soaking up the rays: Antibes belongs to the young, both locals, who scoot, bike and skate like their counterparts in California to *collège* and *lycée*, and visitors, who frequent the mega-white boats that measure over a hundred yards long, moored shoulder to shoulder, vying to see which has the most high-tech communications system. Here the *de rigueur* Riviera poodle has been supplanted by the seadogs' terriers, labradors and spaniels. On the other side of luxurious Cap d'Antibes are the sandy beaches of Juan-les-Pins, where you can swing all night, especially to the tunes of the Riviera's top jazz festival. Inland from here is Vallauris, another ceramics village, this one synonymous with Picasso.

Antibes

Now all the gay decorative people have left, taking with them the sense of carnival and impending disaster that colored this summer...
Zelda Fitzgerald, 1925

Antibes has been a quieter place since the Fitzgeralds and their self-destructive high jinks set a precedent no alcoholic writer or artist has been able to match. The frolicking now takes place over at Juan-les-Pins, which took off as a resort shortly after F. Scott and Zelda's holiday, leaving Antibes to tend its rose nurseries. After the Second World War, when developers cast an eye over Antibes, there were enough building restrictions to keep out most of the concrete. Even so, inlanders regard the town with jaundiced eyes: instead of 'go to hell' they say *'Vai-t'en-à-n-Antibo!'* Yet Antibes still retains an authentic vivacity all its own, drawing in crowds of bright young things who disdain the hollower charms of Juan-les-Pins.

A relic of Antibes' earlier incarnation as France's bulwark against Savoyard Nice are its sea walls, especially the massive 16th-century **Fort Carré** (*Route du Bord-de-Mer, t 06 14 89 17 45; guided tours only; Oct–May 10–4.30; June–Sept 10–6; closed Mon; adm*). Four bastions, called Corsica, France, Antibes and Nice after the places the fort was intended to protect, were added in 1565. The fort provides a decorative backdrop for Antibes' marina, big enough to moor even the 300ft behemoths of the absurdly rich.

Nicolas de Staël lived at the corner of the old port and the Rue des Saleurs ('dry-curers', who made the local dried-fish preserves) before being driven to distraction by the spiky brilliance of the light and throwing himself to his death. The handsome 17th- and 18th-century houses of Vieil Antibes look over their neighbours' shoulders towards the sea, obscuring it from **Cours Masséna**, the main street of Greek Antipolis. Here, the **market** sells a cornucopia of produce, from *fromage de chèvre* to a profusion of cut flowers that leave the paintings in Antibes' galleries pale by comparison.

From the Cours Masséna, Rue Sade leads back to café-filled Place Nationale and the **Musée Peynet** (*t 04 92 90 54 30; open summer 10–6; winter 10–12 and 2–6; closed*

Getting Around

By Train

Antibes' train station, on Place P. Semard, is out at the edge of town, about a 10-minute walk from the centre along Av Robert Soleau towards Nice, **t** 08 92 35 35 35. The station in Juan-les-Pins is very centrally located on Av de l'Esterel. There are frequent Métrazur and TGV trains from Antibes, Juan-les-Pins and Golfe-Juan to Nice and Cannes.

By Bus

Buses (**t** 04 93 34 37 60 and **t** 04 93 64 88 84) for Cannes, Nice, Nice airport, Cagnes-sur-Mer and Juan-les-Pins depart from Place de Gaulle in Antibes; others leave from Rue de la République. From Golfe-Juan buses leave every 20mins for Antibes. Three- and eight-day passes are available, which include round trips to Nice airport. You can get to Vallauris by bus from anywhere along the coast.

By Taxi

Antibes: **t** 04 93 67 67 67.
Juan-les-Pins: **t** 04 92 93 07 07.

Bicycle hire

Azur Bike, 33 Bd Charles Guillaumont, **t** 04 93 61 51 30.

Tourist Information

Antibes: 11 Place Charles de Gaulle, **t** 04 92 90 53 00, **f** 04 92 90 53 01, *accueil@antibes-juanlespins.com, www.antibes-juanlespins.com* and *www.antibes.co.uk. Open daily 9–7 in summer; winter Mon–Fri 9–12.30 and 1.30–6, Sat 9–12 and 2–6.*

Juan-les-Pins: 51 Bd Guillaumont, **t** 04 92 90 53 05, **f** 04 93 61 55 13, *accueil@antibes-juanlespins.com, www.antibes-juanlespins.com. Open daily 9–7 in summer; winter Mon–Sat 9–12 and 2–6.*

Golfe-Juan: Parking du Vieux-Port, **t** 04 93 63 73 12, **f** 04 93 63 21 07, *www.vallauris-golfe-juan.com. Open daily 9–7 in summer; winter Mon–Sat 9–12 and 2–6.*

Vallauris: Square du 8-Mai-1945, **t** 04 93 63 82 58, **f** 04 93 63 95 01, *tourisme.vgj@wanadoo.fr, www.vallauris-golfe-juan.com. Open daily 9–7 in summer; winter Mon–Sat 9–12 and 2–6.*

Internet: **Accès Internet**, 55 Av de Cannes, Juan-les-Pins, **t** 04 93 67 60 60. *Open 11am–8pm. Closed Sun.*

Market Days

Antibes: Cours Masséna, fruit and veg, flowers, rolls of fabric and wicker-work aplenty, June–August daily, otherwise Tues–Sun 6am–1pm sharp. Place Nationale, flea market, Saturday 7–6. Place Audiberti, bric-a-brac, Thursday and Saturday 7–6. Place Barnaud, clothes market, Tuesday and Saturday. Parking de la Poste, clothes market, Thursday morning.

Vallauris: Vegetables, Tues–Sun, Place de l'Homme au Mouton.

Golfe-Juan: Vegetables, Friday am, Parking Aimé Berger. Marché Estival Nocturne, summer evenings (weekends).

Festivals

Jazz tops the bill in Antibes/Juan-les-Pins (the two towns melt into each other without any real boundary); there's the famous **jazz festival** in July, and the gaudy New Orleans-style **Mardi Gras parade** in February/March. Contact the Juan-les-Pins tourist office for details and ticket information.

Europe's largest harbour, the Port Vauban in Antibes, fills up with yachts in June for the celebrated **Voiles d'Antibes**, and there is more sporting fervour in October during the **Antibes Rally**.

Where to Stay

Antibes ✉ 06600

***Thalazur, 770 Chemin des Moyennes Bréguières, **t** 04 92 91 82 00, **f** 04 93 65 94 14,

Mon and hols), housed in a 19th-century school and offering a queasy journey back to the 1960s paved with the love postcards drawn by Raymond Peynet, the father of the genre, who lived in Antibes from 1978. There are sculptures, dolls and models of some of his stage sets for true disciples of kitsch.

www.thalassofrance.com (*expensive*). Combine hedonistic pleasures with thalassotherapy and beauty treatments; four heated pools, saunas and a doctor on duty (*half board compulsory May–Sept*). *Open all year.*

★★★Mas Djoliba, 29 Av de Provence, **t** 04 93 34 02 48, **f** 04 93 34 05 81, *hotel.djoliba@ wanadoo.fr, www.hotel-djoliba.com* (*expensive–moderate*). A serene *mas* in a small garden with a terrace and pool (*half board compulsory in season*). *Closed Nov–Jan.*

Cap d'Antibes ✉ 06160

★★★★Hôtel du Cap Eden Roc, Bd Kennedy, **t** 04 93 61 39 01, **f** 04 93 67 76 04, *edenroc-hotel@wanadoo.fr, www.edenroc-hotel.fr* (*luxury*). Knowns as 'l'Hôtel du Cash', as credit cards are not accepted. This brilliantly white hotel is set in an idyllic park overlooking the dreamy Iles de Lérins, where the rest of the world seems very far away. No hotel on the Riviera has hosted more celebrities, film stars or plutocrats. You could easily shed €150 at the exalted restaurant, the Pavillon Eden Roc. *Closed mid-Oct–mid-April.*

★★★★Hôtel Imperial Garoupe, 770 Chemin de la Garoupe, **t** 04 92 93 31 61, **f** 04 92 93 31 62, *resa@hotelimperialgaroupe.com, www. imperial-garoupe.com* (*luxury*). A peachy villa with impeccable rooms and opulent marble bathrooms set in tranquil gardens above the sea. The staff are friendly and helpful and there is a swimming pool and a private beach. Breakfast can be enjoyed at your private terrace or overlooking the pool. There's also a restaurant (*expensive*). *Closed Nov–Mar; restaurant closed Wed Sept–June.*

★★★★Hôtel La Baie Dorée, 579 Bd de la Garoupe, **t** 04 93 67 30 67, **f** 04 92 93 76 39, *baiedoree@club-internet.fr, www.baiedoree. com* (*luxury–expensive*). Spread out across the waterfront with lovely gardens and a restaurant (*expensive*). *Restaurant closed Nov–Mar.*

★★★Hôtel Garoupe-Gardiole, 81 Bd Francis Meilland, **t** 04 92 93 33 33 or **t** 04 93 61 35 03,

f 04 93 67 61 87, *info@hotel-lagaroupe.com, www.hotel-lagaroupe-gardiole.com* (*expensive*). A venerable white villa, shaded with tall cypresses and set back from the sea in a little pine wood. *Closed Nov–Mar.*

★Nouvel Hôtel, 1 Av du 24-Août, **t** 04 93 34 44 07, **f** 04 93 34 44 08 (*inexpensive*). Near the bus station, and with 20 soundproofed rooms which fill up rapidly in summer.

Juan-les-Pins ✉ 06160

Juan isn't exactly made for sleeping, but it makes sense to stay here if you want to join in the late-night revelry. Everything closes from November to Easter.

★★★★Juana, Av Georges Gallice, La Pinède, **t** 04 93 61 08 70, **f** 04 93 61 76 60, *info@ hotel-juana.com, www.hotel-juana.com* (*luxury*). In a lovely garden facing the pines, a beautiful Art Deco hotel with a luscious white and gold façade, a private beach and heated pool and a restaurant (*very expensive*). *Closed Jan–Mar.*

★★★★Belles Rives, Bd Baudouin, **t** 04 93 61 02 79, **f** 04 93 67 43 51, *info@bellesrives.com, www.bellesrives.com* (*luxury*). Another palace offering de luxe rooms, vintage 1930, facing the sea. There's a private beach and jetty, and a good restaurant (**La Passagère**) with a fine view over the gulf, or you can eat on the beach. *Closed mid-Nov–Feb.*

★★★★Hôtel Ambassadeur, 50–52 Chemin des Sables, **t** 04 92 93 74 10, **f** 04 93 67 79 85, *manager@hotel-ambassadeur.com, www.hotel-ambassadeur.com* (*luxury–very expensive*). A sleekly modern thalassotherapy centre with the usual pools and doctors, as well as a private beach, piano bar and vine-covered terraced restaurant (**t** 04 92 93 74 52; *moderate*).

★★★Hôtel Welcome, 7 Av Docteur Hochet, **t** 04 93 61 26 12, **t** 04 93 61 38 04, *www. hotelwelcome.net* (*expensive–moderate*). Lives up to its name with sunny terraces and a pleasant, well-manicured garden. *Closed Nov–Feb.*

Back towards the sea, Tour Gilli houses the **Musée de la Tour** (**t** *04 93 34 13 58; open Wed and Thurs 2.30–4.30; adm*), devoted to the costumes, furniture, household items and tools of Antibes' fisher-folk of yore. But the best sea views are monopolized by the **Château Grimaldi** – a seaside castle built by the family who ran most of this coast

★★Le Pré Catelan, 27 Av des Palmiers, **t** 04 93 61 05 11, **f** 04 93 67 83 11, *trevoux@club-internet.fr*, *www.precatelan.com* (*expensive–moderate*). Quiet and set back from the hurly burly among palms, with comfortable décor of the candlewick bedspread variety, a shady terrace for breakfast and a little sitting room stuffed full of magazines and books.

★★★Hôtel des Mimosas, Rue Pauline, **t** 04 93 61 04 16, **f** 04 92 93 06 46, *www.hoteldesmimosas.fr.st* (*moderate*). Five hundred metres from the sea, the Mimosa's rooms have balconies overlooking the pool and garden. *Closed Oct–April.*

Eating Out

Antibes

De Bacon, Bd de Bacon, Cap d'Antibes, **t** 04 93 61 50 02 (*very expensive–expensive*). As stylish and elegant as its perfectly prepared seafood and *bouillabaisse*, at classy prices. *Closed Mon and Tues lunch, and Nov–Jan.*

La Bonne Auberge, on the N7 near La Brague, **t** 04 93 33 36 65 (*expensive–moderate*). Chef Jo Rostang's son Philippe has inherited the kitchen, and has already made a name for himself with some of the Côte's finest *nouvelle cuisine*, including his *salade de homard aux ravioles de Romans* and *mille-feuille Bonne Auberge à l'ancienne*; the lunch menu is good value. Reserve far in advance to be sure of a table.

Les Vieux Murs, Promenade Amiral de Grasse, **t** 04 93 34 06 73 (*expensive–moderate*). Cool and spacious, with wooden décor, and serving well-presented traditional food made modern.

Le Sucrier, 6 Rue des Bains, **t** 04 93 34 85 40 (*expensive–moderate*). The chef is proud to be the great-great-nephew of Guy de Maupassant, and spirits up traditional French classics with an exotic twist in a

cavernous stone setting. There is even a vegetarian menu. *Closed Tues and Jan.*

Au Pied dans le Plat, 6 Rue Thuret, **t** 04 93 34 37 23 (*moderate*). The brave can try the house speciality, *tête de veau*, otherwise there's the sublimely simple fish soup or a delicious *blanquette de noix de St-Jacques*. Closing days vary; book.

L'Oursin, 16 Rue de la République, **t** 04 93 34 13 46 (*moderate*). L'Oursin is famous for fresh fish and does particularly fine things with shellfish. *Closed Sun eve, Mon and Tues pm.*

Café Sans Rival, 5 Traverse du 24-Août, **t** 04 93 34 12 67 (*cheap*). A tiny wooden-floored shop and café fitted to the ceiling with coffee beans, teas, herb teas, rice cakes, rye breads, fat sultanas and all things wholesome and *complet*. You can perch outside, drink *real* cappuccino and eat lunch or cake. *Closed Sat and Sun.*

Juan-les-Pins

La Terrasse Morisset, **t** 04 93 61 20 37 (*very expensive*). The resort's top restaurant, in the Hôtel Juana (*see* p.143) boasts delicate dishes imbued with all the freshness and colour of Provence, and excellent wines to match from the region's best vineyards. *Closed Jan–Mar.*

Bijou Plage, Bd du Littoral, **t** 04 93 61 39 07 (*expensive*). An excellent array of sea and land dishes fill the menu, and during the Cannes festival it's a good place to find the stars tucking into a *bouillabaisse*. *Closed Tues eve and Wed.*

Le Grill, Av E. Baudoin, **t** 04 92 93 71 71 (*moderate*). Part of the Eden Casino (*see* below). Try the excellent lunch menu, which includes daily chef's specials, coffee and wine. The delightful terrace looks out over the sea and in the evenings they hold *thés dansants.*

Le Capitole, 26 Av Amiral Courbet, **t** 04 93 61 22 44 (*moderate–cheap*). A charming welcome and generous seafood menus. *Closed Tues lunch in summer, Mon eve and Tues out of season and Nov.*

at one time or another, and who had possession of Antibes from 1385 to 1608. It became a history museum in the 1920s, and for six months in 1946 the owner, Romuald Dor, let Picasso use the second floor as a studio (although the locals say that he had discovered it years previously when it was still in ruins by following some

Sport and Leisure

Marineland, t 04 93 33 49 49. Europe's largest marine park, with 600,000 visitors each year to see the killer whales, sea lions, sea elephants, dolphins, seals and penguins. Luc Besson filmed part of *Le Grand Bleu* here. *Open daily from 10am, performances from 10.30am; July–Aug open till midnight with nocturnal performances at 9.30pm; adm exp.* Other attractions on this site include:

La Petite Ferme: Get closer to the animals. *Open daily 10–6.*

Aquasplash: Complete with a pool with waves. *Open summer daily 10–6.*

Mini-Golf and **Adventure-Golf**: *Open mid-June–Sept daily 10–6; Oct–mid-June, Wed, Sat, Sun and hols 10–6.*

La Jungle des Papillons, t 04 93 33 55 77. A live butterfly zoo. *Open 10–6, July–Aug 10–8. Closed Jan; adm.*

Antibe Land/Luna Park, t 04 93 33 49 49. An amusement/theme park. *Open daily 10–6.*

Parc Exflora, on the N7, Rte de Cannes, Antibes. If you've lost all your money at the gaming or dining tables, this park is free.

Iles de Lérins (*see* pp.165–6). Four to five boats a day between 9am and 4pm, from Ponton Courbet, Juan-les-Pins (**t** 04 93 61 78 84), and Quai Saint-Pierre, Port de Golfe-Juan (**t** 04 93 63 45 94). The fare is €10. *Runs April–Sept.*

Visiobulle, Embarcadère Courbet, Juan-les-Pins, **t** 04 93 67 02 11, www.visiobulle.com. An hour-long boat trip to Cap d'Antibes, with underwater diving.

Entertainment and Nightlife

Antibes

The best fun to be had is in Antibes' **Vieille Ville**, full of *confiseries* and *pâtisseries*; a *mêlée* of locals, lubbers, sailors and who knows who – a mix reflected in the gamut of polyglot newspapers, which includes even the British grubbies.

Cinéma Casino, 6–8 Av du 24-Août, **t** 04 93 34 04 37.

Red Pier Theatre, 15 Rue Clemenceau, **t** 04 93 34 24 30. Theatre with some performances in English.

La Scène sur Mer, Place Nationale, **t** 04 93 61 27 54. Restaurant, with comedy and theatre performances on the first floor.

Geoffrey's of London, Bd Aguillon. If you're homesick, baked beans, Marmite, tea and crumpets are available here.

Antibes Books, Heidi's English Bookshop, 24 Rue Aubernon, **t** 04 93 34 74 11. Heidi's one-word answer to why-did-you-come-to-the-South-of-France is 'hedonism', yet she busily runs the local community centre and a tiny **theatre** below the bookshop (*open daily*). Get the best local maps here.

The nightlife in Antibes tends to keep you moving:

La Siesta, Rte du Bord-de-Mer, on the road to Nice, **t** 04 93 33 31 31. Operating as a beach concession by day, with activities for kids, at night this turns into an over-the-top nightclub and casino where thousands of people flock every summer evening to enjoy five dance floors, fountains and fiery torches.

Juan-les-Pins

Whisky à Gogo, La Pinède, Av Leonetti, **t** 04 93 61 26 40. *Closed Nov.*

Le Village Voom Voom, 1 Bd de la Pinède, **t** 04 92 93 90 00. Haunt of older shakers and movers.

Eden Casino, Bd Baudoin, **t** 04 92 93 71 71.

Le Duc, 142 Bd Wilson, **t** 04 93 67 78 87.

Xtrême Café, 129 Rue Aubernon, **t** 04 93 34 03 90. Young, trendy place with cocktails and an Internet café.

Café Cosy, 3 Rue Migrainier, **t** 04 93 34 81 55. A charming place to sip wine away from the hubbub.

children through a hole in the wall). Picasso, glad to have space to work in, even if it was cold and damp, quickly filled it up in a few months, only later discovering to his annoyance that Dor had intended all along to make his efforts into the **Musée Picasso** (**t** *04 92 90 54 20; open summer Tues, Thurs, Sat and Sun 10–6, Wed and Fri 10–8; winter*

10–12 and 2–6; closed Mon and hols; adm). Because of the post-war lack of canvases and oil paint, Picasso had to find new materials; he began by painting directly on to the château walls and then purloined some 19th-century portraits which had been stashed in an old cupboard and forgotten, and painted over the top of them. Then he discovered the large fibro-cement boards being used for the construction of the prefabricated houses which were being hurriedly thrown up after the war, and painted over these with boat paint using broad house-painters' brushes. You can't help but get the feeling that he was exuberantly happy, inspired by the end of the war, his love of the time (Françoise Gilot) and the mythological roots of the Mediterranean, expressed in *La Joie de vivre*, *Ulysse et ses sirènes* and 220 other paintings, drawings and ceramics. In the same year that Picasso began using the château as a studio, he also visited the local ceramic-producing village of Vallauris (*see* pp.149–50) and, with his usual enthusiastic abandon, began throwing himself into the creation of whimsical clay sculptures, many of which are also exhibited here, including some of the *Tanagra*, an ebullient series of ceramic bottles metamorphosed into curvaceous women. The museum is a deeply civilized space, with room for the imagination, without much effort, to dispense with the crowds and see how Antibes might have been not that long ago.

Outside, the garden is crammed with sculptures by prominent local artists, from skinny bronze and stone statues by Germaine Richier, balanced high in silhouette along the fortified wall, to Arman's *A Ma Jolie*, an alarming eruption of bronze guitars. Miró submerged his enormous *Sea Goddess* in a nearby sea cave, where she languished for 15 years before moving into infinitely more comfortable surroundings here. Among the other artists represented, note the eight striking works on the top floor that Nicolas de Staël painted in Antibes shortly before he committed suicide (or merely fell out of the upstairs window) in 1955. Below, you may see a speedboat cross the sea like a slow rip in a blue canvas.

Just across the street is the **church of the Immaculate Conception**, where a leaflet in your chosen language entreats you to 'Listen...listen to the silent echo of prayers down the ages...', but you'll have to listen hard for silence over the Almighty Muzak. Built over a Greek temple, it's a hotchpotch of art and idols, gawpers, hawkers and rows of burning candles dedicated to St Sebastian, St Roch and Ste Réparate.

Further south, at the end of Promenade Amiral de Grasse, the Vauban-built Bastion St-André houses the **Musée d'Archéologie** (*t 04 92 90 54 35; open June–Sept Tues–Sun 10–6, Wed and Fri 10–8; Oct–May Tues–Sun 10–12 and 2–6; tour Fri 3pm; closed Mon; adm*), where Greek and Etruscan amphorae, monies and jewels dredged up from the sea and soil trace the history of Antibes. More Greek connections are around the corner – at No.8 Rue Bas-Castellet, Nikos Kazantzakis penned *Zorba the Greek*.

Cap d'Antibes and Around

Further south along the peninsula (follow the scenic coastal D2559) the delightful, free, sandy (and therefore packed) beach of **La Salis** marks the start of Cap d'Antibes, scented with roses, jasmine and the smell of money – there's more concentrated here than almost anywhere else in France. Jules Verne was among the first to retreat here, where he found the inspiration for *Twenty Thousand Leagues under the Sea*; nowadays, to maintain the kind of solitude and high-tech luxury enjoyed by Captain Nemo aboard the *Nautilus*, the owners of the Cap's villas need James Bond security systems and slavering Dobermanns. At No. 62 Boulevard du Cap is the lovely **Parc Gustave Thuret**, with a villa which can't be visited, but a free garden (*t 04 93 67 88 00; open daily 8–5.30*), laid out in 1866 as an acclimatization station, where the first eucalyptus was transplanted to Europe (the park now contains over 100 varieties). The botanist Gustave Thuret brought roses, along with his other exotic blooms, to Antibes at the end of the 19th century; the locals scoffed at this *'fada de Parisien'* but, a century later, the garden boasts the creation of a third of the world's rose varieties.

The **Plateau de la Garoupe** is the highest point of the headland, with a lighthouse, a grand view stretching from Bordighera to St-Tropez and the ancient seamen's **Chapelle de la Garoupe**. Its two naves, one 13th-century and one 16th-century, hold a fascinating collection of *ex votos*, the oldest one commemorating a surprise attack on Antibes by Saracen pirates. In the twin chapels are two humble wooden statues: a black virgin, Notre Dame de la Garde, and Our Lady of the Safe Haven.

Back on the coast, the private **Plages de la Garoupe** offer a pricey taste of *la dolce vita*. From behind the beach, the **Sentier Tirepoil** winds spectacularly up to the point at wave-lashed Cap Gros. At the tip of the peninsula is **Villa Eilenroc** (*Av de Beaumont, t 04 93 67 74 33; gardens open Tues and Wed 9–5; part of villa open Wed 9–12 and 1.30–5; closed July–Aug and Christmas–New Year*), which was designed by Charles Garnier (architect of the Paris opera house and the casino at Monte-Carlo) for a Dutch millionaire who spelled his wife's name (Cornélie) in reverse and used it to christen his lavish new seaside home. Jules Verne spent three years here, getting twenty thousand leagues away from it all, and its last owner, a rich and philanthropic American, donated the property to the municipality of Antibes.

Further west, a 12th-century tower holds the **Musée Napoléonien** (*Av Kennedy, t 04 93 61 45 32; open Nov–Sept Mon–Fri 9.30–12 and 2.15–6, Sat 9.30–12; closed Sun and Oct*), with model ships and items relating to Napoleon's connections with Antibes – he left Madame Mère and his sisters here during the siege of Toulon (they were so poor that the girls had to steal figs) and began 'The Hundred Days' at nearby Golfe-Juan.

The Cape is practically synonymous with the **Hôtel du Cap Eden Roc**, originally built in 1870 as the Villa Soleil, a home for impoverished artists founded by newspaper magnate Hippolyte de Vilemessant and the author Adolphe d'Ennery, and one of the very first hotels on the coast to feature an outdoor swimming pool – which, for a princely sum, is still open to the right type of non-resident. After a flurry of popularity with the Russians and the English at the end of the 19th century, when it was the Grand Hôtel du Cap, it sank into a genteel retirement before being resuscitated by the indefatigable New York newspaper magnate James Gordon Bennett (*see pp.19 and 88*). It played a major role in the creation of the Riviera's summer season, when popular American socialites Gerald and Sara Murphy began to come down here from

Paris in 1923, discovering the hitherto unheralded joys of sunbathing on the beach when Antoine Sella, the owner of the Grand Hôtel, kept it open in July and August in an attempt to recoup losses from a bad winter season. They had the place to themselves, along with Picasso's family and a Chinese couple. That same summer, top trendsetter Coco Chanel astonished everyone with her suntan, and a fad was born. In 1925, Sella revamped Eden Roc, which, with its eight unimaginably luxurious *cabanons* (chalets) on the beach, is still rated as the most beautiful place for a swim and a tan on the whole Riviera. The Murphys, famous for holding the very best parties, bought a house on the beach, where they created and lived the carefree but elegant sunny seaside existence that became the essential myth of the Riviera, sharing it with everyone who happened by, including Zelda and Scott Fitzgerald, the latter of whom based his characters Dick and Nicole Diver in *Tender is the Night* on the Murphys.

Juan-les-Pins

When a good idea is in the air, it's not uncommon for different people to pick up on it. In 1924, Edouard Baudoin, a Nice restaurateur, saw a film about Miami Beach and was inspired to recreate it on the Côte. He found his location at Juan-les-Pins among the silver sands and pines of the best natural beach on the Riviera, bought some land, and opened a restaurant and a little casino. As it had suddenly become desirable to bake brown on the beach, Baudoin's investment flourished, attracting the attention of the ever-acquisitive Frank Jay Gould, who bought Baudoin out, built roads and injected the essential money and publicity to help Juan-les-Pins really take off. By 1930 it was the most popular and scandal-ridden resort on the Riviera, where women first dared to bathe in skirtless suits. The presence of Edith Piaf and Sidney Bechet boosted its popularity in the 1950s. It's still going strong, not a beauty but a brash and sassy tart of a resort, with nightclubs, strings of minuscule private beaches and a magnificent jazz festival in the last two weeks of July. All the young come here from Antibes and further (the rich and posh go to Nice).

Golfe-Juan and the Route Napoléon

Next up the coast is **Golfe-Juan**, with its pines, sandy beach and marina; although one might think that there was nothing left that hasn't succumbed to redevelopment fervour, this resort is now undergoing extensive redevelopment of the redevelopment. It is famous as the very spot where Napoleon disembarked from Elba on 1 March 1815, proclaiming that 'the eagle with his national colours will fly from bell tower to bell tower all the way to the towers of Notre-Dame'. Determined to wash away the bitter taste of his abdication a year previously in Fontainebleau, Napoleon intended to overthrow the monarchy of Louis XVIII as rapidly and ruthlessly as possible. An obelisk and a column commemorate the landing, which, in fact, was slightly less than momentous: the locals quickly arrested a few of his men, a cold reception that, along with the substantial garrison at Marseille, decided the eagle to sneak along the back roads to Paris. In one of many Napoleonic coincidences, as Bonaparte landed he met the Prince of Monaco, who informed him that he was on his way to reclaim his tiny realm after being removed during the Revolution. 'Then,

Monsieur, we are in the same business,' Napoleon told him, and each continued on his way, the Prince to his orange groves, Napoleon to Waterloo.

The path he took was repackaged by the French in the early 1930s to become the scenic, touristy **Route Napoléon**, which is marked with the eagle symbol and enough plaques and monuments to satisfy even Napoleon's stupendous ego. The route twists up from Golfe-Juan through Digne and Sisteron and culminates in Grenoble, where the eagle was finally welcomed on 7 March 1815 with cries of 'Vive l'Empereur'.

Vallauris

Two kilometres inland from Golfe-Juan, **Vallauris** has two things in common with Biot: it was given an injection of Genoese in the late 15th century, and it was famous for its pottery, in this case useful household wares. The original village was built in 1138 on land belonging to the Lérins Abbey (see p.165), but the wars, plagues and famines of the 14th century virtually wiped out the unfortunate populace. The monks had always encouraged pottery production, and the influx of Genoese at the end of the 15th century brought new enthusiasm and skill to the art. By the end of the 19th century, almost three-quarters of the town were potters, but half a century later, because of competition with aluminium, the industry was on its last legs.

Then in 1946 Picasso, who was working in his lofty damp studio at the Château Grimaldi (see pp.143–6), rented a small villa in town and met Georges and Suzanne Ramié, owners of the Poterie Madoura. Playing with the clay in their shop, Picasso discovered a new passion, and he spent the next few years working with the medium – although Suzanne, watching his unorthodox methods, remarked that 'an apprentice who worked as Picasso does would never find a job'. He gave the Ramiés the exclusive right to sell copies of his ceramics, and you can still buy them at **Madoura** (t 04 93 64 66 39), just off Rue du 19-Mars-1962. Thanks to Picasso, 200 potters now work in Vallauris, their ateliers lining Avenue Georges Clemenceau.

In 1951 the village asked Picasso if he would decorate a deconsecrated chapel next to the castle. The result is the famous plywood paintings of La Guerre et la Paix, said to have taken Picasso less time to do than if a house-painter had painted the wall. The work was as spontaneous as Guernica was planned, and every bit as sincere. Known as the **Musée National Picasso** (Place de la Libération, t 04 93 64 16 05, www.musee-picasso-vallauris.fr; open Oct–May Wed–Mon 10–12.15 and 2–6; mid-June–mid-Sept 10–12.15 and 2–5; closed Tues and hols; adm), the chapel is dimly lit; Picasso wanted visitors to discover the paintings gradually. On the left is the War panel, painted in numb shades of grey, black and green, with dark silhouetted figures hurling weapons. Skeletal, white-eyed horses drag a cart over blood-red earth; in it, a soldier brandishes a sword dripping with blood at the Guardian of Peace bearing a shield with a white dove. Opposite, on the Peace panel, painted almost entirely in serene blue and white, figures dance and play beneath a blooming tree and a huge vibrant sun. At the furthest end of the chapel is a simple mosaic of four different coloured figures holding aloft a globe marked with a dove, symbol of an ideal society untouched by bigotry.

The same ticket admits you to the **Musée Municipal** (*same details*) in the adjoining 16th-century castle, a former priory of the Lérins monks. Only the 12th-century **Chapelle Ste-Anne** survives from the castle's previous incarnation. It used to have many original pieces by Picasso until art thieves struck in 1989; now to be seen are the winners of the Biennales Internationales de la Céramique d'Art, and paintings and collages by Italian abstract master Alberto Magnelli (1888–1971). There is also a large collection of glowing pieces by the influential Massier family, who began the tradition of decorative ceramics more than a century before Picasso arrived on the scene and took all the glory. On Rue Sicard, there is more pottery and an exhibition of pottery techniques at the **Musée de la Poterie** (*t 04 93 64 66 51; open May–Sept daily 10–12 and 2–6; Oct–April Mon–Sat 2–6*), which forms part of a still-functioning artist's studio. A grumpy bronze man with a sheep glowers out of Place Paul-Isnard: the sculpture was Picasso's gift to the town. Also here, beneath the walls of the Baroque church, is the bustling daily market, which sells the cut flowers and flower-scented perfumes which constitute the second string to Vallauris' economic bow.

In recent years Vallauris has suffered from a spate of thefts, often violent, from cars stuck in traffic, known locally as the 'Vallauris handbag grab'. Visitors are advised to roll up windows and close sun roofs when driving through the town.

Sophia-Antipolis

Meanwhile, as all this modern art appreciation and nightclubbing goes on around Antibes, 15,000 international business people are punching away on their new generation computers in France's Silicon Valley, the spooky new town complex of Sophia-Antipolis, off the D103 north of Vallauris, where cars are directed Scalextrix-style around endless bends and roundabouts. Created in 1969 and funded in part by Nice's chamber of commerce, it is the first stage of the *Route des Hautes Technologies* and seems popular with executives: Air France's international reservations network is here, as well as Dow Corning, Toyota and others. The commune is divided into four sectors, like a spaceship, each dedicated to a different area of business: electronics, communications and computers form one sector; health and biotechnology form the second; teaching and research make up the third; and the fourth is devoted to environmental sciences. Each sector is provided with its own shops and services and almost 1,000 businesses from France and elsewhere have been attracted here. J.G. Ballard's novel *Super-Cannes* explores the psychologically and morally deadening effect of a loosely fictional, artificially created business town just on this spot; how much resemblance his nightmare vision bears to reality would have to be debated.

Grasse

It was Catherine de Médicis (de' Medici) who introduced artichokes to the French and the scent trade to Grasse. Although it may seem obvious that a town set in the midst of France's natural floral hothouse should be a Mecca for perfume-making,

Grasse's most important industry throughout the Middle Ages was tanning imported sheepskins from the mountains of Provence and buffalo hides from her Italian allies, Genoa and Tuscany. Part of the tanning process made use of the aromatic herbs that grew nearby, especially powdered myrtle, which gave the leather a greenish lustre.

In Renaissance Italy, one of the most important status symbols an aristocrat could flaunt was fine, perfumed gloves. When Catherine de Médicis asked Grasse, Tuscany's old trading partner, to start supplying them, the Grassois left the buffalo hides behind to become *gantiers parfumeurs*. When gloves fell out of fashion after the Revolution, they became simply *parfumeurs*, and when Paris co-opted the business in the 19th century the townspeople concentrated on what has been their speciality ever since – distilling the essences that go into that final, costly, tiny bottle. And in that, this picturesque but unglamorous hill town leads the world, with approximately 30 *parfumeries*, even though most of the flower fields that surrounded Grasse only 40 years ago have now been planted with poxy, boxy villas.

Vieille Ville

Grasse's name comes from *grâce* – the state in which its original Jewish inhabitants found themselves once they converted to Christianity. In the Middle Ages it was an independent city-state on the Italian model, with close ties to the republics of Genoa and Pisa – evident in the austere Italian style of its architecture. During the 13th-century turmoil between the Guelphs and the Ghibellines, the town put itself under the protection of the Count of Provence. Today, a large percentage of the population hails from North Africa: the perfume magnates themselves live in Mougins and surrounding villages.

The one place where they often meet is at the morning food and flower market in arcaded **Place aux Aires** near the top of the town, where the handsome Hôtel Isnard (1781), with its wrought-iron balcony, looks as if it has escaped from New Orleans. From here, Rue des Moulinets and Rue Mougins-Roquefort lead to the Romanesque **Cathédrale Notre-Dame-du-Puy**, its spartan façade similar to churches around Genoa and matched by its spartan nave. The art is to the right: the *Crown of Thorns* and *Crucifixion* by Rubens at the age of 24, before he hit the big time; a rare religious subject by Fragonard, the *Washing of the Feet*; and, most sincere of all, a reredos by Ludovico Brea which depicts St Honorat having a chat with Pope Clement and St Lambert, the bishop of Vence between 1114 and 1154.

Across the Place du Petit-Puy, a plaque on the **Tour du Guet** (the former bishops' palace) commemorates the Grassois poet Bellaud de la Bellaudière, whose songs of wine and women, the *Obras et Rimos Provençalos* (1585), are the high point in Provençal literature between the troubadours and Mistral. But then, as now, it's a rare poet who can live off his verse: Bellaud supplemented his income by joining a band of brigands and sang his swan song on a scaffold.

Place du Cours and Four Museums

The Cannes road leads into Grasse's promenade, Place du Cours, with pretty views over the countryside. Close by, at 23 Boulevard Fragonard, is the **Musée Jean-Honoré**

Getting There

There are no trains, but there are frequent buses from Cannes and Nice to Grasse. The gare routière, t 04 93 36 37 37, is on the north side of town, at the Parking Notre-Dame-des-Fleurs. Leave your car here or in one of the other places just outside the centre: Grasse's steep streets are narrow for motorists.

Tourist Information

Grasse: Palais des Congrès, 22 Cours Honoré Cresp, t 04 93 36 66 66, f 04 93 36 86 36, info@grasse-riviera.com; also 3 Pl de la Foux, t 04 93 36 21 68, f 04 93 36 21 07, tourisme. grasse@wanadoo.fr, www.grasse-riviera.com. Open Oct–June Mon–Sat 9–12.30 and 2–6, July–Sept Mon–Sat 9–7, Sun 9–1 and 2–6.

Market Days

General market in the Place aux Aires Tues–Sun; antiques, 1st and 3rd Friday of the month, Cours H. Cresp.

Where to Stay and Eat

Grasse ☒ 06130

★★★Hôtel-Résidence des Parfums, Rue Eugène Charabot, t 04 92 42 35 35, f 04 93 36 35 48, www.odalys-vacances.com (expensive–moderate). Pretty views, a pool, sauna and jacuzzi; it also offers a 1hr 'Introduction to Perfume', lending you a 'nose' to help create your own perfume. Restaurant (moderate).

★★★Auberge du Colombier, 2085 Route Départmentale, Roquefort-les-Pins, t 04 92 60 33 00, f 04 93 77 07 03, info@auberge-du-colombier.com, www.auberge-du-colombier. com (expensive–moderate). Sixteen kilometres east of Grasse, in a delightful white mas with cheerfully decorated rooms, expansive gardens with a swimming pool and an extraordinary restaurant (expensive) – try the ravioli stuffed with wild mushrooms and scattered with roasted hazelnuts. Hotel closed 6–25 Jan, restaurant closed Tues.

★★Charme Hôtel du Patti, Place du Patti, t 04 93 36 01 00, f 04 93 36 36 40, hotelpatti @libertysurf.fr, www.chez.com/hotelpatti (moderate). Very comfortable modern rooms, all with air-conditioning and TV, and a restaurant (moderate), in the centre of medieval Grasse.

Grasse's culinary specialities are rather an acquired taste; typical examples are sous fassoun (cabbage stuffed with pig's liver, sausage, bacon, peas and rice and cooked with turnips, beef, carrots, etc.) and tripes à la mode de Grasse.

Bastide Saint-Antoine, 48 Rue Henri Dunant, t 04 93 70 94 94, www.jacques-chibois.com (very expensive). For a Tuscan feast in glorious al fresco surroundings, try chef Jacques Chibois' sumptuous creations.

Le Mas des Géraniums, Rte de Nice, Quartier San Peyre, Opio, t 04 93 77 23 23 (expensive–moderate). Authentic, aromatic country fare underneath bowers and on the lush garden terrace. Closed Tues and Wed in mid-Nov–mid-Jan.

Brasserie des Arcades, Place aux Aires, t 04 93 36 00 95 (moderate–cheap). Reasonably priced lunch underneath the arches, with Provençal dishes and fishes. Closed Mon out of season.

Fragonard (t 04 93 36 01 61; open June–Sept daily 10–7; Oct–May Wed–Mon 10–1 and 2–5.30; closed Nov; adm), in the 17th-century house of a cousin of Grasse's most famous citizen, Jean-Honoré Fragonard (1732–1806). Son of a gantier parfumeur, Fragonard expressed the inherent family sweetness in chocolate-box pastel portraits and mildly erotic rococo scenes of French royals trying their best to look like well-groomed poodles. Some of these are on display, along with copies of Le Progrès de l'amour dans la cœur d'une jeune fille, which even Fragonard's client, Mme du Barry, Louis XV's most beautiful mistress, rejected as too frivolous (the originals are in the Frick Collection in New York). Losing La Barry's favour was the beginning of the end for Fragonard; he lost most of his clients to the guillotine and in 1790 he washed up in

Up Your Nose

If nothing else, Provence and Languedoc will make you more aware of that sense we only remember when something stinks. The perfumeries of Grasse will correct this 'scentual' ignorance with a hundred different potions; every *village perché* has shops overflowing with scented soaps, pot-pourris and bundles of *herbes de Provence*; every kitchen emits intoxicating scents of garlic and thyme; every cellar wants you to breathe in the bouquets of its wines. And when you begin to almost crave the more usual French smells of Gauloise butts, *pipi* and *pommes frites*, you discover that this nasal obsession is not only profitable to some, but healthy for all.

Aromathérapie, a name coined in the 1920s for the method of natural healing through fragrances, is taken very seriously in the land where one word, *sentir*, does double duty for 'feel' and 'smell'. French medical students study it, and its prescriptions are covered by the national social security. For as an aromatherapist will tell you, smells play games with your psyche; the nose is hooked up not only to primitive drives like sex and hunger, but also to your emotions and memory. The consequences can be monumental. Just the scent of a madeleine cake dipped in tea was enough to set Proust off to write *Remembrance of Things Past*.

Aromatherapy is really just a fashionable name for old medicine. The Romans had a saying, *Cur moriatur homo, cui salvia crescit in horto?* (Why should he die, who grows sage in his garden?) about a herb still heralded for its youth-giving properties. Essential oils distilled from plants were the secret of Egyptian healing and embalming, and were so powerful that there was a bullish market in 17th-century Europe for mummies, which were boiled down to make medicine.

Essential oils are created by the sun and the most useful aromatic plants grow in hot and dry climates – as in the south of France, the spiritual heartland of aromatherapy. Lavender, the totem plant of the Midi, has been in high demand for its mellow, soothing qualities ever since the Romans used it to scent their baths (hence its name, from the Latin *lavare*, to wash). Up until the 1900s, nearly every farm in Provence had a small lavender distillery, and you can still find a few left today. Most precious of all is the oil of *lavande fine*, a species that grows only above 3,000 feet on the sunny side of the Alps; 150 pounds of flowers are needed for every pound of oil.

For centuries in Provence, shepherds were regarded as magicians because of their plant cures, which involved considerable mumbo-jumbo about picking their herbs in certain places and at certain times – and indeed, modern analysis has shown that the chemical composition of a herb like thyme varies widely depending on where it grows and when it's picked. When the sun is in Leo, shepherds make *millepertuis*, or red oil (a sovereign anaesthetic and remedy for burns and wounds), by soaking the flowers of St John's wort in a mixture of white wine and olive oil that has been exposed to the hottest sun. After three days, they boil the wine off and let the flowers distill for another month; the oil is then sealed into tiny bottles.

Still awaiting a fashionable revival are other traditional Provençal cures: baked ground magpie brains for epilepsy, marmot fat for rheumatism, dried fox testicles rubbed on the chest for uterine disease and mouse excrement for bedwetting.

Grasse feeling out of sorts, until one very hot day in 1806 he died from a cerebral haemorrhage induced by eating an ice-cream. Just north of the Cours at 2 Rue Mirabeau, the **Musée d'Art et d'Histoire de Provence** (*t 04 93 36 01 61; same hours as Musée Fragonard*) has its home in the 1770 Italianate mansion built by the frisky sister of Count Mirabeau of Aix, who was married to one of several degenerate marquises who pepper the history of Provence – this one, the Marquis de Cabris, is remembered in Grasse for having covered the walls of the city with obscene graffiti about the local women. Besides Gallo-Roman funerary objects, *santons* and furniture in all the Louis styles, there's Count Mirabeau's death mask, his sister's original bidets, an exceptional collection of faïence from Moustiers and Apt, and paintings by Granet.

At 8 Cours Honoré Cresp, the **Musée International de la Parfumerie** (*t 04 93 36 80 20; same hours as Musée Fragonard*) displays lots of precious little bottles dating from Roman times to the present, plus bergamot boxes of the 18th century and Marie-Antoinette's travel case, while around the corner at 11 Bd du Jeu-de-Ballon the **Musée de la Marine** (*t 04 93 40 11 11, www.musee-amiral-de-grasse.com; open June–Sept daily 10–7; Oct–May Mon–Sat 10–5; closed Nov; adm*) is devoted to the career of the intrepid Amiral de Grasse, hero of the American War of Independence.

Parfumeries

It's hard to miss these in Grasse, and if you've read Patrick Süskind's novel *Perfume* the free tours may seem a bit bland. The alchemical processes of extracting essences from freshly cut mimosa, jasmine, roses, bitter orange, etc. are explained – you learn that it takes 900,000 rosebuds to make a kilo of rose essence, which then goes to the *haute couture* perfume-bottlers and hype-merchants of Paris. Even more alarming are some of the other ingredients that arouse human hormones: the genital secretions of Ethiopian cats, whale vomit and Tibetan goat musk.

Tours in English are offered by: **Parfumerie Fragonard**, in the 18th-century converted tannery at 20 Bd Fragonard (*t 04 93 36 44 65, www.fragonard.com*), or at the spanking-new factory at Les 4 Chemins, on the Route de Cannes; **Molinard**, 60 Bd Victor Hugo (*t 04 93 36 01 62, www.molinard.com*); and **Galimard**, 73 Rte de Cannes (N85) (*t 04 93 09 20 00, www.galimard.com*). The visits are free and they don't seem to mind too much if you don't buy something at the end.

If you want to try your hand at creating your own perfumes, you can study under a 'nose' at the **Studio des Fragrances** (*t 04 93 09 20 00; two-hour course, €34*), or at the **Molinard Atelier** (*telephone same as parfumerie; 90-minute course, €40*). Or you can visit a flower plantation: Mr Biancalana (*t 04 93 60 12 76*) offers guided tours of his, which has been in his family for three generations and offers 'initiation in flower-picking' – jasmine in summer and roses in May and June (*€5 per person*).

Around Grasse: Dolmens and Musical Caves

The Route Napoléon (N85) (*see p.149*), laid out in the 1930s to follow the little emperor's path to Paris, threads through miles of empty space on either side of

Tourist Information

St-Vallier-de-Thiey: 10 Place du Tour, t/f 04 93 42 78 00, *tourisme@saintvallierdethiey.com*, *www.saintvallierdethiey.com*. Open Mon–Sat 9–12 and 3–6, Sun 10–12; shorter hrs in winter.

Market Days
St-Vallier-de-Thiey: Friday mornings and Sundays, Oct–mid-May: Place St-Roch; mid-May–Sept at the Grand Pré.

Where to Stay and Eat

St-Vallier-de-Thiey ✉ 06460

★★Le Préjoly, Place Rougière, t 04 93 42 60 86, f 04 93 42 67 80, *prejoly@wanadoo.fr* (*inexpensive*). Seventeen reasonably priced rooms and an excellent restaurant (*moderate*) frequented by film stars up from the Cannes Film Festival. *Closed mid-Nov–Jan; restaurant closed Sun eve and Mon out of season.*

medieval **St-Vallier-de-Thiey** (12km from Grasse), a popular gathering place for walkers. The ancient plane tree at the centre of the village square is circled by an old stone bench engraved with the words *'Napoléon s'est assis ici le 2 mars 1815'*. Things were busier here around 800 BC, when the people built elliptical walls with stones as high as 6ft. An alignment of 12 small **dolmens**, most of them buried under stone tumuli, stands between St-Vallier and St-Cézaire-sur-Siagne; a flat rock nearby is known as the *pierre druidique* (St-Vallier's tourist office has a map on the wall).

Just to the southwest, signposted on the D5, there's a subterranean lake in the **Grotte de Baume Obscure** (*t 04 93 42 61 63; open July–Aug daily 10–6; May–June, Sept Mon–Sat 10–5, Sun and hols 10–6, Oct–April Tues–Sun 10–5; closed mid-Dec–mid-Feb*), with a hi-tech sound and light show, plus underground pools and waterfalls. More caves can be found just off the D4 south of St-Vallier-de-Thiey: the distinctly less hi-tech **Grottes des Audides** (*t 04 93 42 64 15, www.grottesdesaudides.free.fr; open daily July–Aug 10–6; Nov–mid Feb by appointment only; the rest of the year Wed–Sun 2–5*), where you will have to rely on your own well-shod feet to take you underground. **Cabris**, 6km west of Grasse on the D4, a pretty *village perché* once favoured by Camus, Sartre and Antoine de Saint-Exupéry, is now a town of artisans and perfume executives. The D11 and D13 to the west lead to more caves: the red **Grottes de Saint-Cézaire** (*t 04 93 60 22 35, www.les grottesdesaintcezaire.fr; open June and Sept 10.30–12 and 2–6; July–Aug 10.30–6.30; April–May and Oct 2.30–5; Nov–Mar Sun only 2.30–5; adm*), where the iron-rich stalactites, when struck by the guide, make uncanny music. **St-Cézaire-sur-Siagne** itself is an unspoiled medieval town; its white 13th-century cemetery chapel, built on pure, sober lines, is one of the best examples of Provençal Romanesque on the coast.

Mougins

Cooking, that most ephemeral of arts, is the main reason most people make a pilgrimage to Mougins, a luxurious, fastidiously flawless village of *résidences secondaires*, with more gastronomy per square inch than any place in France, thanks to the magnetic presence of Roger Vergé (*see* 'Where to Stay and Eat', over). But there are a few sights to whet your appetite before you surrender to the table: a **Musée de la Photographie** (*Porte Sarrazine, t 04 93 75 85 67; open Oct and Dec–June*

Tourist Information

Mougins: 15 Av Mallet, **t** 04 93 75 87 67, **f** 04 92 92 04 03, *tourisme@mougins-coteazur.org*, *www.mougins-coteazur.org*. Open June–Sept daily 10–8; Oct–May Mon–Sat 10–5.30.

Where to Stay and Eat

Mougins ⊠ 06250

★★★★Le Moulin de Mougins, Av Notre-Dame-de-Vie, **t** 04 93 75 78 24, **f** 04 93 90 18 55, *info@moulin-mougins.com*, *www.moulin-mougins.com* (*very expensive*). In 1969 chef Roger Vergé bought a 16th-century olive mill near Notre-Dame-de-Vie and made it into this internationally famous restaurant, which also has three rooms and two apartments overlooking the sculpture gardens and wisteria-covered terraces. Of late, France's gourmet bibles have been sniffing that the mild-mannered celebrity chef has lost a bit of his touch – and little faults seem big when you shell out €150 for a meal (though there are menus from €40) But it's still a once-in-a-lifetime experience for most, in the most enchanting setting on the Côte. *Closed Dec–mid-Jan.*

★★★★Les Muscadins, 18 Bd Courteline, **t** 04 92 28 28 28, **f** 04 92 92 88 25, *muscadins@alcyons.fr*, *www.lesmuscadins.com* (*very expensive*). The *nouvelle cuisine* and chocolate desserts at this hôtel-restaurant have received excellent reviews, and the hotel has individually decorated sumptuous rooms of charm and character.

L'Amandier, Place des Patriotes, **t** 04 93 90 00 91 (*expensive*). If you can't get a table at the Moulin de Mougins, Vergé has recently opened this new, simpler restaurant, located up a winding staircase in a 14th-century olive oil mill above his shop in central Mougins. Dishes of the day are chalked up on a huge blackboard, the ivy-covered terrace is utterly romantic and menus start at an excellent €28. In the **shop** below, **Les Boutiques du Moulin**, stock up on crystal glasses, kitchenware and a selection of the master's sauces and *compotes*. For those who still haven't had enough Vergé, he has also opened a **cookery school** above L'Amandier; contact **t** 04 93 75 35 70, **f** 04 93 90 18 55 for details.

Le Feu Follet, Place du Commandant Lamy, **t** 04 93 90 15 78, **f** 04 92 92 92 62, *battaglia@feu-follet.fr* (*moderate*). An affordable restaurant offering several excellent menus – try the *rognons de veau à la graine de moutarde. Closed Mon, and mid-Dec–mid-Jan.*

La Brasserie de la Méditerranée, Place du Cdt Lamy, **t** 04 93 90 03 47 (*moderate*). Serves grilled *gambas* with ginger and other seafood delights accompanied by heavenly home-made bread. *Closed Jan.*

Le Bistrot, Place du Cdt. Lamy, **t** 04 93 75 78 34 (*moderate*). For traditional dishes such as roast quail, beef stew and aubergine caviar, try this vaulted, wooden-beamed bistro. Don't miss the fig tart. *Closed Wed lunch, Thurs lunch and Sat lunch out of season; closed every lunch July–Aug.*

Le Rendez-vous de Mougins, Place du Cdt Lamy, **t** 04 93 75 87 47 (*moderate*). A local favourite, with aromatic dishes like beef with wild mushroom sauce and sea bass with truffles.

Wed–Sat 10–12 and 2–6, Sun and hols 2–6, July–Sept daily 10–8; closed Nov ; adm), with changing exhibitions showcasing both new and established photographers, a collection of photographs of Mougins at the turn of the last century, and a permanent collection which features the work of Jacques Lartigue, who lived in nearby Opio, among others. For the voyeuristic, there is a large number of photographs depicting Picasso at work and at play – André Villars, who was personally responsible for the establishment of the museum, took many of them, and others are by famous names like Robert Doisneau, Jacques-Henri Lartigue and Raph Gatti. Further exhibitions are held in the old village **Lavoir** in the pretty Place de la Mairie.

Two kilometres southeast of Mougins, Picasso spent the last 12 years of his life in a villa next to the exquisite hilltop **Chapelle Notre-Dame-de-Vie** (*open Sun 9–10am*), a 12th-century priory founded by monks from St-Honorat and rebuilt in 1646. Until 1730, when the practice was banned, people would bring stillborn babies here to be brought back to life just long enough for them to be baptized and avoid limbo.

Appropriately located just off the *autoroute* to Cannes, at the Aire des Breguières, the de luxe **Musée de l'Automobiliste** (*Chemin Font-de-Currault, t 04 93 69 27 80; open daily April–Sept 10–7; Oct–Mar 10–6; adm*) is a modernistic cathedral to the car. It has everything from Alfa-Romeos to Zundapps, and a string of very classy Bugattis and Rolls-Royces; every vehicle (and there are almost 100 of them, the oldest dating back to 1838) is in working order.

Just north of Mougins, on the N85 towards Grasse, is the pretty village of **Mouans Sartoux**, which rose from the ashes of two Saracen-beleaguered communities. In the 16th century, feisty Suzanne de Villeneuve fought off the duplicitous duke of Savoy and chased him all the way to Cannes after he had razed her château to the ground despite an earlier promise. The restored 500-year-old château, owned by the town since 1989, has become the **Espace de l'Art Concret** (*t 04 93 75 71 50; open daily June–Sept 11–7; Oct–May 11–6; adm*), the brainchild of a local collector, Sybil Albers-Barrier, and her companion, Gottfried Honegger, the celebrated Concrete artist, who wanted to establish a 'museum imagined by artists'. The exhibits are rotated, rearranged and juxtaposed to inspire visitors to engage actively with the art rather than viewing it passively. Guides will occasionally prod visitors into a strangled reaction to the art which surrounds them, in keeping with the centre's 'didactic and political goals' – but most rather seem to enjoy the experience. Not surprisingly, the gallery is also an education and research centre. A few pieces are fixed, such as the four granite slabs of Ulrich Rückheim's *Africa Nero* in the courtyard and Honegger's carved sculptures *Division 1* and *Division 10* which stand in silhouette in the garden.

Cannes

In 1834 the 3,000 fisherfolk and farmers of Cannes were going about their business when Lord Brougham, retired lord chancellor, and his ailing daughter, stuck in the village because a cholera epidemic in France had closed the border with Savoy, checked into its one and only hotel. As they waited, Lord Brougham was so seduced by the climate and scenery that he built a villa, where he subsequently spent every winter. English milords and the Tsar's family played follow-my-leader and flocked down to build their own villas nearby. 'Menton's dowdy. Monte's brass. Nice is rowdy. Cannes is class!' was the byword of the 1920s. Less enthusiastic commentators mention the dust, the bad roads, the uncontrolled building and the turds bobbing in the sea. If nothing else, the French Riviera proper ends with a bang at Cannes.

As the spunky sister city of Beverly Hills, France's Hollywood and a major year-round convention city (Cannes was the first place on the Côte d'Azur to note that business travellers spend more than three times as much per head as tourists), Cannes offers a

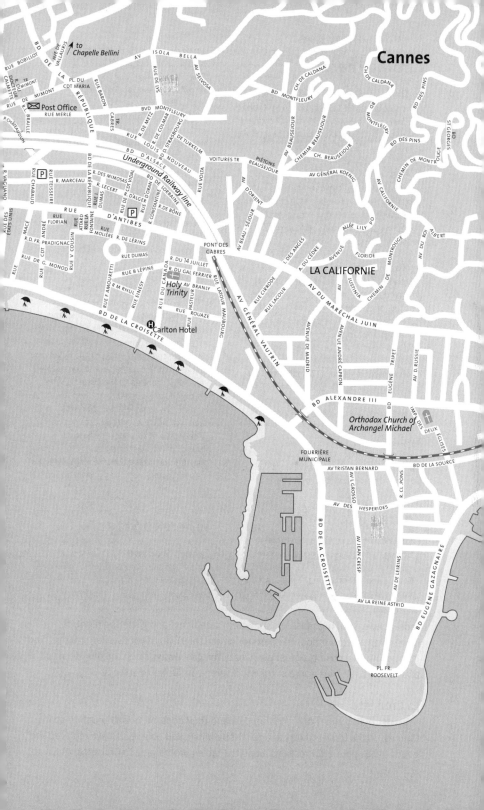

Cannes

to *Chapelle Bellini*

AV. ISOLA BELLA

AV. SELVOSA

RUE BOBILLOT

BD. DE LA

AVE DE VALLAURIS

PL. DU CDT MARIA

RUE DE MIMONT

R.DUE DOCTEUR CALMETTE

R. CHASTEAUDUN

R. BRAILLE

Post Office

RUE MERLE

RUE DE METZ

RUE DE MIMONT

RUE BARON

RUE DE SEZ

RUE LOUIS PASTOUR

RUE DE LA RÉPUBLIQUE

BVD. MONTFLEURY

RUE D. NOUVEAU

RUE LOUIS D

BD. D'ALSACE

RUE DE STRASBOURG

RUE DE TURKELM

RUE DE COLMAR

CH. DE CALDANA

BD. MONTFLEURY

CH. DE CALDANA

MONTFLEURY

BD. DÉS PINS

BD. DÉS PINS

ST GEORGES

AV. BEAUSEJOUR

CHEMIN BEAUSEJOUR

CH. BEAUSEJOUR

AV. BEAU-SÉJOUR

PIÉTONS BEAUSEJOUR

VOITURES TR

Underground Railway line

BD DE LA RÉPUBLIQUE

R. DES MIMOSAS

R. LECERT

R. DALGER

R. DUMAS

RUE GUY DE MAUPASSANT

R. DORAN

R. DE BÔNE

RUE DE LORRAINE

R. CONSTANTINE

RUE VOLTA

CHEMIN DE MONTROUGE

AV. GÉNÉRAL KOENIG

AV. CALIFORNIE

ALLÉE LILY

AVENUE

D'ORIENT

R. DE BÔNE

PONT DES GABRES

RUE P.

RUE DUMAS

RUE MARCEAU

RUE TEISSEIRE

RUE ATTARD

RUE LA FONTAINE

RUE FLORIAN

RUE V COUSIN

RUE ANDRÉ

R.D. FR. PRADIGNAC

R. MACÉ

RUE DR G. MONOD

RUE F AMOURETTI

R M RHUL

RUE B LÉPINE

RUE EINESY

RUE PASTEUR

RUE MOLIÈRE

R. DE LÉRINS

RUE

D'ANTIBES

R. DU 14 JUILLET

R. DU GAL FERRIER

AV. BRANLY

RUE

ROUAZE

RUE DU CANADA

RUE LATOUR MAUBOURG

Holy Trinity

Carlton Hotel

BD DE LA CROISETTE

RUE DES ÉTATS UNIS

R. VACQUNO

P

RUE CHABAUD

P

I. DES ANGÉS

RUE CIRRODE

RUE LACOUR

A. DU CÈDRE

JUSTINIA

CHEMIN DE MONTROUGE

AV. DU ROI

AV. DU ROI

ALBERT

FLORIDE

LA CALIFORNIE

AV. DU MARÉCHAL JUIN

AVENUE DE MADRID

AVENUE ANDRÉ CAPRON

AV EUGÈNE TRIPET

AV. D. RUSSIE

AV. GÉNÉRAL VAUTRIN

BD. ALEXANDRE III

BD.

Orthodox Church of Archangel Michael

IMP. DES DEUX ÉGLISES

BD DE LA SOURCE

FOURRIÈRE MUNICIPALE

AV. TRISTAN BERNARD

AV. L CROSSO

R. CL. PONS

AV. DES HESPERIDES

BD. DE LA CROISETTE

AV. JEAN CRESP

AV. DE LÉRINS

BD. EUGÈNE GAZAGNAIRE

AV. LA REINE ASTRID

PL. FR. ROOSEVELT

Getting There

By Train

The frequent Métrazur between St-Raphaël and Menton, and every other train whipping along the coast, calls into the station at Rue Jean-Jaurès.

By Bus

There is a multiplicity of private bus companies, all arriving and departing from different places; luckily, there is one central number, Bus Azur, t 04 93 45 20 08, at Place de l'Hôtel-de-Ville.

By Boat

Every hour in summer, the glass-bottomed boat *Nautilus*, at Jetée Albert Edouard, departs for tours of the port and its sea creatures. Tickets cost €11, call t 04 93 38 66 33.

Boat trips out to the Iles de Lérins, t 04 93 39 11 82 and t 04 92 98 71 30, *www.trans-cote-azur.com*, depart from Quai St-Pierre approximately every hour (much less frequently between October and June). The general tour is a whirlwind trip , so you're best off going to one island at a time.

By Bicycle

You can rent bikes, cars and scooters at the train station or at Mistral Location, 4 Rue Georges Clemenceau, t 04 93 99 25 25.

Tourist Information

Cannes: Palais des Festivals, 1 La Croisette, t 04 93 39 01 01, f 04 93 99 37 34, *www.cannes.fr. Open daily 9–7 (8 in summer)*. There's another office in the station, t 04 93 99 19 77, f 04 93 39 40 19. *Open Mon–Sat 9–7.*

Also at Cannes La Bocca, Place du Marché. *Open Mon–Sat 9–7.*
Post office: 22 Bivouac Napoléon.
Taxis: daily t 04 92 99 27 27. 24hr service.
Petit Train de la Croisette: Makes a little tour of Cannes in summer 10am–11pm every hour from La Croisette, opposite the Hôtel Majestic.

Market Days

Provençal markets: Tues–Sun, Marché de la Bocca, Marché Forville.
Flower market: daily at Les Allées de la Liberté.
Flea market: Fri 3–7, Place de l'Etang.

Festivals

The **Festival International du Film** erupts for 12 days beginning around the second week of May with a hurricane of hype, *paparazzi*, journalists, movie stars, gawking fans and characters who come every year There are some 350 screenings; most of the tickets are reserved for the cinema people themselves, while 10 per cent go to the Cannois, who bestow the *prix populaire* on their favourite film. The few seats left over go on sale at the Palais' box office a week before the festival.

The month of July sees the **Festival Américain**, with jazz and country music, a long-running **classical music festival** and a **firework festival** (t 04 92 99 33 83 for festival information).

Where to Stay

Cannes ✉ 06400

Although there are discounts if you come to Flash City in the off-season, you can't book too early for the film festival or for

moveable feast of high fashion, showbizzy trendiness and glittering nightlife. Depending on your mood, and perhaps on the thickness of your wallet, you may find it appalling or amusing, or just plain dizzy. You can always catch the next boat to the offshore Iles de Lérins, some of the most serene antidotes to any city.

La Croisette

Besides ogling the shops, the shoppers and their dogs, there isn't much to do in Cannes. Characterless luxury apartment buildings and boutiques have replaced the gaudy Belle Epoque confections along the fabled promenade **La Croisette**, which got

July and August. Cannes' two tourist offices offer a free reservation service, but they won't be much help at that time of year if you want a room that costs less than a king's ransom.

Luxury

★★★★★**Carlton**, 58 La Croisette, t 04 93 06 40 06, f 04 93 06 40 25, cannes@interconti. com, www.cannes.interconti.com (luxury). One of the landmarks of the Riviera, with its two black cupolas, said to be shaped like the breasts of the grande horizontale Belle Otero, the celebrated Andalucían flamenco dancer and courtesan of kings. It has been given a thorough renovation by its Japanese owners, and the 7th floor now boasts a pool, casino and beauty centre.

★★★★★**Majestic Barrière**, 10 La Croisette, t 04 92 98 77 00, f 04 93 38 97 90, www. lucienbarriere.com (luxury). Movie stars' favourite with its classic French décor, heated pool, private beach, etc. Closed 15 Nov–28 Dec.

★★★★★**Martinez**, 73 La Croisette, t 04 92 98 73 00, f 04 93 39 67 82, martinez@concorde-hotels.com, www.hotel-martinez.com (luxury). This hotel has kept its Roaring Twenties character, but now has all imaginable modern comforts, including tennis courts, a heated pool, two new luxury suites and, from the 7th floor, views over the city. Discounts for stays of over five days.

★★★**Bleu Rivage**, 61 La Croisette, t 04 93 94 24 25, f 04 93 43 74 92, bleurivage@wanadoo. fr, www.frenchriviera-online.com/bleurivage (very expensive–expensive). A renovated older hotel on the beach, where rooms overlook the sea or the garden.

★★★**Hôtel Vendôme**, 37 Bd d'Alsace, t 04 93 38 34 33, f 04 97 06 66 80, hotel.vendome@

wanadoo.fr (expensive– moderate). This pink 19th-century villa has recently been beautifully renovated and sits in a private garden in the heart of the town.

★★★**Molière**, 5 Rue Molière, t 04 93 38 16 16, f 04 93 68 29 57, www.hotel-moliere.com (expensive–moderate). Sitting in a garden, with bright rooms and terraces. Closed mid-Nov–end Dec.

If you aren't in Cannes on an MGM expense account, there are other alternatives.

★★**Select**, 16 Rue Hélène Vagliano, t 04 93 99 51 00, f 04 92 98 03 12, hotel-select-06@ wanadoo.fr, www.hotel-select-cannes.com (low moderate). A quiet, comfortable, modern choice with air-conditioned rooms, all with private bathroom.

Chanteclair, 12 Rue Forville, t/f 04 93 39 68 88 (moderate–inexpensive). Good double rooms with showers. Closed Nov–Dec.

Youth hostel, 35 Av de Vallauris, t/f 04 93 99 26 79. To the west, in Cannes La Bocca.

Chalit Auberge de Jeunesse, 27 Av Maréchal Gallieni, t 04 93 99 22 11, f 04 93 39 00 28, le-chalit@wanadoo.fr. Closed Nov.

Eating Out

La Palme d'Or, Hôtel Martinez (see above), t 04 92 98 74 14 (very expensive). The Alsatian chef, Christian Willer, and co-chef Christian Sinicropi prepare succulent dishes served in a fabulous Art Deco dining room. Closed mid-Nov–mid-Dec, and Mon–Tues; open daily during film festival.

Le Fouquet's, Hôtel Majestic (see above), t 04 92 98 77 05 (expensive). Chef Bruno Oger, named as one of France's top chefs, now presides over this sister restaurant to the acclaimed Paris original. **La Villa des Lys**,

its name from a little cross which used to stand on the tip of the Pointe de la Croisette, where pilgrims embarked for the monastery of St-Honorat. The boulevard is now clogged by incessant traffic in the summer, its lovely sands covered by the sun beds and parasols of beach concessions. The shoreline is divided into 32 sections, as memorably named as 'Waikiki', 'Le Zénith' and 'Long Beach' (which is all of several metres long). There is one rare public beach in front of the fan-shaped **Palais des Festivals**, a charmless 1982 construction. **Hand-prints** of film celebrities line the Allée des Etoiles by the Escalier d'Honneur, where the limos pull up for the festival. Outside

t 02 92 98 77 41, remains at the hotel, and is also run by Oger, but in a smaller venue.

Lou Souléou, 16 Bd Jean Hibert, t 04 93 39 85 55 (*expensive–moderate*). For affordable seafood and views of its original habitat; try an authentic *bouillabaisse* and a pretty good *aïoli. Closed Mon and Wed eve, and Nov.*

Brasserie des Artistes, 5 Rue Rouguière, t 04 93 39 09 02 (*expensive–moderate*). Fresh food till late. *Closed Sun.*

Le Baoli, Port Canto, t 04 93 43 03 43 (*moderate*). Indonesian décor, fusion food and glitterati; witih a tree-shaded terrace. *Closed Nov–April.*

Caffé Roma, 1 Square Mérimée, t 04 93 38 05 04 (*moderate*). Decent Italian food served in a brasserie with terrace overlooking the Palais.

Hôtel Brasserie du Marché, 10 Rue Monseigneur Jeancard, t 04 93 48 13 00 (*cheap*). Retains the ambience of the old village and has tasty daily specials.

Café FNAC, 83 Rue d'Antibes, t 04 97 06 29 29 (*cheap*). For good coffee, sandwiches and home-made brownies.

Nightlife

Film

For stars on celluloid, sometimes in their original language (*version originale*, or *v.o.*):

Les Arcades, 77 Rue Félix Faure, t 04 93 39 00 98.

Olympia, 16 Rue Pompe, t 04 93 39 13 93.

Star, 98 Rue d'Antibes, t 04 93 68 81 07.

Casino

The casinos draw in some of the highest rollers on the Riviera, although the adjoining casino discos are fairly staid:

Casino Croisette, Palais des Festivals, t 04 92 98 78 00.

Palm Beach Casino Club, Palm Beach, t 04 97 06 36 90.

Bars and Clubs

To get into the most fashionable clubs (those with no signs on the door) you need to look as if you've just stepped off a 100ft yacht to get past the sour-faced bouncers.

Jimmy'z, at the Casino in the Palais des Festivals, t 04 92 98 78 78. A glitzy showcase billing itself '*La discothèque des stars*'; it's certainly for those with stars in their eyes – gamblers, their ladies and mainstream music. *Open Thurs, Fri, Sat 11.30pm–dawn. Open Sun for* thé dansant.

La Chunga, 24 Rue Latour-Maubourg, t 04 93 94 11 29. There's usually live music to go with the food (*meals expensive*). *Open 8.30pm–dawn. Closed Sun and Mon before Festival, and mid-Nov–end Dec.*

Le Whisky à Gogo, Lady Bird, 115 Av de Lérins, t 04 93 43 20 63. A well-heeled crowd grinding away to the top of the pops.

Cat Corner, 22 Rue Macé, t 04 93 39 31 31. Dance until dawn at the hottest place in town.

Broom's Bar, Hôtel Gray d'Albion. With a piano bar. It also has a disco on Sunday night – **Jane's Club**, t 04 92 99 79 59.

Zanzi-Bar, 85 Rue Félix Faure, t 04 93 39 30 75. A gay bar of long standing. *Open 6pm–6am.*

Disco 7, 7 Rue Rouguière, t 04 93 39 10 36. Dancing and a transvestite show (€15 cover charge). *Open 11.30pm–6am.*

In summer, a number of **discos** erupt on the beach. They change each year. Either just get down there and check them out, look out for flyers or ask around at bars and cafés.

May, this monster disgorges conventioneers attending events such as the Festival of Hairdressing or Dentistry.

For all the present emphasis on glitter, tourist Cannes still remembers its English roots. Behind the Carlton Hotel, at 2–4 Rue Général Ferrié, the **Holy Trinity Church** was rebuilt in 1971 on the site of its 19th-century predecessor, preserving some Victorian odds and bobs: a mosaic, glass medallions of the arms of the Archbishop of Canterbury and the bishop of Gibraltar, and other Anglican paraphernalia. Built from ferro-concrete, the church's glories are its stained glass and seventies style, enough to give points to your collars and make you reach for your platforms.

Birth of a Festival

In 1938, Philippe Erlanger, the Popular Front's minister of tourism, was given the task of finding a suitable venue for a festival to rival Mussolini's new Venice film festival: the French were not about to let the Fascists have all the starlets to themselves. Erlanger went down to the Côte d'Azur, where his Villefranche friends, especially Jean Cocteau, took a close interest in his mission. Erlanger had a weakness for Cannes, but it lacked hotels, and he was about to choose Biarritz instead when Cocteau intervened and insisted on Cannes: it would be more fun, he said.

The first festival, slated to start 1 August 1939, was cancelled owing to a party-pooper named Hitler, spoiling a huge cardboard model of Notre-Dame erected on the beach and forcing a liner full of movie stars sent over by MGM to sail home unrequited. The second festival, in 1946, drew some 50 journalists who hobnobbed and drank complimentary rosé wine. The jury gave every film a prize, which set the tone from the start: the competition bit was only an excuse for a week of carousing and hanky panky; the real festival would always be outside the screenings. Cannes' historians cite 1954 as the year when everything coalesced, when the essential ingredients of sex and scandal were added to the glamour of film: the décolletage of newcomer Sophia Loren made a big impression, grabbing attention and headlines away from Gina Lollobrigida. Another well-endowed starlet (English this time) named Simone Silva went on to the Iles de Lérins for a photo session with Robert Mitchum and removed her brassière. Two hours later she was told to leave Cannes and a few years later, no longer able to find work because of her precocious gesture, she committed suicide. Cannes should have made her an honorary citizen. Two years later, the new sensation was Brigitte Bardot, who coyly spun her skirts around to reveal her dainty *petites culottes*. The atmosphere was so ripe that even the straightest of arrows, Gary Cooper and Esther Williams, had flings during the festival.

These days would-be starlets strip down completely and bump and grind on the Croisette hoping to attract attention, any kind of attention, from the 6,000 journalists. The directors and stars, all carefully groomed in the spirit of Riviera-casual, give the same careful interviews all day. Although the big American studios have traditionally shunned the festival – what's the point, they said, when their own Oscars mean more at the box office than a Cannes Palme d'Or – the importance of the international entertainment market has brought a growing stream over from Hollywood. The wheeling and dealing that goes on can sometimes come from unexpected quarters. In 1993, a ship full of raw Russian sailors caused a sensation by anchoring within spitting distance of the Palais des Festivals with a vast contraband cargo of vodka and smoked salmon. The next day, most of the jurors slept through the screening of the films in competition. Nor was it the last time.

Other European film festivals in Berlin and Venice have of late given Cannes a run for its money, and critics have suggested that Cannes has had its day. After all, the average age of film-makers in the main competition is now 53 years old. But Cannes shouldn't be shrugged off just yet. In true Riviera style it rollicks on, courting controversy wherever possible – if only just for the publicity.

Follies and Fancies

East of La Croisette is **La Californie**, home to some of the most eccentric real estate on the Côte since the mid-19th century, when Eugène Triper, the French consul to Moscow, and his aristocratic young Russian wife built the Villa Alexandra with great flamboyance in an oriental style. It has since been demolished, but there are plenty of other follies to gawp at – like the 'medieval' **Château Scott** at 151 Avenue Maréchal Juin, or the cottagey **Villa Rose-Lawn**, 42 Avenue Roi Albert, with its half-timbering.

There is also the neoclassical palace **Le Californie** at 27 Av Roi Albert, or the **Moorish villa** on Avenue Costabelle. Dating from the early part of the 20th century are the Art Deco **Villa les Ondes** on Bd Stalingrad, and the Villa Fiesole, now known as the **Villa Domergue** after its owners, artist Jean-Gabriel Domergue and his sculptress wife, Odette, who have bequeathed the villa to the town. Among these opulent piles is the **Chapelle Bellini**, once part of a lavish, Tuscan-style palace built at the end of the 19th century. The painter Bellini used it as a studio until his death in 1989, and his paintings are scattered amid the Baroque excess of the chapel interior.

Russian nobility mingled with the playboys, all outdoing each other in architectural eccentricity, in this swanky part of town. The onion-domed Orthodox **church of the Archangel Michael**, on Boulevard Alexandre III, was built to accommodate the substantial court of Tsarina Marie Alexandrovna. Members of the Imperial family wintered here before the Russian Revolution and were buried here after it. The interior is filled with extraordinary glowing icons and bannered messages from the Imperial family; the church choir is rumoured to set spines tingling.

There are more follies on the other side of Cannes in **La Croix des Gardes**, or the *Quartier des Anglais*; this is where Lord Brougham first built the Palladian-style **Villa Eléonore-Louise** (24 Av du Docteur Picaud). English friends followed and were seduced, among them Sir Thomas Woodfield, who built a Gothic castle, the **Château des Tours** (or the Villa Ste-Ursule), with pink gneiss at 6 Av Jean de Noailles. Woodfield's gardener, John Taylor, noted the increasing exchange of properties and set up Cannes' first real-estate agency. Among the other architectural landmarks is the very grand neoclassical **Villa Rothschild**, built by Baron Rothschild in 1881.

The Old Port and Le Suquet

The **Vieux Port**, with its bobbing fishing boats and plush luxury craft, is on the other side of the Palais des Festivals. Plane trees line the **Allées de la Liberté**, where the flower market and Saturday fleamarket take place. Two streets further back, narrow pedestrian **Rue Meynadier** is the best place to buy cheese (Ferme Savoyarde) and fresh pasta (Aux Bons Raviolis), near the sumptuous **Forville** covered market. Cannes' cramped old quarter, **Le Suquet**, rises up on the other side of the port, where the usual renovation and displacement of the not-so-rich is just beginning. At the city's highest point, the monks of St-Honorat built the square watchtower, the **Tour du Mont Chevalier**, in 1088, and their priory is now the **Musée de la Castre** (*t 04 93 38 55 26; open April–May Tues–Sun 10–1 and 2–6; June–Aug 10–1 and 3–7; Sept 10–1 and 2–6; Oct–Mar 10–1 and 2–5; closed Mon; adm, free first Sun of month*), a little museum at a little price, with an archaeological and ethnographic collection donated by a generous Dutch baron in 1873, containing everything from Etruscan vases to pre-Columbian art and a 40-armed Buddha.

The Iles de Lérins

When Babylon begins to pall, you can take refuge on a delightful pair of green, wooded, traffic-free islets just off the coast. Known in antiquity as Lero and Lerina, they are now named after two saints who founded religious houses on them at the end of the 4th century: little **Ile Saint-Honorat** and the larger **Ile Sainte-Marguerite**. (Take water and a picnic, for there is only a smattering of expensive little shops and cafés on Sainte-Marguerite and just one restaurant on Saint-Honorat.)

Saint-Honorat, Isle of Snakes

According to legend, when Saint Honorat landed on the islet that bears his name in 375 he found it swarming with noxious snakes and prayed to be delivered of them. They immediately dropped dead, but the stench of the cadavers was so hideous that Honorat climbed a palm tree and prayed again, asking for the bodies to be washed away. God obliged again, and in memory the symbol of the island became two palm trees intertwined with a snake.

Saint Honorat shares with Jean Cassien of St-Victor in Marseille the distinction of introducing monasticism to France. The island became a beacon of light and learning in the dark ages; by the 7th century the monastery of St-Honorat had 4,000 monks, and 100 priories and lordships on the mainland (including Cannes, which belonged to the monastery until 1788). Its alumni numbered 20 saints, including St Patrick, who, before going to Ireland, trained here and picked up some tips on dealing with pesky snakes. The monastery was also a big boon to local sinners: a journey to St-Honorat could earn a pilgrim an indulgence equal to a journey to the Holy Land. Other visitors, especially Saracen pirates, were not as welcome. To protect themselves, the monks built a fortress, connected to the abbey by means of an underground tunnel. Although the original abbey is long gone, the evocative, crenellated **donjon** remains strong, lapped by the wavelets on three sides. There's a vaulted cloister and chapel, and a terrace with views that stretch to the Alps. In 1869, Cistercians from Sénanque purchased St-Honorat, rebuilt the **abbey** (which still offers accommodation for visitors) and have done all they can to preserve the islet's beauty and serenity, so close and yet so far from the sound and fury of Cannes. The monks who live there continue to cultivate part of the island, producing honey, wine and a liqueur called Lérina, all described in their website, *www.abbayedelerins.com*.

Sainte-Marguerite and the Man in the Iron Mask

Legend has it that Marguerite, sister of St Honorat, founded a convent for holy Christian women on this island, but it broke her heart that her austere brother would only come to visit her when a certain almond tree blossomed. Marguerite asked God to make him come more often and her prayer was answered when the almond tree miraculously began to bloom every month. Ste-Marguerite has nicer beaches than St-Honorat, especially on the south end of Chemin de la Chasse. At the beginning of 2003, the island's forest became a nature reserve.

On the north end stands the gloomy **Fort Royal** (*t 04 93 38 55 26; open April–Sept Tues–Sun 10.30–1.15 and 2.15–5.45; Oct–Mar 10.30–1.15 and 2.15–4.45; closed Mon and hols; adm*), with a little **aquarium** and a **Musée de la Mer** which displays finds from submarine digs. The fort was built by Richelieu as a defence against the Spaniards (who got it anyway) and improved by Vauban in 1712. By then the fortress mainly served as a prison, especially for the mysterious Man in the Iron Mask, who was transferred here from Pigneroles in 1687 and ended up in the Bastille in 1698. Speculation about the man's identity continues at least to divert historians (who insist that the mask was actually leather): was he Louis XIV's twin, as Voltaire suggested, or, according to a more recent theory, the gossiping son-in-law of the doctor who performed the autopsy on Louis XIII and discovered that the king was incapable of producing children? Later prisoners included six Huguenot pastors who dared to return to France after Louis XIV's revocation of the Edict of Nantes; they were kept in solitary confinement until all but one of them went mad.

The Esterel to Bandol

11

The Western Côte d'Azur: The Esterel to Bandol

VAR

Carcès
Le Luc
St-Maximin-la-Ste-Baume
Brignoles
Gonfaron
Cuers
Collobrières
Massif de la Ste-Baume
Le Castellet
Le Beausset
La Cadière d'Azur
St-Cyr-sur-Mer
Les Lecques
La Ciotat
Evenos
Ollioules
TOULON
Bandol
Ile de Bendor
Sanary-sur-Mer
Six-Fours-les-Plages
Les Sablettes
Le Brusc
Ile des Embiez
La Seyne
St-Mandrier
Golfe de Giens
Cap Sicié
Hyères
L'Almanarre
La Capte
Giens
La Tour-Fondue
Ile de Porquerolles

N

10 km
5 miles

Highlights

1 The venerable Cité Episcopale in Fréjus
2 Razzle-dazzle St-Tropez and its beaches
3 Walking and diving in the national park of Port-Cros island
4 Wine and the *pastis* king's island, in Bandol

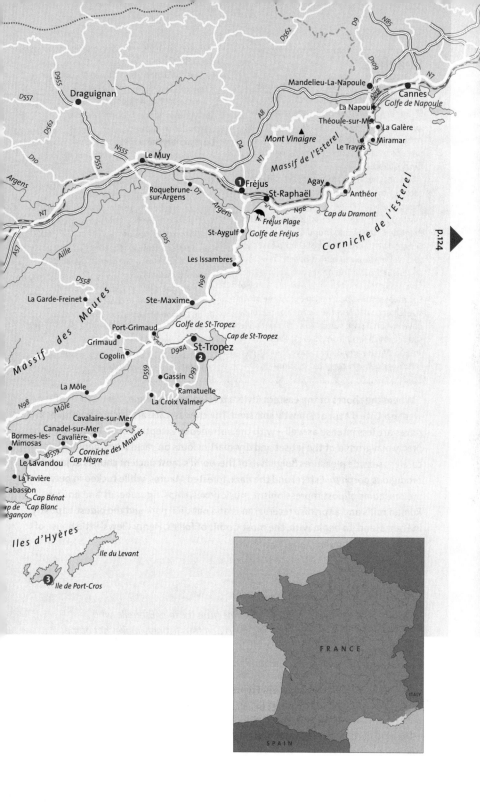

Draguignan

Mandelieu-La-Napoule

Cannes
Golfe de Napoule

La Napoule

Théoule-sur-Mer

La Galère

Miramar

Le Trayas

Mont Vinaigre ▲

Massif de l'Esterel

Le Muy

① Fréjus

Roquebrune-
sur-Argens

St-Raphaël

Agay

Anthéor

Corniche de l'Esterel

Cap du Dramont

St-Aygulf

Fréjus Plage

Golfe de Fréjus

Les Issambres

La Garde-Freinet

Ste-Maxime

Massif des Maures

Port-Grimaud

Golfe de St-Tropez

Cap de St-Tropez

Grimaud

St-Tropez **②**

Cogolin

La Môle

Gassin

Ramatuelle

La Croix Valmer

Môle

Cavalaire-sur-Mer

Canadel-sur-Mer

Corniche des Maures

Bormes-les-
Mimosas

Cavalière

Le Lavandou

Cap Nègre

La Favière

Cabasson

Cap Bénat

Cap Blanc

égançon

Iles d'Hyères

Ile du Levant

③ *Ile de Port-Cros*

FRANCE

ITALY

SPAIN

Beaches

This region contains some of the most enticing beaches in France. From Cannes to St-Tropez the dramatic corniche road offers glimpses down to small sandy coves hiding between jagged rocks. This is, above all, a place to take your time, stopping where fancy dictates.

The beaches of St-Tropez are actually 5km south of the town – Plage de Tahiti is the most infamous, Plage de Pampelonne the least spoiled. True aficionados head south to Plage de l'Escalet and round Cap Lardier to Gigaro. The footpath east of Gigaro takes you to a well-patronized nudist beach.

From St-Trop to Toulon the road climbs and falls along the Corniche des Maures. Some of the most revered beaches in Europe lie off this stretch of coastline – the Iles de Porquerolles have national park status and offer unrivalled sand (catch a ferry from Hyères). West of Toulon, Sanary and Bandol have thin strips, but these get very crowded in summer.

Best Beaches

Esterel coast: dozens of tiny coves between St-Raphaël, Boulouris and Agay, marked with yellow signs along the corniche road.

St-Aygulf: long sand, lots of space, but crowded in summer.

Les Issambres: as above.

Port Grimaud: long beach backing on to Spoerry's *cité lacustre*.

St-Tropez: Plage de Tahiti, Plage de Pampelonne, Plage de l'Escalet.

Gigaro: long beach, a favourite with families.

St-Clair: just outside Le Lavandou; views across to the islands.

Cap de Brégançon: wilder coves, off the beaten track. Cabasson is the French president's summer retreat.

Ile de Porquerolles: Plage de Notre-Dame, or any of the northern coastal beaches.

Ile du Levant: Héliopolis, premier nudist beach.

Hyères: large town beach.

St-Cyr: 2km of fine sand with a gentle slope; perfect for small children.

Where the shores of the eastern Riviera tend to be all shingle, the beaches of the western Côte d'Azur are mostly soft sand. The crowds, cars, art, yachts, boutiques and prices are less intense as well – with the outrageous exception of St-Tropez, the pretty playground of the jet set and dry-martini louts on yachts. Just behind these careless seaside pleasures bulge two of the world's most ancient chunks of land, the prodigious porphyry Esterel and the dark, forested Maures, while tucked in between are museums of postimpressionism, music boxes, ships' figureheads and booze; Roman ruins and a tortoise reserve; an island national park and the oldest baptistry in France; and, to begin with, the most Gothic of follies, Henry Clews' little house of horrors in La Napoule.

The Esterel

The Esterel is supposed to receive its name from the fairy Esterelle, who intoxicates and deceives her ardent lovers and thus fittingly makes her home on the Coast of Illusion.
Douglas Goldring, *The South of France* (1952)

Between Cannes and St-Raphaël this fairy Coast of Illusion provides one of nature's strangest interludes: a wild *massif* of blood-red cliffs and promontories, with sandy or shingle beaches amid dishevelled porphyry boulders tumbling into the blue, blue sea – the kind of romantic landscape where holy hermits like St Honorat (*see* pp.165–6) and unholy brigands like Gaspard de Besse felt equally at home. The handsome

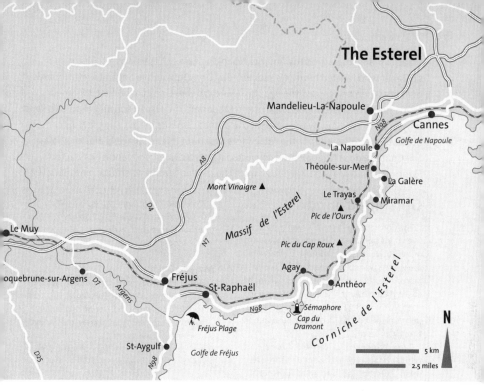

Mandelieu-La-Napoule

Cannes

Golfe de Napoule

La Napoule

Théoule-sur-Mer

La Galère

Mont Vinaigre ▲

Le Trayas

Miramar

Pic de l'Ours ▲

Massif de l'Esterel

Pic du Cap Roux ▲

Le Muy

Agay

oquebrune-sur-Argens

Fréjus

Anthéor

St-Raphaël

Sémaphore

Cap du
Dramont

Fréjus Plage

St-Aygulf

Golfe de Fréjus

Corniche de l'Esterel

N

5 km

2.5 miles

Gaspard, from a bourgeois family of Besse-sur-Issole, was himself the stuff of romance – a generous highwayman with courtly manners, a lover of good food and wine, a scholar who entertained the jury at his trial in Aix by reciting passages of Homer and Anacreon in Greek. When they hanged him anyway, many a woman wept bitter tears (others wondered where he hid all his booty – it has never been found). Unfortunately, the virgin cork forests that once hid Gaspard's band in the Esterel have been ravaged by fire – environmental tragedies with the side effect of clearing sites for property brigands and their grotesque cement-mixers, who race neck-and-neck with the forestry service's gallant attempts to reforest the arid mountain with drought- and disease-resilient pines and ilexes. Come in the spring, when wild flowers ignite this Fauvist volcanic fairyland; in summer, to lower the risk of accidental fires, the internal roads are often closed to traffic.

Mandelieu-La Napoule

Golf is what makes Mandelieu famous. There are nine- and 18-hole courses; the first was laid out a hundred years ago by the nephew of the Tsar, the latest by an American. The brochures speak of 'panoramas to stop you from breathing'. If you recover your breath, down below on the coast, Mandelieu's sister town, La Napoule, has the usual beaches and hotels and the nuttiest folly ever built by a foreigner on this shore, the **Fondation d'Art Henry Clews** (*t 04 93 49 95 05; open Feb–Oct daily 10–6, guided tours daily at 11.30, 2.30, 3.30 and 4.30; adm*), a pseudo-medieval fantasy castle beautifully set near the Pointe des Pendus (Hanged Men's Point), built by a pseudo-medieval artist, Henry Clews.

Born in 1863 into a wealthy American banking family, Clews was a sculptor and designer who fancied himself a modern-day Don Quixote. He began to re-invent his own life when he married the beautiful Elsie Whelen Goelet, whom he renamed Marie because she reminded him of the Madonna. They had a son and moved to Paris, only to be chased out by the noise of the bombardments in 1917. The Clewses came down to the coast, bought the ruined fort first built by the Saracens and known as the Château de la Napoule, and converted it into a crenellated fantasy castle that Henry called La Mancha, his refuge from the modern world, scientists, reformers, the

Getting Around

The Corniche de l'Esterel is well served by five trains per day and buses (at least two an hour) between Cannes and St-Raphaël. Trains are very reasonably priced, but the buses can be considerably more expensive than in the eastern Côte d'Azur. The central number for the SNCF is t 08 92 35 35 35; for buses, call SVA Beltrame on t 04 94 95 95 16 or Bus Azur on t 04 93 45 20 08.

From Mandelieu-La Napoule there are regular boats (€11) to the Iles de Lérins (*see* pp.165–6) from the harbour at **Transports Maritimes Napoulais, t** 04 93 49 15 88, *April–Oct*. For bike hire, try Location 2 Roues, Mandelieu-La Napoule, t 04 92 97 27 37.

Tourist Information

Mandelieu-La Napoule: Rue Jean Monnet, t 04 93 93 64 66, f 04 93 93 64 65. For hotel reservations: centraleresa@ot-mandelieu.fr, www.ot-mandelieu.fr. *Open Mon–Fri 9–12.30, 1.30–6*.
Bd Henry Clews, La Napoule, t 04 93 49 95 31, f 04 92 97 99 57. *Open April–June and Sept–mid-Oct Mon–Fri 10–12.30 and 1.30–6; July–Aug daily 10–7. Closed mid-Oct–Mar*.
Av de Cannes, Termes, t 04 92 97 99 27, f 04 92 97 09 18. *Open mid-Oct–Mar Mon–Sat 9.30–12.30 and 1.30–5.30; April–June and Sept–mid-Oct Tues–Sat 9.30–12.30 and 2–6; July–Aug daily 9.30–12 and 2–6*.
Théoule: 1 Corniche d'Or, t 04 93 49 28 28, f 04 93 49 00 04, www.theoule-sur-mer.org. *Open summer Mon–Sat 9–7, Sun 10–3; winter Mon–Sat 9–12 and 2.30–6.30*.
Agay: Place Giannetti, t 04 94 82 01 85, f 04 94 82 74 20, agay.tourisme@wanadoo.fr,

www.esd-fr.com/agay. *Open Feb–Oct daily 9–6; Nov–Jan Mon–Sat 9–12 and 2–6*.
Internet: Computec, Av de Fréjus, Mandelieu-La Napoule, t 04 92 97 75 00.

Market Days

Théoule: Place Général Bertrand, Friday; Port de Figueirette-Miramar, Tuesday in summer.
Mandelieu-La Napoule: Place St Fainéant, Thursday morning; Wednesday and Friday morning in town centre.
Agay: General market, in front of tourist office, Wednesday morning.

Where to Stay and Eat

Mandelieu-La Napoule ✉ 06210
****Ermitage du Riou, Av Henry Clews, t 04 93 49 95 56, f 04 92 97 69 05, hotel@ermitage-du-riou.fr, www.ermitage-du-riou.fr (*luxury–expensive*). A luxurious refuge built like a Provençal bastide, with a garden and pool overlooking the sea. Restaurant (*very expensive–expensive*).
***Hostellerie du Golf, 780 Av de la Mer, t 04 93 49 11 66, f 04 92 97 04 01, hoteldu golf@aol.com (*moderate*). With a pool, restaurant, and rooms with terraces.
**La Calanque, Av Henry Clews, t 04 93 49 95 11, f 04 93 49 67 44 (*inexpensive*). Much more affordable, with a shady terrace, restaurant (*moderate*) and views of the sea and Clews' folly. *Closed Nov–Mar*.
L'Armorial, Bd Henry Clews, t 04 93 49 91 80 (*expensive–moderate*). In an elegant residence by the sea, this restaurant serves a *bouillabaisse* that must rank among the best to be found in the region, plus immaculately prepared dishes such as Roquefort terrine.

middle class, democrats and everything else (although everyone noticed he didn't extend his hatred to telephones and the other mod cons of the day). Over the door he carved his life's motto: 'Once Upon a Time'.

Once installed, the Clewses rarely left the fairytale world they created. Henry designed the costumes, not only for himself and Marie but also for the maids and the Senegalese butler. They filled the château and garden with peacocks, flamingos and other exotic birds, and loved to stage dramatic, elaborate dinner parties that to the bewildered guests seemed to come straight out of a Hollywood movie. The most

Save room for the chocolate charlotte and truffles. *Closed Wed out of season.*
Le Boucanier, Port la Napoule, t 04 93 49 80 51 (*moderate*). For dinner, try the *soupe de poissons* or *plateau de fruits de mer.* *Closed Thurs in winter, and mid-Nov–Dec.*

Théoule-sur-Mer ✉ 06590
★★★★Miramar Beach Hôtel, 47 Av de Miramar, t 04 93 75 05 05, f 04 93 75 44 83, *reservation@mbhotel.com, www.mbhriviera. com* (*luxury–very expensive*). A luxurious, Provençal-style 'thalasso-energy' centre, spilling down in ochre-coloured balustraded terraces to the water's edge. The grounds include pools, private beaches, beauty treatments and a gastronomic restaurant, **L'Etoile des Mers** (*very expensive–expensive*), which, under chef Laurent Modret, has been garnering a substantial reputation; the many dishes to linger over include lamb with caramelized onions and apricots.
Le Jardin de la Mer, 54 Av de Lérins, t 04 93 49 96 95 (*expensive–moderate*). Fish tanks flash with shoals of exotic fish; some are stocked with langoustines and lobsters heading for the pot. Among the specialities are *crème brûlée* with chestnut *confit*.

Le Trayas ✉ 83700
★★Le Relais des Calanques, Corniche de l'Esterel, t 04 94 44 14 06, f 04 94 44 10 93 (*expensive*). Right on the sea, this hotel has 14 rooms, a pool, two tiny private beaches and a good fish restaurant (*moderate*) on a terrace over the red sea rocks. *Closed Tues and Oct–April.*
Auberge de Jeunesse, 9 Av de La Véronèse, t 04 93 75 40 23, f 04 93 75 43 45 (*moderate*). Superb, but, as usual with youth hostels, as if challenging the hardiness of youth,

hard to reach – 2km uphill from the station (last bus from the train station 7.30pm); has superb views, however. In summer, book (card required). *Closed Jan–mid-Feb.*

Anthéor ✉ 83700
★★Les Flots Bleus, on the N98, t 04 94 44 80 21, f 04 94 44 83 71, *www.hotel-cote-azur.com* (*inexpensive*). All rooms have grandiose views of the sea and the Esterel, though the trains pass close by and it is just off the main road. Good value, however, and the seafood served on the tree-shaded terrace (*moderate*) is fresh and copious. *Closed Nov–Mar.*

Agay ✉ 83700
★★★Sol e Mar, Plage Le Dramont, t 04 94 95 25 60, f 04 94 83 83 61, *hotelsolemar@club-internet.fr* (*expensive*). Right on the sea, with two saltwater pools and an excellent restaurant (*moderate*). *Closed mid-Oct–Mar.*
★★★France Soleil, Bd de la Plage, t 04 94 82 01 93, f 04 94 82 73 95 (*moderate*). In Agay itself, a reliable choice on the beach. *Closed Nov–Easter.*

Inland
★★★★Auberge des Adrets, along the N7, just beyond Mt Vinaigre, t 04 94 82 11 82, f 04 94 82 11 80, *auberge@compuserve.com, www.auberge-adrets.com* (*very expensive*). Once a lonely inn (dating back to 1653) and notorious haunt of bandits like Gaspard de Besse, this has become one of the most romantic hideaways on the Côte. The dining room (*expensive; closed Sun pm and Mon except July–Aug*) has low beamed ceilings and a huge fire, and the bedrooms are the latest in *chi chi chic*, with Christian Dior furnishings. *Closed Nov.*

lasting feature of all is Henry's personal mythology, devoted to something he called Humormystics, amply illustrated in stone throughout the castle, cloister capitals and gardens: weird monsters and grotesques, human figures and animals, many in egg and phallic shapes with cryptic inscriptions and most carved in stone out of his private quarry in the Esterel with the help of 12 stonecutters. Here, too, is Clews' own self-designed tomb and epitaph ('Grand Knight of La Mancha Supreme Master Humormystic Castelan of Once upon a Time Chevalier de Marie'), completed by Marie, who survived until 1959 and made sure all was preserved intact by founding the charitable La Napoule Arts Foundation, where American and French artists and writers can work immersed in Clews' phantasmagoria.

Corniche de l'Esterel

Laid out by the French Touring Club way back in 1903, the Corniche de l'Esterel (N98) is dotted with panoramic belvederes overlooking the extraordinary red, blue and green seascapes below. The largest beaches of sand or shingle are served by snack wagons in the summer and, in between, with a bit of climbing, are rocky coves and nooks you can have all to yourself.

Heading south from La Napoule, **Théoule-sur-Mer**, which claims to be only ten minutes from Cannes' Croisette, has small beaches and an 18th-century seaside soap factory converted into a castle. This isn't bad compared to **La Galère** (the next town south on the same road), infected in the 1970s by a private housing estate which looks as if it were modelled on cancer cells. This is a suburb of fashionable **Miramar**, where the best thing to do is avoid the strings of stuffy private beaches and walk out along **Pointe de l'Esquillon** for the view of the sheer cliffs of Cap Roux plunging into the sea. The nearby slopes and jagged shore, pierced with inlets and secret coves, belong to the villas and hotels of **Le Trayas**.

Beyond Le Trayas, a road at **Pointe de l'Observatoire** ascends to the **Grotte de la Ste-Baume**, where St Honorat resided as a hermit when four-star views were free of charge. Meanwhile the Corniche road itself twists and turns towards **Anthéor,** which has a good little beach, and the Esterel's biggest resort, Agay, a laid-back village set under porphyry cliffs, around a perfect horseshoe bay rimmed with sand and pebble beaches. For all that, a corner of it has sold its soul to the developers, who have constructed a 'model Provençal village': a brash, synthetic concrete lump which has all the charm and authenticity of a TV dinner. In 1944 the American 36th Division disembarked just to the west at the **Plage du Dramont**, where you can pick up the path to the Sémaphore du Dramont (about an hour's walk) for panoramas over the **Gulf of Fréjus** and the two porphyry sea rocks (called the 'Lion de la Mer' and the 'Lion de la Terre') at its entrance. The 'medieval' tower on the minuscule island now called the Ile d'Or was in fact built during the Belle Epoque by an eccentric doctor, who liked to invite celebrities to his 'Kingdom of the Black Isle' and patronize them from his throne. The island and the mad doctor became the inspiration for Hergé's book *Tintin and the Black Isle*. The area also seems to have made an impression in Neolithic times: there's a menhir and other, rather mysterious engraved stones on the ancient road from Dramont to Agay.

The Esterel: Inland Routes

From Cannes, the N7 follows the path of the Roman Via Aurelia, passing through the bulk of the Esterel's surviving cork forest. This is ravishing scenery, ravished by the world that wants to see it. It is possible to see it underneath all its tourists, at least at dawn, in sunny near-silence, when only a few sleepy campers are stirring. The road winds past the old Auberge des Adrets, a 17th-century inn and notorious haunt of bandits like Gaspard de Besse, now the plushest of four-star hideouts (*see* 'Where to Stay', p.173). The high point of the trip, both literally and figuratively, is **Mont Vinaigre**, rising to 1,968ft; from the road a path leads to its summit (about 30 minutes) and a fantastic viewing platform in an old watchtower. Oleander lines the tumbling gorge of the **Ravin de Perthus** further inland, and you can wiggle left off the N7 from Mandelieu at Pont St-Jean and climb up to the Col de la Cadière and the Col Notre-Dame for more vertiginous views over the red rocks and out to sea. Other hairpinning roads begin in Agay and lead to within walking distance of the Esterel's most dramatic features: the hellish **Ravin du Mal-Infernet**, and a scattering of panoramic peaks – the **Pic de l'Ours** and **Pic du Cap Roux** have afforded vision-inspiring views since the 6th century, when the area was littered with hermits. From here the Esterel is at her most stunning, and the Coast of Illusion a flaming vision of colour and light.

St-Raphaël and Fréjus

Between the Esterel and the Massif des Maures, in the fertile little plain of the Argens river, St-Raphaël and Fréjus are the big noises on the coast between Cannes and Hyères. After the fireworks of the Esterel, St-Raphaël has – guess what? – more beaches, holiday flats and yachts, and is swollen so big as to merge with its venerable neighbour Fréjus (Forum Julii), a market town and naval port on the Via Aurelia founded by Julius Caesar himself to rival Greek Marseille. Octavian made it his chief arsenal, to build the ships that licked Cleopatra and Mark Antony at Actium. Even today, Fréjus is a garrison town, with France's largest naval air base.

St-Raphaël

Once the fiefdom of the ambitious François Léotard, leader of the centre-right UDF party, and now run like a tight ship by Mayor Georges Ginesta, St-Raphaël has money, if not much heart. Its once glittering turn-of-the-20th-century follies and medieval centre were bombed to smithereens in the war, sparing only the Victorian-Byzantine church of **Notre-Dame-de-Lépante** in Bd Felix-Martin (with a popular altar to St Antoine, patron saint of lost objects, surrounded with grateful plaques for services rendered) and the **Eglise des Templiers** or St-Pierre (1150), with its Templar watch-tower, in Rue des Templiers (just north of the station). This is the third church to occupy the site, reusing the same old Roman stones – one in the choir vault is carved with something you won't often see in church: a flying phallus, an ancient charm for averting evil (Pompeii has lots of them). In the 17th century, the chapel was fortified

Getting There and Around

By Train

St-Raphaël is the terminus of the Métrazur trains that run along the coast to Menton. Other trains between Nice and Marseille call at both St-Raphaël and Fréjus stations, making it easy to hop between the two towns; St-Raphaël also has direct connections to Aix, Avignon, Nîmes, Montpellier and Carcassonne, and it's 4hrs 30mins on the TGV from Paris.

By Bus

Both towns have buses for Nice airport and Marseille (Cars Phocéens, **t** 04 91 50 57 68, and Beltrane, **t** 04 94 95 95 16), pricier ones for St-Tropez and Toulon (SODETRAV, **t** 04 94 95 24 82), and buses inland for Bagnols, Fayence and Les Adrets (Gagnard, **t** 04 94 95 24 78).

There is an information point at the bus station in St-Raphaël, but It is better to get timetables from the tourist information office opposite the train station.

By Boat

Les Bateaux de St-Raphaël, **t** 04 94 95 17 46, *www.tmr-saintraphael,com*. Depart regularly from the Vieux Port, Centre Ville, to St-Tropez and Port Grimaud, and make day excursions to the Iles de Lérins and Ile de Port Cros (April– Oct), as well as jaunts around the Golfe de Fréjus and its *calanques* (creeks); be sure to reserve in July–Aug.

Taxis

t 04 94 83 24 24.

Bicycle Hire

Action 2 Roues, Fréjus, **t** 04 94 44 48 34.
Cycles Patrick Béraud, Fréjus, **t** 04 94 51 20 20.
Holiday Bikes, Fréjus, **t** 04 94 52 30 65.
Cycles Thierry, St-Raphaël, **t** 04 94 95 48 46. Also does watersport rentals.
A Tout Cycles, St-Raphaël, **t** 04 94 95 56 91.

Tourist Information

St-Raphaël: Rue Waldeck Rousseau (opposite the train station), **t** 04 94 19 52 52, **f** 04 94 83 85 40, *information@saint-raphael.com*, *www.saint-raphael.com*. *Open July–Aug daily 9–7; rest of year Mon–Sat 9–12.30 and 2–6.30.* There is also a hotel reservation service across the road at the station: **t** 04 94 19 10 60, **f** 04 94 19 10 67, *reservation@saint-raphael.com*.

Fréjus: 325 Rue Jean Jaurès, **t** 04 94 51 83 83, **f** 04 94 51 00 26, *frejus.tourisme@wanadoo. fr*, *www.ville-frejus.fr*. *Open summer Mon–Sat 10–12.30 and 2.30–6.30, Sun and public hols during school hols 10–12 and 3–6, winter Mon–Sat 9–12, 2–6, Sun and public hols during school hols 10–12 and 3–6.*

Fréjus-Plage: Bd de la Libération, **t** 04 94 51 48 42. *Open June–Sept Mon–Sat 10–12.30 and 3–6.30; Sun and hols 10–12 and and 3–6.*

Internet: Cyberbureau, 123 Rue Waldeck Rousseau, St-Raphaël, **t** 04 94 95 29 36. *Closed Sat.*

and rebuilt along with the crenellated seigneurial mansion next door. If the church is closed, pick up the key at the adjacent **Musée de Préhistoire et d'Archéologie Sous-marine** (*t 04 94 19 25 75; open June–Sept Tues–Sat 10–12 and 3–6.30; Oct–May Tues–Sat 10–12 and 2–5.30; adm*). For centuries there were rumours of a sunken city off St-Raphaël, apparently confirmed by the bricks that divers kept bringing to shore. Jacques Cousteau went down to see and found, not Atlantis, but a Roman shipwreck full of building materials. Some are displayed here, along with a fine collection of amphorae. There is also a reconstruction of a Roman galley and a room devoted to the strange menhirs and dolmens of the eastern Var region. This is much the prettiest part of town, with a little maze of winding streets hemmed in by peeling houses, and a great place to pick up some very colloquial French at the rowdy food market.

The seafront is popular with ageing *flâneurs* (loafers) and yachting types strolling along the palm- and plane tree-edged boulevard in the footsteps of Alexandre

Market Days

St-Raphaël: General fruit, vegetable and other fresh local produce market in Place Victor Hugo and Place de la République daily; fish market in the Vieux Port daily; flea market in the Place Coullet, Tuesday.

Fréjus: Fresh local produce market in front of the city hall, Wednesday and Saturday mornings; flea market, Saturday morning, and 2nd Sunday in June and Sept.

Where to Stay and Eat

St-Raphaël ✉ 83700

The town of the archangel is rich in pricey campsites and grotesque holiday villages, but a few hotels stand out. The best choices are outside the centre.

***Golf de Valescure, Av Paul L'Hermite, **t** 04 94 52 85 00, **f** 04 94 82 41 88, *info@valescure.com, www.valescure.com* (*expensive*). This has been in the same family for five generations, with tennis and a pool when you're not on the links (*golf packages*).

***Le San Pedro, Av du Colonel Brooke, **t** 04 94 19 90 20, **f** 04 94 19 90 21, *info@hotel-sanpedro.com, www.hotel-sanpedro.com* (*expensive*). Good option in Valescure, which was the old artists' quarter before the First World War. *Restaurant (expensive) closed Tues, and Wed lunch, in winter.*

Les Pyramides, 77 Av P. Doumer, **t 04 98 11 10 10, **f** 04 98 11 10 20, *www.saint.raphael.com/pyramides* (*inexpensive*). This has a little garden. *Closed mid-Nov–mid-Mar.*

Centre International Le Manoir, Chemin de l'Escale, near the Boulouris station, **t** 04 94 95 20 58, **f** 04 94 83 85 06, *manoir@cei4vents.com, www.cei-manoir.com* (*inexpensive*). A youth hostel that is more like a holiday village; by the beach (*ages 18–35 only*). *Closed mid-Nov–mid-Mar.*

L'Arbousier, 6 Av de Valescure, **t** 04 94 95 25 00 (*expensive*). Combines charm and excellent, aromatic gourmet food for half the price you'd pay elsewhere. *Closed Sun eve, Mon and Wed eve out of season.*

Pastorel, 54 Rue de la Liberté, **t** 04 94 95 02 36 (*moderate*). Try the Friday special €26 *aïoli* menu at Pastorel, an excellent address since 1922, with a pleasant, no-nonsense proprietress and an attractive garden terrace. Madame Pastorel's grandson heads the team in the kitchens. *Closed end of Dec–end of Jan, plus Sun eve, Mon and Tues; closed all lunchtimes and Mon in July–Aug.*

Bleu Marine, Port Santa Lucia, **t** 04 94 95 31 31 (*moderate*). An excellent lunchtime menu, including wine, with dishes such as a light cod fillet with shellfish.

Les Terrasses de L'Orangerie, Promenade René Coty, **t** 04 94 83 10 50 (*moderate*). A Belle Epoque brasserie with sea views. *Closed Tues eve, Sun eve and Wed; also closed Jan.*

La Sarriette, 45 Rue de la République, **t** 04 94 19 28 13 (*moderate*). The house speciality is a regal *pied de cochon*, plus plenty of excellent alternatives at this humble, friendly little place. *Closed Sun eve and Mon.*

L'Aristocloche, 15 Bd St-Sébastien, **t** 04 94 95 28 36 (*moderate–cheap*). Friendly and old-

Dumas, Hector Berlioz and F. Scott Fitzgerald (who wrote *Tender is the Night* here). There are brief echoes of the golden days of the Belle Epoque in the handful of regal villas which escaped the bombs, but nowadays St-Raph, as everyone calls it, has hung up its smoking jacket and settled into comfortable middle age, with nondescript apartment buildings overlooking carefully kept lawns and a seafront which looks like a theme park for the over 50s. There is a new **cultural centre**, however (*Place Gabriel Péri, t 04 98 11 89 00, open Tues–Sat 8.30–7*), which hosts exhibitions and concerts.

At the eastern edge of town, heading up to the outlying *commune* of Boulouris, is the monstrous new marina, **Port Santa Lucia**, with a handful of neon-lit bars and restaurants. Behind it, the 8km **Sentier du Littoral** starts to wind its way around the coast, over rough steps cut into the red rock and past tiny pockmarked coves.

fashioned; there is home-made bread to go with the *estouffade provençale de bœuf* and *nougat glacé à la lavande*. Local products are displayed for sale outside the restaurant on market days. *Closed Sun and Mon.*

Piccola Sicilia, 108 Rue de la Garonne, t 04 94 83 11 32 (*cheap*). Enormous platefuls of Sicilian home cooking. Make time for a much needed siesta afterwards. *Closed Mon eve in summer; Mon in winter.*

Fréjus ✉ 83600

***L'Aréna, 139 Rue du Gal. de Gaulle, t 04 94 17 09 40, f 04 94 52 01 52, *www.arena-hotel. com* (*expensive*). Colourful, air-conditioned rooms, a pool and good food (*expensive*) in old Fréjus. *Closed mid-Dec–mid-Jan, restaurant closed Mon eve and Sun eve, and Nov.*

Bellevue, by the cathedral in Place Paul Vernet, t 04 94 17 21 58, f 04 94 51 42 46 (*inexpensive*). The best of the cheapies, with 12 rooms.

Auberge de Jeunesse, t 04 94 53 18 75, f 04 94 53 25 86, *st.raphael@wanadoo.fr*, *www. youth.hostel.frejus.fr* (*inexpensive*). This is 2km from Fréjus' historic centre, in a large park east on the N7; take the shuttle bus from the station at St-Raphaël (platform 7). It also has a small campsite. *Closed mid-Nov–Feb.*

Le Mérou Ardent, 157 Bd de la Libération, t 04 94 17 30 58 (*moderate*). Has a terrace overlooking the beach, a delicious monkfish with prawns, and a rich *fondant au chocolat. Closed Wed eve and Thurs, but check.*

Le Bateau, 1-2 Quai Octave, t 04 94 17 00 00 (*moderate*). A large and modern brasserie, but the service is impeccable and the food remarkably good – try the *choucroute royale* or the salmon.

Les Potiers, 135 Rue des Potiers, t 04 94 51 33 74 (*moderate*). Sparky *nouvelle cuisine* restaurant on a quiet back street in the old town. *Closed Tues, Wed lunch, and 3 weeks Dec.*

Le Cadet Rousselle, 25 Place Agricola, t 04 94 53 36 92 (*cheap*). Eat a filling meal for less money at this popular *crêperie/saladerie*, tucked inside the Place Agricola near the cinema. *Closed mid-Dec–mid-Jan, Mon, and Thurs lunch.*

Entertainment and Nightlife

St-Raphaël

Casino de St-Raphaël, t 04 98 111 777. Gambling and dancing.

Le Seven, 171 Quai Albert Ier, t 04 94 83 93 07. *Closed Mon.*

Coco-Club, Port Santa Lucia, t 04 94 95 95 56. Live music and piano bar.

Le Lido, t 08 36 68 69 28. Cinema with an annual arts festival in September.

Loch Ness, Av de Valescure, t 04 94 95 99 49. Despite the name, a lively Irish pub.

Fréjus-Plage

Maison de la Bière, 461 Bd de la Libération, Fréjus-Plage, t 04 94 51 21 86. Over one hundred beers.

Fréjus

The Roman Town

Founded in 49 BC, Forum Julii (Julius' Market) was the first Roman town of Gaul, but not the most successful; the site was malarial and hard to defend, and eventually the Argens river silted up, creating the vast sandy beach of **Fréjus-Plage** but leaving the Roman harbour, once famous for its size, high and dry a mile from the sea. The port, now smelling rather pungent even for hardy 18th-century noses, was filled in in 1774. A path tracing the ruined quay begins at **Butte St-Antoine**, south of central Fréjus, but it's hard to picture 100 Roman galleys anchored in the weeds. Its one monument, the Lanterne d'Auguste, isn't even Roman, but a medieval harbourmaster's lodge built on a Roman base. Other fragments of Forum Julii are a long hike across the modern town – Fréjus is one place where those ubiquitous tourist trains come in handy. The best preserved is the ungainly greenish **Amphithéâtre Romain**, Rue Henri Vadon (*open Nov–Mar Mon–Fri 10–12 and 1–5.30, Sat 9.30–12.30 and 1.30–5.30, Sun 8–5; April–Oct Mon–Sat 10–1 and 2.30–6.30, Sun 8–7*), flat on its back like a beached whale with the rib arches of its vomitoria exposed to the sky. Arches from a 40km aqueduct still leapfrog by the road to Cannes. North, on Av du Théâtre Romain, the vaults of the **Théâtre Romain** (*open as Amphithéâtre; adm, free Sun*) survive, although the seating has had to be replaced (the coastal road once ran right through its middle). Rock concerts and bullfights now fill the bill.

La Cité Episcopale: the Oldest Baptistry in France

On a map marked with the walls that once contained Forum Julii, modern Fréjus looks like the last lamb-chop on a platter. The Saracens had much of the rest of it in the 10th century, coming back seven times to pillage and destroy the bits they missed. When the coast was clear in the 12th century, the Fréjussiens rebuilt their Cathédrale St-Léonce in Place Formigé, and in the 16th century gave it a superb pair of Renaissance doors carved with sacred scenes, a violent Saracen massacre and portraits of aristocratic ladies and gents, including King François Ier. Inside, over the sacristy door, there's a *Retable de Ste-Marguerite* (*c.* 1450) by Jacques Durandi, of the School of Nice. Ste Marguerite of Antioch is the patron saint of women in childbirth, and her crown of pearls symbolizes her purity and humility.

The cathedral was the centre of a mini **Cité Episcopale,** incorporating a crenellated defence tower, a chapterhouse and a bishop's palace (*t 04 94 51 26 30, www.monum. fr; mid-Aug–mid-May Tues–Sun 9–12 and 2–5; mid-May–mid-Aug daily 9–6.30; adm*), all built with the characteristic warm red stone of the Esterel mountain range. The tour includes the baptistry, the one bit of Fréjus the Saracens missed: late 4th century, octagonal (like all early baptistries it was modelled after the original, built in the 320s by Constantine in Rome) and defined by eight black granite columns with white capitals lifted from the Roman forum. Only adults were baptized in the early days. The pagans would enter the narrow door and have their feet washed at the terra-cotta basin; the bishop would then baptize them in the pool in the centre, and as new Christians they would exit through the larger door to attend Mass. Fairest of all is the 12th-century **cloister**, with slim marble columns and a 14th-century ceiling coffered into 1,200 little vignettes, of which a third still have curious paintings that comprise a whole catalogue of monkish fancies: grotesques, mermaids, animals, portraits and debaucheries. Upstairs, the **Archaeology Museum** (*t 04 94 52 15 78; open Nov–Mar Mon–Sat 10–12 and 1.30–5.30; April–Oct Mon–Sat 10–1 and 2.30–6.30*) has a collection of finds from Forum Julii, among them a perfectly preserved mosaic, a fine head of Jupiter and a copy of the two-faced bust of Hermes discovered in 1970.

Just off Place Formigé, at 53 Rue Sieyès, are two **Atlantes**, all that remains of the house of the Abbé Sieyès (1748–1836), pamphleteer of the Revolution, deputy at the Convention and mastermind of the 18th Brumaire coup that brought Napoleon to power. Later exiled as a regicide, the abbot returned to Paris in 1830, and when asked to sum up his career in politics he gave the famous laconic reply: 'I survived.'

Around Fréjus

Just outside Fréjus stand a scattering of remarkable monuments recalling the rotten days of the First World War, when states supplemented their manpower by importing men from the colonies to fight wars that weren't theirs. In 1917 the Vietnamese built the colourful **Pagode Hong Hien** as a memorial to their 5,000 dead, 2km from the centre on the N7 (*t 04 94 53 25 29; open daily 9–12 and 2–7; adm*), surrounded by protective dragons and white elephants. Almost next door, an imposing necropolis dedicated to the soldiers of the Indonesian wars is slotted into the flanks of the hill, and contains the remains of more than 24,000 soldiers and civilians involved in the terrible collapse of France's former colonial empire.

The Sudanese sharpshooters at the local marine base built the **Mosquée Missiri** (a concrete reproduction of the Missiri Mosque at Djenne, Mali) on Rte de Bagnols-en-Forêt, 5km from Fréjus by way of the N7 and D4 towards Fayence, which, although on a corner of military land, has been sadly abandoned to graffiti. Further along the D4, the **Musée des Troupes de Marine** (*t 04 94 40 81 75; open mid-June–mid-Sept Sun, Mon and Wed–Fri 10–12 and 3–7; winter 2–5; closed Tues and Sat*) covers the history of the marines from 1622 to the present. Another mile further on, at Le Capitou, you can drive and walk through the **Parc Zoologique** (*t 04 98 11 37 37; open June–Aug daily 10–6; Mar–May and Sept–Oct 10–5; Nov–Feb 10.30–4.30*), where parrots and yaks don't look too out of place under the parasol pines.

Just off the N7, in the **Tour de la Mare** district of Fréjus, is Notre-Dame de Jérusalem, the **Chapelle Cocteau** (*Av Nicolaï, La Tour de la Mare, t 04 94 53 27 06; open April–Oct Mon–Fri 2.30–6.30, Sat 10–1 and 2–6.30; Nov–Mar Mon–Fri 1.30–5.30, Sat 9.30–12.30 and 1.30–5.30; adm*), an octagonal chapel of soft grey stone surrounded by cypress, pine and olive trees and grazing donkeys, originally designed by Jean Cocteau in the 1960s. The chapel was to form part of a larger project to build an artists' residence, but, only months after the cornerstone was laid, Cocteau died, and the bold scope of the original idea shrank when faced with municipal apàthy and lack of funds. Finally, in 1988, the city contacted Cocteau's partner and heir, Edouard Dermit, also an artist; after examining Cocteau's original plans and models, he finally painted the chapel himself. Inside is an anarchic flurry of colour and form; limbs radiate from the glass window in the dome (symbolizing the *Resurrection of the Dead*) and colours bounce off the walls from the brilliant stained-glass windows. The frescoes are gentler pastel affairs: among the guests at the *Last Supper* are Cocteau himself, his close friend Francine Weismuller and the handsome face of Cocteau's friend and lover Jean Marais, who appears elsewhere as a blue-winged angel. Scattered throughout the chapel is the sturdy form of the cross of Jerusalem, which also tops the terracotta roof tiles; Cocteau dedicated the chapel to the Jerusalem Order of the Knights of the Holy Sepulchre, who supposedly guarded Christ's tomb. A millstone from an old olive mill, representing the great stone which was rolled away from the tomb, does service as an altar, with a cross and candlesticks also in the form of the Jerusalem Cross. Services are held here on the weekend closest to 15 September, when the holiday of the Tour de la Mare is celebrated.

Ten kilometres up the Argens river from St-Aygulf (Fréjus' resort suburb to the west), the picturesque 16th-century village of **Roquebrune-sur-Argens** offers a break from coastal craziness with a wine and orchid centre that boasts the largest mulberry tree in France. Then there's a comforting maze of higgledy-piggledy streets (markets take place on Tuesdays at the Place Ollier and on Fridays at the Place Alfred Perrin), and the curious 16th-century church of Saints Peter and Paul, which originally had a Gothic twist but was given an awkward facelift in the 18th century. More prehistoric and Roman artefacts are at the **Musée du Patrimoine Roquebrunois** in the Chapelle St-Jacques (*Rue de l'Hospice, t 04 94 45 34 28; open June–Sept Tues–Sat 10–12 and 2–6; Oct–May Thurs and Sat 10–12 and 2–6; adm*). Along the road to Le Muy, the Rochers de Roquebrune form a peculiar red baby massif that toddled away from the Esterel.

The Massif des Maures

Between Fréjus and Hyères, the coast bulges out and up again to form the steep rolling hills and arcadian natural amphitheatres of the ancient Massif des Maures. Although it lacks the high drama of the Esterel, this mountain range (2,300ft at its highest point) is just as much a geological oddball, its granite, gneiss and schist completely unrelated to the limestone that dominates the rest of Provence. The name Maures is derived from *maouro*, Provençal for black, describing its dark, deep forests of umbrella and Aleppo pines, chestnuts and cork. For centuries the latter two trees provided the main source of income of the few inland villages.

Until the 19th century this was the most dangerous coast in France. The Saracens made it their chief stronghold in the area in 846, building forts (*fraxinets*) on each hill

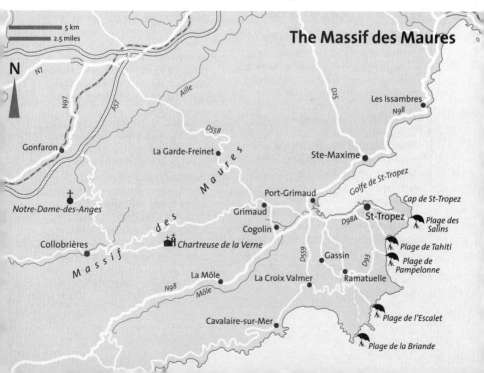

to watch for ships to plunder, and to defend themselves from the Franks. They were finally forced out in the campaign of 972, led by William of Provence, who was greatly assisted by a knight from Genoa named Grimaldi, the first of that family to make waves. But although the pirates had to abandon their *fraxinets*, they hardly abandoned the coast, and maintained a reign of terror that continued until 1830, when the French captured Algiers. A hundred years later, the fashion for seaside bathing spread west from the Riviera, giving every crowded beach a holiday town to call its own.

Ste-Maxime and Port Grimaud

In the seaside conurbation spread between Fréjus and St-Tropez, the only place that may tempt a detour is Ste-Maxime, a modern resort town with a shady, older nucleus by the port and a beach of golden sand facing St-Tropez. It willingly takes the overflow of fashionable and bankable holidaymakers from the latter, and is an attractive proposition as it's easy to commute by frequent boat to the capital of see-and-be-seen (St-Tropez may not look far away, but it's a 2hr traffic jam in high

Tourist Information

Ste-Maxime: 1 Promenade Simon Lorière , **t** 04 94 55 75 55, **f** 04 94 55 75 56. *Open Sept Mon–Sat 9–12 and 2–7; Oct–Mar Mon–Sat 9–12 and 2–6; April–May Mon–Sat 9–12.30, 2–6.30; June Mon–Sat 9–12.30 and 2–7, Sun 10–12 and 4–7; July–Aug Mon–Sat 9–8, Sun 10–12 and 4–7.*

Where to Stay and Eat

Ste-Maxime ✉ 83120

★★★★Belle Aurore, 5 Bd Jean Moulin, **t** 04 94 96 02 45, **f** 04 94 96 63 87, *www.belleaurore. com* (*luxury–very expensive*). Rooms with character as well as the usual four-star comforts and a fine restaurant (*expensive*). *Closed mid-Oct–April; restaurant closed Wed.*

★★★Hôtel Jas Neuf, 112 Av du Débarquement **t** 04 94 55 07 30, **f** 04 94 49 09 71, *info@ hotel-jasneuf.com, www.hotel-jasneuf.com* (*very expensive*). A comfortable huddle of Provençal-style buildings around a swimming pool. *Closed mid-Oct–mid-March.*

★★★Le Petit Prince, 11 Av St-Exupéry, **t** 04 94 96 44 47, **f** 04 94 49 03 38 (*moderate*). A small, modern hotel 50m from the beach, with a parking garage and no-nonsense charm; some rooms have been refurbished and most have balconies.

★★★Domaine du Calidianus, Bd Jean Moulin, **t** 04 94 96 23 21, **f** 04 94 49 12 10 (*expensive*). Glam and newly refurbished hotel, with all mod cons and a decent restaurant (*moderate*). *Closed Jan and Feb; restaurant closed mid-Sept–mid-June.*

★★Mas des Brugassières, Pont-de-la-Tour, **t** 04 94 55 50 55, **f** 04 94 55 50 51, *www.mas- des-brugassieres.com* (*moderate*). A comfortable farmhouse, which doesn't require a king's ransom but makes you feel like royalty anyway. Some rooms open out onto the gardens and swimming pool. *Closed mid-Oct–mid-Mar.*

★★Le Revest, 48 Bd Jean Jaurès, **t** 04 94 96 19 60, **f** 04 94 96 32 19 (*moderate–inexpensive*). Central, with parking, a rooftop swimming pool and food (*half board optional*). *Closed Nov–Mar.*

Le Lotus Bleu, 30 Av Gal Leclerc, **t** 04 94 49 28 00 (*moderate*). One of the best of the 80-odd restaurants in Ste-Maxime. *Closed lunch mid-June– mid-Sept. Closed Wed and Thurs lunch out of season.*

Les Issambres ✉ 83380

★★★★La Villa Saint Elme, t 04 94 49 52 52, **f** 04 94 49 63 18, *info@saintelme.com, www.saintelme.com* (*luxury*). Part of the Small Luxury Hotel group, with a gastronomic restaurant (*expensive*), and a new, less expensive brasserie on the terrace.

season). If you do stay, there's the **Musée des Traditions** (*t 04 94 96 70 30; open Wed–Sun 10–12 and 3–6 (July–Aug till 7), Mon 3–6; closed Sat and Tues; adm*), opposite the port in the 16th-century square tower (Tour Carrée des Dames), built by the monks of the Iles de Lérins, who also named the town after one of their alumni. The remarkable **Musée du Phonographe et de la Musique Mécanique** is in the unlikely setting of the wooded Parc de St-Donat, 10km north towards Le Muy on the D25 (*t 04 94 96 50 52; open Easter–Sept 10–12 and 3–6; closed Mon and Tues; adm*). About half of the music boxes, barrel organs, automata and player pianos still work, as well as some of the rare prizes: one of Edison's original phonographs of 1878, an accordion-like 'Melophone' of 1780, a 1903 dictaphone and an audiovisual '*pathégraphe*' to teach foreign languages, built in 1913. For Côte d'Azur-style R and R, the beaches to the west of town are the nicest: **La Nartelle** is the most popular. The **Plage des Eléphants** appears in the children's book *Voyage de Babar*, written by Jean de Brunhoff (1899–1937), who lived in Ste-Maxime.

From Ste-Maxime, the road passes through **Port Grimaud**, a marina designed in 1968 by Alsatian architect and entrepreneur François Spoerry, inspired by the lagoon complexes around St Petersburg, Florida, where wealthy homeowners, like Venetians, can park their boats by the front door. The tourist office now likes to call it 'Venise Provençale'. The traditionally styled, colourful houses themselves are a preview of the real McCoys in St-Tropez; the pseudo-Romanesque fortified church of St-François, sitting on its own islet, has aggressive and annoying stained-glass windows designed by the late Hungarian Op artist Victor Vasarely (1908–97).

St-Tropez

It made the headlines in France when St-Tropez's mayor forced the discos to close at 2am and declared the beaches off limits to dogs, inciting the fury of 'Most Famous Resident' Brigitte Bardot, that crusading Joan of Arc of animal rights who married a National Front politician and in a recent autobiography referred to her son as a 'tumour'. But then again, BB has always been a bit ahead of the rest of us, ever since she came down here to star in Roger Vadim's *Et Dieu...créa la femme* in 1956 and inci-dentally made this lovely fishing village into the national showcase of free-spirited fun, sun and sex, all boxed in the glitter litter of fashion and wealth. Everyone who wants to be associated with these desirable things tries to squeeze into St-Tropez in the summer, booking one of the few hotel rooms nearly a year in advance, or just coming down for the day for a gawk at the yachts.

Significantly, BB has moved on, miffed at the *commune*'s tolerance for immigrants and its lack of sufficient enthusiasm for animal rights. No one seems to miss her much; in fact, the locals wish other folks would follow suit. St-Tropez, it appears, is a victim of its own success. The French call it 'St-Trop', but pronounce the 'p', so it's not 'St-Too Much' – although in the summer it really is too much: too many people (100,000 on an average day) clogging the roads, lanes and beaches; too much rubbish; too many artists hawking paintings around the port; too many crowded

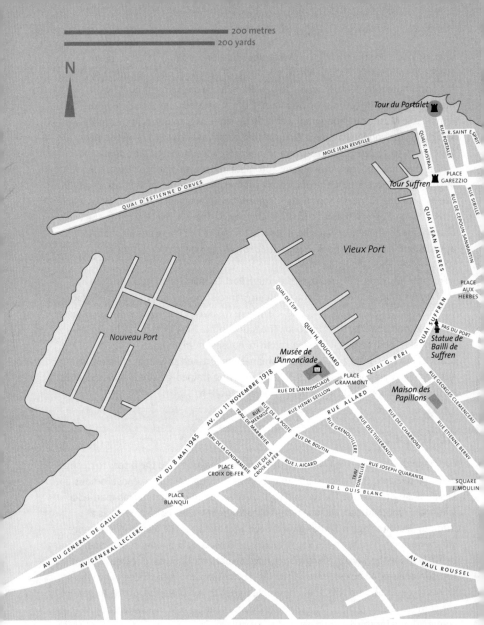

Tour du Portalet

R. SAINT E.SPRIT

RUE PORTALET

QUAI F. MISTRAL

PLACE
GAREZZIO

RUE SIBILLE

Tour Suffren

MOLE JEAN REVEILLE

RUE DE CEPOUN SAN MARTIN

QUAI D'ESTIENNE D'ORVES

QUAI JEAN JAURES

PLACE
AUX
HERBES

Vieux Port

QUAI SUFFREN

PAS DU PORT

QUAI DE L'EPI

Statue de
Bailli de
Suffren

Nouveau Port

QUAI H. BOUCHARD

RUE GEORGES CLEMENCEAU

QUAI G. PERI

Musée de
L'Annonciade

PLACE
GRAMMONT

Maison des
Papillons

RUE DE L'ANNONCIADE

RUE DES CHARRONS

RUE ETIENNE BERNY

RUE HENRI SEILLON

RUE ALLARD

RUE DES TISSERANDS

AV. DU 11 NOVEMBRE 1918

TRAV. DE MERMOT

RUE DE LA POSTE

RUE GRENOUILLERE

TRAV. DE MARBRIER

RUE DR. BOUTIN

RUE JOSEPH QUARANTA

AV. DU 8 MAI 1945

TRAV. DE LA GENDARMERIE

RUE DE LA
CROIX DE FER

RUE J. AICARD

TRAV.
TONNELIER

SQUARE
J. MOULIN

PLACE
CROIX DE FER

BD LOUIS BLANC

PLACE
BLANQUI

AV. DU GENERAL DE GAULLE

AV. GENERAL LECLERC

AV. PAUL ROUSSEL

200 metres
200 yards

N

cafés and restaurants charging unholy prices. Recently, the local newspaper, *Le Bavar*, began a campaign to limit access into the town, erecting a barrier and limiting access by car only to people who are staying at least one night. Other proposals are to freeze the building of new rental accommodation, to decrease the number of places at campsites and to triple the size of the local police to enforce local will. The next elections promise to bring all this to a head, although, curiously enough, the rest of the Var seems to have little sympathy for the Tropéziens' plight.

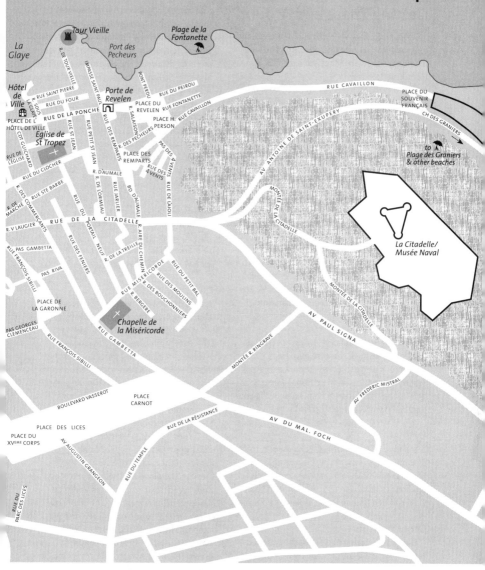

St-Tropez

Tour Vieille

Plage de la Fontanette

La Glaye

Port des Pecheurs

Hôtel de Ville

Porte de Revelen

RUE CAVAILLON

PLACE DU SOUVENIR FRANÇAIS

CH DES GRANIERS

PLACE DE L'HÔTEL DE VILLE

RUE SAINT PIERRE

R. SOUS S GLAYE

RUE DE TOUR VIEILLE

IMPASSE SAINT PAUL

RUE DU FOUR

PONT PEIROU

RUE DU PEIROU

PLACE DU REVELEN

RUE FONTANETTE

RUE CAVAILLON

to Plage des Graniers & other beaches

RUE DE LA PONCHE

R. SALAISON

PLACE H. PERSON

RUE ST JEAN

RUE PETIT ST JEAN

R. DES PECHEURS

RUE DES REMPARTS

AV ANTOINE DE SAINT-EXUPERY

Eglise de St Tropez

RUE DE L'ÉGLISE

PLACE DES REMPARTS

PAS DES 4 VENTS

RUE DES 4 VENTS

RUE DU CLOCHER

R. D'AUMALE

RUE DE L'ORMEAU

RUE DE LAIOLI

RUE DES COMMERCANTS

RUE STE BARBE

RUE JARLIER

BD D'AUMALE

R. DE MARCHE

RUE DES FENIERS

MONTÉE DE LA CITADELLE

R. V LAUGIER

RUE DE LA CITADELLE

R. AIRE DU CHEMIN

La Citadelle/ Musée Naval

RUE PAS GAMBETTA

R. DE LA TREILLE

RUE TORRAIL NEUF

PAS RIVA

R. MISÉRICORDE

RUE DU PETIT BAL

MONTÉE DE LA CITADELLE

RUE FRANÇOIS SIBILI

R. DES BOUCHONNIERS

RUE DES MOULINS

AV PAUL SIGNAC

PLACE DE LA GARONNE

R. BERGERE

PAS GEORGES CLEMENCEAU

RUE GAMBETTA

Chapelle de la Miséricorde

MONTÉE R. RINGRAVE

RUE FRANÇOIS SIBILI

AV FREDERIC MISTRAL

BOULEVARD VASSEROT

PLACE CARNOT

RUE DE LA RÉSISTANCE

AV DU MAL. FOCH

PLACE DES LICES

PLACE DU XVème CORPS

AV AUGUSTIN GRANGEON

RUE DU TEMPLE

RUE DU PARC DES LICES

Outside high season, it's much easier to understand what started all the commotion in the first place – St-Tropez is a dishy little place, full of colour and character. Only beware that in winter it's the only town on the Côte d'Azur that faces north, and can be extremely blustery.

History: Proto-National-Front Ligurians and Celebrity Cosmetics
One of the strangest but most prophetic legends along the coast has it that St-Tropez's first incarnation, the Greek colony Athenopolis, was founded by Praxiteles'

Getting There and Around

On its peninsula, St-Tropez is a dead end; the one road leading into it (D98A), and the lanes leading off to the beaches are packed solid from June to August.

By Air

Nice airport is about 90km away; Toulon–Hyères airport is about 50km. If you planned to flit in on your chopper, think again: St-Tropez's airport has closed. However, this has caused enough consternation in the right places for a new project: a summer-only floating heliport, 4km offshore, with a fleet of speedboats to race passengers to the shore.

By Train

There is no train station in St-Tropez. The nearest TGV stop is at Les Arcs (t 04 94 99 60 00), from where shuttle buses take travellers into St-Tropez twice a day. Call SODETRAV on t 04 94 97 88 51 for timetable information.

By Bus

Besides the St-Raphaël–Hyères coastal bus (t 04 94 97 88 51, or the *gare routière* in St-Tropez, t 04 94 54 62 36), there's a bus in season linking Toulon to St-Tropez (t 04 94 18 93 40). Note that there's no place to leave your luggage if you want to stop en route.

By Boat

You may be better off catching a boat from St-Raphaël (*gare maritime*, t 04 94 95 17 46) or Ste-Maxime (MMG t 04 94 96 51 00). There are boat-taxis which also offer tours of the Gulf: call **Taxi Bateau Vasse**, t 04 94 54 40 61.

Other Transport

The ghastly traffic makes bike and moped hire an attractive alternative: try **M.A.S**, 3 Rue Quaranta, near St-Tropez's Place Carnot, t 04 94 97 00 60 (*closed mid-Oct–Mar*).

Tourist Information

St-Tropez: Maison du Tourisme du Golfe de St-Tropez/Pays des Maures, t 04 94 55 22 00, f 04 94 55 22 01, *www.golfe-infos.com*, *tourisme@golfe-infos.com*, at the N98/D559 junction just before the traffic gridlock, is a tourist's godsend. With fountains and sculptured pools, this is the Var tourist board's *pièce de résistance*. The helpful staff will call ahead to St-Tropez to book hotels, advise on restaurants and book excursions (both coastal and inland) and wine tours. If you accidentally whizz past, head into St-Tropez and the office at Quai Jean Jaurès, t 04 94 97 45 21, f 04 94 97 82 66. *Open summer Mon–Fri 9–7.30, Sat 9.30–6.30, Sun 10–6; spring and autumn Mon–Fri 9–7, Sat 9.30–6; winter Mon–Fri 9–6.30, Sat 9.30–5.30.*

Market Days

General market: Place des Lices, Tuesday and Sunday morning.
Fish market: Place aux Herbes, mornings, except Monday in winter.

Festivals

Not to be missed if you're anywhere in the vicinity, the **Bravade des Espagnols** (15 June) sees St-Tropez's finest lads and lasses in 18th-century uniforms and Provençal costumes for a morning procession of the relics of St Torpes. At every square the band stops playing as the 'soldiers' fire an earsplitting fusillade from their blunderbusses straight into the stone pavement, while clouds of acrid smoke choke bystanders.

St Torpes himself is honoured with an even more important two-day shooting-spree *bravade* in the middle of May.

Besides the *bravades*, the most exciting annual event in St-Tropez is **Les Voiles de St-Tropez**, the last French yacht race, '*pour fêter la fin de la saison et de l'été*' (first week of October). The oldest and most beautiful yachts in the world take on the autumn billows. There are two crowds: them and us (sailors and lubbers). Lubbers can follow the course by sea in special boats, or by helicopter.

Shopping

Although many of the once trendsetting boutiques are now owned by design chains, a few exclusive shops remain for die-hard fans.

Autour des Oliviers, 2 Place des Oliviers. Provençal specialities, especially olive oil.

Galeries Tropéziennes, 55 Rue Gambetta. For fabrics, espadrilles, garden furniture and everything else.

Gas Bijoux, Rue Garonne. Specializing in costume jewellery made of coral and turquoise.

La Pause Douceur, 11 Rue Allard. De luxe chocs.

Rondini, 16 Rue G. Clemenceau. For the famous *sandales tropéziennes*, invented in 1927 on the gladiator model. If they don't have your size they may be able to make them.

Rues Allard and Sibilli: All the top-notch designers, from Lacroix and Versace to Donna Karan and Calvin Klein.

Sugar: Rue Victor Laugier. Upmarket cotton tops, shorts and sandals.

For wine, there are several *domaines* which are open to the public for tours and tastings:

Cave de Saint-Tropez, Av Paul Roussel, t 04 94 97 01 60.

Château Minuty Maton-Farnet, Route de Ramatuelle-Gassin, t 04 94 56 12 09, *www.nova.fr/minuty*. Offers tastings and tours of the *caves. Open summer Mon–Fri 9–12.30 and 2–6.30, Sat and Sun 10–12 and 3–6.30; closed weekends in winter.*

Domaine du Bourrian: 2496 Chemin du Gourrian-Gassin, t 04 94 56 16 28. A big operation, with Côtes de Provence and Pays de Maures wines. *Closed Sun in winter.*

Maîtres Vignerons de Saint-Tropez: Carrefour de la Foux-Gassin, t 04 94 56 32 04. A shop with a varied selection of what is available in the Maures; it also sells regional produce.

Where to Stay

St-Tropez ✉ 83990

If you haven't already booked a hotel long before, forget about arriving in St-Tropez on the off chance between July and September.

There are acres of campsites in the area, although in the summer they are about as relaxing as refugee camps; the tourist offices keep tabs on which have a few inches to spare. As for prices, expect them to be about 20 per cent higher per category than anywhere else on the coast. And if you come in the off season, beware that most hotels close in the winter.

Luxury

★★★★Le Byblos, Av Paul Signac, t 04 94 56 68 00, f 04 94 56 68 01, *www.byblos.com*. Built by a Lebanese millionaire and designed like a *village perché*, with rambling corridors, patios and opulent rooms. In the middle there's a magnificent pool, and the night-club is one of most desirable to be seen in. There is now a *nouvelle cuisine* restaurant, **Spoon**, t 04 94 56 68 20 (*very expensive*). *Closed mid-Oct–Easter.*

★★★★Résidence La Pinède, Plage de la Bouillabaisse, t 04 94 55 91 00, f 04 94 97 73 64, *residence.pinede@wanadoo.fr, www.residencepinede.com*. The *luxe, charme et volupté* of this Relais & Châteaux place has given it the current edge. Dining *à la carte* in its gourmet restaurant comes at an appropriate price. *Closed Oct–Easter.*

★★★★La Bastide de Saint-Tropez, Rte des Carles, t 04 94 55 82 55, f 04 94 97 21 71, *bst@wanadoo.fr, www.bastidesaint-tropez.com*. Similarly swish, but perched on a hill, this has an even better, Michelin-starred restaurant, **L'Olivier** (*very expensive*). Served in a garden of oleander, figs and parasol pines, the food is flamboyant, generous and exceptionally delicious. *Closed Jan–mid-Feb.*

★★★★Le Yaca, 1 Bd d'Aumale, t 04 94 55 81 00, f 04 94 97 58 50, *hotel-le-yaca@wanadoo.fr, www.hotel-le-yaca.fr*. Once home to Colette, and before her to Paul Signac. A rambling, but very chic, fusion of three small cottages; most of the rooms look on to a courtyard bursting with flowers. *Closed Oct–Easter; restaurant closed Mon.*

★★★★La Ponche, 3 Rue des Remparts, t 04 94 97 02 53, f 04 94 97 78 61, *hotel@laponche.com, www.laponche.com*. Picasso's old watering hole, in the old town – a charming, romantic nook to entice your special darling. The rooms overlooking the street can be noisy, but there is double glazing and air-conditioning. *Closed Nov–mid-Feb.*

Very Expensive–Expensive

★★★Le Sube Continental, 15 Quai Suffren, t 04 94 97 30 04, f 04 94 54 89 08. The oldest hotel in town and a historic monument to boot, with views over the port. *Closed Jan–mid-Feb.*

Expensive
***Lou Troupelen, Chemin des Vendanges, **t** 04 94 97 44 88, **f** 04 94 97 41 76, *www.nova. fr/lou-troupelen*. Quiet rooms in an old farmhouse. *Closed mid-Oct–Easter.*

Moderate
Les Lauriers, Rue du Temple, **t 04 94 97 04 88, **f** 04 94 97 21 87. Modern, pleasant rooms with air-conditioning, in a garden setting. *Closed Jan.*

Eating Out

While in St-Trop, you may want to try a *tropézienne*. This local speciality is a sponge cake sliced horizontally and filled with raspberry or strawberry jam, and topped with whipped cream.

Very Expensive
Leï Mouscardins, Tour du Portalet, **t** 04 94 97 29 00. For pure atmosphere and the best creative food in town, book a table overlooking the harbour at Leï Mouscardins; it may be one of the high points of your holiday. *Closed Dec–Jan, and Tues and Wed, except summer. Closed lunch June–Sept.*

Expensive
Le Club 55, Plage de Pampelonne, **t** 04 94 55 55 55. One of the oldest and best-known beach-restaurants. *Closed .*
La Voile Rouge, Plage de Ramatuelle, **t** 04 94 79 84 34. The current fashionable favourite.
La Ramade, Rue du Temple, **t** 04 94 97 00 15. Fish specialities, served in a garden terrace. *Closed Jan–mid-Feb, and Mon except July–Sept.*

Moderate
Tahiti Plage, Le Pinet, **t** 04 94 97 18 02. Also very fashionable. *Closed Oct–Easter.*
Moorea, Rte de Tahiti, **t** 04 94 97 18 17. More down-to-earth. *Closed Nov–Easter.*

Chez Maggi, 5 Rue Sibille, **t** 04 94 97 16 12. A busy, fashionable, gay bar/restaurant serving up good Franco-Italian cuisine, such as delicious *petits farcis provençaux*, to a youthful clientele in a small room adjoining the raucous bar area. *Closed mid-Oct–Feb*
Plage des Jumeaux, **t** 0494 55 21 80. If you want to eat right on the beach, head here for lunch.
Bar du Soleil, Rte de Tahiti, **t** 04 94 97 81 24. Another more modest beach joint.
L'Echalote, 35 Rue du Général Allard, **t** 04 94 54 83 26. Here you can beef up on your black puddings and all things meaty. *Closed mid-Nov–Dec and Thurs lunch.*
Café des Arts, Place des Lices, **t** 04 94 97 02 25. A quiet alternative on this popular square, with seafood specialities. *Closed mid-Oct–mid-April.*

Entertainment and Nightlife

The bars in Place des Lices provide an entertaining sideshow in which to pass the early part of the evening.
Sénéquier, by the port, **t** 04 94 97 09 00. A St-Trop institution. *Closed Nov.*
La Bodega du Papagayo, Quai de l'Epi, **t** 04 94 97 76 70. An attractive bar haunted by a younger clientele. Has an equally attractive restaurant (*moderate*). *Restaurant closed Wed in season.*

Dancing and much besides goes on until dawn at St-Trop's clubs. Don't take it personally if you have trouble getting in; St-Tropez's bouncers have a formidable reputation to uphold.
VIP Room, by the new port, **t** 04 94 97 14 70. *Closed Oct–Easter.*
Les Caves du Roy, Hôtel Le Byblos (*see* p.187), **t** 04 94 97 16 02. Full of stars.
Cabane Baiy-Bou, west edge of Pampelonne beach, **t** 04 94 79 84 13. Fantastic Thai food, open late in the summer.
Le Pigeonnier, Rue de la Ponche, **t** 04 94 97 84 26. One of the best-known gay clubs, open till 4am.

famous model Phryne, who had a face like a toad but the body of a goddess. Put on trial in Athens for unseemly behaviour, she lifted up her skirt, astonishing the jury with her charms, and was acquitted on condition that she leave Athens. She ended up out here in the Wild West of antiquity, married to a Ligurian chieftain. Together they founded Athenopolis, but the story has a sad end: Phryne was sacrificed to the Ligurian gods with the request that they should please keep foreigners away in the future.

In AD 68, Torpes, a Christian officer of Nero, was beheaded in Pisa. As anyone who has studied the *Lives of the Saints* knows, the Romans had no lack of ingenuity in dealing with martyrs; in this case, they buried Torpes' head in Pisa and put his body in a boat with a dog and a cock, who were to slowly devour it. But the animals had no appetite and their boat floated safely to Athenopolis (the Roman Heraclea Cacabria) which eventually adopted St Torpes' name. The saintly trunk was hidden and lost during the Saracen attacks, one of which destroyed St-Tropez in 739.

St-Tropez was repopulated in 1470 with settlers imported from Genoa. Good King René of Provence exempted them from taxes in return for defending the coast, and until the 17th century the Tropéziens enjoyed a special autonomous status under their Capitaines de Ville. Their most glorious moment came on 15 June 1637, when they courageously beat off an attack by 22 Spanish galleons, an event annually celebrated in the Bravade des Espagnols. Later invaders were more successful. The first famous visitor from the outside world, Guy de Maupassant, drifted into the port in 1880s and in his pre-syphilitic madness gave the villagers a preview of the 1960s. In 1892 the post-Impressionist painter Paul Signac was forced by the weather to anchor his yacht at St-Tropez; enchanted, he bought a villa called La Hune and invited his friends down to paint. St-Tropez was a revelation to many: Matisse, who had previously worked in a rather dark style, came down in 1904 and produced his key, incandescent picture of nudes on a St-Tropez beach, *Luxe, calme et volupté*, and joined the Fauvist revolution begun by Signac's friends Derain, Vlaminck, Van Dongen and Dufy; today their hot-coloured canvases illuminate the town's local museum.

Writers, most famously Colette, joined the artists' 'Montparnasse on the Mediterranean' in the 1920s, but, even then, thoughts of making a franc out of fashion and beauty were in the air; Colette herself had a shop in the port selling Colette-brand cosmetics in the 1930s. The third wave of even more conspicuous invaders – Parisian existentialists and glitterati – began in earnest in the 1950s, when Françoise 'Bonjour Tristesse' Sagan and Bardot made it the pinnacle of chic. Back then, Sartre could sit in the Café Sénéquier and write *Les Chemins de la Liberté* in peace, but these days he'd be hard put to it even to think, with all the showbiz comets who come to be seen and the paparazzi who dutifully come to snap them when they appear. Joan Collins has a house here, so has George Michael, and Elton John's manager paid £7m in 1995 to join the set. Guest appearances have been made by Prince Albert of Monaco, Clint Eastwood, Naomi Campbell, Robert De Niro, Jack Nicholson, Rupert Everett and even a cavorting once-royal British duchess (for an oral pedicure).

Musée de l'Annonciade

*Quai de l'Epi, t 04 94 97 04 01; open June–Sept 10–12 and 3–7;
Oct–May 10–12 and 2–6; closed Tues, holidays and Nov; adm.*

If everything about St-Tropez in the summer fills you with dismay, let this be your reason to visit. Housed in a 17th-century chapel next to the port, the museum concentrates on works by painters in Paul Signac's St-Tropez circle, Postimpressionists and Fauves who began where Van Gogh and Gauguin left off and blazed the trail for Cubism – and blaze their works do, saturated with colour that takes on a life of its own with Vlaminck (*Le Pont de Chatou*) and Derain (*Westminster Palace* and *Waterloo Bridge*). Seurat's small but fascinating *Canal des Gravelines* (1890), the oldest painting of the collection, gives an idea of his mathematical, optical treatment of Impressionism, a style from which his disciple, Signac, moved away while in St-Tropez.

The collection started out in a one-room gallery in the town hall, known by its Provençal name, the Museon Tropolen, but soon outgrew its cramped quarters and was moved to the disused chapel by the port. It had belonged to the Pénitents Blancs, who took care of fishermen maimed in fishing accidents, but was taken over during the anti-clerical fervour of the Revolution and used first for storing sails, then for building boats, and finally to house orphans, before sinking into disuse. After the Second World War the chapel was gutted and restored, uncovering lovely original features like the nave and choir.

Other highlights include Braque's *Paysage de l'Estaque*, painted in homage to Cézanne; Matisse's *La Gitane* (1906); Vuillard's *Deux Femmes sous la lampe*; Bonnard's *Nue devant la cheminée* and *La Route rose*; and key works by Van Dongen, Friesz, Dufy, Marquet and Cross. Upstairs, loafers lounge in leather armchairs among Aristide Maillol's graceful sculptures and gaze out through windows framing sky and sea far above the crowds and bustle.

From the Port to the Citadelle

Just outside the museum, the port is edged with the colourful pastel houses that inspired the Fauves, a scene that regains much of its original charm if you can get up before the trippers and the scores of hack painters who block the quay. It was demolished during the war and, by the time it was rebuilt, the bohemian élite from Paris had already chosen the town as their summer quarters, with the result that new shops and restaurants took the place of the old boathouses and storing sheds. The view is especially good from the **Môle Jean Réveille**, the narrow pier which encloses the yacht-filled port and looks out, so they say, across the bay to Sardinia and back towards the Alps on very clear days. In the street above, the 19th-century **church of St-Torpes** contains a gilt bust of St Torpes and a sculpture of his little boat, carried in the *bravades*.

Seek out Place de l'Ormeau, Rue de la Ponche and Place aux Herbes, poetic corners of old St-Tropez that have refused to shift into top gear. The rambling little **Quartier de la Ponche**, with several coolly chic restaurants and bars, folds itself around the shore and the tower of the now defunct **Château de Suffren**. Suffren was an

18th-century admiral who spent two years battling in the East Indies and could never reconcile himself to the boredom of his life afterwards; his statue overlooks the port. The narrow Rue de la Ponche leads out to a point surmounted by the **Tour Vieille**, usually crawling with unfeasibly acrobatic children, with a little beach which is very nice for a quick dip.

You can look down on shiny roof tiles from the 16th- to 18th-century *citadelle* at the top of town (or visit its little **Musée Naval**, *t 04 94 97 59 43; open May–Sept 11–5.30; Oct–April 10–12.30 and 1.30–5.30, guided tours 2pm; closed Tues and Nov; adm*). Another essential ingredient of St-Tropez is the charming Place Carnot, better known by its old name of **Place des Lices**, an archetypal slice of Provence with its plane trees, its Tuesday and Saturday markets, its cafés and eternal games of *pétanque*.

Beaches and St-Tropez's Peninsula

Although the beaches begin even before you enter St-Tropez, those famous sandy strands where girls first dared to bathe topless (circumventing local indecency laws by placing Coke bottle tops over their nipples) skirt the outer rim of the peninsula. In the summer, minibuses link them with Place Carnot, a good idea as beach parking is as expensive as the beaches themselves. (Note that St-Tropez lost its Blue Flag status in 2001, although most of the crowd here don't bother with swimming.) **Plage des Graniers** is within easy walking distance, but it's the most crowded. A path from here skirts Cap de St-Tropez and, in 12km, passes **Plage des Salins** (4km direct from St-Tropez) and the gay beach **Neptune**, and ends up at the notoriously decadent **Plage de Tahiti**, the movie stars' favourite. Tahiti occupies the north end of the 5km **Plage de**

Where to Stay and Eat

Ramatuelle ✉ 83350

****Château Hôtel de la Messardière**, Rte de Tahiti, t 04 94 56 76 00, f 04 94 56 76 01, *www.messardiere.com* (*luxury*). For sheer self-indulgence you can't beat this: a late 19th-century folly on a height overlooking the sea, ultra-comfortable, with a superb panoramic restaurant (*very expensive– expensive*) and exquisite, exotic dishes. *Restaurant open eves only. Closed mid-Oct–mid-Mar.*

***Hostellerie Le Baou**, Av Gustave Etienne, t 04 98 12 94 20, f 04 98 12 94 21, *www. chateauxhotels.com* (*luxury–very expensive*). Though it has become part of a luxury chain with modern rooms, the views are enchanting, and it also has a heated pool and a restaurant serving delicious sunny Provençal treats. *Closed mid-Oct–mid-April.*

***La Figuière**, Rte de Tahiti, t 04 94 97 18 21, f 04 94 97 68 48 (*expensive*). An old farm-house in a vineyard, with tennis, a pool and restaurant. *Closed Oct–mid-April.*

***La Ferme d'Augustin**, Route de Tahiti, t 04 94 55 97 00, f 04 94 97 40 30, *vallet. ferme.augustin@wanadoo.fr, www.fermeau-gustin.com* (*expensive*). Set in a garden, a stone's throw from the sea. *Closed mid-Oct–mid-Mar.*

Gassin ✉ 83580

***Bello Visto**, Place deï Barri, t 04 94 56 17 30, f 04 94 43 45 36, *www.bello-visto.com* (*moderate*). Simple and charming rooms next to Gassin's magnificent belvedere; book early for a chance of staying in one. The restaurant has a pleasant terrace. *Closed Nov–Mar; restaurant closed Tues.*

Auberge La Verdoyante, 866 Rte de Coste-Brigade, t 04 94 56 16 23 (*moderate*). On the outskirts of Gassin, this seems lost in the countryside, an old Provençal manor serving traditional old Provençal dishes. *Reservations advised; closed Wed and mid-Oct–Mar.*

Pampelonne, lined with cafés, restaurants and luxury concessions where any swimming costumes at all are optional.

On the other side of Cap Camarat, **Plage de l'Escalet** is hard to reach, but much less crowded and free (take the narrow road down from the D93). From L'Escalet you can pick up the coastal path and walk in an hour and a half to the best and most tranquil beach of all, **Plage de la Briande**.

The centre of the peninsula, swathed with Côtes de Provence vineyards, is dominated by two villages of sinuous vaulted lanes and medieval houses: **Gassin**, up a dizzy series of hairpin turns, and below it the larger **Ramatuelle**. Both were Saracen *fraxinets*, and both have caught serious cases of artsy fashion flu from St-Trop, but they still make refreshing escapes from the anarchy down below. In Ramatuelle's cemetery you can see the romantic tomb of actor Gérard Philippe (*Le Diable au corps* and *Fanfan la Tulipe*), who was only 37 when he died in 1959.

Into the Massif des Maures

Beckoning just a short drive from the coastal pandemonium are the quiet chestnut woodlands of the Massif des Maures, or at least what's left of them after a quarter of the forest burned to the ground in 1990; note that some of the few roads that penetrate the mountain may be closed in dry summers. The main walking path through the hills, the GR9, begins at Port Grimaud and passes through La Garde-Freinet on its way west to Notre-Dame-des-Anges; if you're going by road, the most rewarding route is the D14, beginning at Grimaud.

Cogolin and Grimaud

Perhaps by now you've noticed signs advertising pipes from **Cogolin**, not an especially pretty town but a busy one. For once the craftsmen are not just loose ends from Paris selling artsy gimcracks to tourists; for over two centuries the famous pipes of Cogolin have been carved from the thick roots of the briars (*erica arbores*) that grow up to 20ft high in the Maures. Visit **Courrieu Pipes** (*58 Av G.-Clemenceau, t 04 94 54 63 82, www.courrieupipes.fr; open daily 9–12 and 2–6*). A second craft was started up in the 1920s by Armenian immigrants, who introduced their ancestral art of hand-knotted wool rugs, the origin of a local industry that now sells its *tapis de Cogolin* to the best addresses in Paris and the Arab emirates. Another important industry harvests an ancient swamp to make top-quality reeds for saxophones. And Provence's only bamboo forest provides the raw material for Cogolin's furniture.

Cogolin's church of **St-Sauveur** has some pretty Renaissance art inside, in particular a Florentine wood *triptyque* (1540), but the pilgrims who come to Cogolin are more likely to be French film buffs: the granddaughter of Pagnol's favourite character actor has opened the **Musée Raimu** in his memory, in the basement of the local cinema (*18 Av Georges-Clemenceau, t 04 94 54 18 00, www.musee-raimu; open summer daily 10–12 and 4–7; winter 10–12 and 3–6; closed Sun am, plus all Tues exc during school hols; adm*), packed full of posters and re-creations of favourite scenes (like the card game in

Getting Around

Grimaud and Cogolin are stops on the St-Raphaël–St-Tropez **bus** routes.

Other villages are much harder to reach by public transport: two buses a day go from Le Lavandou to La Garde-Freinet, and there's but one linking La Garde-Freinet and Grimaud to Toulon. There is a nearby helipad for Grimaud, however, t 04 94 43 39 30, *www.helicopter-saint-tropez.com*.

Tourist Information

Cogolin: Place de la République, t 04 94 55 01 10, f 04 94 55 01 11, *www.cogolin-provence.com*. Has a list of *chambres d'hôtes* and *gîtes*. *Open mid-June–mid-Sept Mon–Sat 9–1 and 2–7; mid-Sept–mid-June Mon–Fri 9–12.30 and 2–6.30, Sat 9.30–12.30.*

Grimaud: 1 Bd des Aliziers, t 04 94 55 43 83, f 04 94 55 72 20, *bureau.du.tourisme. grimaud@wanadoo.fr, www.grimaud-provence.com*. *Open Oct–Mar daily 9–12.30, and 2.15–5.30; April–June daily 9–12.30 and 2.30–6.15; July–Aug daily 9–12.30 and 3–7.*

La Garde-Freinet: 1 Place Neuve, t 04 94 43 67 41, f 04 94 43 08 69, *ot_lgf@ club-internet.fr, www.lagardefreinet-tourisme.com*. *Open July–Aug Mon–Sat 10–12.30 and 3–6.30, Sun 9.30–12; Nov–Feb Mon–Sat 10–12.30 and 2–5.30; Sept–Oct and Mar–June Mon–Sat 10–12.30 and 2.30–6.*

Collobrières: Bd Caminat, t 04 94 48 08 00, f 04 94 48 04 10, *ot@collotour.com, www. collotour.com*. *Open July–Aug Mon 2–6, Tues–Sat 10–12.30 and 3–6.30; Sept–June Tues–Sat 10–12 and 2–6.*

Market Days

Cogolin: Place Victor Hugo, Wednesday morning; Place de la République, Saturday morning.

Grimaud: Thursday, Place Vieille; Thursday; wool market on Ascension Thursday.

La Garde-Freinet: Wednesday and Sunday morning, Place Neuve.

Collobrières: Thursday morning in summer, larger on Sunday morning; Place de la Mer, chestnut market, last three Sundays of October; annual fair 1 Nov.

Gonfaron: Thursday am, Provençal market.

Where to Stay and Eat

Grimaud ✉ 83310

Le Verger, Route de Collobrières, t 04 94 55 57 80, f 04 94 43 33 92 (*expensive*). A Provençal building a kilometre west of Grimaud. French windows lead out into the quiet gardens and dinner is served by the pool. *Closed Nov–Easter.*

★★★**La Boulangerie**, Rte de Collobrières, t 04 94 43 23 16, f 04 94 43 38 27 (*expensive*). For more great views and silence. Swimming pool and tennis. *Closed mid-Oct–Easter.*

★★★**Hostellerie du Coteau Fleuri**, Place des Pénitents, t 04 94 43 20 17, f 04 94 43 33 42, *www.coteaufleuri.fr* (*moderate*). A comfortable stone inn, almost hidden by flowers and ivy, built in the 1930s on the quiet western outskirts of town, with grand views over the vineyards and the Maures; its restaurant (*expensive*) serves reliably good Provençal dishes. *Closed mid-Nov–mid-Dec; restaurant closed Tues exc in July–Aug, closed lunch in July–Aug.*

Les Santons, Rte Nationale, t 04 94 43 21 02 (*expensive*). Indulge in a gourmet spread of lobster salad, seafood or thyme-scented *selle d'agneau* in dining rooms full of *santons*. *Closed Nov–Mar.*

Café de la France, Place Neuve, t 04 94 43 20 05 (*moderate*). Pennywise, the best bet for food, in an old stone house with a summer terrace. *Closed Nov–Feb and Sun eve in Mar.*

La Garde-Freinet ✉ 83680

La Sarrazine, Route Nationale, t/f 04 94 55 59 60 (*expensive*). With very filling menus, and specializing in *gâteau d'agneau*.

Collobrières ✉ 83610

Notre-Dame, 15 Av de la Libération, t 04 94 48 07 13, f 04 94 48 05 95 (*inexpensive*). Adequate rooms, a garden and a restaurant (*moderate*). *Closed mid-Dec–Jan and Tues.*

Hôtel Restaurant des Maures, 19 Bd Lazare Carnot, t 04 94 48 07 10 (*inexpensive*). Has a decent restaurant.

La Petite Fontaine, Place de la République, t 04 94 48 00 12 (*moderate*). Dine on polenta, rabbit in garlic, mushrooms and the local wine. Book. *Closed 15–30 Sept and school hols; restaurant closed Mon and Sun eve.*

César). Raimu made more than 50 films between 1912 and 1946, among them the Pagnol adaptations *Marius, César, Fanny*, and *La Femme du boulanger*. The letters and photographs are given a personal touch with the commentary of Isabelle Nohain, Raimu's granddaughter, who recounts her memories of this notoriously difficult but well-loved comedian, whom Orson Welles called the 'greatest actor in the world'.

Unlike Cogolin, **Grimaud** is all aesthetics and boutiques. A former Saracen and Templar stronghold, it can hold its own among the most perfect *villages perchés* on the coast, crowned by the ruined castle of the Grimaldis, after whom the village is named. From its rubble you can look down on the old windmill which has recently been restored and is now in working order. The Romanesque church of **St-Michel** is in surprisingly good nick; from here, Rue des Templiers (formerly Rue des Juifs), lined with arcades from 1555, passes the **House of the Templars**. This is one of the few surviving structures in Provence built by that religious and military order of knights founded in Jerusalem during the First Crusade in 1118. Before their wealth, influence and secret rites incited the deadly envy of King Philip the Fair of France and Pope Clement V, the Templars acquired extensive properties in exchange for their military services. They often built their castles and churches in Jewish or Saracen quarters, both to learn from their ancient wisdom and to protect them from the Christians – hence the damning charge of heresy raised against them by pope and king, who conspired together to dissolve the order in 1307. At the top of the village is the dark and dank **Chapelle des Pénitents**, with damp stone walls, an incongruous, brilliantly gilded altar and a gruesome statue of martyred Saint Theodori, gazing out with an expression of mild reproach despite the seven knives sticking out of her chest.

La Garde-Freinet

When Charles Martel defeated the Moorish invaders at Poitiers in 732 and pushed them back to Spain, a few managed to give the Franks the slip and escape into Provence, where they generally made a nuisance of themselves (but are also credited with introducing the tambourine, medicine and flat roof tiles). Their strongholds, or *fraxinets*, gave their name to La Garde-Freinet, a large village full of medieval charm and British ex-pats. A path, past chestnuts said to be 1,000 years old, ascends to the site of the **Saracen fortress** (the standing walls are from the 15th century); from here lookouts would signal the approach of fat merchant ships down to the pirates' cove of St-Tropez.

One of the arts brought to Provence by the Saracens was working in cork, which involves stripping the tree of its outer layer of bark during certain years when the tree can survive the loss; the bark is then boiled, cut into strips, boiled again and set to dry and season for six months before being carved into bottle stoppers. This was the chief industry in the 19th century, and in 1851 the cork workers of La Garde-Freinet, men and women, formed a co-operative that stood up to the bosses, beginning an experiment in socialism in the same dark year as Louis Napoléon declared himself emperor; you don't have to be an historian to guess what happened. Things are quieter now in La Garde-Freinet. There is a small exhibition on the bottle stopper above the tourist office (*open Tues–Sat 10–12.30 and 3–6*). The only other thing to do in La Garde-Freinet, according to the tourist office, is walk (at least they provide very helpful pamphlets).

Collobrières and Around

Six kilometres off the D14 from Grimaud stands the moody, ruined **Chartreuse de la Verne** (*t 04 94 43 45 41; http://la.verne.free.fr; open summer 11–6; winter 11–5; closed Tues, religious hols and Jan; adm*), founded in 1170 in one of the most romantically desolate corners of France. Rebuilt several times before it was abandoned and burned in the Revolution, the vast and impressive Carthusian complex (great and small cloisters, guest house, church and porch) is mostly of interest for its use of local stone – a combination of reddish schist and hard greenish serpentine. Since 1983, restoration work has been carried out by the Brothers of Bethlehem. The back gate of the larger cloister leads up to the remnants of an old windmill and another lovely view across the chestnut trees and oaks.

Near the crossroads for the Chartreuse, a minor road leads to the *garde forestière* Ferme Lambert, where you can ask permission to see the two largest **menhirs** in Provence (11ft and 10ft high) and the largest chestnut tree, the **Châtaignier de Madame** (33ft in circumference).

The air is sweet in the biggest settlement of the western Maures, **Collobrières**, an attractive old village full of quirky fountains (the oddest is of a small boy carrying a large fish in the village square) and scented with chestnuts being ground into paste and purée or undergoing their apotheosis into delectable *marrons glacés*. In late October there is a chestnut festival for true devotees – and parades of cows to be judged and admired at the **Fête de la Transhumance** in spring. The village's name comes from *couleuvre* (grass snake), owing to the snake-like patterns in the prevalent serpentine stone. But the thick forests all around are known for other natural delights: boar and deer (and their hunters), not to mention a fabulous array of mushrooms.

Due north of Collobrières, narrow roads squiggle up through the forests to **Notre-Dame-des-Anges**, a sanctuary constructed on an ancient pagan site which has drawn pilgrims since long, long before the vogue for Our Lady took off. It sits on top of the highest point in the Var (2,500ft), with brave views over the Maures.

Further squiggles north will bring you to **Gonfaron** where, according to legend, donkeys fly. At the time of the annual village procession of St Quinis (whose chapel perches above the village on an isolated hill), the local people used to clean their porches in his honour; in the 17th century, one recalcitrant shopkeeper refused and scoffed that he would only toe the line when the statue flew over his refuse heap. Moments later he found himself and his donkey at the top of a nearby hill before both were hurled into a ravine. There's a **donkey sanctuary** (*hameau des ânes*) out on Route des Mayons (*call t 04 94 78 32 10 for information*), where most of the inmates manage to stay on the ground and obligingly pull tourists around on traps, and a local museum, the **Eco-musée du Liège** (*t 04 94 78 25 65; open Mon and Wed–Sat 9–12 and 2–5, Sun 9–12; adm*), dedicated to the art of cork production, where the craftsmen scoff at the introduction of plastic wine corks which has put many a Portuguese family out of work recently. The villagers also boast that both Julius Caesar and Louis XIV demanded to taste the local wine; you can try it yourself at a tour of a local wine production centre run by the proudly named **Maîtres Vignerons de Gonfaron** (*t 04 94 78 30 02*).

Just east (off the N97 or the A8 and near the donkey sanctuary), the **Village des Tortues** (*t 04 94 78 26 41, www.tortues.com; open daily 9–7, closed Dec–Feb, when a notice on the gates explains that 'the tortoises are sleeping'; adm*) is devoted to saving France's last native land tortoise, the yellow and black Hermann's tortoise of the Maures. Some 1,200 tortoises live at this non-profit-making centre until they reach the age of three, when they are released into the Maures, where the lucky ones will live to be 80. Occasionally, the dafter ones amble ponderously across the motorway, bringing breakneck drivers to a screeching halt. The best months to visit the centre are April and May when the tortoises mate, June when they lay their eggs and September when the eggs hatch.

From the Corniche des Maures to Hyères

Apart from fashionable pockets like Bandol and Cassis, the Corniche des Maures is the last glamorous hurrah of the Côte d'Azur, where celebrities and other big money types have villas among the pines and flowers by the silver sand. No railways come between the towns and the sea, and the main road in season is a slow purgatory of fed-up motorists and bus passengers.

Baie de Cavalaire

The bay on the underside of the St-Tropez peninsula, with its clear coves and large beaches of silken sand, has been given lock, stock and barrel to the property promoters. **La Croix-Valmer** is all new, although the story of its name dates back to Emperor Constantine who, as mere co-emperor of Gaul, was on his way to Rome when he saw a cross lit against the sky here, telling of his future destiny as the victor at the Milvian bridge in Rome – where he would see another cross – and his role as the first Christian emperor. The longest beach in the bay is at **Cavalaire-sur-Mer** which, like La Croix-Valmer, is more popular with families than movie stars.

Between Cavalaire-sur-Mer and Le Rayou Canadel, the **Domaine du Rayol** (*Av des Belges, t 04 98 04 44 00, www.domainedurayol.org; open 25 Jan–Mar Tues–Sun 9.30–12.30 and 2–5.30; April–Sept Tues–Sun 9.30–12.30 and 2,30–6.30; Oct–21 Nov Tues–Sun 9.30–12.30 and 2–5.30; closed 22 Nov–24 Jan; adm*) is well worth a stop for its Mediterranean gardens with global flora: South African, New Zealand, Mexican and Californian species thrive and abound among avenues and steps, a chance to glut your eyes on greenery after the Côte de Cement.

For a quiet detour inland, take the narrow D27 from Canadel-sur-Mer, west of Cavalaire, to **La Môle**, a tiny village with a two-towered château, where Antoine de Saint-Exupéry (pilot, and author of *The Little Prince*) spent much of his youth. Behind the 18th-century village is the site of its ancient counterpart, tucked under the massive basalt Rocher de Sainte-Magdeleine, with the still discernible ruins of the 11th-century church.

Bormes-les-Mimosas and Le Lavandou

Persevering west past Cap Nègre and the exclusive villages of **Pramousquier** and **Cavalière** you find the big boys on the Corniche-des-Maures, the fishing port and resort of Le Lavandou and **Bormes-les-Mimosas**, a cute hyper-restored medieval enclave that added the mimosas to tart up its name in 1968, although the honour of first planting and commercializing these little yellow Mexican ball blooms goes to Cannes, where in 1880 a gardener carelessly tossed a branch someone had given him into a pile of manure and *voilà*, the next morning he had the lovely flowers that are now the totem of the Côte d'Azur.

At the summit of the village is the **Château de Pos**, now a private residence and displaying the last word in restoration techniques; far nicer is the footpath which leads up to the delightful, austere **Chapelle Notre-Dame-de-Constance**, built at the insistence of Constance de Provence in the 13th century. The 18th-century church of **St Trophyme** is packed out in summer with rubber-neckers trying to get a glimpse of the President of France, whose summer residence is out on Cap de Brégançon, and the **Chapelle St-François** is full of *pétanque*-players praying for good fortune in the World Pétanque Championships, which take place annually in September in the

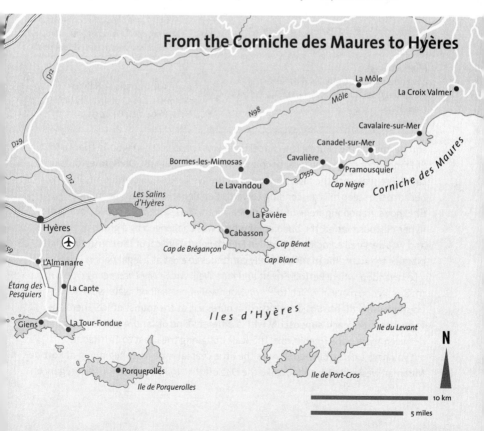

Getting Around

Besides slow and expensive **buses**, there are summer **boat** connections from Cavalaire-sur-Mer and year-round services from Le Lavandou to the Iles d'Or. Call the Vedettes Iles d'Or, t 04 94 64 18 17. To explore the hinterland, you can rent bicycles or scooters at **Holiday Bikes**, Rue du Port, t 04 94 15 19 99. Parking is at a premium in both Cavalaire-sur-Mer and Bormes-les-Mimosas.

Tourist Information

Cavalaire-sur-Mer: Maison de la Mer, t 04 94 01 92 10, f 04 94 05 49 89, *www.golfe-infos. com/cavalaire.*

Bormes-les-Mimosas: Place Gambetta, t 04 94 01 38 38, f 04 94 01 38 39, *mail@bormesles mimosas.com, www.bormeslesmimosas.com. Open Oct–Mar Mon–Sat 9–12.30 and 2–6; April–Sept daily 9–12.30 and 3–6.30.*

Le Lavandou: Quai Gabriel Péri, t 04 94 00 40 50, f 04 94 00 40 59, *info@lelavandou. com, www.lelavandou.com. Open Oct–April Mon–Sat 9–12 and 3–6; May–Sept daily 9–12 and 3–7.*

Market Days

Cavalaire: Place Jean Moulin, Wednesday morning. Fish market, at the harbour, every morning.

Bormes-les-Mimosas: Wednesday morning, Saturday morning in season, in the old village.
Pin-de-Bormes: Tuesday morning.
Le Lavandou: All year mornings only, in Le Lavandou. June–Sept, Plage de Cavalaire.

Where to Stay and Eat

Cavalaire-sur-Mer ✉ 83240
★★★**Hôtel La Calanque**, Rue de la Calanque, t 04 94 01 95 00, f 04 94 64 66 20, *mario. lacalanque@wanadoo.fr, www.hotel-la-calanque.com (luxury–very expensive).* Modern, and 20ft above the sea on the cliff edge, with smart, balconied rooms, a swimming pool, jacuzzi, tennis courts and a pretty seafood restaurant on a shady terrace. *Closed Jan–mid-Mar, and Mon out of season.*
★★**Hôtel Raymond**, Av des Alliés, t 04 94 01 95 95, f 04 94 01 95 96, *www.hotel-raymond. com (expensive–moderate).* An earthy Logis de France establishment with a dollop of old-fashioned charm. It has a little pool and a children's play area, and a decent restaurant, Le **Mistral**, specializing in *bouillabaisse. Closed Oct–Mar; restaurant closed Sun lunch and Mon; winter open eves only.*

Bormes-les-Mimosas ✉ 83230
★★★**Les Palmiers**, 240 Chemin du Petit Fort, t 04 94 64 81 94, f 04 94 64 93 61,

---

square outside the church. The chapel itself was constructed in 1560, in thanks to St François for saving the local people from the plague in 1481. On Bormes' outskirts, **La Favière**, was once the favourite resort of the White Russian community in Paris, because the steep hills descending towards Cap Bénat reminded the founder – Chekhov's granddaughter – of the Crimea. All this has since been spoiled by Bormes' hyper-hideous marina, the building of which was challenged by a group of residents and was declared completely illegal in French courts. Typical of the corruption that plagues the coast, the marina blithely continues to exist as a legal fiction.

Le Lavandou, where Bertolt Brecht and Kurt Weill wrote *The Threepenny Opera* in 1928, is a good place in which to empty your wallet on seafood, water sports, boutiques and nightclubs; for glossy brochures ask at the tourist office. There are 12 beaches here, each, supposedly, with a different kind of sand. A *petit train* trundles between them. For a freebie, take the walk out along the coast to Cap Bénat.

If you have a car or bike, don't miss the little coastal wine road, beginning at **Port-de-Miramar**, west of Le Lavandou (take the D42 off the N98); it passes Cap de Brégançon

les.palmiers@wanadoo.fr (*luxury–moderate*). The best hotel in the *commune* is a steep drive south along the D41 to Cabasson, and is only a few minutes from the sea; its restaurant serves solid classic food, which is a good thing as half board is obligatory in the summer. *Closed mid-Nov–Jan.*

★★★**Grand Hôtel**, 167 Rte de Baguier, t 04 94 71 23 72, f 04 94 71 51 20, *www.augrandhotel. com* (*moderate–inexpensive*). Splendid sea views and characterful yet modern rooms. Very good value. *Closed Nov–mid-Feb.*

Lou Portaou, 1 Rue Cubert-des-Poètes, t 04 94 64 86 37, t 04 94 64 81 43 (*expensive*). In a 12th-century guardhouse, serving excellent seasonal regional dishes. Book early in summer. *Closed Tues out of season and mid-Nov–20 Dec; closed lunch June–Sept.*

La Tonnelle, 23 Place Gambetta, t 04 94 71 34 84 (*moderate*). Tables are set under a gallery of vines and the food is made entirely from local ingredients with the finesse of a master and perfectionist. The prices are very reasonable by Côte standards. *Closed lunch July–Aug, Wed and Thurs in Oct–April, and Wed and Thurs lunch in May–June and Sept.*

Le Lavandou ✉ 83980

★★★★**Les Roches**, 1 Av des Trois-Dauphins, Aiguebelle-Plage, t 04 94 71 05 07, f 04 94 71 08 40, *info@hotellesroches.com, www.hotel-prestige-provence.com* (*luxury*). Set magnificently over the *calanques* 4km east of Le Lavandou, Les Roches has modern rooms furnished with Internet access, as well as a private beach, a pool and tennis-courts. The hotel and restaurant have recently been bought and renovated by a luxury hotel chain, with corresponding drop in friendliness. *Closed Jan–Feb.*

★★★**Belle Vue**, Chemin du Four-des-Maures, St-Clair, t 04 94 00 45 00, f 04 94 00 45 25, *hotelbellevue@wanadoo.fr, www.lelavandou. com/bellevue* (*expensive–moderate*). Charming and as good as its name, with views over the coast. *Closed Nov–Mar.*

★★★**Auberge de la Calanque**, 62 Av du Général de Gaulle, t 04 94 71 05 96, f 04 94 71 20 12, *lacalanque@wanadoo.fr* (*very expensive–expensive*). Large airy rooms with wonderful views, very affable staff and a decent restaurant (*expensive–moderate*). *Half board obligatory in summer. Closed Nov–Mar; restaurant closed Wed lunch and Thurs lunch in summer.*

★★**L'Escapade**, 1 Chemin du Vannier, t 04 94 71 11 52, f 04 94 71 22 14, *hotelescapade@wanadoo.fr* (*inexpensive*). A small but very cosy hotel in a quiet lane, with air-conditioning and TV. *Half board obligatory in summer.*

Tamaris, Plage St-Clair, t 04 94 71 79 19 (*expensive*). Fresh grilled fish, *bouillabaisse* and *langoustes* that will warm the cockles of your heart. *Closed Nov–Mar.*

and its fortified château (the official summer retreat of the President of France), and leads southeast to the delicious beach at **Cabasson** (*free, but you must pay for parking*), with a campsite and hotel.

Hyères

Known as Olbia by the Greeks from Marseille, who founded it in 350 BC, as Pomponiana by the Romans and as Castrum Arearum ('town of threshing floors') during the Middle Ages, Hyères claims to be the original resort of the Côte d'Azur, with a pedigree that goes back to Charles IX and Catherine de Médicis, who wintered here in 1564. It knew its greatest fame in the early 19th century, when people like Empress Josephine, Pauline Borghese, Victor Hugo, Tolstoy and Robert Louis Stevenson built villas here and invited one another to teas and soirées, before it faded genteelly from fashion in the 1880s. For despite its mild climate and lush gardens, Hyères was, unforgivably, three miles from the newly popular seaside. But the town had more

Getting There and Around

By Air

Hyères–Toulon Airport is served by Air France from Paris (for national information, call **t** 0802 802 802) and sometimes by various budget airlines from London.

By Train

Hyères is a dead end, linked to Toulon but nowhere else; the station is 1.5km south of town, but there are frequent buses into the town centre.

By Bus

Buses can be tricky. Call first. SODETRAV, 47 Av Alphonse Denis, **t** 04 94 12 55 12, serves routes west to Toulon and east to Le Lavandou. City buses (from the *gare routière* in the town centre) link Hyères to Hyères-Plage and the Giens peninsula.

By Boat

Boats for all three of Hyères' islands – Porquerolles, Port-Cros and Le Levant – depart at least twice a day, year-round, from **Port Saint-Pierre** in Hyères (**t** 04 94 12 54 40) and **Le Lavandou** (**t** 04 94 71 01 02), with additional sailings in the summer. There are more frequent connections from **La Tour-Fondue**, at the tip of the Giens peninsula, to Porquerolles (**t** 04 94 58 21 81), and in summer boats also sail from Toulon to Porquerolles.

Note that inter-island connections are more rare; check the schedules before setting out.

By Bicycle

Bicycles can be hired from **Holiday Bikes**, Centre Commercial Nautique, **t** 04 94 38 79 45.

Tourist Information

Hyères: 3 Av Ambroise Thomas, **t** 04 94 01 84 50, **f** 04 94 01 84 51, *info@ot-hyeres.fr*, *www.ot-hyeres.fr*. *Open winter Mon–Fri 9–6, Sat 10–4; summer Mon–Sat 8.30–7.30, Sun 9–1 and 3–7.*
Porquerolles: on the port, **t** 04 94 58 33 76, **f** 04 94 58 36 39, *www.porquerolles.com*. *Open April–Sept 9–5.30; Oct–Mar 9–12.30.*

Market Days

Hyères: Farmers' market, Place de la République and Av Gambetta, Tuesday and Saturday; organic produce, Place de la Vicomtesse de Noailles, Tuesday, Thursday and Saturday; large market, Av Gambetta, Saturday; flea market, La Capte, Sunday morning.

Local Wine

The local wine to look out for is **Côte des Iles**, which is exquisite but rare. Try some at: **Domaine de la Courtade**, at La Courtade, **t** 04 94 58 31 44, *www.la-courtade.com* (*open for visits by appointment only*).

Where to Stay and Eat

Hyères Town ✉ 83400

★★Hôtel du Soleil, 2 Rue des Remparts, **t** 04 94 65 16 26, **f** 04 94 35 46 00, *soleil@hotel-du-soleil.fr*, *www.hotel-du-soleil.fr* (*moderate*). A pleasant, quiet choice near Parc St-Bernard. It's very difficult to drive through this part of town, so park and walk.

★★Les Orangers, 64 Av des Iles d'Or, **t** 04 94 00 55 11, **f** 04 94 35 25 90, *orangers@var-provence.com*, *www.var-provence.com* (*inexpensive*). A sturdy Provençal-style building near the restaurants and brasseries just to the east of the Rue Gambetta, and one of the prettiest and most comfortable hotels in town.

★Reine Jane, Ayguade, between Bormes-les-Mimosas and Hyères, **t** 04 94 66 32 64, **f** 04 94 66 34 66, *reine.jane@wanadoo.fr*, *www.perso.wanadoo.fr/hotel.reine.jane*

than one egg in its basket, and has since made the most of its salt pans on the peninsula, exploited since ancient times, and its nurseries of date palms (developed from a Californian species adaptable to sand and salinity), most of which are exported to Saudi Arabia and the Arab emirates. Now 'Hyères-les-Palmiers', if you please, it has recently won a national award for its parks and gardens.

(*inexpensive*). Good rooms and food (*moderate*) at bargain prices. *Closed first two weeks in Jan; restaurant closed Wed.*

La Colombe, Impasse Vieille, Bayorre, t 04 94 35 35 16 (*moderate*). For a more elaborate dinner, try the delicious *turbot au beurre d'herbe tendre*. Service on the patio in summer. *Closed Sat lunch, Sun eve and Mon lunch.*

Le Bistrot de Marius, 1 Place Massillon, t 04 94 35 88 38 (*moderate*). A tiny stone establishment with big platefuls of Provençal favourites, a very jolly host and tables out on the main square in summer. *Closed mid-Nov–mid-Dec and Jan.*

Les Jardins de Bacchus, 32 Av Gambetta, t 04 94 65 77 63 (*moderate*). Pulls out all the stops with its rich, flavoursome Provençal dishes and quietly elegant surroundings. *Closed Sun eve and Mon in winter; Sun lunch and Mon in summer and one week in Jan.*

Ile de Porquerolles ✉ 83400

There are seven hotels on the island, all priced above the odds and all booked months in advance in the summer. The best are:

★★★★**Mas du Langoustier**, t 04 94 58 30 09, f 04 94 58 36 02, langoustier@compuserve.com, www.langoustier.com (*luxury–very expensive*). A romantic old inn between the woods and a long sandy beach, with lovely rooms and a superb restaurant (*expensive*), where the chef imaginatively combines the best ingredients of Provence. The wine list includes Porquerolles' famous rosé. *Closed mid-Oct–April.*

★★**Sainte-Anne**, t 04 98 04 63 00, f 04 94 58 32 26, steanne.porquerolles@wanadoo.fr (*expensive*). A bit dilapidated, but stays open longer than the rest; half board is compulsory in season, but the food is good. *Closed mid-Dec–Feb.*

★★**Auberge des Glycines**, 22 Place d'Armes, t 04 94 58 30 36, f 04 94 58 35 22, www.aubergedesglycines.net (*expensive–*

moderate). A small and charming inn, with rooms decorated in Provençal fabrics and set around a tranquil courtyard.

★★**Relais de la Poste**, Place d'Armes, t 04 98 04 62 62, f 04 94 58 33 57, relaisposte@aol.com, www.lerelaisdelaposte.com (*moderate*). This was the island's first hotel and has pleasant Provençal-style rooms with loggias and a simple *crêperie*. *Closed Oct–Mar.*

Il Pescatore, t 04 94 58 30 61 (*moderate*). For all things fish: not just the predictable *bouillabaisse*, but *carpaccio* and *sashimi*. Eat on the restful terrace overlooking the boats bobbing in the port. *Closed Nov–Feb.*

Port-Cros ✉ 83400

There is only one choice on paradise, and it needs to be booked long in advance.

★★★**Le Manoir d'Hélène**, t 04 94 05 90 52, f 04 94 05 90 89 (*luxury–expensive*). An 18th-century mansion set among the eucalyptus groves, with an outdoor pool and a fine little restaurant (*expensive*). *Closed Oct–Mar.*

Ile du Levant ✉ 83400

La Brise Marine, Corniche des Arbousiers, t 04 94 05 91 15, f 04 94 05 93 21, info@labrisemarine.fr, www.labrisemarine.fr (*moderate*). At the summit of the islet, with pretty rooms situated around a patio with a swimming pool. *Closed mid-Sept–April.*

Entertainment and Nightlife

With bar life in Toulon restricted to seedy sailors' bars and nefarious goings-on in the old town, most Toulonnais head to Hyères for a night out, crowding the many bars and clubs.

For a bop, try the newly reopened **Casino des Palmiers**, t 04 94 12 80 80, in the centre of Hyères-les-Palmiers.

'Mit Palmen und mit Ice-cream, ganz gewöhnlich, ganz gewöhnlich...' (With palms and ice-cream, quite usual, quite usual...) So Bertolt Brecht, and so Hyères. There isn't much to do but take a brief wander into the Vieille Ville, beyond **Place Massillon**. Here stands the **Tour des Templiers**, a remnant from a Templar's lodge, and, on top of a monumental stair, the collegiate church of **St-Paul** (1599) (t 04 94 65 83 30; open

April–Sept Wed–Mon 10–12 and 4–7; Oct–Mar 10–12 and 2–5.30), with 400 *ex votos* dating back to the 17th century. Inside also is a set of *santons* too large to move. The Renaissance house next to St-Paul doubles as a city gate, through which you can walk up to **Parc St-Bernard**, with Mediterranean plants and flowers.

At the upper part of the park, the so-called Château St-Bernard, or **Villa Noailles** (*open summer Wed–Sun 10–12 and 4–7; winter Wed–Sun 10–12 and 2–5; closed Tues*), was designed as a *château cubiste* by Robert Mallet-Stevens in 1924 for art patron Vicomte Charles de Noailles, the financier of the first film by Cocteau, *Blood of the Poet* (1930), and of Salvador Dalí and Luis Buñuel's *L'Age d'or* – which nearly got Noailles excommunicated, not to mention thrown out of the Jockey Club. Austere cement on the outside, furnished with pieces commissioned from Eileen Gray and designers from the Bauhaus, this vast villa, with 15 guest rooms and a covered pool, was a busy hive of creativity between the wars – it even stars in Man Ray's murky 1929 film *Le Mystère du Château de Dé*. You can visit the house during exhibitions, or the exotic garden, the **Parc St-Bernard**, any day for free. The garden has recently been linked to that of Edith Wharton, author of *The Age of Innocence*, who lived on the same slope in a former convent of Ste-Claire. The **Parc Sainte-Claire** is spread over 28 terraces (*open summer daily 8–7; winter 9–5*) and encompasses the little house, **La Solitude**, where Robert Louis Stevenson stayed and wrote *A Child's Garden of Verses*. Further up the hill are the hollow walls and towers of the **Vieux Château**, with an overview of Hyères' peninsula and jumble of hills.

In 1254, when Louis IX returned to France from the Crusades, he disembarked at Hyères and went to pray in the 13th-century Franciscan church in Place de la République, now named **St-Louis** in his honour. Below, in Place Th. Lefebvre, the heart of 19th-century Hyères, a **Musée Municipal** (*t 04 94 00 78 42; open 10–12 and 2.30–5.0; closed Tues, Sat and Sun*) houses the fragmentary remains of Hyères' Greek and Roman seaside predecessors, as well as two engraved menhirs and a Celto-Iberian figure holding two heads, similar to the statues at Roquepertuse in Aix. Further south, on Av Gambetta, you can relax in the **Jardin Olbius-Riquier** among the palms, rare tropical and semi-tropical trees and cacti. There is a lake and a small **zoo** (*open 9–6*) for the kids, with birds, ponies, etc. Two neo-Moorish villas from the 1880s remain in this part of town: the **Villa Tunisienne** in Avenue Beauregard and the **Villa Mauresque** in Avenue Jean Natte.

The Giens Peninsula

Over the centuries, the island that was Giens has been anchored to the mainland by two sand bars whose arms embrace a salt marsh, the **Etang des Pesquiers**. Although the link has historically been dodgy – Giens became an island again in the storms of 1811 – it hasn't stopped people from building villas and hotels, especially on the isthmus at **La Capte**.

The barren west arm, dotted by shimmering white piles of salt, is traversed by the narrow *route du sel* beginning at **Plage de l'Almanarre**. In 1843 the archaeologist king, Frederick VII of Denmark, excavated the ruins of the Greek-Roman town at **Almanarre**. Most of it has been reclaimed by the sand, but the remaining sites are open (*t 04 94*

57 98 28; open April–Sept Sat 10–12 and 2–5, Sun 10–12 and 2–5; closed Oct–Mar). There are Merovingian tombs in the 12th-century Chapelle St-Pierre.

The 'salt road' ends in **Giens**, a quiet little hamlet under a ruined castle that was the last home of the 1961 Nobel-prize-winning poet St-John Perse, who is buried in the cemetery; further up are views from the ruined castle. To the south, **La Tour-Fondue** is the principal port for Porquerolles, although the often violent seas around the peninsula have caused scores of shipwrecks. In 1967 an intact cargo ship dating from the time of the Roman republic was found in the Golfe de Giens, with sealed amphorae containing a clear liquid with reddish mud on the bottom – the ultimate fate of red wine aged too long.

The Iles d'Hyères

Known as the Stroechades, or 'chaplet', by the ancient Greeks, and in the Renaissance as the Iles d'Or owing to the shiny yellow colour of their rock, Hyères' three islands are voluptuous little greenhouses that have seen more than their share of trouble. In the Middle Ages they belonged to the monastery of St-Honorat, and attracted pirates like moths to a flame; in 1160, after the Saracens carried off the entire population, the monks gave up and just let the pirates have the islands.

The expansion of the Ottoman Empire throughout the Mediterranean in the 16th century made the kings of France sit up and notice the Saracens, and in 1515 an attempt was made to preach a crusade against the Hyères pirates, but the crusading spirit was long past. François Ier had a golden opportunity to install the then homeless Knights of St John on Porquerolles, but the two parties couldn't agree on terms and the Knights settled for Malta, which then belonged to Spain, paying their famous rent of one golden falcon. François had to build his own forts and send settlers to man them against Charles V and other sea predators, but again the pirates carried everyone off.

Henri II, son of François, thought he had a good idea in populating the islands with criminals and malcontents. By this time, however, France had found the solution to her piracy problem: becoming allies with them and the Turks. On one memorable occasion in 1558, the French navy had a big party on Porquerolles to help the notorious Barbarossa and his cut-throats celebrate the end of Ramadan. Then the new inhabitants of the islands spoiled Henri's plans by following their instincts and becoming pirates themselves, capturing numerous French ships and once even pillaging the naval base in Toulon. It took another century to eradicate them.

Later rulers rebuilt the island's forts. In the late 19th century they were variously used to quarantine veterans of the colonial wars and as sanctuaries for homeless children: Le Levant and Porquerolles became Dickensian orphanages and juvenile penal colonies. In both cases the young inmates rebelled, and many were killed. Industrialists opened sulphur plants on the islands that no other place in France would have tolerated, and the navy bought Le Levant in 1892 and blew it to pieces as a firing range. In the 1890s fires burned most of the forests on Porquerolles and

Port-Cros. Fortunately, in this century, the French government has moved to protect the islands; strict laws protect them from the risks of fire and developers.

Porquerolles

Largest of the three, Porquerolles stretches 7km by 3km and has the largest permanent population, which in the summer explodes to 10,000. Its main village, also called Porquerolles, was founded in 1820 as a retirement village for Napoleon's finest soldiers and invalids. It still has a colonial air, especially around the central pine-planted **Place d'Armes**, the address of most of Porquerolles' restaurants, bars, hotels and bicycle hire shops. Even the village church was built on the orders of the Ministry of War, and has military symbols on the altar. Although the cliffs to the south are steep and dangerous for swimming, there are gentle beaches on either side of the village, especially the white-sand **Plage Notre-Dame** to the east and **Plage d'Argent** to the west. The previous owner of the island (an eccentric Belgian, who discovered Mexico's largest silver lode) took a special interest in acclimatizing flora, such as the *bellombra*, a Mexican tree with huge roots and elephant-skin-like bark, but today green thumbs concentrate on vines.

Between Porquerolles and Giens the now deserted little islet of **Grand Ribaud** was used in the early 1900s for 'spiritualist experiments' and other research by one Dr Richet, who also imported kangaroos. The kangaroos liked the islet, we are told, but banged themselves to untimely deaths by jumping too exuberantly on the sharp rocks.

Port-Cros

Although barely measuring a square mile, Port-Cros, rising to 640ft, is the most mountainous of the three islands. Since 1963 it has been a national park, preserving not only its forests of pines and ilexes, recovered from a devastating fire in 1892, but nearly a hundred species of birds; brochures will help you identify them as you walk along the mandatory trails. There is a selection of trails: the *sentier botanique* is for visitors pressed for time, while at the other end of the scale there's a 10km *circuit historique* for the lucky ones who have a packed lunch and all day. Two curiosities of the island are its abundant native catnip and its *euphorbe arborescente*, which loses all its leaves in the summer and grows new ones in the autumn. Like the national park in the Florida Keys, Port-Cros also protects its surrounding waters, rich in colourful fish and plant life. There's even a 1,000ft 'path' which divers can follow from Plage de la Palud to Rascas islet, clutching a plastic guide sheet that identifies the underwater flora. Of late, some of the more fragile plants around the island have suffered as a result of Port-Cros' extraordinary popularity – from the emissions and anchors of the thousands of pleasure craft that call here each year.

Ile du Levant

The French navy still hogs almost all this flowering island, but they no longer use it for target practice. Nowadays, they test aircraft engines and rockets, which are marginally quieter. The island's remaining public quarter is occupied by **Héliopolis**,

France's first nudist colony (1931). Anyone who's been to St-Tropez and other fashionable Côte beaches will find the idea of a specially reserved nudist area quaint by now, but Héliopolis still has its determined Adams and Eves, especially because it's so warm: 60 members of the colony stick it out here all year.

The West Coast of the Var

Toulon

If Provençal traditionalists (and they are landlubbers all) look upon the cosmopolitan Côte d'Azur as an alien presence, they feel equally ill at ease in the south's two great ports, Toulon and Marseille: to the Provençal they are dangerous, salty cities, populated by untrustworthy strangers and prostitutes. But while Marseille is essentially a city of merchants and trade, Toulon has always been the creature of the French navy. Whatever piquant charms it once had were bombed into oblivion in the Second World War and are only now slowly being restored.

History

For some reason the deepest, most majestic natural harbour in the Mediterranean tempted neither the Greeks nor the Romans. Instead Toulon (originally Telo Martius) was from Phoenician times a centre for dyeing cloth, thanks to its abundant murex shells (the source of royal purple) and the dried red corpses (*kermès*) of the *coccus illicis*, an insect that lived in the surrounding forests of oaks. Toulon's destiny began to change when Provence was annexed to France in 1481. The first towers and walls went up under Louis XII in 1514; Henri IV created the arsenal, but it was Louis XIV who changed Toulon forever, making it the chief port of France's Mediterranean fleet, greatly expanding the arsenal and assigning Vauban the task of protecting it with his star-shaped forts, built by forced labour. It was during this period that Toulon became the most popular tourist destination in Provence, when well-heeled visitors came to see not the new navy installations, but the miserable galley slaves – Turkish prisoners, African slaves, criminals and, later, Protestants – chained four to an oar, where they worked, ate and slept in appalling conditions. The 17th century was such a rotten time that there were even volunteers for the galleys, distinguished by their moustaches and less likely to feel the cat o' nine tails.

Toulon's history is marked by three disasters. In 1720 nature's neutron bomb, the plague, killed 15,000 out of 26,000 inhabitants. The second disaster began after the execution of Louis XVI, when Toulon's royalists had confided the city to the English and their Spanish and Sardinian allies. In 1793 a ragamuffin Revolutionary army of volunteers and ruffians under the painter Carteaux, fresh from massacring 6,000 people in Lyon, arrived at the gate of Toulon and began an ineffectual siege of two months. A young Napoleon Bonaparte came on the scene and convinced the commissioners to put him in charge of the artillery. Bonaparte turned his guns to the west side of the harbour, on the English redoubt of Mulgrave, so well fortified that it was

Central Toulon

Cemetery

RUE GIMELLI

BD DE TESSE

i

RUE D'ANTRECHAUS

RUE VICTOR CLAPPIER

RUE TRUGUET

RUE PICOT

RUE FR. FABIE

BD DE STRASBOURG

BD DE TESSE

BD RAYNOUARD

BD DE LA DEMOCRATIE

AV CDT MARCHAND

RUE MOLIERE

RUE CORNEILLE

RUE RAIMU

Fontaine des 3 Dauphins

PL PUGET

RUE HOCHE

RUE PYAT

RUE BAUDIN

RUE P. LANDRIN

RUE DE LORGUES

RUE MAIRAUD

RUE DES REMPARTS

RUE ST-BERNARD

AV GEORGES CLEMENCEAU

AV PHILIPPE LEBON

AV MARCEL CASTIE

AV COL FABIEN

AV COL FABIEN

POL

PL ST-VINCENT

Jardin du
Champ de Mars

RUE D'ASTOUR

Halles

COURS LAFAYETTE

RUE J. ALCARD

Square
Kennedy

RUE ZOLA

PL DE LA CATHEDRALE

Cathédrale
Ste-Marie

M

RUE V. COURDOUAN

ALL DE LA
LEGION ETRANGERE

A DAUMAS

RUE BASTIDE

Musée du
Vieux Toulon

RUE GARIBALDI

RUE ST-ANDRIEUX

St-Pié X

PL DE LA
POISSONERIE

COURS LAFAYETTE

PL DU
MURIER

PLACE
POMPIDOU

AV F. ROOSEVELT

H. SEILLON

Hôtel
de Ville

RUE POMME DE PIN

AV DE BESAGNE

RUE DU MURIER

RUE H. PERTUS

St-François-
de-Paule

AV DE LA REPUBLIQUE

QUAI DE LA SINSE

Stade Mayol

AV. F. ROOSEVELT

Darse Vieille

N

Customs

To Tour Royale

ROND-POINT
BONAPARTE

Pedestrian Street

200 metres
200 yards

Getting There and Around

Toulon is the major local transport hub.

By Air

Toulon's airport (t 04 94 00 83 83) is out near Hyères (for information, call t 08 25 01 83 87; for domestic flight reservations, call the airlines. Budget airlines from London sometimes fly the route; check **Travel**.

By Train

The train station is on the northern side of Toulon in Place Albert Ier, with four daily TGVs to Nice and Marseille, four direct to Paris (taking just over 4hrs), and frequent connections up and down the coast and to Hyères. SNCF: t 08 92 35 35 35.

By Bus

For St-Tropez and the coast between Hyères and St-Raphaël, catch an (*expensive*) SODE-TRAV bus from the *gare routière* (which is right next to the train station), t 04 94 12 55 12. Buses run by Ouest Littoral Cars (which leave from Av Vauban, running south from the station), t 04 94 74 01 35, will take you to Bandol, La Seyne, Six-Fours and Sanary.

From Quai Cronstadt, pleasant and very reasonably priced sea-buses go to La Seyne, Les Sablettes and St-Mandrier.

City bus and sea-bus info can be obtained from RMTT on t 04 94 03 87 03.

By Boat

From May to August there are daily sailings (weekly in September) to Corsica and frequent sailings to Sardinia (SNCM, Av de l'Infanterie-de-Marine, t 0825 801 701; Corsica Ferries, t 0825 095 095).

Companies departing from Quai Cronstadt offer tours of Toulon's anchorages and battleships, the Grande Rade and Petite Rade, and the surrounding coasts and islands:

Trans-med 2000, t 04 94 92 96 82. Tours to the Ile de Porquerolles, July–Aug.

Les Bateliers de la Rade, t 04 94 46 24 65. Also has crossings to all three Iles d'Hyères, June–Aug.

Transport Maritime Toulonnais, t 04 94 23 25 36.

Catamaran Alain II, t 04 94 46 29 89.

SNRTM, t 04 94 62 41 14. Tours of the *rades*. For sea-buses, *see* above.

Bicycle and Scooter Hire

Espace Vélo/Cycles Cutaia, 395 Av Franklin Roosevelt, t 04 94 42 61 90.

Motard Service, 282 Bd Léon Bourgeois, t 04 94 03 94 04. Motorcycles and scooters.

Tourist Information

Toulon: Place Raimu, t 04 94 18 53 00, f 04 94 18 53 09, *infos@toulontourisme.com*, *www.toulontourisme.com*. Open June–Sept Mon–Sat 9–6, Sun 10–12; Oct–May Mon–Sat 9.30–5.30, Sun 10–12. The tourist office can also help finding *chambres d'hôtes*.

Post office: The main post office is at Rue Ferréro (behind the Galeries Lafayette), t 04 94 18 51 00. There's another at Place de la Poissonnerie (behind the City Hall).

Internet: **Cap Games**, 7 Rue Corneille, t 04 94 93 92 52.

Market Days

On Cours Lafayette every morning except Monday – don't miss it; big flea markets on

nicknamed 'Little Gibraltar' (now Fort Caire), and had captured it by 19 December. In spite of the opposition of the English commander Samuel Hood, the allies decided to abandon Toulon to its fate. The thousands who couldn't escape were mercilessly slaughtered by the Jacobins. The hitherto unknown Bonaparte, promoted to brigadier-general, became the darling of the Convention. Although the Revolutionaries hailed the galley slaves as 'the only decent men of the infamous city', convicts (like Jean Valjean in *Les Misérables*) continued to be sentenced to the *bagnes* (penal camps) in Toulon until the 1850s. Chained in pairs, with rats for pets, the cons envied the lucky few who made a fortune as executioners: 20 *livres* for breaking a

the eastern (industrial zone) outskirts of the city on Sunday morning.

Festivals

The **Fête de la Musique** takes place through June and July, with concerts in town and surrounding areas. July also sees the **Festival de Jazz**, t 04 94 09 71 00.

Rhythm' Estival, in early August, is a world music festival (**t** 04 94 09 71 00).

Sports

Toulon's **rugby** team is one of the best in France and passions can run high; for tickets at the home pitch, Stade Mayol, call **t** 04 94 41 08 10.

Where to Stay

Toulon ✉ 83000

Prices are about one-third less than on the fashionable Côte, and fall even lower in the low season.

***La Corniche, 17 Littoral F. Mistral, Le Mourillon, **t** 04 94 41 35 12, **f** 04 94 41 24 58, info@cornichehotel.com, www.cornichehotel.com (expensive–moderate). Part of the Best Western chain, this cleverly designed modern Provençal hotel is near the beach. There is a restaurant built around the massive trunks of three maritime pines, serving refined seafood and meat dishes. Restaurant closed Sat lunch and Sun eve.

Résidence du Cap Brun, 192 Chemin de l'Aviateur-Gayraud, off Corniche Gal. de Gaulle, **t** 04 94 41 29 46, **f** 04 94 63 16 16, www.gaudefroy-receptions.com info@gaudefroy-receptions.com (moderate). A magical

old white villa set on a cliff top beyond the beaches of Mourillon. Surrounded by pine and plane trees and a world away from the urban hubbub of Toulon, it has a small swimming pool and a steep stone path down to the shore. No restaurant. Closed Nov–Mar.

Grand Hôtel du Dauphiné, 10 Rue Berthelot, **t 04 94 92 20 28, **f** 04 94 62 16 69, www.grandhoteldauphine.com (inexpensive). In the pedestrian zone, not far from the opera, this is a comfortable, friendly older hotel, air-conditioned, with discounted parking.

*Le Jaurès, 11 Rue Jean Jaurès, **t** 04 94 92 83 04, **f** 04 94 62 16 74, www.hoteljaures.fr (inexpensive). The top bargain choice; the rooms all have baths.

*Molière, 12 Rue Molière, **t** 04 94 92 78 35, **f** 04 94 62 85 82 (inexpensive). Another good bargain place. Closed Jan.

Eating Out

Le Lingousto, Rte de Pierrefeu, Cuers, **t** 04 94 28 69 10 (expensive). Toulonnais in search of a special meal drive 20km northeast to Cuers to eat at Le Lingousto, located in an old bastide, where the freshest of fresh local ingredients are transformed into imaginative works of art – langoustines with pasta, omelettes with oursins (sea urchins), cheeses that have 'worked' to perfection and divine desserts. Closed Sun eve and Mon, and Jan.

Le Jardin du Sommelier, 20 Allées Amiral Courbet, **t** 04 94 62 03 27 (expensive). Gastronomic Provençal cuisine with wines to match in a small, intimate dining room, perfect for 'un tête-à-tête en amoureux'. Closed Sat lunch and Sun.

nobleman (crushing all his bones, but not shedding a drop of his noble blood), 15 for a hanging or burning alive, down to two for cutting off a nose. They were forced to wear chains weighing 7kg day and night and to wear coloured hats: red for those who were under a short-term sentence, green for those condemned for life and brown for deserters. In 1860 the convicts were packed off out of sight to Devil's Island in French Guyana and in 1874 the penal colonies of Toulon shut up shop for good.

The city's most recent sufferings began in 1942, when the Germans took the city by surprise and the Vichy Amiral Laborde blocked up the harbour by scuttling the entire Mediterranean fleet to keep it from falling into the hands of the enemy.

Les Pins Penchés, 3182 Av de la Résistance, t 04 94 27 98 98, *www.restaurant-pins-penches. com* (*expensive*). A new gourmet restaurant with plenty of accolades and acres of gardens. *Closed Sun eve, Mon all day and Tues lunch in winter.*

Le Cellier, 52 Rue Jean Jaurès, t 04 94 92 64 35 (*expensive–moderate*). Jovial and friendly, with good menus. *Closed Sun.*

Le Lido, Littoral Frédéric Mistral, t 04 94 03 38 18, *www.lelidodetoulon.com* (*moderate*). A restaurant with nice nautical décor and a window on to the kitchen where you can watch your fresh fish being prepared. *Closed Sun eve and Mon in winter.*

La Chamade, 25 Rue Denfert-Rochereau, t 04 94 92 28 58 (*moderate*). Another local favourite which offers a serious fixed three-course menu prepared by chef Francis Bonneau. *Closed Sun and first three weeks in August.*

Le Village, 10 Rue Dumont-d'Urville, t 04 94 22 03 03 (*moderate*). Southwest and Provençal cuisine, with live jazz and theatre. *Closed Sat lunch, Sun and Aug.*

Les Enfants Gâtés, 7 Rue Corneille, t 04 94 09 14 67 (*moderate–cheap*). Traditional Provençal cuisine in a trendy setting in the centre of town. *Closed Sun in winter, weekends in summer.*

Entertainment and Nightlife

Pick up a paper or copy of the monthly *Fiesta* to tell you what's really going on. Toulon has some good theatre, dance and jazz, but it's not very easy to find out what.

Northwest of Toulon (Ollioules), a 17th-century tower was converted in 1966 into a handsome theatre, to host cultural events. The mayor infamously stamped down on its artistic freedom in the mid-1990s, but it has recently reopened as the **Châteauvallon Theatre**, with a varied and experimental programme of performing arts. It hosts the Festival de la Danse et de l'Image.

Music

Opéra, Place Victor Hugo, t 04 94 92 70 78. For opera, ballet and inane comedies in winter.

Zénith-Oméga concert hall, Place des Lices, t 04 94 22 66 77. Rapidly becoming the number one rock venue in the south of France – hosting the likes of Elton John and Lenny Kravitz.

Bar à Thym, 32 Bd Cunéo, t 04 94 41 90 11. Live rock and DJs on a more relaxed scale.

Cinemas

Pathé Liberté, 4 Place de la Liberté, t 08 92 69 66 96. Six screens and comfortable seats.

Pathé Grand Ciel, opposite the university at La Garde, t 08 92 69 66 96. Twelve screens and films in their original language (*v.o.*).

Le Royal, Rue Bertholet, t 08 92 68 03 89. Films in their original language.

Bars and Clubs

There is no lack of **bars**, especially around Rue Pierre Sémard, but in general they're not places where you'll feel comfortable alone. Toulon society prefers the bars along Littoral Frédéric Mistral on Mourillon beach, or drives to Hyères or Le Lavandou.

Boy's Paradise, 1 Bd Pierre Toesca, t 04 94 09 35 90. One of the Riviera's most famous gay nightclubs.

On 15 August 1944, after flattening the picturesque old port with aerial bombing raids, the Allies landed and the French army, under Général De Lattre de Tassigny, recaptured Toulon, but not before the entrenched Germans blew up the citadel, the harbour and the dockyards. Toulon was rebuilt quickly, although without a great sense of design or beauty. The end of the 20th century was not kind to Toulon. The shipbuilding yards in La Seyne closed down, putting thousands out of work, and the ugly forces of reaction succeeded in electing France's first National Front deputy, followed by the election of a National Front mayor whose xenophobic, anti-cultural antics were a national affront until his defeat in the last few years by one of Jacques

Chirac's allies, Hubert Falco. Now, with the opening of several restaurants and new museums, Toulon is beginning to rise from its own ashes.

Central Toulon

From the train station, Av Vauban descends to Av du Maréchal Leclerc; on the right at No.113 is the grandly gloomy municipal museum and library: inside are the **Musée d'Histoire Naturelle** (*t 04 94 36 81 10; open Mon–Fri 9.30–12 and 2–6, Sat and Sun 1–8*) and the **Musée d'Art** (*t 04 94 36 81 01; open daily 1–6.30; closed hols*). The natural history museum has all kinds of stuffed birds and beasts – from stately 'Clem', a lioness who was once a popular attraction at Toulon zoo, now come down in the world and playing to a much diminished audience, to a tiny, ratty *Musareigne etruseque*, the smallest mammal in the world, hiding behind a magnifying glass. The art museum contains an above-average collection of paintings and sculptures, including a Fragonard and some sculptures by Vernet and Pierre Puget. There's also an especially strong contemporary collection upstairs with Bacon, Arman, Yves Klein and Christo, among others, but you will be lucky if you see it all together; the museum usually focuses on local artists and lends out the heavyweights of its collection.

Next door is the quiet, spacious **Jardin Alexandre Ier**, with lovely magnolias and cedar trees. In the centre is an indomitable bust of Puget and a monument to the soldiers of the First World War. The Toulonnais do pretty well for local free museums: across the road, heading towards the centre of the town, the **Hôtel des Arts** (*236 Av du Maréchal Leclerc, t 04 94 91 69 18; open Tues–Sun 11–6*), is a lofty, elegant building devoted to modern art which, again, usually puts the spotlight on the work of local artists.

Avenue J. Moulin continues down to the large bleak square of **Place d'Armes**, decorated with ordnance from the adjacent arsenal, one of the biggest single employers in southeast France with some 10,000 workers. Alongside the arsenal in Place Monsenergue are miniature versions of the ships that it once made, displayed in the **Musée de la Marine** (*t 04 94 02 02 01; open Wed–Mon 10–12 and 2–6; closed Tues; adm*). France's great Baroque sculptor and architect Puget started out in Toulon carving and painting figureheads for the ships, and the museum has works by his followers. The grand Baroque entrance to the building itself is the original Louis XIV arsenal gate of 1738.

The best surviving works of Puget in Toulon are the two **Atlantes** (1657) on Quai Cronstadt, *Force* and *Fatigue*, whose woe and exhaustion may well have been modelled on the galley slaves. (You can see early copies of them in the Musée d'Art, *see* above.) They once supported the balcony of the old Hôtel de Ville, and were packed off to safety just before the bombings in the last war. Off the Quai, Rue d'Alger, now a popular evening promenade, used to be the most notorious street in Toulon's **Vieille Ville**, or '*le petit Chicago*', the pungent pocket of the pre-war town. Some of the narrow streets off here – known locally as 'the gut' – are still distinctly unsavoury after dark. However, blocked off from the sea by rows of ugly new buildings, the shifty bars and shabby flats are giving way to fashionable cafés and boutiques. Adding further swish to the neighbourhood is the **Maison de la Photographie** (*Rue Nicholas Laugier,*

Place du Globe, t 04 94 93 07 59; open Tues–Sat 10–12.30 and 1.30–6), which showcases local talents alongside legends such as Robert Doisneau and Bernard Faucon.

Further east, at 69 Cours Lafayette there's the dingy **Musée du Vieux-Toulon** (*t 04 94 62 11 07; open 2–5.45; closed Sun and hols*), with sketches by Puget, historical odds and ends, Provençal costumes and a 19th-century model of the town. Around the corner is the cathedral of **Ste-Marie**, 17th-century on the outside and Romanesque-Gothic within, although its features are barely discernible in the gloomiest interior in the south of France; during the Revolution an attempt to convert it into a stable failed when the horses threw their riders rather than enter it. Cours Lafayette itself used to be known as '*le pavé d'amour*', a favourite trysting spot, but young lovers today would have a hard time fighting their way through the babel of the colourful daily market that now runs its length. Come early in the morning to take it in, along with the fish market in Place de la Poissonnerie.

In attractive, café-lined Place Puget, at the top of the adjacent pedestrian quarter, is Toulon's prettiest fountain, the **Fontaine des Trois Dauphins**, sculpted by two young Toulonnais in the 18th century and now almost hidden by foliage. North of the three dolphins is Toulon's main street, Boulevard de Strasbourg, site of the **Opéra** (*see* 'Entertainment and Nightlife'), the biggest opera-house in Provence, noted for its acoustics, with an interior inspired by Charles Garnier. In Place Victor Hugo, in front of the Opéra, there is a wistful statue of the actor Jules Muraire, affectionately known as 'Raimu' (*see* pp.192–4), who was born at 6 Rue Anatole France, off the Place des Armes, in 1883. A bronze reconstruction of a famous scene from the hugely popular film, *César*, based on a Pagnol novel, sits outside the tourist ofice.

Mont Faron

Toulon looks better seen from a distance. Bus no.40 will take you to Bd Amiral Vence in **Super-Toulon** (bus stop *Téléphérique*), site of the terminus of the little blue funicular (*t 04 94 92 68 25; open Tues–Sun 9.30–12 and 2–5.30; not advisable in high winds; adm*) that runs to the top of 1,755ft Mont Faron (which means 'lighthouse mountain' in Provençal). There's a narrow hairpin road circuit as well, beginning in Av Emile Fabre. Besides a tremendous view over the city and its harbours, there's the **Musée Mémorial du Débarquement** (*t 04 94 88 08 09; open Tues–Sun 9.45–11.45 and 1.45–4.30; adm*), devoted to the August 1944 Allied landing in Provence, with models, uniforms and breathless 1944 newsreels. It shares the summit with a **zoo** (*t 04 94 88 07 89; open daily 2–5.30; closed mornings in winter on rainy days; adm; combined tickets for the funicular and the zoo are available*), which specializes in breeding wild-cats, including jaguars, tigers and lions. In 1997 a 'discovery path' was created among the wooded parks of the peak, with well-marked walking trails and picnic spots (the tourist office has a booklet with a map) where you can escape the city stickiness in summer.

Around the Harbour

The first stop should be the new **Musée des Arts Asiatiques** in Villa Jules Verne (*106 Bd Eugène Pelletan, t 04 98 00 41 00; open May–mid-Oct Tues–Sun 1–7; mid-Oct–April*

Tues–Sun 12.30–6; closed Mon), which includes 18th- and 19th-century pieces from Southeast Asia and Tibet (many from the collection of Baron de Rothschild). Bus nos.3 and 13 from in front of the station or on Av du Maréchal Leclerc will take you to the **Plage du Mourillon**, Toulon's largest beach and site of the city's oldest fort, Louis XII's 1514 Grosse Tour or Tour Royale, which once guarded the eastern approaches to Toulon with its rounded walls, 16–24ft thick. In later years the lower part, excavated out of the rock, was used as a prison; it now contains an annexe of the **Musée de la Marine** (*t 04 94 02 02 01; open Mon–Sat 10–6.30; adm*), with more figureheads in a baleful setting. Two beautiful coastal paths – the Sentier des Douaniers and the gentler Promenade Henri Fabre – leave from the Plage du Mourillon (both were damaged by severe storms in September and December 1999). They offer glimpses of tiny, hidden rocky coves shaded by umbrella pines and are about as near as you will get to an empty beach.

The west shore of the Petite Rade is Toulon's business end: although the yards of **La Seyne** are now closed, there is a dense mass of factories and industry. To the south, at L'Aiguillette, stood 'Little Gibraltar' near **Fort Balaguier**, another English stronghold that fell to Bonaparte; this now contains the **Musée Naval Municipal du Fort Balaguier** of Napoleana (*t 04 94 94 84 72 ; open winter Tues–Sun 10–12 and 2–6; summer Tues–Sun 10–12 and 3–7; adm*).

Further south is the residential suburb of **Tamaris**, once the home of officers and their families, where George Sand wrote her novel *Tamaris* in 1861. In the 1880s the mayor of nearby Sanary purchased much of Tamaris in the hope of turning it into a resort. This mayor had a more exciting career than most: born Michel Marius in Sanary in 1819, he was employed by the Ottoman Empire as a builder of lighthouses, a job he performed so well that the Sultan made him a pasha before sending him home in 1860 with a fat pension. Inspired by what he had seen in Turkey, Michel Pasha commissioned a number of fantasy neo-Moorish buildings in the area. In 1890 he decided to create a palace for his wife, inspired by Florentine villas. It has a lavishly garlanded façade, Italian balustrades and an unhappy ending: three years after work had begun, Michel Pasha's wife was knifed by a madman and, as a consequence, he dropped the project and the house remained unfinished and abandoned for a century. Now the **Villa Tamaris Pacha** (*t 04 94 06 84 00 ; open Tues–Sat 2–6.30*) is an elegant art gallery. The resort was a flop, but a fad for neo-Moorish confections swept across the Riviera at the turn of the century.

Beyond the fine sands of **Les Sablettes** beach, the hilly St-Mandrier peninsula closes off the west end of the Grande Rade, which was an island until the mid-17th century. The quiet and unassuming fishing village and marina of **St-Mandrier-sur-Mer** is easily accessible by sea bus (no.28M) from Quai Cronstadt in Toulon and has a little sandy beach by the port and a wonderful, wild (if pebbly) beach, **Plage de la Cadoulière**, on the opposite side of the isthmus, popular with windsurfers and without a beach concession in sight.

Coastal paths (*sentiers littoraux*), which are marked with yellow painted signs, leave from here to the equally unravaged **Plage de Cavalas** and the more sophisticated **Plage de St-Asile**, a favourite with families. In the woods on the hills above the fishing village is a Franco-Italian cemetery with wide views over the *rades* – and the flat grey forms of the frigates and aircraft carriers of the navy fleet. The tip of the peninsula belongs to the French navy and is out of bounds.

Toulon to Les Lecques

West of Toulon, the coast tosses out the curious peninsula of Cap Sicié, with the old town of Six-Fours, before ending in a string of small towns with sandy beaches, including Sanary, fashionable Bandol (one of the coast's great wine towns) and Les Lecques. Offshore, you can be entertained on Paul Ricard's two little islets, or amuse yourself inland exploring the hills, woods, vineyards and gorges around Ollioules, La Cadière-d'Azur and Le Castellet.

Around Cap Sicié: Six-Fours

Cap Sicié, like a clenched fist punching the sea, takes the brunt of the wind and rough swells from the west. If you can, avoid the depressing main roads and urban sprawl that cut across the peninsula from Les Sablettes to Sanary, and take the **Corniche Varoise**, a minor road that circles the cliffs of the Cap (not recommended on windy days, however). The cliffs tower up to 1,100ft over the sea at **Notre-Dame-du-Mai**, named after a sanctuary much esteemed by sailors, who always approached it barefoot.

On the west side of the peninsula, the little port of **Le Brusc**, set amid cliffs and pines, has two or three departures every hour for the **Ile des Embiez**, owned by Paul Ricard, the *pastis* baron. Ricard has left the seaward side of the island alone, but facing the mainland he is developing what he calls 'the leisure centre of the future', a vast marina and the **Fondation Océanographique Ricard** (*t 04 94 34 02 49; open July–Aug daily 10–12.30 and 1.30–5.30; Sept–June Wed and Sat 2–5.30, Mon, Tues, Thurs, Fri and Sun 10–12.30 and 1.30–5.30; adm*), with 100 Mediterranean species.

The rough winds and waves off Cap Sicié's west coast offer an exciting challenge to surfers and windsurfers, who get their kicks at **Brutal Beach** and **Plage de Bonnegrâce**, part of the commune of **Six-Fours-les-Plages** (from the Latin *sex furni*, six ovens). The village once stood on the isolated mountain nearby, but was destroyed in the 19th century to build the **fort** (no entry, but you can drive up to the barbed wire outside for the view). Two churches were spared: a 10th-century **oratory** on the road to Le Brusc, commemorating a victory over Saracen pirates, and the 12th-century Collegiate church of **St-Pierre-aux-Liens** (*t 04 94 34 24 75; open Oct–May Mon–Sat 2–6, Sun 10–12 and 2–6; June–Sept Mon–Sat 3–7, Sun 9–12 and 3–7*), built in pure Provençal Romanesque over a 5th-century baptistry; Palaeo-Christian coins and gems found here are displayed in a case. The church has a number of medieval works of art, including a polyptych of Provence's favourite saints by Jean de Troyes (1520). The niche behind the altar, built to hold the Eucharist, was until 1914 (when the practice was banned) used by the faithful to deposit scraps of cloth taken from the clothes of dead relatives when they came to pray for their souls.

Le Castellet
Le Beausset
La Cadière d'Azur
D559B
▲ Le Gros Cerveau
La Ciotat
Les Lecques
St-Cyr-sur-Mer
D559
Evenos
Gorges d'Ollioules
D2
TOULON
Bandol
Ollioules
Ile de Bendor
Sanary-sur-Mer
Six-Fours-les-Plages
La Seyne
Le Mourillon
Le Brusc
Les Sablettes
St-Mandrier
Ile des Embiez
Notre-Dame-du-Mai
Cap Sicié
Golfe de Giens

N

10 km
5 miles

North of here off the D63 is the stone-built **Chapelle Notre-Dame-de-Pépiole** (*usually open 3–6, and for services Sun 9.30–11*), with three little barrel-vaulted naves modelled after the earliest Syrian churches. It dates back to at least the 8th century, the date of fragments of Islamic ceramics found inside, and may even be Carolingian.

Sanary-sur-Mer, Ollioules and the Big Brain

Provençal for St-Nazaire, **Sanary** is a little resort of pink and white houses and a sandy beach, once picked out by the Kislings and Aldous Huxley as a good place to live, far from the Babylon further east. After 1933, Huxley was joined by the cream of anti-Nazi German intelligentsia, led by Thomas and Heinrich Mann and Bertolt Brecht. But Sanary was not far enough away, and under the Vichy régime many Germans were rounded up and imprisoned in an internment camp near Aix. On Sanary's promontory, the chapel **Notre-Dame-de-Pitié** has a delightful collection of naïve *ex votos*.

Ollioules' name comes from olives, although these days it's better known for its wholesale Mediterranean flower market. The town itself has the typical Provençal charms – arcaded lanes, a medieval castle and a Romanesque church – and numerous artisans who make barrels, birdcages, nougat, olive woodwork, goat's cheese and the like, a welcome respite from the lavender sachets and *santons*. Three signposted walks head out of town into the hills and up to the Gorges d'Ollioules.

Getting Around

By Train
The train station for Ollioules is halfway between the town and Sanary, with bus connections to both. Bandol is on the Toulon–Marseille TGV. For train information, the general SNCF number is **t** 08 92 35 35 35.

By Bus
Six-Fours and Sanary are easiest reached by bus from Toulon. SODETRAV buses, **t** 04 94 18 93 40, run from Toulon to St-Tropez and St-Raphaël, and Littorals Cars, **t** 04 94 74 01 35, leave Toulon from Rue Vauban for Sanary and Bandol.

Bicycle and Surfboard Hire
In Bandol you can hire a bike to explore the beautiful hinterlands at **Holiday Bikes**, 127 Route de Marseille, **t** 04 94 32 21 89. Or catch some waves by hiring windsurfers and surf boards from the **Société Nautique de Bandol**, **t** 04 94 29 42 26.

Tourist Information

Ollioules: 116 Rue Philippe de Hauteclocque, **t** 04 94 63 11 74, **f** 04 94 63 33 72, *office-tourisme@ollioules.com, www.ollioules.com. Open summer Mon–Sat 9–12 and 4–8; winter Mon–Fri 9–12 and 3–6, Sat 9–12.*
Bandol: Allée Vivien, **t** 04 94 29 41 35, **f** 04 94 32 50 39, *otbandol@bandol.fr, www.bandol.fr. Open winter Mon–Fri 9–12 and 2–6, Sat 9–12; summer daily 9–7.*

Internet: Boss, Rue des Ecoles, Bandol, **t** 04 94 29 03 03.

Market Days
Le Brusc: Thursday morning.
Sanary: Wednesday morning.
Ollioules: Thursday and Saturday.
Bandol: Daily, with a bigger market on Tuesday morning.
La Cadière-d'Azur: Thursday morning.

Where to Stay and Eat

Le Brusc ✉ 83140
Le Saint-Pierre, 47 Rue de la Citadelle, **t** 04 94 34 02 52 (*moderate*). Marcel, 'the king of *bouillabaisse*' will fill you to the brim with the well-priced offerings on the delicious menu, which is mostly fish. *Closed Tues eve, Wed and Jan.*

Bandol ✉ 83150
★★Hôtel Bel Ombra, 31 Rue de la Fontaine, **t** 04 94 29 40 90, **f** 04 94 25 01 11, *hotel. bel.ombra@wanadoo.fr (inexpensive).* Quiet, friendly and unassuming. *Closed mid-Oct–Mar.*
★★L'Oasis, 15 Rue des Ecoles, **t** 04 94 29 41 69, **f** 04 94 29 44 80, *www.oasisbandol.com (inexpensive).* West of the port, with a cool, shady garden and just a short walk from the beach. However, rooms can be stuffy and the street is noisy in high season. Restaurant (*moderate*); half or full board compulsory mid-June–mid-Sept. *Closed Dec; restaurant closed Sun eve.*

A kilometre north of town, just past the romantic ruins of an 18th-century oratory, the Celto-Ligurian Iron Age *oppidum* of **La Courtine** is built on a basalt rock and covered with wild roses planted by two frustrated amateur archaeologists when they got tired of excavating. You can still make out the dry-stone walls and wells. Over 300 Greek coins engraved with the features of Hercules and Hecate were discovered here, donated to a sanctuary destroyed by Romans in 123 BC.

Evenos is an extraordinary *village perché* just to the north off the N8; a granite-grey huddle of houses patched with the remains of the 16th-century château which glowers byronically at the summit of the village. A footpath leads around the castle ruins and offers glimpses of the the dramatic scenery, especially the fantastical yellow-tinted **Gorges d'Ollioules**, a natural Gothic landscape much admired by Victor

L'Auberge du Port, 9 Allée J. Moulin, t 04 94 29 42 63, *www.ile-rousse.com* (*expensive–moderate*). Bandol's gourmet rendezvous, specializing in seafood; you can go the whole hog on a *menu dégustation*, or pick from the extensive menu of local fish specialities.

Le Jérôme, on the waterfront, near the tourist office, t 04 94 32 55 85 (*moderate*). A restaurant and pizzeria serving huge portions at attractive prices with cheerful, genuine service.

Ile de Bendor ⊠ 83150

***Delos**, t 04 94 29 11 60, f 04 94 32 41 44 (*expensive*). Big, comfortable rooms decorated in extravagant bad taste – but the views of the sea and the watersports make up for it. *Closed Jan–Feb.*

***Hôtel Soukana**, t 04 94 25 06 06, f 04 94 25 04 89 (*expensive*). This has lots of activities and an occasionally raucous but cheerful clientele, plus a restaurant (*moderate*). *Closed Nov–mid-June.*

La Cadière-d'Azur ⊠ 83740

***Hostellerie Bérard**, Av Gabriel Péri, t 04 94 90 11 43, f 04 94 90 01 94, *berard@hotel-berard.com, www.hotel-berard.com* (*expensive*). The one hotel in the village is a charming and luxurious place to stay: a 16th-century convent building with a shady terrace, a heated swimming pool, gardens and a good restaurant with splendid views, serving delicately perfumed dishes. You may want to avoid it in July, August and November, when all the bus tours arrive

for **cookery courses** with the master chef – or you may want to arrange to join them. *Closed mid-Jan–mid-Feb; restaurant closed Mon lunch and Sat lunch.*

Le Castellet ⊠ 83330

***Le Castel Lumière**, t 04 94 32 62 20, f 04 94 32 70 33, *www.lecastellumiere.com* (*moderate*). Next to the medieval gate in the village, Le Castel Lumière has six rooms and an excellent restaurant (*expensive*), partially funished with antiques, with panoramic views. The staff can be a little sniffy. *Closed Sun eve, Mon in summer and Jan.*

***Castel Sainte-Anne**, 81, Chemin de la Chapelle, 2km northwest on the D26, t 04 94 32 60 08, f 04 94 32 68 16, *castelsaintanne@hotmail.com* (*inexpensive*). A cosy niche that won't break the bank, with a terrace, garden and pool.

Les Lecques ⊠ 83270

***Grand Hôtel des Lecques**, 24 Av du Port, t 04 94 26 23 01, f 04 94 26 10 22, *www.lecques-hotel.com* (*expensive–moderate*). A white villa with a gastronomic restaurant set in lovely gardens just a stone's throw from the beach. The staff can be snooty. Half-board only in season. *Closed Nov–mid-Mar.*

**Le Chanteplage, Place de l'Appel-du-18-Juin, t 04 94 26 16 55, f 04 94 26 25 71 (*moderate*). Right on the seafront, with great views of the coastline and a genial host. *Closed mid-Nov–Feb.*

Hugo. The strange strains of the *tambourin provençal* and the Provençal flute might well be heard from the local bar, hotel and restaurant, a tiny establishment called La Voute which clings to the cliffside amid a flurry of chickens and ducks. The owner and his family are staunch upholders of Provençal traditions and language and, if you are lucky, Patrick, the charismatic local *musicien felibre*, will be there enjoying a drink, playing his drum and whistle and regaling his friends with stories.

The D220 from Ollioules leads on to the wooded mountain ridge of **Le Gros Cerveau**, or 'Big Brain', a curious name of uncertain derivation and site of another *oppidum*. It, too, has strange rock formations and is pitted with caves, where 'witches' hid in the time of Louis XIII – in 1616 three were sentenced to be strangled, hanged, and then burned for good measure.

Bandol

Travellers will find Bandol, sheltered from the mistral, either a preview or a *déjà vu* of the typical Côte d'Azur town: pretty houses and lanes festooned with flowers, palm trees, boutiques, a casino, the morning market in Place de la Liberté, and an over-saturation of villas on the outskirts.

But Bandol has something most of the Riviera hotspots lack – its own excellent wine and a little island, **Ile de Bendor**. A barren 6-hectare rock when Paul Ricard bought it with his *pastis* fortune in 1950, it is now an adult playground, a masterpiece of architectural dissonance from the 1950s and '60s – Ricard himself hopes that it will some day fall in ruins and become 'a 20th-century Delos'. There's a diving and windsurfing school, a nautical club, an art school and gallery, a business centre, hotels and the **Exposition Universelle des Vins et Spiritueux** (*t 04 94 29 44 34; open Easter–Sept 10.30–12.30 and 3–7, closed Wed and Sat am*). The building is decorated with frescoes by art students and the displays of 8,000 bottles and glasses from around the world will whet your thirst for some Bandol AOC.

Apart from wine, Bandol offers its visitors pink flamingos, toucans, cockatoos and disgusting Vietnamese pigs in a lovely garden of tropical flora, the **Jardin Exotique et Zoo de Sanary-Bandol**, Route du Beausset, 3km east on the D559 (*t 04 94 29 40 38, www.zoosanary.com; open summer daily 8–12 and 2–7; winter 8–12 and 2–6; adm*). It's near the Moulin de St-Côme, where you can tour the most important olive press in the Var (or, in December and January, watch it at work) and buy a bottle of oil to take home.

North of Bandol are a pair of medieval wine-producing *villages perchés*, both restored, both lovely nonetheless, and neither as virgin as their olive oil. **La Cadière-d'Azur**, definitely a lesser perched village in terms of height, sits on a hill with cliffs sliced sheer on the north side, enjoying views out to the Massif de Ste-Baume and the noisy *autoroute*. Noisiest of all is a local mynah bird who has trained himself to mimic car alarms. **Le Castellet** is perched more precariously over its sea of vines. Much refurbished, it looks like a film set, and indeed has often been used as such (Marcel Pagnol got here first, for his *Femme du boulanger*); its 12th-century church is attractively austere, although the same cannot be said of the streets full of arty shops.

East of here (follow the D26 towards the N8), the 16th-century agricultural village of **Le Beausset** sits on a plain 2.5km from the 12th-century **Chapelle Notre-Dame-du-Beausset-Vieux** (*t 04 94 98 61 53; open Mon, Thurs and Fri 2–5.30, Tues, Wed and Sun 9.30–5.30, Sat 9–5.30*), with a basalt altar that once served as a millstone in an olive press, and *santons* from the 16th century.

Les Lecques and St-Cyr-sur-Mer

West of Bandol, Les Lecques is an unassuming family resort with a long fine sand beach, set in front of the old Bandol AOC town of **St-Cyr-sur-Mer**, which has something in common with New York – a Statue of Liberty, a scale model of Bartholdi's *grande dame* in Place Portalis, just cleaned up and looking splendid. It's a bustling little place, with a popular market and a formal rose garden, created after France won

Bandol Wine

When a courtier asked Louis XV the secret of his eternal youth, the king replied, 'The wines of Rouve (in Bandol), which give me their vigour and spirit.' They had to have a certain vigour to survive the journey to Versailles, sloshing about in barrels in slow boats from the Mediterranean to the Atlantic and up the Seine. Today Bandol still flexes its charming muscle; averaging €6–9 a bottle, it gets top marks in Provence for value for money.

The arid, wine-coloured *restanques* (terraces) cut into the mountain flanks in the eight *communes* around Bandol have produced wines since 600 BC. Dominated by small, dense mourvèdre grapes (which account for at least 50 per cent of the blend) mixed with cinsault and grenache, the reds are sombre of tone and require patience to reach their peak. Top vintages from **Domaine Tempier** and **Château de Pibarnon** are widely acknowledged as some of the best reds in the world. Bandol also comes in pale salmon-hued rosés, known for their delightful perfume, and dense whites that are to the taste what wild roses are to the nose, and make the ideal accompaniment to grilled fish – 1997 and 1998 were great years.

Some Bandols have extraordinary pedigrees: **Château des Salettes**, at La Cadière-d'Azur (**t** 04 94 90 06 06, **f** 04 94 90 04 29), has been in the same family since 1602. The **Domaine Tempier**, up in Le Plan-de-Castellet, **t** 04 94 98 70 21, **f** 02 04 94 90 21 65, is widely recognized to produce some of the finest wines in the area.

Other estates to visit are the organic **Domaine de la Tour du Bon**, at Le-Brulat-du-Castellet, **t** 04 94 32 61 62, **f** 04 94 32 71 69 (by appointment only), the rising superstar estate, and **Domaine Ray-Jane**, at Le-Plan-du-Castellet, **t** 04 94 98 64 08, **f** 04 94 98 68 72, where, besides wine, visitors can examine France's largest collection of cooper's tools. The Comte de Saint-Victor's estate of **Château de Pibarnon**, at La Cadière-d'Azur, **t** 04 94 90 12 73, **f** 04 94 90 12 98, is sculpted into rugged limestone flanks geologically millions of years older than their neighbours, which give its spicy reds, charming rosés and fruity whites a personality all their own.

Domaine de la Laidière, at Sainte-Anne d'Evenos, **t** 04 94 90 37 07, **f** 04 94 90 38 05, *www.laidiere.com*, is one of the most quality-conscious estates of the area, producing red, white and rosé, with the red wine the finest.

Next to the tourist office, the **Maison des Vins de Bandol** sells most of the labels and has a list of estates open for visits, **t** 04 94 29 45 03.

See www.vins-de-bandol.com.

the football World Cup in 1998. In the middle of it is a life-size poster of local hero Franc LeBœuf, who comes from the town, arms spread in victory. It also offers the cool, wet delights of **Aqualand** (*t 04 94 32 08 32; open June–Sept*).

Les Lecques itself is one of several places that claim to be ancient Tauroentum, a colony of Greek Marseille where Caesar defeated Pompey in a famous naval battle and gained control of Marseille. But most of the finds in Les Lecques so far have been Roman, as displayed in the **Musée de Tauroentum** on the road to La Madrague (*t 04 94 26 30 46, www.saintcyrsurmer.fr/culture/tauroentum/musee.htm; open*

June–Sept 3–7, closed Tues; other times weekends and hols only 2–5; adm). The museum protects the remains of two Roman villas built around the year 1 AD, with mosaics and bits of fresco, vases and jewellery, and, outside, an unusual two-storey tomb of a child. Ancient Tauroentum itself is supposed to be somewhere just offshore, lost under the sea. You can look for traces of it along a lonely coastal path (marked with yellow signs) that begins near the museum and continues to Bandol; along the way are little *calanques* for quiet swims.

Language

Even if your French is brilliant, the soupy southern twang may throw you. Any word with a nasal *in* or *en* becomes something like *aing* (*vaing* for *vin*). The last vowel on many words that are silent in the north get to express themselves in the south (*encore* sounds something like *engcora*).

What remains the same as anywhere else in France is the level of politeness expected: use *monsieur*, *madame* or *mademoiselle* when speaking to everyone (and never *garçon* in restaurants!), from your first *bonjour* to your last *au revoir*.

For Food vocabulary, *see* pp.49–55.

Pronunciation

Vowels
a/*à*/*â* between *a* in 'bat' and 'part'
é/*er*/*ez* at end of word as *a* in 'plate' but a
   bit shorter
e/*è*/*ê* as *e* in 'bet'
e at end of word not pronounced
e at end of syllable or in one-syllable word
   pronounced weakly, like *er* in 'mother'
i as *ee* in 'bee'
o as *o* in 'pot'
ô as *o* in 'go'
u/*û* between *oo* in 'boot' and *ee* in 'bee'

Vowel Combinations
ai as *a* in 'plate'
aî as *e* in 'bet'
ail as *i* in 'kite'
au/*eau* as *o* in 'go'
ei as *e* in 'bet'
eu/*œu* as *er* in 'mother'
oi between *wa* in 'swam' and *wu* in 'swum'
oy as 'why'
ui as *wee* in 'twee'

Nasal Vowels
Vowels followed by an **n** or **m** have a nasal sound.
an/*en* as *o* in 'pot' + nasal sound
ain/*ein*/*in* as *a* in 'bat' + nasal sound
on as *aw* in 'paw' + nasal sound
un as *u* in 'nut' + nasal sound

Consonants
Many French consonants are pronounced as in English, but there are some exceptions:
c followed by *e, i* or *y*, and *ç* as *s* in 'sit'
c followed by *a, o, u* as *c* in 'cat'
g followed by *e, i* or *y* as *s* in 'pleasure'
g followed by *a, o, u* as *g* in 'good'
gn as *ni* in 'opinion'
j as *s* in 'pleasure'
ll as *y* in 'yes'
qu as *k* in 'kite'
s between vowels as *z* in 'zebra'
s otherwise as *s* in 'sit'
w except in English words as *v* in 'vest'
x at end of word as *s* in 'sit'
x otherwise as *x* in 'six'

Stress
The stress usually falls on the last syllable except when the word ends with an unaccented **e**.

Useful Phrases

hello *bonjour*
good evening *bonsoir*
good night *bonne nuit*
goodbye *au revoir*
please *s'il vous plaît*
thank you (very much) *merci (beaucoup)*
yes *oui*
no *non*
good *bon* (*bonne*)
bad *mauvais*
excuse me *pardon, excusez-moi*

Can you help me? *Pourriez-vous m'aider?*
My name is... *Je m'appelle...*
What is your name? *Comment t'appelles-tu?*
(informal), *Comment vous appelez-vous?*
(formal)
How are you? *Comment allez-vous?*
Fine *Ça va bien*
I don't understand *Je ne comprends pas*
I don't know *Je ne sais pas*
Speak more slowly *Pourriez-vous parler plus
lentement?*
How do you say ... in French? *Comment dit-on
... en français?*
Help! *Au secours!*

WC *les toilettes*
men *hommes*
ladies *dames* or *femmes*

doctor *le médecin*
hospital *un hôpital*
emergency room *la salle des urgences*
police station *le commissariat de police*

No Smoking *Défense de fumer*

Shopping and Sightseeing

Do you have...? *Est-ce que vous avez...?*
I would like... *J'aimerais...*
Where is/are...? *Où est/sont...*
How much is it? *C'est combien?*
It's too expensive *C'est trop cher*

entrance *l'entrée*
exit *la sortie*
open *ouvert*
closed *fermé*
push *poussez*
pull *tirez*

bank *une banque*
money *l'argent*
traveller's cheque *un chèque de voyage*
post office *la poste*
stamp *un timbre*
phone card *une télécarte*
postcard *une carte postale*
public phone *une cabine téléphonique*
Do you have any change? *Avez-vous de la
monnaie?*

shop *un magasin*
central food market *les halles*
tobacconist *un tabac*
pharmacy *une pharmacie*
aspirin *l'aspirine*
condoms *les préservatifs*
insect repellent *l'anti-insecte*
sun cream *la crème solaire*
tampons *les tampons hygiéniques*

beach *la plage*
booking/box office *le bureau de location*
church *l'église*
museum *le musée*
sea *la mer*
theatre *le théâtre*

Accommodation

Do you have a room? *Avez-vous une chambre?*
Can I look at the room? *Puis-je voir la
chambre?*
How much is the room per day/week? *C'est
combien la chambre par jour/semaine?*
single room *une chambre pour une personne*
twin room *une chambre à deux lits*
double room *une chambre pour deux
personnes*
... with a shower/bath *... avec douche/salle de
bains*
... for one night/one week *... pour une
nuit/une semaine*

bed *un lit*
blanket *une couverture*
cot (child's bed) *un lit d'enfant*
pillow *un oreiller*
soap *du savon*
towel *une serviette*

Directions

Where is...? *Où se trouve...?*
left *à gauche*
right *à droite*
straight on *tout droit*
here *ici*
there *là*
close *proche*
far *loin*
forwards *en avant*
backwards *en arrière*

up *en haut*
down *en bas*
corner *le coin*
square *la place*
street *la rue*

Transport

I want to go to... *Je voudrais aller à...*
How can I get to...? *Comment puis-je aller à..?*
When is the next...? *Quel est le prochain...?*
What time does it leave (arrive)? *A quelle heure part-il (arrive-t-il)?*
From where does it leave? *D'où part-il?*
Do you stop at...? *Passez-vous par...?*
How long does the trip take? *Combien de temps dure le voyage?*
A (single/return) ticket to... *un aller* or *aller simple/aller et retour) pour...*
How much is the fare? *Combien coûte le billet?*
Have a good trip! *Bon voyage!*

airport *l'aéroport*
aeroplane *l'avion*
berth *la couchette*
bicycle *la bicyclette/le vélo*
mountain bike *le vélo tout terrain, VTT*
bus *l'autobus*
bus stop *l'arrêt d'autobus*
car *la voiture*
coach *l'autocar*
coach station *la gare routière*
flight *le vol*
on foot *à pied*
port *le port*
railway station *la gare*
ship *le bateau*
subway *le métro*
taxi *le taxi*
train *le train*

delayed *en retard*
on time *à l'heure*
platform *le quai*
date-stamp machine *le composteur*
timetable *l'horaire*
left-luggage locker *la consigne automatique*
ticket office *le guichet*
ticket *le billet*
customs *la douane*
seat *la place*

Driving

breakdown *la panne*
car *la voiture*
danger *le danger*
driver *le chauffeur*
entrance *l'entrée*
exit *la sortie*
give way/yield *céder le passage*
hire *louer*
(international) driving licence *un permis de conduire (international)*

motorbike/moped *la moto/le vélomoteur*
no parking *stationnement interdit*
petrol (unleaded) *l'essence (sans plomb)*
road *la route*
road works *les travaux*

This doesn't work *Ça ne marche pas*
Is the road good? *Est-ce que la route est bonne?*

Numbers

one *un*
two *deux*
three *trois*
four *quatre*
five *cinq*
six *six*
seven *sept*
eight *huit*
nine *neuf*
ten *dix*
eleven *onze*
twelve *douze*
thirteen *treize*
fourteen *quatorze*
fifteen *quinze*
sixteen *seize*
seventeen *dix-sept*
eighteen *dix-huit*
nineteen *dix-neuf*
twenty *vingt*
twenty-one *vingt et un*
twenty-two *vingt-deux*
thirty *trente*
forty *quarante*
fifty *cinquante*
sixty *soixante*
seventy *soixante-dix*

Friday *vendredi*
Saturday *samedi*
Sunday *dimanche*

Time

What time is it? *Quelle heure est-il?*
It's 2 o'clock (am/pm) *Il est deux heures (du matin/de l'après-midi)*
... half past 2 *...deux heures et demie*
... a quarter past 2 *...deux heures et quart*
... a quarter to 3 *...trois heures moins le quart*
it is early *il est tôt*
it is late *il est tard*

month *un mois*
week *une semaine*
day *un jour/une journée*
morning *le matin*
afternoon *l'après-midi*
evening *le soir*
night *la nuit*
today *aujourd'hui*
yesterday *hier*
tomorrow *demain*
day before yesterday *avant-hier*
day after tomorrow *après-demain*
soon *bientôt*

r
février
mars
April *avril*
May *mai*
June *juin*
July *juillet*
August *août*
September *septembre*
October *octobre*
November *novembre*
December *décembre*

Days

Monday *lundi*
Tuesday *mardi*
Wednesday *mercredi*
Thursday *jeudi*

Glossary

abbaye abbey

anse cove

arrondissement a city district.

auberge inn

aven natural well

bastide taller, more elaborate version of a *mas*, with balconies, wrought-ironwork, reliefs, etc; also a medieval new town, fortified and laid out in a grid.

beffroi tower with a town's bell

borie dry-stone shepherd's hut with a corbelled roof

buffet d'eau in French gardens, a fountain built into a wall with water falling through levels of urns or basins

cabane simple weekend or holiday retreat, usually near the sea; a *cabane de gardian* is a thatched cowboy's abode in the Camargue

calanque narrow coastal creek, like a miniature fjord

capitelles the name for *bories* in Languedoc

cardo the main north–south street in a Roman *castrum* or town

caryatid column or pillar carved in the figure of a woman

castrum rectangular Roman army camp, which often grew into a permanent settlement

causse rocky, arid limestone plateaus, north of Hérault and in the lower Languedoc

cave (wine) cellar

château mansion, manor house or castle

chemin path

chevet eastern end of a church, including the apse

cirque round natural depression created by erosion at the loop of a river

cloître cloister

clue rocky cleft or transverse valley

col mountain pass

commune in the Middle Ages, the government of a free town or city; today, the smallest unit of local government, encompassing a town or village

côte coast; on wine labels, *côtes, coteaux* and *costières* mean 'hills' or 'slopes'

cours wide main street, like an elongated main square

couvent convent or monastery

crèche Christmas crib with *santons*

donjon castle keep

écluse canal lock

église church

étang lagoon or swamp

Félibre member of the movement to bring back the use of the Provençal language

gare train station (SNCF)

gare routière coach station

gisant sculpted prone effigy on a tomb

gîte shelter

gîte d'étape basic shelter for walkers

Grande Randonnée (GR) long-distance hiking path

grau a narrowing, either of a canyon or a river

halles covered market

hôtel with *particulier*, originally the town residence of the nobility; by the 18th century the word became more generally used for any large, private residence

hôtel de ville town hall.

lavoir communal fountain, usually covered, for the washing of clothes

mairie town hall

maquis Mediterranean scrub. Also used as a term for the French Resistance during the Second World War

marché market

mas a farmhouse and its outbuildings

mascaron ornamental mask, usually one carved on the keystone of an arch

modillon stone projecting from the cornice of a church, carved with a face or animal figure

motte hammock, or a raised area in a swamp

oppidum pre-Roman fortified settlement

parlement French juridical body, with members appointed by the king; by the late *ancien régime*, parlements exercised a great deal of influence over political affairs

pays region or village

pont bridge

porte gateway

predella small paintings beneath the main subject of a retable

presqu'île peninsula

puy hill

restanques vine or olive terraces

retable carved or painted altarpiece, often consisting of a number of scenes or sculpted ensembles

rez-de-chaussée **(RC)** ground floor

santon figure in a Christmas nativity scene, usually made of terracotta and dressed in 18th-century Provençal costume

source spring

tour tower

transi on a tomb, a relief of the decomposing cadaver

tympanum sculpted semicircular panel over a church door

vieille ville historic, old quarter of town

village perché hilltop village

Further Reading

Ardagh, John, *France Today* (Penguin, 1982, revised 3rd ed. 1995). One of Penguin's informative paperback series on politics and life in contemporary Europe.

Barr, Alfred, *Henri Matisse: His Art and His Public* (Museum of Modern Art, NY, 1951).

Blume, Mary, *Côte d'Azur: Inventing the French Riviera* (Thames and Hudson, 1992) Delightful anecdotal account of the creation of the myth.

Cameron, Roderick, *The Golden Riviera* (Weidenfeld & Nicholson, 1975). One of the best travelogues of the region.

Colette, *Letters from Colette*, (Farrar, Straus & Giroux, 1980). Follow the progress of St-Tropez from idyll to mass tourism.

Donnelly, Honoria, *Sara and Gerald* (Holt, Rinehart & Winston, out of print). Biography of the Murphys.

Fitzgerald, F. Scott, *Tender is the Night*, many editions. 1920s Riviera decadence based on personal research.

Fortescue, Winifred, *Perfume from Provence* (1935, but recently reprinted). Poor, intolerable Lady Fortescue's misadventures with the garlicky peasants near Nice.

Greene, Graham, *J'Accuse: The Dark Side of Nice* (The Bodley Head, 1982). The late Graham Greene, resident of Antibes, discovers the mafia connections and graft in the government of discredited mayor Jacques Médecin.

Goldring, Douglas, *The South of France* (Macdonald, 1952). Travels and comments by another English resident.

Haedrich, Marcel, *Coco Chanel: Her Life, Her Secrets* (Little, Brown, 1972). All about the queen of fashion, who helped create the Côte d'Azur.

Hugo, Victor, *Les Misérables*, many editions. Injustice among the galley-slaves and basis for the hit musical.

de Larrabeiti, Michael, *The Provençal Tales* (Pavilion, 1988). Troubadours' tales, legends

and stories told by shepherds around the camp fire.

Lyall, Archibald, *Companion Guide to the South of France* (Collins, 1978). Personal, well-written but dated guide of the entire Mediterranean coast.

Mistral, Frédéric, *Miréio and Poème de la Rhône*, epic poems by the Nobel prize-winning Félibre, widely available in French or Provençal.

Morris, Edwin T., *Fragrance: The Story of Perfume from Cleopatra to Chanel* (Charles Scribner & Sons, 1984).

Pagnol, Marcel, *Jean de Florette and Manon of the Springs, The Days were too Short* (Picador, 1960). Autobiography by Provence's most beloved writer. Many of his books were filmed and starred the Toulon-born actor affectionately known as Raimu.

Raison, Laura, compiler, *The South of France: An Anthology* (Cadogan, 1985).

Smollett, Tobias, *Travels through France and Italy* (Penguin, 1979). The irrepressible, grouchy Tobias 'Smelfungus' makes modern travel writing look like advertising copy.

Süskind, Patrick, *Perfume* (Penguin, 1989). Thrilling and fragrant murder in the 18th-century perfume industry in Grasse.

Vergé, Roger, *Cuisine of the Sun*, (London, 1979). The owner of the Moulin de Mougins tells some of his secrets of nouvelle Provençal cooking.

Whitfield, Sarah, *Fauvism* (Thames and Hudson, 1991). A good introduction to the movement that changed art history.

Worwood, Valerie, *Aromantics* (Pan, 1987). An amusing look at aromatherapy.

Zeldin, Theodore, *France 1845–1945* (Oxford University Press, 1980). Five well-written volumes on all aspects of the period.

Index

Main page references are in **bold**. Page references to maps are in *italics*.

Also available from Cadogan Guides in our European series...

France

France
Dordogne & the Lot
Gascony & the Pyrenees
Brittany
Loire
South of France
Provence
Côte d'Azur
Corsica
Short Breaks in Northern France

Italy

Italy
The Bay of Naples and Southern Italy
Lombardy and the Italian Lakes
Tuscany, Umbria and the Marches
Tuscany
Umbria
Northeast Italy
Italian Riviera and Piemonte
Bologna and Emilia Romagna
Central Italy
Sardinia
Sicily
Rome Venice Florence

Spain

Spain
Andalucía
Northern Spain
Bilbao and the Basque Lands
Granada Seville Córdoba

Greece

Greece
Greek Islands
Athens and Southern Greece
Crete

The UK and Ireland

England
London–Paris
London Markets

Scotland
Scotland's Highlands and Islands

Ireland
Ireland: Southwest Ireland

Other Europe

Portugal
Madeira & Porto Santo
Malta, Gozo & Comino

The City Guide Series

Amsterdam
Barcelona
Bruges
Brussels
Edinburgh
Florence
London
Madrid
Milan
Paris
Prague
Rome
Venice

Flying Visits

Flying Visits France
Flying Visits Italy
Flying Visits Spain
Flying Visits Switzerland
Flying Visits Scandinavia
Flying Visits Germany
Flying Visits Ireland

Cadogan Guides are available from good bookshops, or via **Littlehampton Book Services,** Faraday Close, Durrington, Worthing, West Sussex BN13 3RB, **t** (01903) 828800, **f** (01903) 828802; and **The Globe Pequot Press,** 246 Goose Lane, PO Box 480, Guilford, Connecticut 06437–0480, **t** (800) 458 4500/**t** (203) 458 4500, **t** (203) 458 4603.